Family Resource Management

THIRD EDITION

This book is dedicated to our families, students, and friends.

To the littles who would keep us young, our grandchildren—Aiden, James, Owen, Norah, Benjamin, and the new little one on the way. You renew our faith in the future.

Family Resource Management

THIRD EDITION

Tami James Moore

Sylvia M. Asay

University of Nebraska at Kearney

Los Angeles | London | New Delhi
Singapore | Washington DC | Melbourne

FOR INFORMATION:

SAGE Publications, Inc.
2455 Teller Road
Thousand Oaks, California 91320
E-mail: order@sagepub.com

SAGE Publications Ltd.
1 Oliver's Yard
55 City Road
London EC1Y 1SP
United Kingdom

SAGE Publications India Pvt. Ltd.
B 1/I 1 Mohan Cooperative Industrial Area
Mathura Road, New Delhi 110 044
India

SAGE Publications Asia-Pacific Pte. Ltd.
3 Church Street
#10-04 Samsung Hub
Singapore 049483

Acquisitions Editor: Joshua Perigo
Editorial Assistant: Adeline Wilson,
                Alexandra Randall
Content Development Editor: Sarah Dillard
Production Editor: Tracy Buyan
Copy Editor: Laureen Gleason
Typesetter: C&M Digitals (p) Ltd.
Proofreader: Victoria Reed-Castro
Indexer: Terri Morrissey
Cover Designer: Rose Storey
Marketing Manager: Kara Kindstrom

Printed in the United States of America

Library of Congress Cataloging-in-Publication Data

Names: Moore, Tami James, author. | Asay, Sylvia M., author.

Title: Family resource management / Tami James Moore, Sylvia M. Asay.

Description: Third edition. | Thousand Oaks : SAGE, [2018] | Includes bibliographical references and index.

Identifiers: LCCN 2017022151 | ISBN 9781506399041 (pbk. : alk. paper)

Subjects: LCSH: Family life education—United States. | Families—Study and teaching.

Classification: LCC HQ10.5.U6 M66 2018 | DDC 372.37/4—dc23
LC record available at https://lccn.loc.gov/2017022151

This book is printed on acid-free paper.

SUSTAINABLE FORESTRY INITIATIVE
Certified Chain of Custody
Promoting Sustainable Forestry
www.sfiprogram.org
SFI-01268

SFI label applies to text stock

17 18 19 20 21 10 9 8 7 6 5 4 3 2 1

BRIEF CONTENTS

Preface: Structure, Understanding, and Application   xv

Acknowledgments   xx

UNIT I • THE STUDY OF FAMILY RESOURCE MANAGEMENT   1

CHAPTER 1 • The Complexity of Managing Family Resources   3

CHAPTER 2 • Understanding Families   21

CHAPTER 3 • The Management Process   49

UNIT II • DISCOVERING FAMILY NEEDS   67

CHAPTER 4 • Categorization of Needs   69

CHAPTER 5 • Values, Attitudes, and Behaviors: Understanding Family Choices   89

UNIT III • UNDERSTANDING RESOURCES   111

CHAPTER 6 • Identification of Family Resources   113

CHAPTER 7 • Families Within the Economic Environment   133

CHAPTER 8 • The Impact of Society on Family Decisions   157

UNIT IV • MAKING CHOICES   185

CHAPTER 9 • Managing the Future   187

CHAPTER 10 • Communication Within the Decision-Making Process   209

CHAPTER 11 • The Individual Within Family Decision Making   229

UNIT V • IMPLEMENTING AND EVALUATING DECISIONS 251

CHAPTER 12 • Making It Happen 253

CHAPTER 13 • Defining Success 277

CHAPTER 14 • Current and Future Challenges 303

Case Family Information 321

Glossary 335

Web Resources 345

References 347

Index 365

About the Authors 383

DETAILED CONTENTS

Preface: Structure, Understanding, and Application xv

 Family Resource Management Is Flexible and User-Friendly xvii

 Understanding Family Diversity xvii

 Real-World Examples xviii

 Case Application Opportunity xviii

Acknowledgments xx

UNIT I • THE STUDY OF FAMILY RESOURCE MANAGEMENT   1

CHAPTER 1 • The Complexity of Managing Family Resources 3

Objectives 3

What Is a Family? 5

How Do Families Use Resources? 5

 ➡ In the News 6

Managing Families 7

The Decision-Making Process 7

Contextual Influences in Family Resource Management 8

 Historical Influences 8

 Environmental Influences 10

 ➡ Reality Check 10

 Cultural Influences 13

 ➡ Worldview 16

Multidisciplinary Perspectives 16

 Psychology 17

 Sociology 17

 Social Psychology 17

 Cultural Anthropology 18

 Economics 18

 Biology 18

Summary 19

Questions for Review and Discussion 19

CHAPTER 2 • Understanding Families 21

Objectives 21

History of the Family 22

The Family Today 23

Defining the Family 23

Theoretical Definitions   24

Variations on a Definition of Family—When Numbers
 Are Necessary   25

The Gray Areas   27

➡ Worldview   28

Changes in the Family   29

➡ In the News   30

Family Functions   31

Families Within Cultural Contexts   32

➡ Reality Check   33

Researching the Family   35

Family Systems Theory   36

Social Exchange Theory   37

Symbolic Interactionism   38

Conflict Theory   39

Feminist Perspective   41

Family Ecological Theory   42

Family Strengths Framework   43

Family Development Theory   44

Family Research Design   45

Summary   47

Questions for Review and Discussion   47

CHAPTER 3 • The Management Process   49

Objectives   49

Management as a Field of Study   50

Parallel Histories   51

**The Evolution of Home and Business Management: The 20th
 Century   52**

Era One (ca. 1900–1930s)   53

Era Two (ca. 1940s–1950s)   54

Era Three (ca. 1950s–1960s)   54

Era Four (ca. 1970s–1980s)   55

Contemporary Movements   56

➡ Reality Check   56

**The Interface of Business Management and Family Resource
 Management in the Context of the Family   57**

The Foundation of Family Resource Management   58

Specific Applications of Management to the Family Unit   60

➡ Worldview   61

Time Management   61

➡ In the News   62

Family Planning   62

Dependent Care   63

Financial Management   64

Summary   65

Questions for Review and Discussion   65

UNIT II • DISCOVERING FAMILY NEEDS   67

CHAPTER 4 • Categorization of Needs   69

Objectives   69

Needs and Wants   70

Hierarchy of Needs   71

➡ Worldview   72

Applying the Hierarchy of Needs to the Family   73

The Consumer Resource Exchange Model (CREM)   75

Categorization of Needs   76

Measuring Satisfaction of Needs   77

Changing Perceptions of Needs   78

Circumstances   78

Personality   80

Economic Status   80

Technology   81

Culture   81

Life Span   82

Gender Differences   83

➡ Reality Check   84

Needs Assessment   85

➡ In the News   86

Individual Needs Versus Societal Needs   86

Summary   87

Questions for Review and Discussion   88

CHAPTER 5 • Values, Attitudes, and Behaviors: Understanding Family Choices   89

Objectives   89

Values   90

Personal Values   91

Family Values   93

➡ Reality Check   93

Values Across the Life Span   97

Value Congruence Across Generations   98

Attitudes   99

Behaviors   101

Values, Attitudes, and Behaviors in the Decision-Making Framework   103

➡ In the News   103

Values and Behaviors in Family Purchasing Decisions   104

Brand Preference   105

Quality Preference   105

Price Preference   106

Design Preference   106

Impact of Culture on Values, Attitudes, and Behaviors   107

➡ Worldview   107

Impact of Socioeconomic Factors on Values, Attitudes, and Behaviors   108

Consistency Over Time and Situation   109

Summary   110

Questions for Review and Discussion   110

UNIT III • UNDERSTANDING RESOURCES   111

CHAPTER 6 • Identification of Family Resources   113

Objectives   113

Resource Availability   114
➡ Worldview   114

Resource Theory   115

Human Resources   116

Economic Resources   118
➡ Reality Check   121

Environmental Resources   122

Social Resources   123
➡ In the News   126

Measurement of Resources   126

Resource Allocation and Use   128

Summary   132

Questions for Review and Discussion   132

CHAPTER 7 • Families Within the Economic Environment   133

Objectives   133

Beginnings of Consumerism   134

Economic Principles   137
➡ In the News   137
Supply and Demand   138
Pricing   139
Income Fluctuations   141
Changes in Preference   143
Employment   144
Money   150
➡ Reality Check   150
Exchanging Nonmonetary Resources   153

Families in the Economy   154
➡ Worldview   155

Summary   156

Questions for Review and Discussion   156

CHAPTER 8 • The Impact of Society on Family Decisions   157

Objectives   157

Individuals and the Tax System   158
Federal Taxes   158
State and Local Taxes   160

Social Security   161

Medicare   165

Unemployment Insurance   166

Government-Supported Assistance Programs   166

➡ **Worldview   167**

Health and Human Services   167

The Department of Agriculture   168

The Food and Drug Administration   169

➡ **In the News   170**

Consumer Protection   172

➡ **Reality Check   177**

Privately Funded Programs   178

Compulsory Education   178

History   178

The Federal Level   179

The State Level   180

The Community Level   180

Family Involvement   180

Alternatives to Public Education   181

Making Educational Choices   183

Supply and Demand: An Application in Education   183

Summary   184

Questions for Review and Discussion   184

UNIT IV • MAKING CHOICES   185

CHAPTER 9 • Managing the Future   187

Objectives   187

Goals, Objectives, and Standards   188

The Planning Process   190

Types of Plans   193

➡ **Worldview   194**

Schedules   197

Budgeting   197

Family Financial Planning   201

➡ **Reality Check   203**

Creating the Financial Plan   204

➡ **In the News   206**

Emergency Action Plans   207

How Plans Emerge   208

Summary   208

Questions for Review and Discussion   208

CHAPTER 10 • Communication Within the Decision-Making Process   209

Objectives   209

Communication Theory   210

Family Communication 210
➡ **In the News 218**
Communication and Conflict 218
➡ **Worldview 220**
Communication and Information Technology 221
Radio and Audio Streaming 221
Television and Online Media 221
Telephones and Mobile Devices 222
➡ **Reality Check 224**
Computers and the Internet 225
Application to Family Decision Making 227
Summary 227
Questions for Review and Discussion 228

CHAPTER 11 • The Individual Within Family Decision Making 229

Objectives 229
Group Dynamics 229
Groupthink 233
➡ **Reality Check 236**
Leadership 238
Theories 240
Leadership and Parenting Styles 242
➡ **In the News 248**
➡ **Worldview 249**
Summary 250
Questions for Review and Discussion 250

UNIT V • IMPLEMENTING AND EVALUATING DECISIONS   251

CHAPTER 12 • Making It Happen 253

Objectives 253
Implementation 254
Strategies 255
Delegation 258
Accountability 259
Motivation 260
Estate Planning 261
Family Business Succession 264
Risk Management 265
Insurance 266
Health Insurance 267
➡ **Reality Check 268**
Life Insurance 270
Automobile Insurance 271

Home Insurance 272

➡ **Worldview 274**

Completion and Reflection 274

➡ **In the News 275**

Summary 276

Questions for Review and Discussion 276

CHAPTER 13 • Defining Success 277

Objectives 277

Societal Responsibility 278

➡ **Reality Check 278**

➡ **Worldview 287**

Family Responsibility 288

Social Wellness 289

Occupational Wellness 290

➡ **In the News 293**

Spiritual Wellness 293

Physical Wellness 294

Intellectual Wellness 296

Emotional Wellness 297

Individual Responsibility 299

Summary 302

Questions for Review and Discussion 302

CHAPTER 14 • Current and Future Challenges 303

Objectives 303

Technology 304

Lifestyle Changes 304

➡ **Worldview 305**

Healthcare 306

Education 307

Impact of Technology 307

➡ **In the News 308**

Family Structure 309

Marriage and Committed Relationships 309

Children 310

Divorce 311

➡ **Reality Check 312**

Natural Resources 313

Changing Demographics 314

Diversity and Immigration 315

Economic Divide 316

Aging Population 316

Geographic Location and Housing 317

Summary 319

Questions for Review and Discussion 319

Case Family Information   321

Glossary   335

Web Resources   345

References   347

Index   365

About the Authors   383

PREFACE

Structure, Understanding, and Application

The goals of *Family Resource Management* are focused on structuring the concept of the topic in an understandable format that allows students and instructors to apply both knowledge and theory to the study of how families manage their resources for both survival and fulfillment. Multiple perspectives are used to broaden the base of understanding in a contemporary environment.

Family Resource Management unlocks the complexity of family decision making for students, enabling them to grasp both the concepts and underlying explanations of family behavior. A strong theory base and the organization of material within the decision-making process framework facilitate both understanding and retention.

The third edition has been enhanced through both surveys of educational professionals using the last edition in academic programs and extensive research of contemporary challenges emerging after the 2008 recession and the 2016 election. Although the material is based in and focused on the realities of managing families within the context of the United States, the examples provided illuminate the diversity of families within the nation and the impact of globalization on the resources available and the utilization of those resources.

Unit I, "The Study of Family Resource Management," presents a framework for understanding the discipline of family science/family studies in the context of the decision-making process. Past textbooks used by family resource management professionals had that common thread of need recognition and relevant resource decisions. An in-depth analysis of the concept of family and family structure presents the complexity of how families identify and fulfill their needs. Students are also provided with a structured approach for comprehension of how cultural diversity and differing worldviews impact that decision-making process. Another important concept explored in this unit is that of the contextual influences that impact family resource management. Management—principles and application—is presented in both historical and contemporary contexts. The interdependence of family management and business management is explored and synthesized through theory and practice. Although solid theory evolves slowly, the third edition has incorporated more recent statistical information and changing definitions and societal norms. Family structures continue to become more complex and complicated. The concept of cohabitation and family formation is included as a contemporary issue relevant to resource management. Resources, both economic and human, have been challenged by dynamic social changes nationally and globally. Families have become more resourceful and more dependent on new advancements in technology. This resourcefulness draws from and adds to discipline-based work in the field of family and business management.

Unit II, "Discovering Family Needs," requires recognition of how needs and wants differ and how families determine priorities when necessary. This includes a discussion of Maslow's hierarchy and an analysis of how values, attitudes, and behaviors impact need recognition and the actual perception of need. It also includes an understanding of how external forces, such as marketing and social changes, impact family value sets over time. The field of social psychology continues to add new theory and application to explain and predict human behavior in the social context. This new knowledge enhances the understanding of family choices in contemporary situations.

Unit III, "Understanding Resources," presents economic and social resources in a family-based framework. Although students may have been exposed to the field of economics and financial planning in previous courses, it is essential that practicing family service providers and educators understand the reciprocal relationships between families and these social systems. Financial problems are often cited as catalysts in family dissolution, and the complexity of social services, especially Social Security and Medicare, has created a new family service niche—family life education programs and consulting services. Emerging from a period of recession, the national economy has stabilized once again. The dramatic shift in proposed policy of a new political administration will force families to adapt to many possible changes. The impact of these changes on the global, national, state, and community levels will require adaptation and resourcefulness of family groups. This unit has been purposefully strengthened by the feedback received from educators in the classroom.

Unit IV, "Making Choices," moves the decision-making process into the action mode. The planning process and implementation of choices are presented through real-life applications, such as financial planning and emergency action preparation. The importance of communication in the family decision-making process is validated with strong theoretical support and clear illustrations. Understanding the choices made by families and the diversity of those choices requires an understanding of leadership concepts and group dynamics as they apply to family units.

Unit V, "Implementing and Evaluating Decisions," wraps up the five-step decision-making process. Reflection on actions and behaviors, as well as evaluation of the actual impact these decisions have on the family, are perhaps the most important steps, although often neglected. Breaking the cycle of bad choices requires post-decision analysis. Life satisfaction and the impact of decisions on individuals, the family unit, the community, and society are essential to student learning and professional development. The definition of success continues to evolve, and the rapid changes in products and technology create even higher levels of complexity in resource selection and implementation to address needs and problems in the family context.

FAMILY RESOURCE MANAGEMENT IS FLEXIBLE AND USER-FRIENDLY

After decades of experience in the undergraduate classroom and discussions with students as to their preferences, the authors selected a conversational style of material presentation, rich in application and discussion. Understanding that the core concepts within this topic are complex and dynamic, the decision to include descriptive scenarios at frequent intervals strives to connect new material to existing student understandings. This method encourages readers to control their own learning process. Drawing from multiple disciplines and preparing university students for personal, career, and possible graduate study success, it is imperative that material be drawn from scholarly resources and properly referenced in an academic fashion.

The abundance of material and the multiple opportunities for application in this text allow the instructor the opportunity to provide a structure for presentation and the possibility of gearing the material to any college/university course level needed. The material can be integrated into a multiple-level approach of studying family resource management, or it can stand alone as a one-term principles course. The flexibility of material and the presentation style used allow usage in both the degree-specific study of this topic and the more generalized elective courses across multiple major programs of study. The authors recognize that all students in postsecondary education are members of existing families and that they will find the material applicable to both personal and professional experiences, current and future.

UNDERSTANDING FAMILY DIVERSITY

Presenting a framework for students to use as they explore the challenges presented by an increasingly diverse clientele is essential for positive development of diversity skills and understanding. The authors have chosen the worldview framework introduced by Kluckhohn and Strodtbeck (1961). Others have built on this over the last five decades, but the original remains most adaptable to multidisciplinary approaches.

Although difficult when presenting diversity within scenarios, the use of ethnic names has been deliberate as a purposeful effort to be inclusive. The examples created for explanation of complex concepts are not always negative, nor are they positive. No stereotypes are implied through the use of these names. Families of all races, ethnicities, income levels, and other defined characteristics experience similar decision-making situations. The worldview framework helps students realize that decision making will differ between and within family units based on how situations are defined and viewed by the individuals involved. This framework is helpful both with intra-national diversity of groups and international group differences.

REAL-WORLD EXAMPLES

Each chapter strives to present current, reality-based supporting information for the chapter's objectives and content. *Reality Checks* include information from contributing families or media accounts of real individuals and families in specific circumstances. *Worldview* pieces are drawn from both the media and academic sources to provide concrete examples of how families from different cultures might perceive similar concepts differently. *In the News* features have been extracted from contemporary news sources to further inform students of issues facing society on a daily basis that are directly connected to the material they have just been presented.

CASE APPLICATION OPPORTUNITY

The concept of "experiential learning" has become a central part of university experiences over the last few years. Preparing professionals to work with real families presents unique challenges in the experiential domain because of the vulnerability of these family members. It is unethical to expect undergraduate students to actively provide case management without proper training and supervision. The use of cases, or simulations, provides an acceptable alternative. The casebook available for use with this text provides students with the opportunity to explore what it is like to be part of family structures that might be different from their family of origin and to work with a specific family through a series of family resource management challenges. In this casebook, there are five different families, each with unique strengths and problems inherent to family resource management. Ten case application assignments, designed specifically for each family, are provided to use with individual chapters. Students may be assigned one specific family for the course term. Then students can participate in community groups, where classmates representing the other four families can share their success and concerns in working with the other four challenging case families. This approach to application of concepts has proved effective with past courses. Each section of the text presents complementary information that can be used to problem solve in hypothetical situations presented. The cases use writing and practical skill-building assignments. An accompanying instructor's guide with detailed teaching notes makes the use of this pedagogy manageable across one semester.

When appropriate, instructors have the flexibility to adapt the casebook material included in this edition to meet the needs of upper-level students by adding assignments and activities that enhance higher-order thinking skills and application. The ten situations specifically engage the student in the application of knowledge and skills required to navigate the creation of a monthly budget addressing fixed expenses (housing, insurance, taxes) and expenditures related to lifestyle choices (memberships, soft and durable goods, travel, entertainment, gifting).

INSTRUCTOR SUPPORT

SAGE offers a robust set of offerings for instructor resources, all accessible from title's companion website. The Instructor Teaching Site is verified and password protected, offering you both peace of mind and a wealth of support for your courses. It can be accessed directly at **study.sagepub.com/moore3e.**

Password-protected Instructor Resources include the following:

- A Microsoft® Word® test bank is available containing multiple choice, true/false, and short answer for each chapter. The test bank provides you with a diverse range of prewritten options as well as the opportunity for editing any question and/or inserting your own personalized questions to effectively assess students' progress and understanding.

- Editable, chapter-specific Microsoft® PowerPoint® slides offer you complete flexibility in easily creating a multimedia presentation for your course.

- A Teaching Guide for the family resource management casebook is included within the text.

- An Interactive Budgeting Sheet with embedded formulas can be distributed to students in accompaniment with the casebook.

ACKNOWLEDGMENTS

We are grateful to those at SAGE who have encouraged us in this journey, for the guidance and patience necessary to complete this new edition. We are thankful for the substantial contributions of the original reviewers of the book. We also appreciate the feedback, criticism, and suggestions that were essential for this new edition to further address the market's need for this textbook. The authors are grateful to the following reviewers:

Soo Hyun Cho, South Dakota State University

Jeannie Frazier, Jacksonville State University

Mary Junot, Nicholls State University

Ashley Martin-Cuellar, University of New Mexico

Robert B. Nielsen, University of Georgia

M. Angela Nievar, University of North Texas

Kim Holdbrooks Townsel, Jacksonville State University

Our students continue to be an important source of direction, providing suggestions and critique when necessary. They have been instrumental in the development of this book, adding their own unique perspective to balance that of their more "seasoned" faculty. Finally, our colleagues at the University of Nebraska at Kearney have been both supportive and understanding.

THE STUDY OF FAMILY RESOURCE MANAGEMENT

The Decision-Making Process

- Recognize existing needs
- Identify alternatives to fulfill needs
- Evaluate identified alternatives
- Select and implement alternatives
- Reflect on and evaluate the alternatives selected

Chapter 1. The Complexity of Managing Family Resources

Chapter 2. Understanding Families

Chapter 3. The Management Process

CHAPTER ONE

THE COMPLEXITY OF MANAGING FAMILY RESOURCES

Objectives
What Is a Family?
How Do Families Use Resources?
In the News
Managing Families
The Decision-Making Process
Contextual Influences in Family Resource
    Management
    Historical Influences
    Environmental Influences
Reality Check
    Cultural Influences
Worldview
Multidisciplinary Perspectives
    Psychology
    Sociology
    Social Psychology
    Cultural Anthropology
    Economics
    Biology
Summary
Questions for Review and Discussion

Objectives

- Be aware that the family is the basic unit of society that has continued and is maintained over time.

- Recognize that the family is in transition as a result of changes outside the family and in family structure.

- Understand that family resource management is a process that requires decision-making and evaluation skills.

- Acknowledge that families need education about the opportunities and limitations of resources.

- Be familiar with how the words *family*, *resource*, and *management* identify the study of family resource management.

- Comprehend the five-step decision-making process.

- Acknowledge the impact that contextual influences have on family resource management.

**Family Resource Management is an understanding
of the decisions individuals and families make about
developing and allocating resources, including
time, money, material assets, energy, friends,
neighbors, and space, to meet their goals.**

**—National Council on Family Relations
(2014, www.ncfr.org)**

Despite the challenges facing families across time, the family remains the world's oldest form of relationship, a universal phenomenon (Sokalski, 1994). For centuries, families have been organized as a basic unit of society. This social unit has continued to be maintained over time, and, until recently, the family unit was generally considered to be a private institution. The contemporary family is now, more than ever before, a political entity. Family values are emerging in campaign slogans, drawing increased attention to the importance of family units within the social framework of communities, locally, nationally, and globally. This surge of interest in the family unit has resulted in increased research, expanding our knowledge base of family functions and evolution over time.

Although family life does give individuals a strong sense of continuity, Skolnick and Skolnick (2014) call attention to the fact that the family is in transition. Emerging communications and technology capabilities have accelerated this transition. Families of the future will not only need to be aware of changes that are taking place; they will also need the skills to adapt resource management to fit new realities.

Paralleling the changing social, political, and economic climates surrounding families are changes in the structure of families. Coontz (2000) points out that favored traditional family structures carry privilege, whereas Doherty (1997) speculates that as a result of environmental changes, our current society may be the first in history that cannot clearly define the family. These complexities necessitate the need for ongoing education and evaluation about the ways in which families function.

Management:
the act of directing and controlling a large group of people for the purpose of coordinating and harmonizing the group toward accomplishing a goal beyond the scope of individual effort

The key concepts of family resource management include an interdependency of individuals, a dynamic environment, and a conscious effort to meet basic needs for all individuals within the family unit. Managing family resources has always been a process, requiring individuals to recognize that effective decisions cannot be made quickly and that the evaluation of those decisions is essential for future decisions.

Families cannot effectively manage resources without an awareness of their opportunities as well as a consideration of their limitations. They need to be aware that living in the 21st century presents numerous challenges to the family. Families will continue to consume large amounts of resources, be engaged in the global economy, and provide safety and security for their members. Each of these functions requires management. Thus, the concept of family resource management is embedded in those three individual words: family, resource, and management.

WHAT IS A FAMILY?

Contemporary families are diverse in nature, reflecting the socioeconomic environments surrounding them. The idea that a traditional family exists, from which students can compare and contrast other nontraditional family units, is nonproductive to the goals and objectives of family service providers. It is necessary, however, to categorize and define families when public and private programs assess needs and determine qualified services for citizens based on that designation. Chapter 2 presents a framework for understanding contemporary family definitions and structures.

Nontraditional family: a family that doesn't fit the social norm of the traditional family

> *Joe and Rocia have three children. Joe recently lost his job. To qualify for financial assistance through various local and state programs, the couple must meet the criteria of those programs in terms of how a family is defined. Some programs may be available to them only if they are legally married. Other assistance programs may provide more resources if Rocia is unmarried. These discrepancies challenge ethical decision making and may result in a weakening of family structure. Some assistance may be available based on their household status, regardless of whether they share a home. If Joe is not the biological father of the children, his assistance may be based on only what is deemed necessary for a single male.*

In terms of family resource management, it is assumed that families are units in which members strive to meet the needs of all members while maintaining that family unit over a period of time. Thus, families have both individual and group needs. Identification and communication of these needs are continual. To satisfy these needs, resources must be identified and secured. Money and material possessions are easiest to identify as important family resources; however, the human resources available among all family members are just as important, if not even more essential, to the family's survival and maintenance.

Family: the basic unit in society, traditionally consisting of two parents rearing their children

The processes of identifying needs and securing resources are dynamic within a family unit. Situations arise in frequent, repetitive ways that allow many decisions to become subconscious and almost habitual. Family members shopping for a weekly supply of groceries may cruise down the store aisles, identifying and purchasing an assortment of products with little deliberation. These products have been identified through previous decision-making processes; until family members decide that these basic products are no longer meeting their needs, they are habitual purchases. Other situations require more deliberation and information seeking. The working parent who is confronted on Monday morning with an ill childcare provider must find a specific resource to meet an acute need. The stress level involved in this type of decision is much higher, because this decision impacts the family unit on multiple levels.

Resources: commodities and human resources used in the production of goods and services; anything identified to meet an existing or future need

HOW DO FAMILIES USE RESOURCES?

Humans consume and require massive amounts of resources for survival, physical growth, and personal growth. Basic needs, such as food, water, shelter, and clothing, are obvious. Other resources are necessary to facilitate education, community, and recreation. The study of family resource management considers both consumption of resources and the availability/expenditure of human resources by family members.

The identification of resources to meet specific needs is guided by culture, availability, and accessibility. Tap water quenches thirst, yet an individual may choose to buy bottled water for family drinking purposes. A single-family detached house may be preferred, but if an apartment is the only choice available, a family may make do until other options surface. An Ivy League college may be a student's top choice, but if he or she does not meet the requirements for admission, another selection must be made.

As families identify needs, their focus turns to finding ways to fulfill those needs. The number of possible solutions will vary depending on the particular need. These solutions, however, always require resources. The larger the pool of resources, the higher the probability that needs will be met with efficiency and effectiveness. In managing family resources, sufficiency is also an important consideration. Will family members accept a solution that meets just their minimum expectations? Old newspapers suffice for bathroom use, but not everyone would accept this choice. Because family needs are dynamic and ongoing, any one particular resource may prove useful on some occasions, but not even be considered at other times.

Families may substitute some resources for others, depending on the situational variables. Lunch may consist of a peanut butter sandwich when time is limited but may be a multicourse feast when time is not an issue. Money is often substituted for time in resource selection. Fast food, airline travel, and lawn-care services are examples of this resource transfer or exchange. The complexity of individuals and families elevates the complexity of resource identification and selection when compared to resource management in the business setting.

Availability: the ability to be used as needed

Accessibility: the ability to obtain something when needed

Efficiency: being or involving the immediate agent in producing an effect

Effectiveness: producing a decided, decisive, or desired effect

Sufficiency: judged as being adequate

Substitute: to replace something with another similar product or good

Cohabitation: to live together as or as if a married couple

IN THE NEWS

What's a Plus One?

The practice of cohabitation among adults in the United States and globally has increased greatly over the last few decades. The impact of cohabitation on family formation has been addressed in recent census gathering. The U.S. Census Bureau refers to an "unmarried partner" as someone over the age of 15 who is not related to the householder, but shares living quarters and has a close personal relationship with the householder (U.S. Census Bureau, 2015). For some, this is viewed as a stepping stone to legal marriage, but to others, it serves as a formalized union without the trappings or legal benefits of marriage.

Because cohabitation is now a recognized part of family formation and maintenance, traditional definitions have had to change. That has been true in the insurance industry and in the workplace. As competition for good employees increased, the insurance benefit packages offered by employers became increasingly important as a recruitment incentive. If an employer did not offer "family benefits" to employees who had chosen cohabitation over traditional marriage, the competition would offer that to lure new or to retain existing employees. Many insurance companies allow policy extensions to unmarried partners, regardless of sexual orientation. The issue became whether or not an individual employer would allow that in their benefit package.

Bindley (2012) points out that cohabiting heterosexual partners ultimately benefited from something originally intended to address workplace acknowledgment of employee sexual orientation rights. She reports that marriage rates are at an all-time low and the practice of cohabiting jumped by 13% between 2009 and 2010. The unintentional benefit for cohabiting heterosexuals is the ability to have the same insurance benefits enjoyed by their colleagues who are married or in same-sex domestic partnerships. Many employers have created criteria that must be met to participate in the unmarried yet cohabitating category. Many refer to these criteria as "plus one" benefits. Employees can include partners, and often children whom those partners bring into the family unit.

MANAGING FAMILIES

The history of family science is closely linked to that of business management. Both fields emerged in academia at about the same time, and both began with efforts to facilitate efficient and effective use of resources. Many of the management theories that are applied to individual and family resource management stem from business management. Many human resource theories are supported by research in family science and other social sciences. Business management focuses on planning, organizing, leading, and controlling the use of resources to accomplish performance goals. The goal of any business is the maximization of this process. It is a conscious effort and a constant process. Choices must be made and evaluated continually.

Although the family is not a **business**, it does have many of the same goals that a business addresses. Management theories are explored from both the business and family conceptual frameworks in Chapter 3. Business decisions generally have a stronger hierarchical base and more tangible factors available in the decision-making process. Most family management activity begins with that same decision-making process, but family management exists on a higher personal level, with more emotional, intangible types of factors to consider. The decision-making process is a major concept addressed and explored throughout this text.

Business: a commercial or mercantile activity engaged in as a means of livelihood

THE DECISION-MAKING PROCESS

There are many ways in which individuals and families go about making decisions. Janis (1989) proposes the rational model, presuming that in the process of making decisions, there are purposeful goals and objectives. Rational decision making involves searching for alternatives, assessing consequences, estimating risk or uncertainty, determining the value of consequences, and selecting the action that maximizes attainment of the desired objectives. Decisions that have long-lasting impact on a family unit would benefit from this type of structure. Selection of educational programs and disease treatment options are often approached within this type of framework.

▶ **Photo 1.1**
Technology
enhances a
family's search for
alternatives.

**Five-step
decision-making
process:** a flexible
decision-making
framework that
incorporates
recognizing existing
needs, identifying
alternatives to
fulfill needs,
evaluating identified
alternatives,
selecting and
implementing
alternatives, and
reflecting on and
evaluating the
alternatives selected

Pfeffer (1987) proposes another model that draws from rules, procedures, and processes, rather than the effort to maximize values. The bureaucratic model relies on habitual ways of doing things and is appropriate only for low-risk and uncontested decision situations. Although this model is more appropriate for business decisions, there are some frequent, low-risk decisions that must be made by families. Grocery shopping, especially for staple items, often operates this way.

The political model of decision making (Pfeffer, 1987) produces outcomes that are related to the power of individuals within the group. This model recognizes that individuals within the unit may have differing interests and acknowledges that conflict is normal or at least customary. Although decisions made within this model are seldom perfect for all members, the acts of bargaining and compromising result in member support for the final decision. Decisions specific to family relocation are often reached using this approach. Although children are greatly affected by such moves, it is generally more of a negotiation among the adults, where power becomes a crucial influence.

Realizing that family decision making may be served by any, all, or a combination of these basic models, it is necessary to create a flexible framework for analysis of a variety of individual situations. The **five-step decision-making process** is the framework chosen for this text. Although family decisions are not always methodical, they follow a general framework of need identification and clarification, identification of alternative resources available, analysis and comparison of those resources, selection and implementation of resources chosen, and post-implementation evaluation. This model also gives the family the tools for rational, bureaucratic, or political thought found in the other decision-making models. By analyzing these steps separately and then synthesizing them as a process, the learner can more fully understand the complexity and occasional unpredictability of family choices and behaviors.

CONTEXTUAL INFLUENCES IN FAMILY RESOURCE MANAGEMENT

Families do not exist in a vacuum. Outside influences come into the family environment to change the way the family thinks and behaves. These influences come from history, culture, and the environment.

Historical Influences

Throughout history, there have been ideas and circumstances that have influenced the way in which families manage their resources. New ideologies and ways of thinking have impacted existing family behaviors. New childcare practices, new medical discoveries, and even changing marriage expectations may alter the way in which a family carries out its functions. Historical events also influence the family. Wars, recessions or depressions, terrorist attacks, and other events all have an impact on families. The most recent national recession and global financial crises have illuminated the vulnerability and the strengths of contemporary family structures in times of economic difficulties. The ultimate impact of unemployment on a dual-earner family unit has been very different from that experienced in earlier recessions, where the sole paycheck-earning adult may have lost all earning potential. Families change as history evolves, reflecting and impacting the larger economic environment.

The history of family resource management has influenced the way a family manages today. The early Greek and Roman cultures left a wealth of information about family management that can be found in the writings of the ancient philosophers. The word *economy* comes from the ancient Greek *oikos nomos*, which means *house* and *management*. Hesiod (ca. 715 BCE) wrote, "You should embrace work-tasks in their due order, so that your granaries [grain storage] may be full of substance in its season" (Hesiod, 1999). The 13th-century Church of England also left a legacy of instruction for management. As the church experienced a reform movement, more clergy were encouraged to speak out on marriage and family issues (Murray, 1987). One of the earliest recorded writings was by Robert Grosseteste, Bishop of Lincoln. This was written for his friend, Countess Margaret of Lincoln, after the death of her husband to help her manage his vast estate. He wrote,

> And with the money from your corn, from your rents, and
> from the issues of pleas in your courts, and from your stock,
> arrange the expenses of your kitchen and your wines and your
> wardrobe and the wages of servants, and subtract your stock.
> (Henley, Lamond, Cunningham, & Grosseteste, 1890)

In contemporary terms, he was suggesting how this new widow might balance her budget—income and expenses.

By the end of the 20th century, the world was changing at a rapid pace. Social mobility and invention would change the way many families managed. Although the Western family was still patriarchal, the Industrial Revolution had forced men and women to move into different spheres of influence. Men gave their energies to their work, now outside the home, whereas women gained more power over the household. Isabella Beeton's *Book of Household Management* (cited in Hughes, 2006) sold thousands of copies in England. Her ideas have been compared to modern small-business management techniques. According to Mrs. Beeton, good management included setting an example for and giving clear guidance to the staff, controlling the finances, and applying the benefits of order and method in all management activities (Wensley, 1996).

In the United States, another reference during this time was Beecher's (1869) *The American Woman's Home*. This volume was written as a training manual for women on the duties of the home, in the same fashion as training for other trades at that time. According to Beecher, a woman's profession included

> care and nursing of the body in the critical periods of infancy and sickness, the training of the human mind in the most impressionable period of childhood, the instruction and control of servants, and most of the government and economies of the family state. (p. 14)

The United States experienced massive immigration, overcrowding of urban centers, unsanitary food and water sources, and deplorable working conditions for many citizens at the turn of the 19th century (Gentzler, 2012). These social dilemmas, influenced and addressed by science (ecology and biology) and technology (invention) in the home, precipitated the Lake Placid Conferences in 1899 and 1909. The progressive attendees of these conferences created an interdisciplinary body of knowledge that eventually became the home economics profession. With the creation of the American Home Economics Association in 1909, it was determined that colleges and universities should establish courses of study beyond the existing food preparation and house sanitation offerings. Before the closing of the last Lake Placid conference, home economics was linked to funding for federal vocational programs. The curriculum included nutrition, safe food handling, clothing and textiles, personal finance, home management, and child and human development.

Since the early 1900s, many changes have taken place in living conditions, equipment, and values and standards. During this time, the development of management has also changed. The way in which today's egalitarian family acquires and uses resources is radically different from what was done in previous decades.

Environmental Influences

The resources that are available for use also influence family management. Some families may have a limited number of resources available because of their geographic location or economic status. The needs of a family may not be met because necessary resources are not available. In other cases, if a resource is limited, the family may have to pay more to get that resource than they would if it were plentiful. The availability and accessibility of resources greatly influence how they are used. These factors also influence how resources are managed. More discussion about how resources influence family management can be found in Unit III.

REALITY CHECK

When Uncle Sam Calls

What impact does military deployment of a parent have on a family? The United States has fought many wars in the past, but the most recent efforts in Iraq and Afghanistan have disrupted families in ways that were not typical of past deployments. For these recent wars, the majority of soldiers did not come through a draft of young men. In the Vietnam and Korean Wars, the average soldier spent less than a year overseas and was a young recruit or draftee. In Iraq and subsequent deployments, much of the burden has fallen on older reservists, National Guardsmen—family men and women (Skipp, Ephron, & Hastings, 2006). As deployed family members return home, the Arrendos' experience may be common across the nation.

The Arrendos (name changed for privacy) agreed to share their experience with our readers. Kathy and Mike were young professionals with two small children, ages 2 and 3, when Mike was called to duty. Kathy shares how her needs and resources changed during the course of her husband's absence. Payne's (1998) five resource categorizations are used as a framework for understanding.

▶ **Photo 1.2** Family members serving in the military leave more than emotional voids behind them.

Financial Resources

My husband's income increased through deployment. He made more money as a major than he was making as a civilian. Our expenses changed also with his absence. He was not spending money and was no longer part of the budget for food, clothing, gasoline, and entertainment. I continued to work, and with both of our incomes and this decreased spending, we were able to accumulate a large savings account.

This situation is much different from previous wars, when young men entered the service at much lower pay rates and, if married, their wives were usually not professional career women, so money was often tight for those military families. Kathy shared her initial discomfort in this situation.

I met many military wives in a support group. They were in similar economic situations, and their spending was unbelievable. I think I tried hard not to increase spending with our savings goal in mind. Some spending, I believe, is tied to emotions. When I was feeling angry about our situation, I spent money. As the savings account grew, I relaxed a little and spent a little more on myself—haircuts, dining out, clothing, and makeup. Other wives were remodeling their entire homes, buying new homes, and getting new vehicles. When my husband returned, we went

on a bit of a spending spree, and we don't feel the same financial pressures we did before we accumulated the savings account.

Not all military families experience such increased financial resources. However, without the draft, enlistment demands have changed the level of incentives currently offered.

Emotional Resources

Initially, I couldn't focus or concentrate. How am I going to be a single parent? We always did everything together! When he left, it was almost easier, because the anticipation of his departure was so emotionally draining. I went into automatic [mode], doing what had to be done. I realize now that I did take some of my frustration out on my daughter. My mother recognized this early on and set me straight. I had relaxed control over both children, and I needed to reclaim it. Eventually, the kids and I were functioning normally again.

At the 6-month point, I quit feeling sorry for us and changed my thinking. The hardest thing emotionally is the loss of companionship. I was very lonely and found myself grasping every opportunity to converse with another adult. I found myself drinking alcohol more frequently, not more, just one or two drinks each night.

His return was much more emotionally taxing than I anticipated. It took at least 3 months for the kids and me to get used to another adult making and enforcing some of the rules. I didn't deal well with his disciplining of the children, and he seemed to be talking down to the children. It had been 18 months, and the three of us seemed to have grown and matured, but he returned at the same level he was at when he

(Continued)

left. He resumed managing all bills and the checking account. It drove me nuts for a while! It seemed like when he had called me from over there almost every day, we really talked! He listened. At home he was returning to his old routine of avoiding conflict and controlling things. I was unwilling to go back to that relationship. We have had to work through a lot, and that probably should include counseling.

When asked to discuss how her relationships with family and friends changed during Mike's deployment, Kathy noted several things that surprised her.

My father, who hates emotions, came with me to the "send off" and came to visit us every 3 months from his home in another state. Usually, on past visits, he wanted to be taken care of and entertained, but not during this time. He mowed, fixed things, winterized our home, and did everything that needed to be done. My mom watched the kids when I needed to be away for days at a time for work. I didn't hear from my mother-in-law at all, but I didn't before the deployment, either. No one from his family really stepped up to help. His little brother called more than usual, but never spent time with us. My siblings were supportive, my sister most. My brother did take my children to his home for 2 weeks over Christmas and made it an incredible holiday for all of us.

Friends . . . well, I really learned who my friends were. Most of those we believed to be friends before Mike left disappeared. Some we had never really done a lot with suddenly appeared and gave me tremendous support. When Mike returned, his old buddies started calling. I insisted that we had new friends, and he was understanding enough to change friendships himself.

Mental Resources

At first it was difficult to go from two adults making decisions to one adult in a high-stress, emotional state solving problems. However, as time went on, I was more and more confident in solving problems myself, and I think that I actually grew and became more independent and better at decision making.

I became a very good time manager. I was forced to be more efficient. I think the hardest thing was being a working parent and wanting to spend as much time with the children as possible, but cleaning, mowing, laundry, cooking still had to be done.

I simply decided to choose my battles. We ate out a lot, and we found more time to play together on the weekends.

Spiritual Resources

I am not a real spiritual person. I think through deployment you have to maintain a high level of trust and believe that our troops are well trained and that your spouse will make good decisions. I wasn't able to even think about what if. . . . I maintained a level of confidence that things would be OK, and I had a greater appreciation for God. During this time, my 18-month-old neighbor was diagnosed with cancer. I couldn't play the "poor me" card after that. I developed an ability to focus on the positives in life.

Although my husband is the religious member of my family, I continued to take my children to church each week. At first, it was nothing more than a hassle with a 2-year-old and a 3-year-old to watch and control. I got nothing out of the sermon. Over time, they became more manageable, and, although I did not receive support from the church, it was a nice quiet time to reflect.

Physical Resources

At first I was exhausted, but after about 6 months, my stamina improved. I did hit a wall at 12 months. I had had enough. I was frustrated and angry, and I wanted it to be over! We all stayed in very good health through this time. When the kids did get sick, I brought them to work, or they went to a neighbor's house. I felt neglectful, but I didn't have a choice. Once I got sick myself, and had to ask for help, but I actually was the most physically fit I have ever been during this time. Cooking for me and two little ones was easy. The kids and I walked every day.

Kathy and Mike did what had to be done and coped in the best ways available to them. Their resources expanded with increasing needs. Sources of support shifted and changed completely in some ways. They will never be able to return to the same relationships and decision-making style present before deployment. Time, circumstances, and priorities have changed their family unit markedly. The year following a service member's return to civilian life will often determine the family's ultimate adjustment.

The toll on families caught up in the wars in Iraq and Afghanistan and the effort to end global terrorism will be analyzed for years to come. Divorces in the military increased by 100% in 2004 (Skipp, Ephron, & Hastings, 2006). The army has spent millions of dollars on programming designed to positively enhance the marital relationships of deployed men and women. All branches of the military have engaged in conscious efforts to strengthen support systems on both sides of the globe. Kathy appreciated this:

The army family support group meetings were helpful, and I really respected the army chaplains and their wisdom. It was a good place to air frustrations and anger, but it was only once a month.

Cultural Influences

Any study of individuals and families in the context of a global community could not ignore the enormous impact that **culture** and **diversity** have on the identification, use, and production of both material and human resources.

One cultural influence is family experience. When individuals marry, they bring with them a wide array of experiences from their own family of origin, including their unique cultural heritage, which ultimately influences their expectations for the new family. The way in which the family of origin managed resources will follow people into their newly formed relationship, and the two individuals will explore these experiences as they formulate their own unique way of managing resources together.

> *Yuki and Eric have been married for 4 years. They are planning to begin a family soon. Eric announces that they must find a larger, two-bedroom apartment before a baby arrives. Yuki doesn't understand this need. In her home country, Japan, it is not uncommon for infants to share their parents' bed for the first few years.*

Another important cultural influence on family resource management is **worldview**. Kluckhohn and Strodtbeck (1961) developed a framework for comparing and contrasting the different value systems between and among different cultural groups. The assumptions underlying their work include the following:

- There is a limited number of common human problems for which all people at all times must find some solution. Most families, at one time or another, must match needs and resources to feed, clothe, educate, and protect their members.

- There is variability in solutions to all the problems; it is neither limitless nor random, but definitely variable within a range of possible solutions. Each family and each situation is unique; however, experiences have common factors between and among families.

- All alternatives of all solutions are present in all societies at all times, but are differentially preferred. Choices made by any family at any given time may differ from those of others because of cultural expectations and beliefs. (p. 10)

Culture: a set of learned beliefs, values, and behaviors of the way of life shared by the members of a society

Diversity: the inclusion of diverse people (as people of different races or cultures) in a group or organization

Worldview: the common concept of reality shared by a particular group of people, usually referred to as a culture or an ethnic group; an individual as well as a group phenomenon

As a result of these different value frameworks, Kluckhohn and Strodtbeck identified five distinctive **orientations** that exist within any particular cultural group, yet differ between groups. These orientations are human nature, humans and nature, time, activity, and relations.

The orientation of human nature may be viewed by a cultural group as evil, a mixture of good and evil, or basically good. Often, cultural practices are based on these beliefs. Consider the judicial system. The practice of imprisoning criminals for certain periods of time with rehabilitative treatment suggests a culture that believes that humans are basically good but can be misled. Religions that believe in original sin purport human nature as basically evil, with possible salvation through ritual.

©iStockphoto.com/martin-dm

▶ **Photo 1.3**
Family traditions draw heavily from the concepts of worldview.

The relationship between humans and nature is an orientation that can be categorized in three perspectives. Humans can be subjugated to, be in harmony with, or have mastery over nature. Refusal of medical treatment is illustrative of a subjugation orientation. Air-conditioning and heating systems are used by many to gain mastery or control over the weather elements. Today, emerging concerns over environmental quality and the sustainability of natural resources have forced a reconsideration of harmony between man and nature.

Every cultural group must deal with all three time orientations—past, present, and future—to maintain existence over time. The preference or dependence on a particular time orientation separates cultural groups. To participate in a financial savings plan implies that an individual is preparing for the future. Investing four or more years to obtain a college degree is another example of future-time orientation. Cultural groups that devote a great deal of time to the study and practice of past rituals, art forms, and doctrine are reflective of past-time orientation.

The value placed on human activity is an orientation that also differs between cultural groups. Some focus on being or living only for the day. Others focus on becoming, searching, and working for self-growth and improvement. A third orientation places more emphasis on accomplishments that are measurable by external standards. All three orientations may exist within any large group of people; however, the group as a whole shows a preference for one. Members who show evidence of that preferred activity are then deemed to be successful.

The last orientation identified to differentiate between cultures is that of human relations. Three different patterns emerge: lineal, collaborative, and individualistic. The lineal pattern is characterized by dominant group goals, a chain of command, and a commitment to maintaining the group over time. A collaborative pattern is reflected in the concept of a team. Someone operating from the individualistic pattern will place primary emphasis on personal goals and objectives and on personal autonomy.

How does this worldview framework impact family decision making? Each and every decision made by a family reflects cultural preferences at multiple levels. For instance, when a parent decides to participate in a college savings plan for his or her child, this decision reflects core beliefs that education is important, that sacrificing today for something that might come to be in the future is a worthy action, and that a college degree is an accomplishment viewed positively by the larger social group.

A human service professional operating from his or her own worldview will find that his or her ability to serve individuals and families functioning within another orientation is problematic. When an individual is devoted to collaborative relationships (i.e., family, gang, religion), he or she will not consider solutions that involve competitive actions or individualistic accomplishments. If a parent believes that children are inherently good or bad, behavior modification plans will be viewed as illogical. A family struggling for many generations with intense poverty may see no value in saving or planning for the future when surviving each day requires so much of its resource base.

As Payne (1998) states,

> The role of the educator or social worker or employer is not to save the individual, but rather to offer a support system, role models, and opportunities to learn, which will increase the likelihood of the person's success. Ultimately, the choice always belongs to the individual. (p. 149)

Awareness and understanding of cultural differences or different worldviews provide the human service professional with increased options and heightened objectivity.

Table 1.1 Selection of Family Housing: Same Ages, Income, Location, and Educational Levels		
Orientation	**Family A**	**Family B**
Humans and nature	Harmony considerations: energy conservation; natural building materials; simplicity of furnishings	Mastery over considerations: comfort regardless of weather; popular building materials; high-tech, personalized interiors
Time	Present considerations: provide for the present; meet current needs	Future considerations: invest for the future; plan for future needs
Activity	Being considerations: housing is merely shelter; changing situations will require moving	Accomplishing considerations: housing reflects social position; neighborhood implies status
Possible decisions	Modest rental unit that is conveniently located	Purchase of acceptable home with mortgage commitment

WORLDVIEW

Using the structured form below (Table 1.2), analyze the following family decisions in terms of differing worldview perspectives:

- A dual-career couple decides that the wife will leave the workforce until the youngest child enters middle school.

- Your neighbor refuses to use weed killer on his or her lawn because it is harmful to the environment.

- A 16-year-old high school student drops out of school to take a full-time job to help support his or her family during an economic crisis.

- A high school graduate decides to attend a 4-year college instead of entering the workforce immediately.

Table 1.2 Worldview Applications

Orientation	Perspective	Possible Decisions
Human nature	Humans are evil? Humans are good? Humans are a mixture of good and evil?	
Humans and nature—the relationship	Humans are subjugated to nature? Humans are in harmony with nature? Humans have mastery over nature?	
Time orientation	Look to the past? Look to the future? Live in the present?	
Human activity—what is valued	Focus on being? Focus on becoming? Focus on accomplishments?	
Human relations—what is expected	Lineal decision making? Collaborative decision making? Individualistic decision making?	

MULTIDISCIPLINARY PERSPECTIVES

Discipline: academic area of research and education

The study of families and behaviors of individuals and family units depends on research methods and **disciplines** that provide a variety of perspectives. The field of family studies integrates existing theory, new research findings, and cross-disciplinary works into a framework for understanding the complexities of family study. Using that framework, professionals are able to engage in further research or practical application of knowledge in the field. Although the following discussion illustrates a few specific disciplines that contribute to this knowledge base, several others are possible contributors over time.

Psychology

In ancient Greek, the word *psyche* meant *soul* or *mind*, and *logos* was the study of something. Psychology, as a field, has evolved into an academic and applied field focusing on the study of the mind and behavior. In the applied sense, psychology also refers to the use of the knowledge accumulated through that study to treat mental illness and do behavioral analysis. Psychologists study the mental processes and behavior of individuals, alone or in a group, not the group itself. Wilhelm Wundt opened the first psychological laboratory in 1879.

Sociology

Sociology is the study of society, with a focus on the study of the social interactions of people, groups, and entire societies. This academic discipline emerged in the early 1800s and evolved through that century as struggles for global leadership emerged. Scientific methods were used to understand how and why groups come together and continue across time. From this inquiry, theories about social rules and governing structures give insight into why individuals are motivated to be a part of groups. In an applied form, sociological research benefits educators, lawmakers, administrators, families, and others who seek resolution of social problems and creation of public policy.

Social Psychology

The ancient philosopher Plato believed that humans organize themselves into groups and form governments to solidify their groups because they cannot achieve all of their individual goals alone (Goethals, 2003). Through the ages, students have pondered this question: How much of our behavior is determined by external constraints versus internal drives? Triplett (1898) put social psychology into the realm of academic discipline by conducting studies that focused on the impact of other people on the individual. Allport's textbook *Social Psychology* (1935) grounded the study of social psychology in scientific methods. Many studies have focused on the development of norms within groups and the transmission of those norms across groups—that is, interpersonal influence.

Social psychology is a field devoted to understanding how individuals impact the groups they associate with and how groups impact their individual members. Research within this discipline includes studies of marriage, religion, and parenting, as well as adolescent behavior.

Cultural Anthropology

Anthropology is the study of humanity. The cultural branch of anthropology seeks to make sense of difference or variation among humans. Because culture is acquired through learning, people living in different, separate places or under differing circumstances will develop different ways of thinking about similar things. This belief is exemplified by the earlier discussion of worldview.

Although understanding the differences among cultures is important to understanding how families manage their resources, it is also important to this discipline to seek universalities among humans across cultural and geographic boundaries. Are beliefs and behaviors completely learned, or is there a biological, hereditary basis to them? Anthropologists have surmised that people adapt to their environments in nongenetic ways—through culture. Current concern for the global environment and international relationships has redirected study in this field to the tensions among cultures.

Economics

The study of economics is not only about business, but also about human behavior within existing structures of production, distribution, trade, and consumption of goods and services. As a science, it functions to predict and explain the consequences of choices made by consumers and producers. Economics is a quantified field of research that depends on numerical methods of analysis.

Microeconomics studies individual agents, such as households and businesses. Macroeconomics focuses on the economy as an entirety. Key concepts include supply, demand, competition, and pricing. The research and models derived from the study of economics help explain how families identify and evaluate resources in their decision-making processes.

Behavioral economics is an emerging field of study that focuses on application of scientific principles to human and social dimensions of decision making. Research questions seek to answer how consumer decisions impact pricing and the allocation of resources in a society.

Biology

The field of biology is the study or science of living things. Family resource management derives important information on reproduction, physical health, and safety from biological findings, and implements biological research methods and theories to answer questions about how the environment and humans interact. Genetics is an associated field that provides families with guidance when making important reproductive and health decisions. Medicine is also a related field that plays an important part in family decisions and resource allocation.

Professionals in family studies use multidisciplinary research methods and integrate research generated by all of these fields, which allows a multifaceted exploration of topics. For instance, if we want to understand maternal employment and its impact on the family, we can approach the question from multiple frameworks. Psychologists might focus on the emotional and cognitive impacts on family members—parents and children. Sociologists may consider the motivations that lead to the mother's participation in the workforce and how social expectations influence that behavior.

Social psychologists may view the topic in terms of how employment impacts the female's self-esteem or power base, or how females impact the working environment they occupy. Cultural anthropology might be more interested in how maternal employment participation varies between and among different cultures and across time. Economics would be interested in how maternal employment impacts resources available to families and how that, in turn, impacts their consumption. Another topic of interest to economists is the potential for increased production through more fully participating adult female labor pools. Biology might study the issue from a physical perspective. The spread of contagious diseases through on-the-job contact or within childcare centers might be of interest.

In combination, these disciplines provide us with a holistic view of family resource management. All are important to the study and understanding of family behavior.

SUMMARY

The family unit has been and continues to be the basic unit of society. As such an integral part of the larger social system, the family is impacted by all social, economic, political, and environmental changes. Thus, the family is dynamic in nature, responding and adapting to change. To allow such flexibility, families must engage in the management process, using basic decision-making tools and accessing necessary resources to maintain over time.

QUESTIONS FOR REVIEW AND DISCUSSION

1. Why and when is it necessary to create limiting definitions of the family?

2. Other than money, how many resources can you list that would be important in the management of families?

3. How have culture and worldview influenced your decision to study family resource management?

4. Individuals and families use the basic decision-making steps for even small situations. Trace your most recent eating experience through this process.

5. Using the worldview framework in this chapter, determine your personal combination of the five dimensions.

6. Marriage, cohabitation, and divorce are important topics in this field. How might researchers in economics and social psychology differ in the way in which they approach these topics? How would those in psychology and sociology differ?

CHAPTER TWO

UNDERSTANDING FAMILIES

Objectives
History of the Family
The Family Today
Defining the Family
   Theoretical Definitions
   Variations on a Definition of Family—When
      Numbers Are Necessary
   The Gray Areas
Worldview
Changes in the Family
In the News
Family Functions
Families Within Cultural Contexts
Reality Check
Researching the Family
   Family Systems Theory
   Social Exchange Theory
   Symbolic Interactionism
   Conflict Theory
   Feminist Perspective
   Family Ecological Theory
   Family Strengths Framework
   Family Development Theory
Family Research Design
Summary
Questions for Review and Discussion

Objectives

- Be aware of the history and origins of the family.

- Recognize that the family today is in transition.

- Acknowledge the variety of definitions of *family* and the sources of those definitions.

- Be familiar with the functions of the family both in the past and today.

- Be aware of the purpose and usefulness of theory in understanding families.

- Be familiar with the basic family theories, or conceptual frameworks.

- Acknowledge the strengths and weaknesses of family theories/perspectives.

- Be aware of the two basic types of research methodology, both quantitative and qualitative.

The family. We were a strange little band of characters trudging through life sharing diseases and toothpaste, coveting one another's desserts, hiding shampoo, borrowing money, locking each other out of our rooms, inflicting pain and kissing to heal it in the same instant, loving, laughing, defending, and trying to figure out the common thread that bound us all together.

—Erma Bombeck

The most basic unit of society is the family. It is hard to imagine someone who has never experienced being part of a family. In fact, almost everyone can tell a story about his or her family. For most, family is where we learn strength and courage to face the outside world. Effective management of the family is critical not only to the family, but to the individual members within the family. The family is where we learn to make good decisions and experience the consequences of bad decisions. A study of the family begins with the history of the family.

HISTORY OF THE FAMILY

The origins of the family are unclear. Some have suggested that there is evidence that families have existed for thousands, perhaps millions, of years (Gough, 1971). Anderson (1997) speculates that although prehistoric clans were organized around a patriarch, with the development of agriculture, it became necessary to organize around geographic areas ruled by political figures, rather than by the head of the family. In medieval Europe, the family was influenced by the church and feudalism, generally extended in form (Seufert-Barr, 1994). Tadmor (1996) studied the definition of a family as it appeared in 18th-century English writings. She found that the term included not only immediate blood relatives in the household, but also servants and other relatives in residence. The criterion for inclusion as a family unit at that time was an individual's dependence on the head of household for basic needs.

The institution of marriage within the family is also varied. As early as 1922, Westermarck described the origin of marriage as follows:

> It was, I believe, even in primitive times, the habit for a man and a woman to live together, to have sexual relations with one another, and to rear their offspring in common, the man, being the protector and supporter of his family and the woman being his helpmate and the nurse of his children. This habit was sanctioned by custom, and afterwards by law and was thus transformed into a social institution. (1971, pp. 27–28)

Polygyny: the practice of a man having more than one wife at the same time

Gibbs and Campbell (1999) reported that religious and social groups experimented with different forms of familial social bonds in America during the 19th century. The practice of **polygyny**, having multiple wives, existed in certain religious factions and in some Native American cultures. Larger households meant an increase in children and wealth. Multiple adult members provided the resources necessary to fulfill the many daily needs of large family units.

In America, the preindustrial family was largely an economic unit. Those who lived together were needed to help provide for existence. Families sometimes included nonfamily members whose purpose was to care for the children or carry out household work. Children, once old enough, were often sent to help other families if they were not needed at home.

After the Industrial Revolution, work was no longer centered in the home. Men went away from the home to work, and family roles were more defined. As the middle class emerged, the family became a symbol of stability and the domestic ideal (Skolnick, 1993). The modern family consisted of a breadwinning husband, a housewife, and their children. According to Aulette (2002), the modern family included two distinct phases. First, the democratic family emerged at the end of the 18th century as a separate and private group in society where mates were selected through preferences and children were nurtured. Creating and maintaining a family was an expected, almost obligatory, role for adults. Husbands went to work outside the home, and wives were expected to stay home. By the 20th century, the second phase, the companionate family, had become the most common family form. In the companionate family, husbands and wives were partners who married because they loved each other, rather than out of a sense of moral duty (Mintz & Kellogg, 1988).

The postmodern family implies that families at this time in history are so diverse that comparison with those in the past is impossible. Another implied concept within the term *postmodern* is that in trying to rely on past research and theory, one would be unable to study current family structures and relationships.

THE FAMILY TODAY

Throughout history, researchers have been unable to find a picture of family that would represent what it has come to mean today or what it will be in the future. How we define the family today must be broad and flexible. One definition would not be able to accurately characterize every family in the United States. The traditional family or nuclear family implies a husband, wife, and children in one household. Although this idea has come to symbolize the American family, it is far from actually representing the vast majority of families today.

The functions of the family will lead us into our discussion throughout the text. Before we look at these functions, it is helpful to look at the diverse ways in which family units are defined.

DEFINING THE FAMILY

The word *family* still brings to mind the image of an intact, two-parent home with two children, a dog, and gray-haired grandparents. In reality, we have just learned that in the United States we can no longer define the family in this way. In the past, the definition of family has been selective and often rigid in description, leaving many to wonder about the validity of their own family. Given the various configurations of families today, creating a contemporary definition of family can

Modern family: a family that consists of a breadwinning husband, a housewife, and their children

Democratic family: a family that emerged at the end of the 18th century as a separate and private group in society where mates were selected through preferences and children were nurtured

Companionate family: a family where husbands and wives were partners who married because they loved each other, rather than out of a sense of moral duty

Postmodern family: the contemporary family that is more diverse than in the past in terms of family structure and relationships

Traditional family: a married couple and their biological child or children in one household

Nuclear family: the family group consisting of parents (usually a father and mother) and their children in one household

Figure 2.1　Family and Living Arrangements, 2016

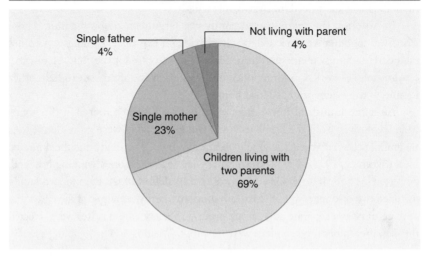

Source: United States Census Bureau, 2016.

be a difficult task. The definition of family takes on diverse meanings, depending on the context from which it comes.

Theoretical Definitions

Within the study of family resource management, the interdependence of members and the continual need for decision making to meet the needs of members are key concepts. Although no single definition meets all situational needs, those within the field of family sciences incorporate core concepts founded not only as a result of research and the development of family theory, but in response to the changes that have taken place within society. Existing definitions that address the study of families include the following:

> A group of persons united by the ties of marriage, blood, or adoption; constituting a single household; interacting and communicating with each other in their respective social roles; and creating and maintaining a common culture. (Burgess & Locke, 1945)

> A range of household structures that meet people's needs at various points in their lives or that are forced on them by circumstances. (Hess, 1995)

> A consuming unit that is highly dependent on the economic system beyond the home, over which the family members have little control. (Hess, 1995)

> Two or more persons who share resources, share responsibility for decisions, share values and goals, and have a commitment to one another over time. (American Association of Family and Consumer Sciences, 2001)

As families search for public and private resources, they must navigate the multitude of definitions held by different institutions. It is hard to put the family into one philosophical box. Throughout history, the family has changed to meet the needs of its members. **Family** will be defined in this text based on three core concepts drawn from Lamanna, Riedmann, and Stewart (2015):

Family: the basic unit in society, traditionally consisting of two parents rearing their children

1. Any sexually expressive or parent-child or other kin relationship in which people, usually related by ancestry, marriage, or adoption, form an economic unit and care for any young,

2. Consider their identity to be significantly attached to the group, and

3. Commit to maintaining that group over time.

All three criteria have major implications for resource identification, access, and management.

Variations on a Definition of Family—When Numbers Are Necessary

U.S. CENSUS BUREAU: The *family* is a group of two or more people (one of whom is the householder) related by birth, marriage, or adoption and residing together (U.S. Census Bureau, 2015).

Data gathered by the U.S. Census are used in a multitude of ways. Business institutions focus on these households as consuming units, further categorizing them into socioeconomic, cultural, age-specific, and other target market groups. Financial analysts use these data to forecast the economic health of the country. Social scientists apply these data to the analysis of behavioral shifts and actual or possible impacts of such changes.

PUBLIC OPINION: Surveys administered to the general public collect information about behaviors and configurations of family units that are then presented as being acceptable or deemed to be normal in that particular society. Depending on the scientific rigor of the instruments used in these polls, results may be generalized to the larger population or may be biased and unreliable.

Policy-Specific Definitions

THE LEGAL SYSTEM: The legal definition of *family* has become much more flexible and nonspecific and not limited to people linked by legal marriage, blood, or adoption. Judges use these criteria: common residence, economic interdependency, stability, and commitment (Scanzoni & Marsiglio, 1993).

> Based on the functional and psychological qualities of the relationship: The "exclusivity and longevity" of relationship; the "level of emotional and financial commitment"; the "reliance placed upon one another for daily family services"; and how the members "conducted their everyday lives and held themselves out to society." (New York Supreme Court; see Gutis, 1989)

Life Insurance

Employers offering life insurance in their benefits package will usually limit coverage of an employee's family members by defining such terms as *spouse* and *child*. For example, the University of Nebraska (2017) gives the following definitions:

Spouse
- Husband or wife, as recognized under the laws of the state of Nebraska
- Common-law spouse if the common-law marriage was contracted in a jurisdiction recognizing a common-law marriage

Child
- The following dependent children may be eligible for coverage:
  - Natural-born or legally adopted child who has not reached the limiting age of 26
  - Stepchild who has not reached the limiting age of 26
  - Child for whom the employee has legal guardianship and who has not reached the limiting age of 26
  - Child with a mental or physical disability who has attained the limiting age of 26 may continue coverage beyond age 26 if proof of disability is provided within 31 days of attaining age 26

The Family and Medical Leave Act (FMLA)

Under the FMLA, employees working for qualifying employers have the legal right to take unpaid leave to care for infants, ill children, spouses, or parents or to take new parental bonding time with adopted or foster children. The following definitions illuminate qualifying situations:

- Birth and care of a newborn child

- Placement with the employee of a child for adoption or foster care and to care for the newly placed child

- Care for an immediate family member (spouse, child, or parent—but not a parent-in-law) with a serious health condition

- Any "qualifying exigency" arising out of the fact that the employee's spouse, son, daughter, or parent is a covered military member on or called to active duty (American Federation of State, County and Municipal Employees, 2017)

U.S. Income Tax/Internal Revenue Service

To determine tax liability, U.S. citizens file annual tax returns. The terms used in this process are defined by accompanying literature. A **head of household** is an unmarried or "considered unmarried" person who pays more than one half the cost of keeping up a home for a qualifying person, such as a child who lived with that person or a parent whom the person can claim as a dependent. There are five tests that must be met for a person to qualify as another's **dependent**:

1. *Relationship test.* The person must either be a relative or have lived in your home as a family member all year.

2. *Age test.* The person must be under age 19 or a student under age 24 at the end of the year and younger than you or permanently and totally disabled at any time during the year, regardless of age.

3. *Residency test.* To meet this test, your child must have lived with you for more than half the year. There are exceptions for temporary absences, children who were born or died during the year, kidnapped children, and children of divorced or separated parents.

4. *Support test.* To meet this test, the child cannot have provided more than half of his or her own support for the year, and you generally must provide more than half of a person's total support during the calendar year.

5. *Joint return test.* To meet this test, the child cannot file a joint return for the year. An exception to the joint return test applies if your child and his or her spouse file a joint return only to claim a refund of income tax withheld or estimated tax paid. (www.irs.gov)

> **Head of household:** the person whose name appears first in the census enumeration of a family or group of people living together

> **Dependent:** a person who relies on another for support

©iStockphoto.com/Juanmonino

▶ **Photo 2.1**
Same-sex parenting challenges some definitions of family.

The Gray Areas

Other definitions of *family* tend to be influenced by social factors. Family definitions include arrangements that may be seen as gray areas by some, but are becoming more socially accepted, and these families are often granted "family" legal rights.

Cohabitation or an *unmarried couple* is defined as "two unrelated adults of the opposite sex (one of whom is the householder) who share a housing unit with or without the presence of children under 15 years old. Unmarried couple households contain only two adults" (U.S. Census Bureau, 2015). Despite some concerns, this form of the family has gained widespread social acceptance over the past

> **Cohabitation:** to live together as or as if a married couple

Domestic partners: the personal relationship between individuals who are living together and sharing a common domestic life together, but are not joined in any type of legal partnership, marriage, or civil union

Mutual definition: a definition shared by or common to two or more people or groups

30 years. Current legal debate has centered on **domestic partners** being entitled to legal rights and/or employee benefits. Loosely, two people who have chosen to share one another's lives in an intimate and committed relationship, live together, and are jointly responsible for basic living expenses qualify for such programs in states that recognize this designation. As of 2009, federal employees in domestic partnerships gained some benefits following a new policy enacted by the Obama administration (Phillips, 2009). In addition, since July 9, 2015, married same-sex couples throughout the United States have had equal access to all the federal benefits given to married opposite-sex couples (Lynch, 2015).

Yorburg (2002) defines *families* as groups related by marriage, birth, adoption, or **mutual definition**. According to this definition, when people define themselves as a family, they essentially are a family. Within that mutual definition are elements of emotional involvement and identity attachment that connect individuals at the present time and create a need for continuation or maintenance of that family unit over time. This maintenance function requires acquisition and utilization of resources.

WORLDVIEW

World Family Map: Mapping Family Change and Child Well-Being Outcomes

The World Family Map, sponsored by Child Trends and a range of educational and nongovernmental institutions from across the globe, provides important and current indicators about the family in developing countries. This project points individuals, families, communities, NGOs, and governments to significant factors affecting family well-being that programs and policies can use to build strong families. Scholars around the world contribute to the project to provide reliable data and research on families and children. The following are indicators of family structure around the world:

- In spite of marked family changes around the globe over the last half-century, children are still most likely to live in two-parent families in all countries except South Africa.

- One of five children are living without either of their parents in South Africa and Uganda, and at least one of eight children do so in other sub-Saharan African countries, including Ghana, Tanzania, Kenya, and the Democratic Republic of the Congo. About one of 10 children live apart from both parents in several countries in Central/South America (Bolivia, Chile, Colombia, and Nicaragua), while less than one in approximately 20 do so in other regions of the world.

- Growing up with a single parent is especially common in sub-Saharan Africa, in Central and South America, and in several English-speaking Western countries; in the United States, the United Kingdom, New Zealand, and Canada, one fifth or more of children do so. Asia, the Middle East, and Eastern Europe have the world's lowest rates of single parenthood.

- Extended families, which can compensate for the absence of one or both parents from the household, are most commonly found in sub-Saharan Africa, followed by Asia and Central/South America.

- Although marriage rates for adults ages 18 to 49 are declining worldwide, they remain high in Asia and the Middle East (between 47% in Singapore and 80% in Egypt), and are particularly low in Central/South America. The rate of cohabitation for adults ages 18 to 49 tops 30% in some Central/South American countries and 20% in some European nations.

- While fertility rates are also declining worldwide, nonmarital childbearing is increasing in many regions, with the highest rates found in Central/South America and Western Europe.

Source: Child Trends. *The World Family Map.* © 2014.

CHANGES IN THE FAMILY

Changes in family expectations serve to alter the emphasis of the family within society. The Pew Research Center (2015) reports that expectations differ by age, with older adults more likely to believe that society is better off when people value marriage and children. The American family is becoming increasingly more diverse, and family structures are constantly evolving, with less than half of all children living with two married parents (Pew Research Center, 2015). Marriage rates continue to decline. In 1960, 9% of adults had never been married, but by 2012, that percentage increased to 17% for women and 23% for men. There are several reasons for these changes, including more people waiting to marry later in life and a rise in cohabitation. Another reason for the decline in marriage could be that previously married adults show less interest in marrying again (Pew Research Center, 2015). There are fewer two-parent households, and families are smaller (Pew Research Center, 2015).

There is no doubt that cohabitation has increased as a family structure, and it is estimated that the majority of couples now live together before getting married. There are still cultural and religious traditions that view cohabitation as unacceptable, and research continues to point out concerns for those who cohabitate. Lundberg, Pollak, and Stearns (2016) report an economic inequality among those who cohabitate; those who are college-educated follow more traditional patterns of marriage and parenting than do men and women with less education. Childbearing in cohabiting unions is higher among high school graduates and those with some college, and their marital and cohabiting unions are less stable. Children of less-educated parents are more likely to grow up in a single-parent household or to experience instability. This increasing inequality has contributed to inequality in household income.

Stanley, Rhodes, and Markman (2006) coined the term "sliding versus deciding" to illustrate an important implication of the transition from cohabitation to marriage. Those couples who slide into cohabitation may also remain in a relationship or move toward marriage regardless of the quality of or commitment to the relationship. In contrast, those couples who have discussed their future intentions and what cohabitation means to their relationship—the "deciders"—are more successful as they move into marriage.

The National Marriage Project (Hymowitz, Carroll, Wilcox, & Kaye, 2013) reports that the institution of marriage has also changed. Continuing to support earlier trends of delayed married for young adults, research finds that while some may see this as evidence that marriage is becoming undesirable, a large majority of young adults say they hope to marry in the future. There are several benefits of marriage delay, which include better economic opportunities and a lower divorce rate. However, more women are now becoming mothers before getting married, with 47% of twentysomethings giving birth outside of marriage. The result of these changes can include economic, social, and family stability consequences, especially for children.

Americans are sharply divided when it comes to recent structural changes in the family, such as cohabitation, single parenting, mothers working outside the home, intercultural marriage, and so forth. The Pew Research Center reports that about one third of people accept these changes, one third reject or believe these changes are harmful for families, and one third are tolerant of the changes but believe they may not be good for the family (Morin, 2011).

Although many changes have taken place and the family may be difficult to define, the concept of family is an integral part of the fabric of American culture. Policymakers, educators, and service providers acknowledge the importance of the family as the core of individual well-being and growth.

IN THE NEWS

The TV Family

The American family has been at the core of many media productions—radio, TV, movies, and even music videos. The family has been portrayed as comical, cynical, dysfunctional, and even macabre. The public is easily drawn to these odd yet interesting imaginary families—so much so that when these shows are discontinued, viewers mourn their loss, as if the characters were real, not imaginary, friends.

Father Knows Best ran on network television from 1954 to 1963. The main actor was less like a formal father and more like a "dad," and the TV audience related to his character and his traditional family. He loved his wife and kids, and family came first, but it was difficult to balance each week. Father Knows Best was so popular that when production ended, it continued to be shown on the prime-time TV network schedule for three years.

The Addams Family debuted in 1964 as a weekly prime-time comical, yet dark, production. Scripts were focused on the traditional family of Gomez, his wife Morticia, and their two young children, Pugsley and Wednesday. Living with this family in the frightening mansion were Uncle Fester, Grandmama, Cousin Itt, and Thing, under the faithful care of the butler, Lurch. This family unit became so beloved and well known that even though the original series lasted for only 2 years, subsequent animated series and full-length movies based on these characters brought them back to life again and again.

Growing Pains, a family sitcom, ran from 1985 to 1992. The show's premise set up a more modern dynamic, as the father in the family moved his psychiatry practice into the family's home when his wife returned to the workforce. Viewers became so attached to the Seavers that two full-length movies have been made since the show's departure from prime time more than 25 years ago. The movies' writers attempted to continue the original storyline while allowing the cast members and their characters to have interesting adult experiences.

The Simpsons, one of the most successful and critically acclaimed TV shows of all time, has built its reputation on the bizarre interpretation of real-life family and social issues. Because it is an animated series, none of the characters is required to age, allowing the pseudo-middle-American family great freedom of interpretation of current social issues through almost three decades.

Everybody Loves Raymond, a long-running comedy from 1996 to 2005, is about a sports writer and his family; they live just across the street from Raymond's overbearing parents. The writers poke fun at Raymond's inability to set boundaries with his parents, and the audience feels sorry for him because his wife is smarter than he is. However, the show's popularity comes from the fact that many people can identify with Raymond and his family life.

Modern Family, a more recent television situational comedy that began in 2009, depicts three diverse families that are all part of a larger extended family. They include anxious and stressed Claire and her husband, fun-loving Phil; gay partners Mitchell and Cameron, who have decided to adopt; and Jay and his Colombian wife, Gloria, who despite being in love have obvious differences in age and culture. Although the show embraces diversity in all forms of relationships, it also acknowledges the challenges that result from those differences.

The list of old and new media hits based on the family is long. What makes viewers so anxious to follow the escapades of imaginary families? Some might say that it is an attempt to make sense of their own. Others might suggest that it is an attempt to escape their own, if only for a few minutes each week.

FAMILY FUNCTIONS

Perhaps it would also be beneficial to look at the various structures of the family and concentrate on the critical functions of the family. As noted earlier, families provide individuals with a sense of belonging and emotional security, and also provide for their physical needs. The family is the most basic economic unit in society and is responsible for reproduction. The family is also the principal component in the socialization process. It is in the family setting that a child learns his or her place in society, as well as the roles and behaviors that give him or her status in that society.

In the past, one of the most popular theories about family was the structural-functional theory. This theory views individuals as members of many interrelated systems, one of which is the family. Talcott Parsons (1968), one of the creators of this theory, believed that four basic functions were necessary for any system to survive. These functions help explain duties that families perform and that have caused the family to continue throughout history. These functions are latent pattern maintenance, or loyalty; adaptation, or ability to adjust to change; integration of members; and goal attainment, or the ability to mobilize resources. This theory has been criticized for its patriarchal views, as well as for not being able to explain the differences between culture and ethnicity (Aulette, 2002).

Juliet Mitchell (1984) suggested that families provide four activities or functions: production (producing or purchasing food and shelter, preparing workers to earn wages, and consumption of goods and services), reproduction (bearing and raising children), socialization (teaching the rules of society), and sexuality ("legitimate" sexual activity).

Although some social scientists have acknowledged that many families have lost some of the functions of previous generations, such as growing their own food and educating their own children, they generally agree on three basic functions: to raise children responsibly, to provide economic support, and to give family members emotional security (Lamanna, Riedmann, & Stewart, 2015). Reproduction, meaning bearing and raising children, has been largely the responsibility of the family. Although the family is no longer self-sufficient in the production of goods, the family is responsible for meeting the basic economic needs (food, clothing, and shelter) of its members. In addition, families can provide individuals with an important source of emotional support, which includes affection and companionship. Identification of the functions of families describes the family by defining the work of families.

FAMILIES WITHIN CULTURAL CONTEXTS

Families exist within the cultural contexts of race, ethnicity, religion, politics, and economics. These frameworks impact how individuals and families define and evaluate their relationships. As the global community continues to evolve, it is important to recognize, understand, and be responsive to cultural differences between and among cultural groups.

Families pass learned behaviors and experiences, or a cultural heritage, from generation to generation (Johnson, 1998). Drawing from the worldview framework introduced in Chapter 1, the values held by cultural groups are expressed in unique patterns through the formation and perpetuation of family units. Kluckhohn and Strodtbeck (1961) propose that the three primary cultural expressions of group membership are lineal, collaborative, and individualistic. Family units within these cultural groups reflect the orientation of the larger social group. For instance, Native American families reflect stronger lineal relationships, often defining family membership based on a clan

©iStockphoto.com/Satoshi-K

▶ **Photo 2.2**
Traditional dress and ceremony express cultural beliefs about marriage.

or group of related families (Johnson, 1998). However, few cultural groups will fit neatly into any one of the three orientations. Although many Native Americans may have a more developed awareness of their tribal membership (lineal), the basic functions of these tribes have historically been collaborative in nature.

As cultural groups coexist within a larger society, and because more than one quarter of the U.S. population is now made up of immigrants, individuals from different racial, ethnic, and religious groups have begun drawing life partners from distinctly different cultural groups. Interracial marriages include the joining together of individuals from the white, African American, Asian, and Native American races with people from outside their race. Interethnic marriages consist of partners who marry within their ethnic groups, such as unions between Hispanic groups or between Asian groups. Today, 15.5% of new marriages represent two people from diverse cultural backgrounds (Restuccia, 2014).

Although religious homogamy is still important for some, **interfaith** marriages are increasing in the United States. The U.S. Religious Landscape Survey (Pew Research Center, 2014c) reports that 39% of Americans are married to a spouse with a different religious affiliation. In contrast, 49% of people who are cohabitating are in an interfaith relationship. The report also points out that religion is much more fluid, meaning that although individuals may not identify with any particular religion, spirituality or religious ideals are at least somewhat important in their lives. Certain religious groups are more likely to marry within their faith, such as Hindus, Mormons, and Muslims. Religious orientations often affect decisions about money, children, social networks, and relationship issues.

Interfaith: involving or occurring between people of different religious faiths

REALITY CHECK

Arranged marriage is a common practice in many Indian cultures, yet among non-Indians in the United States, it is widely misunderstood. Vani is an undergraduate university student who moved to the United States with her parents 10 years ago. Her family operates a retail business, and she is an education major. Vani was anxious to share marriage customs from her homeland.

Interviewer: Are you considering an arranged marriage when it is time?

Vani: It is very likely. My parents want me to return to India when it is time to begin looking for marriage. We visit about once a year, and family members who remain there would help me through the process.

Interviewer: Can you describe that process?

Vani: Most marriages where I come from are "arranged"; that is to say, the parents choose their children's mate. A key point is making sure that the mate is from the appropriate caste and is able to pay the dowry price.

(Continued)

(Continued)

Interviewer: What is a dowry?

Vani: Dowry is the payment in cash or kind by the bride's family to the groom's family when they give the bride away. The bride's family can give land, jewelry, and/or money as the gift.

Interviewer: Dowry is a very unfamiliar concept for many. Having lived in the United States, do you still think the dowry system is a good idea?

Vani: The Hindu religion is more likely to practice the dowry system, so it has religious history in my family. This practice has been responsible for many crimes against women in India, including domestic violence, bride burning, and wife murder. But my family and the families from our area are not as violent.

Interviewer: What purpose does a dowry serve?

Vani: There are three purposes. First, it is like a gift from the bride's family to the groom's, a friendship bond. Second, it is a means of compensating the groom and his family for taking on the economic burden of the bride. Third, it is a pre-mortem inheritance for the bride.

Interviewer: You mean, it is like a life insurance policy. If the groom dies, the bride will get that back?

Vani: Maybe not exactly the same things back, but she will be assured some assets if her husband dies.

Interviewer: Let's get back to the "arranged" part of arranged marriage.

Vani: My friends in the United States have a real problem with that concept. I think people have the idea that parents find a girl for their son, and that the two never meet until their wedding day—that they have to take whatever they are given. That rarely happens. Those types of arranged marriages may still happen in smaller, conservative communities, but it's not likely.

Interviewer: How do you think your marriage will be arranged? What is the process?

Vani: Don't get me wrong. Some couples in India marry for love, but most are arranged. Since I am here, going to school, my family back in India will look for a possible husband for me. They talk to people—uncles, cousins, neighbors—and find out if anyone knows of a suitable man. Eventually someone will say, "My friend's brother has a son. . . ." The girl's side always takes the first steps, making everyone aware that they have a marriageable female family member. When a family has a possible husband, they will ask questions and get information to help them decide if I might be good for him.

Interviewer: So, if they think you are a possible match, what happens?

Vani: We will meet. If we like each other, arrangements will start.

Interviewer:	You have seen your U.S. friends date. What do you think of dating?	
Vani:	I think it is a lot of bother. My friends seem to be attracted to guys for the wrong reasons—cars, clothes, looks.	
Interviewer:	How quickly do marriage arrangements happen?	
Vani:	Maybe half a year. During that time, sometimes, the couple finds out they are not compatible. They can stop the process when that happens. They get together a few times, not overly much. Maybe two times a month, minimum.	
Interviewer:	What about divorce?	
Vani:	I have had a few classes that explore "love." That seems like a very shaky thing to me. In my country and in my group, marriage and family is built on more strong points—compatibility and possibilities. Marriage isn't expected to be	

perfect or always joyful. I think our way is more realistic.

Interviewer: Then there are no divorces?

Vani: No, there are. I know some people who have divorced. The reasons aren't about love or stopping love; it is usually about drunkenness or violence. I approve if it's needed—if he's a drunk or if he's beating her. Many of my American friends have divorced parents. Children back home don't have that kind of insecurity.

The United States has citizens from many religious and cultural backgrounds. Dating and mating behaviors will differ between and among groups—even within the same group. These behaviors have evolved over long periods of time, reflecting values and experiences of group members. They are all valid on some level. It is difficult, if not impossible, to evaluate behaviors from outside your group without the necessary context for understanding why those practices continue.

RESEARCHING THE FAMILY

Those who study the family recognize that the field is diverse. Not only are there many structural variations that describe families and numerous ways of defining the family; there are many ways to explain how families function and operate in society. Formal **theory** involves a set of propositions that can be tested or proved to explain a phenomenon in society, such as the family. Borrowing from various fields of study, family theory depends on multiple **theoretical perspectives** or **conceptual frameworks**. Some of these involve scientific explanations, whereas others are based on personal experience and observation. All seek to understand the family.

There are several reasons why it is necessary to examine the theoretical perspectives of families. These perspectives help explain "why" or "how" families work. They help us make sense of how families behave. This information is helpful to those who assist families as well as those who guide policy that affects families. Theory also provides structure for future studies—a place to start when looking for answers. They give the researcher a guide for his or her inquiry.

Theory: a broad generalization that explains a body of facts or phenomena

Theoretical perspective: one's preference for a particular theory

At this point, it becomes important to explore eight theoretical perspectives that help in understanding families. Particular attention is given to how these perspectives relate to family resource management.

Family Systems Theory

Family systems theory (also referred to as the family systems framework) is a popular perspective among professionals who work with families. This theory grew out of the general systems theory developed by Bertalanffy (1969) in the 1960s in the science field. Several components of this theory are distinctly applicable to the family as a system. According to family systems theory, when something happens to one family member, all members of that family are affected. It is assumed that the members are part of the group or system and function as a system. Family therapists find this theory especially helpful in working with individual family members, and their treatment may need to include the whole family.

> *Charles and Bonnie have always enjoyed the finer things of life, and throughout their married life they have rationalized their need for expensive clothing, fine dining, and a lavish lifestyle. They frequently have spent more than their income to support their habits, not being able to build savings or retirement as a safety net for the future. For Charles, this way of living was a model that he saw from his own parents. When Bonnie, who grew up in a very poor family, met Charles, she was enamored by the lifestyle and quickly adopted his principles of the "good life." Although they recognized that their way of living was probably not responsible, they were not willing to change. They often remarked, "Most people have no idea how to live!" They knew that others did not approve of their lifestyle, but Charles would announce, "We are not hurting anyone. . . . I wish they would mind their own business!" After a few years, Charles and Bonnie's son graduated from college and announced his engagement. The newlyweds were married in a lavish ceremony and began their new lives in a beautiful new home in one of the finest areas of town. After a few months, their son called to tell them that he and his wife were getting a divorce and that he would have to declare bankruptcy. Charles was shocked and replied, "How could this happen? You have everything you want!"*

This story illustrates the idea that the actions of individuals within a family affect all the family members. Parents model behavior that is passed down from generation to generation, unless there is a conscious effort to change. If Charles and Bonnie's son is ever going to make responsible decisions about his financial future, he will have to make a conscious decision to make changes that will help him learn new strategies about spending and saving money.

Another aspect within the family systems framework is the assumption that what families do within their units impacts not only other family members, but also their communities.

Social Exchange Theory

Utilitarian thinking shares a common theme that humans are moved to act and behave based on what they value the most. This utilitarian thinking is part of the microeconomics of the family (White, Klein, & Martin, 2015). Family members have individual motivations influencing the behaviors they select. These differences between and among members create situations where personal resources can be bartered or exchanged to further one's self-interests. Family members bring to the family unit personal resources that can be used to maintain that unit. Infants and children are heavily dependent on the resources of older family members, but will be expected, at some future time, to contribute their own time, energy, and skills to the family's functioning. Adolescent and adult family members may participate in a type of cost-benefit analysis when they feel uncomfortable or unappreciated by other members. The degree of self-sufficiency perceived by individuals will impact their decisions to either leave or stay within the family group.

The exchange framework is often used to study power bases within the family. Obviously, the ability to provide necessary resources to the family unit will increase one's value in that group. Depending on the circumstances or the types of resources necessary at any one time, an individual family member's personal power may increase or decrease. That power base may impact an individual's role in the decision-making process. When a parent has the money and ability to make a purchase contract, he or she will have more actual power in the decision process for buying a teenager an automobile. Whether or not he or she exercises that power will depend on the family's communication process and the history of that particular child–parent relationship.

Application of social exchange theory also emerges in the study of courtship, mate selection, and implementation of the decision-making process across family life situations. By the end of the 1970s, exchange theory had become one of the most widely used theoretical frameworks in family research (Edleson & Tan, 1993).

> *Monty and Frank are brothers in their mid-40s. After the death of their father, Bill, they have jointly inherited the family farming operation. Monty is married with three children. Frank is single and has no children. Their mother is to receive an annual living allowance from their operational profits. This change of ownership has created a great deal of stress between the brothers and between Monty's wife and her mother-in-law. They decide to bring the conflicting issues before their lawyer for advice.*
>
> *"I know Bill meant well," Monty's wife offers, "but we have children to support, and Frank is single. Surely he didn't mean for his grandchildren to go without at the expense of their uncle."*
>
> *"Having children was a choice you and Monty made," her mother-in-law responds. "We wanted our hard-earned estate to be equally divided between the two boys."*
>
> *"How does this inheritance continue, then?" asks Monty's wife. "When Monty and Frank die, is the entire farm operation split equally among our kids?"*

Inheritance:
the succession of money, property, or a title that has been passed on from generation to generation

Inheritance can be viewed as a set of long-term exchange relationships, linking different generations of the farming family (Kennedy, 1991). Land and earning power are both examples of resources that are used as bargaining capital in the exchange process within families. Historically, this division of farming lands among surviving heirs seriously compromised the ability of farm families to make a living on shrinking pieces of land. Much of what used to be family farm ground is now part of large corporate-owned businesses. The increasingly complex legal ramifications of such actions has made the creation of legal wills and trusts a common action of families with inheritance that is to be passed from generation to generation.

Symbolic Interactionism

Symbolic interactionism has a long-standing tradition in family theory, tracing back to the early 1900s and continuing to add to the theoretical framework through the last century (LaRossa & Reitzes, 1993). Social and psychological concepts are woven into this conceptual framework. This theoretical perspective looks within families at the process that creates a family unit in the minds of those family members.

Drawing from both qualitative and quantitative research studies, theorists avoid identifying any natural or typical family structure. Instead, families are viewed as unique creations of participants as they spontaneously relate to one another. Interactions of family members, such as talk, gestures, actions, and shared beliefs, create that family's particular reality. Individuals develop a sense of self through these interactions. Family identities emerge over time as the family creates rituals and shared meanings or **symbols** (Bossard & Boll, 1943).

Symbol:
something that represents something else by association, resemblance, or convention

The shared meanings that emerge through interactions and defining of member roles allow the family unit to define situations in unique ways. Behaviors, such as decision making and resource identification, are based on meanings that group members have created regarding both the situation and possible actions that individuals and family units have available to handle that particular situation (Mead, 1964).

Impression management:
the process by which people try to control the impressions that other people form of them

This theory does not ignore the impact of larger social groups on the family unit. Researchers have sought ways to explain how family units and members within families seek to present themselves to others. Turner (1970) refers to this as **impression management**. As consumers of goods and services, individuals within the family unit are aware that the choices they make will be interpreted by other social groups outside the family, and social value judgments will result.

> *Samuel, a PeeWee baseball player, and his parents are shopping for shoes to wear during practices and games. Prices range from $30 to $120 in Samuel's size range.*
>
> *"I've got to have those white ones on the top shelf. My favorite professional baseball player talks about them on television, and Bobby said he was going to get them, too."*

"But those are twice as much as these," his father counters, pointing to a similar-looking pair on a lower shelf.

What are the odds that Samuel will walk out of the store with the more expensive shoes?

Shoes are shoes. Why is it that some consumers will pay higher prices for athletic shoes that are similar in construction to less expensive choices, merely for an athlete's endorsement or a company's insignia? Building on the symbolic interactionist theory, Laverie, Kleine, and Schultz (2002) explored how and when consumption and products purchased impact a person's self-identity or "how products make the person." The results of this study found that not only do the actual possessions (e.g., apparel and equipment used during athletic activities) lead to more positive self-evaluations; social ties and the media promotion of those products also enhance the owner's feeling of self-definition. A contemporary term, **conspicuous consumption**, is used to describe situations that result from purposeful selection of products to create an image of the self when judged by others. Designer labels, expensive automobiles with identifying symbols, and even specially bred pets are examples of this concept.

Conspicuous consumption: spending large quantities of money, often extravagantly, to impress others

The media's advertising implications and peer pressure may have a significant impact on Samuel's ultimate possession of new baseball shoes. The process utilized by his parents to decide which shoes to buy will include the possible impact of this purchase on young Samuel's self-identity, as well as the reflection such a purchase will have on the entire family, as decision-making criteria. Prioritizing such criteria will determine the ultimate impact such factors will have on the shoes selected.

Conflict Theory

Although conflict theory surfaced as a popular framework in the 1960s, its roots are in the 19th-century works of Karl Marx (Marx & Engels, 1967). Marx revolutionized the way in which human society was viewed, focusing on the negative impact of the European Industrial Revolution. He felt that the capitalistic environment encouraged the exploitation of the workers. To combat this, he purported that when those being oppressed join forces and challenge their oppressors, conditions can be changed.

©iStockphoto.com/ranplett

▶ **Photo 2.3**
Young adolescents emulate sports celebrities and often seek group identities.

Conflict theorists agree that conflict is natural and expected in human interaction. Family units are no different from other organized groups in this respect.

There are unequal power bases within each family, resulting in situations of competition, coercion, and conflict.

Conflict theory can be analyzed through three central themes: (a) humans are driven to want and to seek certain things, (b) power is at the core of all social relationships, and (c) groups have self-interests that they use to advance their own goals, rather than those important to the entire society. Thus, families are social institutions where some members benefit more than others from the existence and maintenance of the family unit. Marriage is often viewed as a relationship ripe with inequality, subordination, and male dominance. Other family situations that are often studied using this framework are domestic violence, divorce, and single parenting.

Application of conflict theory challenges the presentation of families as stable, harmonious, and peaceful social units. For that reason, many researchers avoided using this framework in family research until society experienced stressful change periods, such as the civil rights movement of the 1960s and the dramatic increase of women in the workplace over the last four decades. It emerged as a major player among theories in the late 1960s, and the body of research since that time has established this framework as a strong base for the study of contemporary family issues. Feminist theory is often considered to be rooted in basic conflict theory thought.

Marta and Pete are disagreeing more and more about day-to-day parenting decisions concerning their twin daughters. Frequent struggles over power within their personal relationship have ensued since Marta returned to her job after the girls started grade school. Marta had left her flight attendant career when she became pregnant. Pete is beginning to feel that his job as a travel agent is becoming a dead-end endeavor. The advancement of travel arrangement via the Internet has brought about lower commission earnings at his current office. Marta has been very pleased to be able to supplement his declining earnings with her own paycheck. Recently, she was promoted to a higher level of crew management and received a large raise in pay.

When the girls are exposed to chicken pox at school and have to spend a few days recuperating at home, tension boils over.

"Pete, can't you stay home with them and do your work on your computer, here?" Marta pleads when she gets a call for a well-paying flight.

"The girls want you, and you know that they are impossible. You've spoiled them rotten," he retorts as he grabs his bag and heads toward the door.

"They're just not used to you being so involved with them," Marta continues. "If you'd just spend more time with them—"

Pete is already out the door.

When parents are struggling within their own relationship over power issues, how are relationships with their children affected? Lindahl and Malik (1999) found that clashes over power and control in the marriage were associated with diminished support of the children. Mental and physical resources are limited, and when couples are channeled into negative discourse, they are unavailable for other tasks. Pete may be trying to regain his earlier power base of breadwinner by forcing Marta to choose between her daughters' well-being and her job at the economic detriment of the entire family unit.

Feminist Perspective

Although the field of family sociology has been in existence for decades and women's rights emerged as early as the late 1800s, originally the study of the family was largely dominated by men. Since the early 1970s, feminists have stressed that the widely used frameworks that describe families are often void of the women's point of view or experiences.

Gordon (1979) identified three essential themes within the feminist perspective: the "emphasis on women and their experiences; recognition that under existing social arrangements women are subordinated or oppressed; and commitment to ending that unjust subordination" (p. 107). Osmond and Thorne (1993) suggest that, as a result of these themes, a fourth theme has emerged: "attention to gender and gender relations as fundamental to all of social life, including the lives of men as well as those of women" (p. 592).

Although the feminist perspective has gained some popularity in the past few years, there are others who argue that the theory isolates the role of women in relationships and forgets that both genders should have equality within family relationships. There is no doubt that gender plays a large role in family studies or that researchers should take both genders into account.

Charlotte was recently widowed after a long and happy marriage of 48 years. Following the shock of losing the only man she ever loved, she was faced with the overwhelming task of taking care of the financial affairs of the estate.

Realizing how helpless his mother felt, John decided to help her sort through the papers. "Where did Dad keep all the insurance policies and the statements from your retirement account? Did he have a safety deposit box, or did you have a savings account?"

Charlotte responded, "I don't know where anything is! Your dad took care of all our finances. . . . I guess he never thought I would need to know. I was only a housewife."

Charlotte is not alone. Many older women have had similar experiences. Macdonald (1995) suggests that the very nature of economics is male-dominated, and thus the two spheres of paid labor market economics and unpaid/informal household economics are separate. In this case, the feminist perspective could help understand how these two spheres interact and impact each other.

Family Ecological Theory

Family ecological theory joins the concepts of human development and family relationships with the structure of family resource management to identify a wide range of problems that families face, given the environment in which they live. Bubolz and Sontag (1993) suggest that this theory is particularly useful today because it is not limited to certain groups, and it applies to a wide range of family configurations and cultural backgrounds.

The origin of ecological theory as it relates to the family began as the ideas of human ecology were being promoted by Haeckel in 1873 (Bubolz & Sontag, 1993). According to Haeckel, who was intrigued by Darwin's theories of evolution, there is a link between science or biology and the environment. During this same time, Ellen Swallow Richards announced the beginning of the science of oekology (derived from the Greek word meaning *household management*), which she described as the "science of living" (Clarke, 1973). Oekology was a way of using scientific principles to improve the lives of families. The name that eventually became associated with this science was *home economics*.

Although ecological theory does not have a formal set of theoretical propositions, Hawley (1986) put up some general propositions that describe the family within the surrounding ecosystem. Some of the propositions Hawley suggested are that change and growth occur through experiences with outside systems, new information from the outside causes change to the relationships within the family, and the family is closed to the ecosystem around it to ensure stability.

> *Sheila and Michelle are cousins and are both single mothers. Their children are the same age, but have responded to the demands of life in very different ways.*
>
> *Michelle reports, "Ben is getting into trouble at school almost every day, but I just don't know what to do. It has upset me so much that I started seeing a therapist. He suggested that I take an antidepressant to help me."*
>
> *Although Sheila is sympathetic, she doesn't agree with the way that Michelle is handling her situation. Sheila replies, "Michelle, have you talked to Ben about what is bothering him? Have you met with his teachers? Are you sure that medication will solve this problem? I know that when Ethan gets in trouble, it helps to get all the information I can in order to help him."*
>
> *Sheila silently wonders if Michelle is making decisions about medications that are based on societal expectations without knowing the consequences to herself and her family. Is Michelle neglecting to address her own physical, emotional, and even spiritual needs?*

Ecological theory requires that the whole person within a series of systems— the external environments—is taken into account when a problem is presented. Bronfenbrenner (1994) used ecological systems theory to explain how the external environment influences how the child will grow and develop. Meyers, Varkey, and Aguirre (2002) found a significant association between these systems and family functioning. In this case, Michelle opts to solve the problem at hand by taking an antidepressant drug instead of examining the various systems involved in her son's behavior as well as her own.

Family Strengths Framework

The focus of the family strengths framework is on what is right rather than what is wrong with families. According to Olson and DeFrain (2003), one advantage of this framework is that the focus of study is changed from just solving problems to emphasizing what is working well in that family. Once strengths are identified, a foundation is established for continued growth and change in that family. As a result, strong families can become a model for families that want to succeed.

The strengths perspective can be traced back as early as the 1930s, but Herbert Otto's work in the 1960s is often credited with building a foundation for the current work in family strengths (Otto, 1962). Within the structure of the family strengths framework, there are six major qualities of a strong or healthy family (Stinnett, 1981; Stinnett, DeFrain, & DeFrain, 1999): commitment to the family, spending enjoyable time together, spiritual well-being, successful management of stress and crisis, positive communication, and showing appreciation and affection to each other. Researchers continue to study family strengths and have found that these qualities have been reported by more than 21,000 family members in the United States and more than 38 other countries around the world. Families everywhere are unique in their own cultures, yet strong families commonly seem to be guided by these basic qualities.

> Greg and Cindy are newlyweds. They thought that they had prepared for marriage in every way. They attended premarital sessions, talked to other newlyweds about their experiences, and read several books about marriage. Six months into their marriage, they began to see differences in the way they each wanted to spend money. After realizing this, Cindy said, "This doesn't change the way I feel about you, but I am concerned that when we have children, we will have trouble deciding on how to save for their education, and other expenses." They began to talk about the origin of these differences and traced many of their ways of thinking back to the models that they saw while growing up. Will Cindy and Greg ever be able to work through this issue in their marriage?

DeFrain and Stinnett (2002) identified several propositions of the strengths perspective that are illustrated here. Greg and Cindy were able to look at their own families and identify differences focused on the issue of money. Instead of continuing to disagree and argue about who was right, they focused on the positive by appreciating the values that the other person brought to the discussion. They also used positive communication to discuss ways to change and manage positive growth in this area. Through their discussions, they started to realize that neither one had an inherently flawed idea of money, and that they needed to understand each other's views and develop financial goals that met the needs of their own newly formed family.

Understanding family strengths requires understanding the cultural contexts in which families live. People live within the context of their family, their extended family, the community, and the broader national culture that cannot be easily understood, labeled, or judged. Numerous external factors enmesh and influence families, sometimes proving helpful and useful to individual families, but at other times proving harmful and demanding. A positive and useful approach to conceptualizing families from a global perspective links family strengths, community strengths, and cultural strengths and demonstrates how families use these strengths to meet the many challenges they face. Researchers in 38 countries, to date, have found remarkable similarities from culture to culture when studying family strengths (DeFrain & Asay, 2007). This framework has been used in multidisciplinary research, including family science, social work, nursing, psychology, and other fields of study.

Family Development Theory

Of all the theories introduced in this chapter, family development theory is the only one that is based solely on the discipline of family studies. The two major components within this theory are time and history, focusing on the changing social expectations unique to each stage of a family's existence. Thus, it views the family as a dynamic system and focuses on the family's changing forms. When it is combined with other theories, some have used the name *life course development framework* to describe this way of thinking about the family (White, Klein, & Martin, 2015).

Tracing back as far as the American Revolution (1770s), the definition of a family and the life course of individual families were recorded and reflected on. White, Klein, and Martin (2015) refer to this phase as the descriptive phase of the theory. Shortly after World War II, research on family stress ensued. Within this research, the family unit is described as having social roles and relationships within itself that change as the family moves through stages over time. The theory was embraced, and research efforts further solidified it as a major theoretical idea.

Most recently, family development theory has struggled to maintain a distinctive position in family theory. Proponents have tried to answer criticisms and incorporate new methodologies. Core to this current theoretical framework are the ideas that families are identifiable groups that mature and change as they move through a time continuum. Time is measured in stages. A **family stage** is an interval of time in which the roles and relationships within the family change in observable ways. The theory works most easily with traditional families—wife, husband, and two children. Considering the current diversity in family constructs, this theory becomes problematic. Even traditional family structures with several children become confusing as the number of stages and the overlapping of stages increase.

Family stage: an interval of time in which the roles and relationships within the family change in observable ways

Alvin has recently retired from his lifelong career and is making adjustments to his daily schedule. He has spent the last 40 years in a fast-paced, 60-hours-per-week position and has been looking forward to relaxing and pursuing his special interests that have long been postponed. He is also anxious to spend more time with his family and to travel extensively.

Martha, Alvin's wife of 42 years, has devoted most of her time to managing the home and family and actively volunteers for several charity organizations. She has been anxiously awaiting Alvin's retirement and looks forward to spending more time with him. As a couple, these two are transitioning from one family stage into the next—retirement. They adjusted to the empty-nest stage years ago.

After 2 weeks, Martha explains to Alvin, as he places his breakfast dishes into the sink, "Let me show you how to load the dishwasher and run it. I've been wanting to talk about how you could help me more around the house, anyway."

Housework was not one of the things Alvin had been planning to add to his new role. "But I already take care of the yard and the car."

As families move from one stage to the next, roles must be renegotiated. Gupta (1999) studied the effects of transitions in marital status on men's performance of housework. One conclusion from that study was "with respect to housework time at least, the formation of households with adult partners of the opposite gender remains more to men's than to women's advantage" (p. 710). This notion would lead us to believe that Alvin will probably not rise to meet his wife's new expectations. However, family member roles may be age- and stage-graded (White, Klein, & Martin, 2015). If the surrounding culture views cleaning as a more acceptable expectation for a retired male than for a working male, Alvin may likely accept these new duties willingly.

The theoretical or conceptual framework utilized in a research project will both enhance and constrain the information collected. All the theories and perspectives presented in this chapter have a history within the study of families. Each has its strengths and weaknesses (see Table 2.1). Together they have created a broad, useful knowledge base for family problem solving and understanding.

FAMILY RESEARCH DESIGN

Questions about how families work lead to research. Research methods are selected to answer these questions and are chosen based on the researcher's theory preference. Research traditions fall along the lines of either quantitative or qualitative methodology (see Table 2.2). **Quantitative research** is used when quantifiable data are needed to show a measurable relationship between phenomena. One example of a research project that would require a quantitative design involves a researcher who wants to find out whether an increase in single-parent homes

Quantitative research: research that examines phenomena through the numerical representation of observations and statistical analysis; data can be collected through structured interviews, experiments, or surveys and are reported numerically

Table 2.1 Theory Strengths and Weaknesses

Theory/Perspective	Strength	Weakness
Family systems theory	Focuses on the interconnectedness of family members and their experiences	Assumes that all family members are functioning as active participants of the family system
Social exchange theory	Focuses on individual resources and the bartering of these resources, seeking to explain the power bases within families	Not all rewards are stable over time; some behavior doesn't seek rewards
Symbolic interactionism	Combines social and psychological concepts, and views families as uniquely self-created units	Focuses on the uniqueness of family realities and lessens the generalizability of research findings
Conflict theory	Recognizes that conflict is natural and expected in human interaction	Challenges the view of families as stable social units
Feminist perspective	Incorporates women's views and experiences into the research framework	Isolates the role of females and ignores male experiences
Family ecological theory	Links the family's experiences to its environment	Broadens research efforts and raises level of complexity for findings
Family strengths framework	Focuses on emphasizing what is working well for the family rather than problem solving	Focusing only on the positives may not lead to needed change
Family development theory	Views the family as a dynamic system	Becomes difficult with nontraditional family structures

Qualitative research: a research method that measures information based on opinions and values as opposed to statistical data; data can be collected through open-ended interviews, review of documents and artifacts, participant observations, or practice

has a possible connection to an increase in juvenile delinquency. The researcher would need to have a large sample and collect enough data to show statistical significance between two or more variables. In contrast, qualitative methodology is used to develop a deeper understanding of something about which little is known. **Qualitative research** involves descriptive details that are difficult to present in quantitative terms. An example of a qualitative study with families would include describing the complexities of homelessness (Marshall & Rossman, 1995). This study could involve the researcher conducting interviews, observation, or both in an effort to understand the families' lived experiences. Whatever methodology is chosen, the results of research are meant to inform and contribute to existing literature. This new information can then be used to prompt new questions for further research, improve education, or change policies in that particular area.

Table 2.2 Family Research Design

Quantitative	Qualitative
• Data are collected with an instrument.	• The researcher is the instrument.
• The search is for a relationship.	• The search is for a pattern.
• Results are reported using numbers or percentages.	• Results are reported using words or description.
• Findings are generalized.	• Findings are centralized, but specialized.

SUMMARY

The family is one of society's most basic institutions. Historically, the family has existed for centuries and was organized for economic purposes. Today, the family has changed. Although it is still an organization that depends on economics, family members may also rely on each other for emotional support and security. Throughout history, researchers have been unable to find a common definition that would describe the family. It is still hard to find a definition that would represent what the family has come to mean today or what it will be in the future. Such a definition must be broad and flexible. The family has also experienced a change in function. Although functions such as the production of goods and services have changed to the procurement of goods and services, basic functions of emotional security and economic support still apply. Family theory is another way to define and understand how families work, and family researchers draw from one or more of these theories or conceptual frameworks. Today, family researchers use quantitative and qualitative methodology to lead to a better understanding of the family.

QUESTIONS FOR REVIEW AND DISCUSSION

1. What is the history of the family?

2. What are some examples that illustrate how the family today is in transition?

3. Why are there so many different definitions of family?

4. How have the functions of the family changed over time?

5. What is the purpose of theory in understanding families?

6. What are the strengths and weaknesses of each family theory?

7. What are the two types of research methodology used in family research? What are the differences between the two?

CHAPTER THREE

THE MANAGEMENT PROCESS

Objectives
Management as a Field of Study
   Parallel Histories
The Evolution of Home and Business
   Management: The 20th Century
   Era One (ca. 1900–1930s)
   Era Two (ca. 1940s–1950s)
   Era Three (ca. 1950s–1960s)
   Era Four (ca. 1970s–1980s)
   Contemporary Movements
Reality Check
The Interface of Business Management
   and Family Resource Management in the
   Context of the Family
The Foundation of Family Resource
   Management
Specific Applications of Management to the
   Family Unit
Worldview
   Time Management
In the News
   Family Planning
   Dependent Care
   Financial Management
Summary
Questions for Review and Discussion

Objectives

- Be familiar with the common history of business management and family management.

- Acknowledge the importance of management to family success.

- Recognize the need for active management processes in the decision-making process.

- Understand the connections between management and family choices.

American families have always shown remarkable resiliency, or flexible adjustment to natural, economic, and social challenges. Their strengths resemble the elasticity of a spider web, a gull's skillful flow with the wind, the regenerating power of perennial grasses, the cooperation of an ant colony, and the persistence of a stream carving canyon rocks. These are not the strengths of fixed monuments but living organisms. This resilience is not measured by wealth, muscle or efficiency but by creativity, unity, and hope. Cultivating these family strengths is critical to a thriving human community.

—Ben Silliman, Family Life Specialist with the University of Wyoming's Cooperative Extension Service

Management is an ongoing process. It involves matching resources and needs on a continual basis. It could be argued that management continues until failure is accepted. The largest, most successful companies in the United States have survived because their management approaches have evolved with the social, political, and economic changes characteristic of the business environment.

Families also exist within a dynamic environment. Because family members experience personal, individual growth and development, managing a family unit requires high levels of flexibility and resourcefulness. Although business and family management differ in many ways, they share many threads, in both historical development and contemporary application.

MANAGEMENT AS A FIELD OF STUDY

Management is essential to human existence. One could argue, then, that management has been practiced since the beginning of humankind. The word *manage* has its roots in two distinctive sources. The Italian word *manageggiare* is defined as handling things, especially horses. However, it is believed that at the turn of the 16th century, that word became confused with the French word *menager*. This new meaning was to be used carefully, especially in a household. Also of interest is the fact that the word *economy* can be traced to ancient Greek, where it meant *house management* (Wensley, 1996).

R. Stone (1998) suggests that even as late as the 1940s, management as a discipline of study was yet undeveloped: "Most managers did not realize that they were practicing management" (p. xi).

Crainer (2000) believes that management, as a profession, came of age during the 20th century, but it would be foolish to assume that it did not exist before that time. Obviously, management was involved in the creation of all historic civilizations, evident in their cultural expressions of arts and political structures.

In Weir's (2001) biography of King Henry VIII of England (1491–1547), she presents several managerial scenarios within this single royal court. Managing a kingdom and a court of great size required both structure and recordkeeping. To maintain a royal blood line, it was necessary to exert high levels of control over even the most personal aspects of the royal family's life.

> Back in his nursery, the Prince was subject to an orderly regimen.... Henry's Lady Mistress supervised his wet-nurse and dry nurse, who were assisted by four chamberers known as rockers, whose chief duty was to lull their charge to sleep by rocking his cradle.... A physician stood by to supervise every feeding. (p. 137)

Surely, the construction of ancient artifacts, such as the pyramids and the Great Wall, required massive management campaigns. Management, as a process used by humans, is evident in historic written records as well as artifacts left behind from each great civilization. To accomplish goals and objectives, resources must be managed, either consciously or subconsciously. The same is true of both businesses and families. If a business or family unit is to maintain, grow, and be productive, it must be managed well.

Parallel Histories

The post–Civil War United States was heavily involved in reconstructing the country and its government. These activities required a great deal of organization and resource management. During this time, the culture of the United States remained dependent on the family unit. Commerce and industrialization were rising, yet the transfer of wealth from one generation to the next was still connected to inheritance through family lines. Families lived in household units that required management of facilities, food, clothing, and education. As early as 1861, a publication on how to manage such a unit was released and received by the general public quite favorably. As mentioned in Chapter 1, Beeton's *Book of Household Management* (cited in Hughes, 2006) presented three principles of good management:

- Set an example and provide clear guidance to your staff.

- Control the finances of the family carefully.

- Strive for order and method in all management activities.

Some argue that Mrs. Beeton was the first author of the operations management perspective (Wensley, 1996).

Not long after this publication, Fayol (1949) proposed four key managerial concepts: plan, organize, lead, and control. Although these concepts were intended for business management, they were equally applicable in household management. When viewed as a social organization and a productive unit, the family resembles the business unit in many ways. As the discipline of business management emerged during the 20th century, there were several parallel developments in the field of home economics, in which family resource management has its roots.

Two influential people lived and worked for similar things at the turn of the 20th century. Frederick Taylor was busy applying scientific analysis to the workplace and the nature of work itself, and Ellen Swallow Richards was working diligently toward a similar end—the application of science to the family and the household.

Ellen Richards

Richards was the first woman admitted to the Massachusetts Institute of Technology, as a special student in chemistry. In 1876, she became head of the science section of the Society to Encourage Studies at Home. Her scholarly contributions included the study of sanitation of the home, nutrition, and health, and the management of the home in terms of time, energy, and money. As a contributor in the noted Lake Placid Conferences at the turn of that century, Ellen ensured that the field of home economics was recognized by the academic community. She was also instrumental in the formation of the American Home Economics Association (now the American Association of Family and Consumer Sciences), formally organized in 1908 and devoted to improving living conditions in the home, the institutional household, and the community (Pundt, 1980).

Frederick Taylor

Frederick Taylor had a passion for efficiency. Perhaps his greatest contribution was to invent management as science. He focused on the nature of work, proposing that any change in the process of work that brought about increased efficiency and resulted in increased productivity was worthy of both study and implementation. In 1911, he published his beliefs in *The Principles of Scientific Management*. Taylor also believed that the fundamental principles of scientific management were applicable to all human activities (Crainer, 2000).

©iStockphoto.com/shotbydave

▶ **Photo 3.1**
Family farm management is heavily dependent on emerging technologies.

Both Richards and Taylor were working toward similar ends at about the same time in history. They wanted their personal passion for scientific study of management to be legitimatized as a field of study, recognized, and appreciated by the scientific minds in higher education. The realms of application differed, however. Home economics would strive to improve the lives of individuals and families where they lived, the home, whereas business management would strive to improve efficiency and productivity in the workplace, the assembly line, and other production venues.

THE EVOLUTION OF HOME AND BUSINESS MANAGEMENT: THE 20TH CENTURY

Aspects of both home and family management and business management have continued to coexist and to even thread together on occasion through the last

100 years. Vickers (1984) delineates this period of time into four separate eras of household production and consumption patterns. Because the changes in the social, political, and economic environments of the United States had a profound impact on both household management and business management, the changes emerging within the science of business management are presented within the discussion of each era that follows.

Era One (ca. 1900–1930s)

Building on the foundation set forth by Richards, the study of household management continued, focusing on health, sanitation, and hygiene. The study of how households function as units of consumption and production in the overall economy was also considered. Programs and curriculum in both high schools and universities were built around cleaning, cooking, meal planning, and organizing housework.

> In 1918, the first Home Management House opened (at the University of Nebraska), where students actually lived and received practical instruction in keeping up a home as part of their coursework . . . in 1922, the Home Management House grew to include a baby, giving the women opportunity to have practical training in childcare. The babies were "borrowed" from the State Home for Children. . . . Each baby stayed about four months before it was adopted. (Kroesche, 2002)

> Pietrykowski, a professor of economics at the University of Michigan–Dearborn, illuminated the fact that home economists extended the scope of economics and consumer behavior through their use of time surveys and production diaries. He reported that home economics programs of the 1920s and 1930s were quite empowering to women, an opposing view to the idea that they just reaffirmed gender stereotypes. (Boscia, 2013)

Another illustration of how the fields of both family and business management became intertwined is the story of Lilian Gilbreth. Lilian and her husband Frank were pioneers in "motion study." When Frank died in 1924, companies that had employed the couple as consultants refused to continue employing a widowed woman in that capacity. Lilian turned her study of efficiency to what was possible, her family's home life. She charted her 12 children's daily activities—chores, hygiene, and education.

The field of business management underwent several important changes in direction during this era of time. Max Weber moved beyond Taylor's work in efficiency to the development of a highly structured **bureaucratic** system. Chester Barnard introduced rational decision making into the management process, proposing that the chief officer of any company is more of a parent than a dictator, nurturing the values and goals of the organization. He also incorporated the systems theory into his framework. A woman, Mary Parker Follet, worked within

Bureaucratic: of, relating to, or having the characteristics of a bureaucracy or bureaucrat

the business management field to humanize industry at a time when her male colleagues were moving in the other direction. She saw the manager's tasks as coordination, defining the purpose, and anticipation (Crainer, 2000).

To summarize Era One, both fields of study embraced the idea that units, whether family or company, operate within a greater system, impacting and being impacted by that system. Both fields focused on the value of application of their emerging sciences through simulated learning opportunities, and both factions were continuing to establish their relevance to the society in general.

Era Two (ca. 1940s–1950s)

World War II and the emergence of the United States from the Great Depression years combined to bring intense change to the environment surrounding homes and businesses. Invention and production of goods and services were at an all-time high. The attitudes and imaginations of the American public were equally charged. Demand for and consumption of goods and services quickened to a frantic pace. The entire nation was in a consumption mode.

The study of home economics came into direct alignment with the field of business management during this time. New household equipment was tested, improved, and incorporated into the vision of the modern home. Efficiency of completing household tasks, saving wasted steps and movements in the process, and simplifying and standardizing work units became key research and application projects.

The U.S. business sector was frantically involved in keeping up with product development, production, and marketing. Although the rebuilding of Japan at this time was changing management thought at a basic level, it was not really apparent to the American business realm until much later.

Era Three (ca. 1950s–1960s)

This era is best characterized as the time when home economics, as a discipline and field of study, began the metamorphosis to better serve the changing needs of its mostly female constituency and the changing social scripts of both men and women. As the nation struggled with civil rights issues and the escalating women's movement, traditional female roles were being questioned, and the definition of family was being modified to align with emerging social programs and practices. Reflective of the broadening worldviews across the nation, home economics was divided into five different but interrelated areas: human development and the family, home management and family economics, food and nutrition, textiles and clothing, and housing.

Optimization: the process of finding the solution that is the best fit to the available resources

In response to these environmental and curricular changes, the focus of this discipline moved heavily into what is now characterized as family resource management—family values, goals, standards, resources, decision making, organization and process, and optimization of families. Less emphasis was placed on work performance within the home, and more energy was devoted to understanding the family unit and its interaction with the greater social structure. This family structure, or family culture, became a model for new developments in the field of business management.

Schein (2004) coined the phrase *corporate culture* to explain how companies were becoming both self-contained and self-perpetuating. He proposed that employees within a company slowly create norms, acceptable behaviors, role expectations, and unique communication processes that differentiate that company from others. In essence, they create a faux family unit at the workplace. Executives and workers at the time were primarily men, and this emerging devotion and expected loyalty to the company has often been portrayed as "men in flannel suits."

It was also during this time that Abraham Maslow presented his theory of motivation, with its famous visual pyramid of needs. This pyramid has since been applied to the study of psychology, sociology, economics, families, and business. It is explored in more depth in later chapters. Maslow was also interested in how values and goals impacted the behavior of workers and how teamwork may be used in the realm of business.

Era Four (ca. 1970s–1980s)

It was during these two decades that many long-standing home economics programs in universities across the nation were threatened with elimination during budget crises. It became increasingly important to shore up the mission, objectives, and curriculum of these programs. A key approach was to illustrate how essential these programs were to society in terms of employment and social impact. One outcome was the development of a systems framework that emphasized the interconnections among family, home, and society.

Another outcome of this time was the movement toward a closer alignment of home economics programs with vocational education. The Carl D. Perkins Vocational Education Act was passed in 1984 with financial support in the form of state-based grants for secondary and postsecondary educational vocational programs. The vocational framework within this alignment is obvious in the program restructuring at this time. The five majors (or fields of study) within home economics programs were (1) food and nutrition, (2) human development and the family, (3) clothing/textiles, (4) family economics, and (5) home economics education. Each had elements from the field's original foci—food selection and preparation, raising children, sewing, and managing the home. The topics, however, were encased in possible job or career clusters.

Vocational: relating to, providing, or undergoing training in a special skill to be pursued in a trade or occupation

The realm of business management during this time was evolving into two distinctive camps: protecting and empowering employees. The success of Japanese business was intriguing American business leaders. Quality control, especially in the form of quality circles, became a popular management technique. The principle underlying quality circles was that when employees participate in decision making and problem solving, the quality of work is enhanced.

Quality circle: a group composed of workers who meet together to discuss workplace improvement and make presentations to management with their ideas

Kanter (1985) reintroduced the humanistic approach to management. She proposed that the corporation is merely a minisociety that shapes individuals to meet collective ends. Another concept illuminated in her works was empowerment of employees. While the home economics discipline was moving to connect the field with business in terms of specific jobs and career training, the business world was looking at research in the area of personal growth and development from a holistic perspective.

Contemporary Movements

The field of home economics has undergone many transformations since the 1980s. One obvious change is in the way the field identifies itself. Few programs still exist under the title of home economics. In 1993, five leading associations recommended changing the name from home economics to family and consumer sciences. As it became necessary to reposition and reframe its mission, the discipline found the old title too restrictive and too laden with incorrect assumptions about contemporary research, application, and curriculum. In spite of the general change to family and consumer sciences, the field continues to evolve and to align with other disciplines across campuses. One problem emerging from that evolution is a lack of consistency in program names. Students, professionals, and the general public can be confused by the variety of titles used (see Table 3.1). In spite of all of the growing pains within this profession, Gentzler (2012) believes that there will always be a need for the core of home economics, a field that has made a positive difference for more than a century.

The field of business management continues to struggle with its quest for efficiency and its need to avoid depersonalization of employees. The technology explosion of the past two decades has presented new problems for managers. They and their subordinates must be able to think differently, frequently seek additional training, and respond to change in positive ways.

Table 3.1 Diversity of Program Titles

Family and Consumer Sciences	Family Science
Human Sciences	Family Studies
Human Ecology	Family and Community Studies

REALITY CHECK

It is not unusual for business and family to become intertwined. The United States, like many other countries, has a strong economic base of family-operated businesses. Some have evolved over several generations. New family businesses often arise from perceived needs within a family. The Burns family launched a large-scale specialty service business to fulfill a personal need.

Jan Burns, owner and manager of her own small business, catered to the pet grooming needs of her community. For 15 years, she had been moderately successful, establishing both her skills and relationships with loyal customers. The flexibility of her schedule and the home-based location allowed her to raise her two children with little outside childcare. Joanna, Jan's daughter, was now in high school, and what had been a syndrome of learning and developmental difficulties was becoming an obvious problem for both her teachers and her parents. Jan shares the decision-making process that followed this recognition.

Joanna's teachers are wonderful. They are very supportive and have challenged her in the special education classrooms as best they could. When she was a junior in high school, her classmates began talking about college and future careers. Her father and I hadn't really accepted the fact that she wouldn't be capable of at least some training program in the local community college. Joanna was even more belligerent. She insisted on sending in college postcards that were coming in the mail on a daily basis. She even signed up to take the ACT test. Her father and I had never applied to a junior or a regular college, so we had no idea what that really was.

Of course, we weren't prepared for Joanna's reaction—frustration and despair—when she went to take that test. Her coursework in middle and high school had been modified, and although she performed adequately in those specially designed situations, she had elementary math skills and science comprehension. Reality hit us all hard. Joanna would never be fully independent and socially functional. Her counselor began talking to her and us about group home living and vocational work programs in the area. We were devastated.

While her parents dealt with their new realization, Joanna turned to self-therapy and began spending more and more time at her mother's grooming shop. Jan took notice and expanded her customer services to include short-term boarding. Joanna was given the responsibility of taking care of boarded dogs and cats at night and on weekends. She was both capable and responsible in these duties. Jan started thinking about a possible future for her daughter in her own business field.

I don't remember just when it hit me, but one day a customer told me about a pet resort she had toured in a neighboring city. I did some surfing on the Internet and realized that there was a growing market for high-service pet care. Within the year, we had expanded my small business with the construction of a large grooming, retail, training, and boarding facility— Jan's Pet Resort!

Like many new businesses, this endeavor started slowly. However, within the first year, it proved to be a huge success.

Our grooming business more than tripled, and the boarding is at capacity every holiday season. Joanna feeds these pampered pets, plays with them, and even does some front desk customer relations. I can see her working full time here when she graduates. We, as a family, have accepted the fact that she will always need our attention and support. The increased income from this new business takes some of the stress off, however.

Creating a business to meet the needs of one family member proved to be both a positive family experience and a profitable business endeavor. Basic management skills provided Jan with answers to both personal and professional challenges.

THE INTERFACE OF BUSINESS MANAGEMENT AND FAMILY RESOURCE MANAGEMENT IN THE CONTEXT OF THE FAMILY

Why is it important to understand the history of business management and its connection to family resource management? Both have a parallel developmental dateline. Because both are concerned with sustainability and improvement of a group of people, it is natural that they will reflect one another at any period in time. Both borrow new and old ideas from the other. One only has to compare the popularized family living programs of the last few years with the management gurus and their programs to see the connections. Authors apply the same basic core concepts of management to family and business structures.

Technology has also had a profound effect on both business management and family management. Historically, the United States has moved through periods of overdependence on labor, materials, and fuels. Its greatest challenge in the future may be that of information acquisition. Knowledge may be the most important resource available to both families and companies as computerization continues to expand on both fronts.

Another factor that connects these two fields closely is the interdependence of the family unit and business. Families realize that the wages and status earned through employment have an enormous impact on their success. Businesses realize that employees are members of families and their obligations to the family unit will impact their motivation, loyalty, and willingness to commit to company objectives. A great deal of mutual research has been done in the areas of childcare, job design flexibility, and family-friendly benefit packages.

THE FOUNDATION OF FAMILY RESOURCE MANAGEMENT

As mentioned previously, the study of family resource management has a long history woven throughout home economics. Originally based in microeconomic theory, theorists moved toward sociology in the 1960s and 1970s, connecting to systems theory (Buckley, 1967; Key & Firebaugh, 1989). Cushman (1945) structured her textbook, *Management in Homes*, around case studies. Her cases presented traditional family units across the life span, focusing on resource identification and problem solving. Everything from kitchen space planning to values and body mechanics were part of the proposed curriculum. Knoll (1963) encouraged the development of a conceptual framework for the field of home management. Her framework centered on the "decision-making organization process" (p. 335).

Hill (1971) presented the family household as a semi-closed system composed of a group of individuals with responsibility to maintain the group and a level of interdependency that made the group cohesive. The family, as a social system, was viewed as transforming energy, information, and matter that enter that system into outcomes that the family needs and wants. To accomplish this goal, families participate in decision making and communication, which leads to goal setting, planning, implementation, and evaluation.

Deacon and Firebaugh (1975) included events in their model of family resource management. The family is viewed as a decision-making unit that requires human and material resources to fulfill demands. Demands are specific objectives based on the family's value structure. Events are unexpected,

Figure 3.1 Family Systems

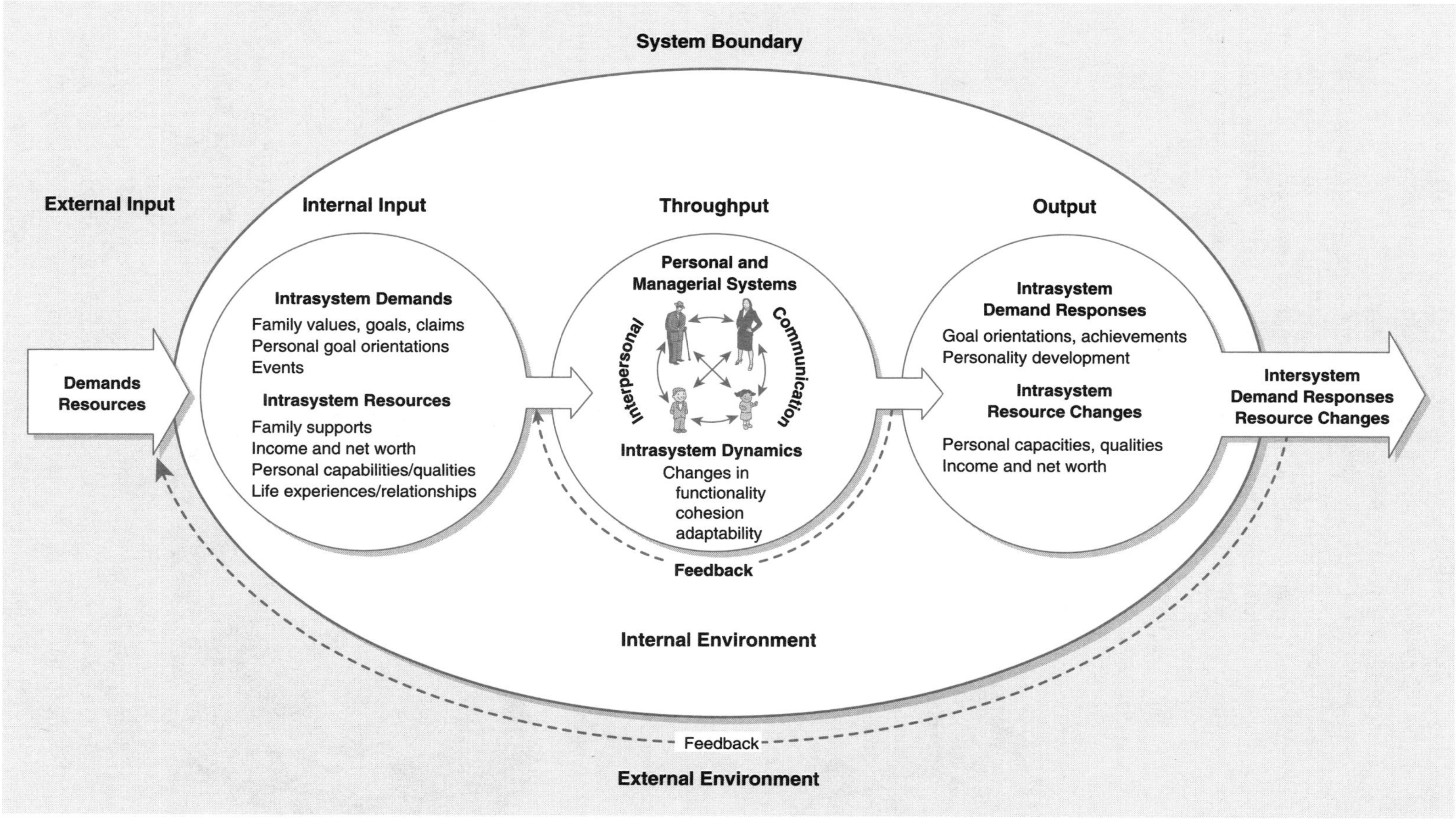

System Boundary

Internal Input

Throughput

Output

External Input

Intrasystem Demands
Family values, goals, claims
Personal goal orientations
Events

Intrasystem Resources
Family supports
Income and net worth
Personal capabilities/qualities
Life experiences/relationships

Personal and Managerial Systems

Communication

Interpersonal

Intrasystem Dynamics
Changes in
functionality
cohesion
adaptability

Feedback

Intrasystem Demand Responses
Goal orientations, achievements
Personality development

Intrasystem Resource Changes
Personal capacities, qualities
Income and net worth

Intersystem
Demand Responses
Resource Changes

Internal Environment

External Environment

Feedback

Demands
Resources

Source: Deacon, Ruth E.; Firebaugh, F.M., *Family Resource Management*, 2nd, © 1988. Printed and Electronically reproduced by permission of Pearson Education, Inc., Upper Saddle River, New Jersey.

low-probability situations that must be met with action. Meeting objectives and responding to these events require the use of human and material resources, with a constant tension between the two.

Paolucci, Hall, and Axinn (1977) designed their textbook around the decision-making process within the family ecosystem. Their premise was that families have decisions to make and a certain level of freedom in that process. However, decisions are influenced by many things, most significantly, in their estimation, the environments within which individuals and families operate. A central concept of their discussion was the "family as an energy driven organization" (p. 25), which coincides with the emergence of computer terminology—inputs and outputs—in academia during that decade.

Although a great deal of time and energy had been exerted in the attempt to create a theoretical foundation for family resource management prior to 1990, Key and Firebaugh (1989) reflected on the shift from economics to systems theory and the ultimate impact on the theoretical foundation of the field. They proposed that the 21st century would present unique and challenging problems for families. Specific issues in their discussion were changing family structures, uncertain economic times, and demographic changes of the U.S. population. W. Bryant (1990) published an entire book on the *Economic Organization of the Household*, thus igniting more research on families in the economic systems of their environments. He based his work on the emerging interest of economics courses and women's issue courses on the family unit.

Avery and Stafford (1991) presented a new theory—the scheduling congruity theory of family resource management—incorporating works from behavioral psychology, cognitive psychology, economics, business management, and Deacon and Firebaugh's seminal work in family resource management. Their intent was to design a theoretical structure that would both explain and predict family resource-allocation behavior. The strengthening of existing theoretical structures in family resource management continues. A common theme drawn from all these past approaches is the inherent need for families to make decisions. Thus, this textbook focuses on and organizes information within that process.

©iStockphoto.com/fotosipsak

▶ **Photo 3.2**
Organic foods have a limited shelf life, impacting food and meal planning.

SPECIFIC APPLICATIONS OF MANAGEMENT TO THE FAMILY UNIT

Family members possess many types of resources that are discussed in detail in later chapters. To understand the importance of managing those resources, time management, family planning, dependent care, and financial planning are discussed briefly.

WORLDVIEW

In the United States, many choose to buy their groceries on a weekly or monthly basis. The ability to stock up on some items, made possible by having disposable income and the ability to store large quantities, seems to be an American practice. In contrast, many families in European countries shop for their food on a daily basis. Being able to use the freshest produce is one reason why many of these families choose to buy food so often. Another reason is limited storage space. Many European kitchens have small refrigerators and limited counter and cabinet space.

In the days following the fall of communism in the late 1980s, there were other reasons why people in Eastern European countries bought their food on a daily basis. One reason was that the devaluation of currency left many families uncertain about their purchasing power for necessities such as food. In addition, shortages in goods, including food, were common during this time in many areas. Many previously government-run food sources were no longer in business, and makeshift markets were set up in vacant lots, empty buildings, and street corners. One never knew whether the man who was selling eggs (by the piece, rather than by the dozen) would be on that same corner the next day. The availability of fresh fruits and vegetables during the winter and other foods not readily available in the local area was especially dismal. One author of this book experienced this in the spring of 1994 in Romania. Fresh vegetables were so scarce that the markets were selling tiny carrots that were pulled out of the ground prematurely, just to make this product available as soon as possible. Grocery shopping around the world can be very different.

Time Management

Although not all cultures believe that time is manageable, the general belief in American culture is that time is a **commodity**. One can measure time, keep time, save time, and waste time. Major activities that require the expenditure of time in the family setting include sleeping, eating, grooming, learning, working, maintaining the environment, and relaxing. A common problem expressed by working parents is the lack of sufficient time to accomplish all of these tasks. It is often a fine line on which working parents balance.

Commodity: an economic good

Imagine that Maggie and John are both employed outside of the home and they have two children, a toddler and a grade-school child. Not only is this family juggling schedules for four different individuals; it is also trying to mesh the schedules of two workplaces, an elementary school, and a daycare provider. Even with the highest commitment to organization and planning, there will be times when one change in one of these schedules causes intense discomfort for one or more family members.

If both parents work 40-hour weeks and work 8-hour shifts each workday, they must make arrangements to ensure that each child will be delivered to the child-care or school setting as needed daily. These children may need to be picked up and delivered to multiple locations at times. The flexibility of parents' work hours enhances a family's ability to juggle such arrangements. Stringent, depersonalized work schedules and demands can elevate the pressure the family must endure.

Designer Families

From the world of journalism, not science, the term *designer baby* made its entry into the *Oxford English Dictionary* in 2004, where it was defined as "a baby whose genetic makeup has been artificially selected by genetic engineering, combined with in vitro fertilization to ensure the presence or absence of particular genes or characteristics." As early as 1999, magazine reports of scientific breakthroughs allowing parents to select the sex of their unborn child to avoid sex-linked birth defects and genetic diseases made headlines (Lemonick, Bjerklie, Park, & Thompson, 1999). The question at that time centered on the possibility of preselection of appearance and intelligence characteristics. By 2009, the focus of discussion had shifted to the ethical implications surrounding such possibilities. A prolific display of twins among celebrity parents pushes those ethical questions to new heights. If the technology is available to create "designer babies," and professionals in the medical field are not afraid to offer such options to clients, does wealth create a new line of superhumans?

Nowhere in the history of mankind has the ability to manage parenthood been so user-friendly. Parents can decide when to reproduce and what kind of children will become their offspring. Women are postponing motherhood to facilitate career and personal goals. They are selecting whether they wish to couple with another parental figure or to parent alone. They are using the right to abortion and the ability to conceive outside of the body to ensure that their children will exhibit desired characteristics. This contemporary ability to create "designer families" raises many new questions for future generations to monitor.

In vitro fertilization (IVF) involves the joining of eggs and sperm outside the body in a laboratory setting. Once an embryo or embryos form, they are then relocated in the uterus. IVF is a complicated and expensive procedure; even so, since its introduction in the United States in 1981, more than 200,000 babies have been created using IVF and similar techniques (Nihira, 2009).

To address the infertility issue of uterine failure, recent organ transplant techniques have presented the option of uterine transplants. Such transplants have been conducted in medical settings; however, the success has been problematic to date. Catsanos, Rogers, and Lotz (2013) examined the ethics of uterus transplantation. They concluded that while uterus transplantation may allow a woman to conceive and gestate a pregnancy, thereby fulfilling a desire to have her own child and her own pregnancy, the reality of infertile women's subjection to painful, possibly debilitating, risky, and uncertain outcomes should undergo intense ethical debate. The research and practice of this new approach to infertility nevertheless have been moving forward.

Controversy around the ethics of all artificial reproductive methods will continue. Legislation to control the use of such reproductive assistance has been considered, especially because of the publicity surrounding births of four, five, six, and more babies resulting from implantation of multiple IVF embryos. The medical profession has issued ethical guidelines but has no legal abilities to enforce these recommendations. But the issues of creating "designer babies" and the long-term consequences to the social and moral fabric of humanity loom large over the next generation of world leaders.

Family Planning

Never before in the history of science has a woman had as much control over childbearing decisions as she does today. However, not every woman finds herself in a position to exercise all options available to her. Nevertheless, it is assumed by many that having one child or multiple children is something that can be managed or planned. The average age of women giving birth in the United States has gradually increased over the last few decades. Lamanna, Riedmann, and Stewart (2015) suggest that there are four emerging trends for those of childbearing age: remaining child-free, postponing parenthood, having only one child, and nonmarital births. These options are discussed in more detail later in this book but serve as important references in this discussion of management.

The choice to have one child or multiple children has a substantial impact on the resources needed by a family and how those resources will be managed. Each additional member creates multiple ripples in the family system. The roles and expectations of children have also been changed in light of new childbearing attitudes and behaviors. A child within a large agricultural family during the 1920s may have been viewed as another source of labor for family farming operations, whereas a child today may be viewed more as a visible extension of his or her family's social position.

Dependent Care

Adults who do choose to have children are faced with competing needs for time and energy resources. Working parents must secure adequate childcare, and those who leave the workforce to care for children in the home must adjust income and expense expectations. Seventy-four percent of women with children between the ages of 6 and 17 and 90% of fathers are employed outside the home (Mannes, 2006). A two-career household juggles multiple work, childcare, school, and activity schedules. Time management is essential.

Working parents appreciate family-friendly employer efforts. Onsite or contracted childcare, flextime, and job sharing are becoming more common. When the pool of qualified employees is tight, employers realize the long-term cost savings that such options provide. Workers who worry about their children and struggle with competing needs at home and at work are less productive and less satisfied with their jobs. Inflexible work hours may add to the stress faced by employees with family obligations, resulting in more sick time and more frequent job turnover.

Mothers who leave their careers to care for young children must realize that their loss of income will have an impact on family dynamics and financial resources. Women who take more than one year off to have children experience a persistent wage gap, even after returning to their jobs. A recent study reports that a woman faces a 3% future salary penalty per year of absence from the workplace (Mazurkewich, 2010). A mother making $60,000 in after-tax income would see a lifetime salary loss of more than $325,000 if she takes 3 years off for childbearing. Opportunity costs are associated with all decisions. Although they can be difficult to assess, there are lost possibilities with every choice made.

Janell has a college degree in marketing. She has been working for 5 years for her current employer and has risen to middle management. When she discovers that she is expecting her first child, Janell decides to leave her job and stay home with her young family until the children are school age. Her cousin, Sara, has two small children but chooses to continue working full time after her maternity leave ends. Both women must adjust to changes in financial resources. Janell no longer has a steady income and must rely on her husband's income and accumulated savings. Sara, while still bringing a paycheck home, must pay for daycare. At the end of 5 or 6 years, both cousins have sacrificed financially for their decisions to have children. However, Sara has continued her career path and statistically will earn about one third more over the course of her working years than will Janell. Each will have to individually determine how her decision impacted the level of life satisfaction achieved.

Caring for dependents—children, parents, and other family members—is a responsibility facing many adults within family units. Cost, quality, and availability are weighed against the family's resources. Matching the needs to the resources is an important and often frustrating management task.

©iStockphoto.com/doble-d

▶ **Photo 3.3**
Working parents based at home have unique time management challenges.

Financial Management

Families must manage the flow of resources into and out of the family unit to maintain the needs of the group. Long-term financial management is explored in Chapter 9, but it is important to understand the impact of purposeful, continual management on a family's monetary resources. Money, once earned and received, must be exchanged as cash, check, or electronic transfer funds. This transformation of income into expendable forms is a management procedure.

Payne (1998) has explored the difference in management styles inherent in differing socioeconomic levels. Those with a tremendous amount of financial security actively manage their money through investments or allocate financial resources to pay others to manage their money. Middle-class families focus on shorter-term savings plans and are more active in the management of their monthly cash flow with checking and savings accounts. Middle-class families also save for retirement, but in passive ways, most often through employer plans. Individuals and families operating at or below the poverty line depend much more heavily on cash and much less on bank-centered transactions. Savings are lower in priority, and money is more easily shared among family and friends.

SUMMARY

Management is a key process for any group's survival, whether in business or family units. There are limited resources and limitless needs of group members, and the matching, evaluation, and distribution of resources within the unit present a continual challenge. Whereas businesses measure success in terms of financial gains and losses, families must focus on less tangible things, like relationships, health, and wellness. Financial security is important to both businesses and families, but interpersonal linkages are more essential to families. The decision-making process is the key to the management success of both types of groups.

QUESTIONS FOR REVIEW AND DISCUSSION

1. Do you believe that business management and family management continue to impact each other in this century? If so, how?

2. The number of women with children participating in the workforce has increased greatly during the last 50 years. Do you think that the workplace has incorporated major changes that reflect their needs? If so, what? If not, what might be changed?

3. Explain how management is a culturally defined behavior.

DISCOVERING FAMILY NEEDS

The Decision-Making Process

- Recognize existing needs

Chapter 4. Categorization of Needs

Chapter 5. Values, Attitudes, and Behaviors: Understanding Family Choices

- Identify alternatives to fulfill needs

- Evaluate identified alternatives

- Select and implement alternatives

- Reflect on and evaluate the alternatives selected

CHAPTER FOUR

CATEGORIZATION OF NEEDS

Objectives
Needs and Wants
  Hierarchy of Needs
Worldview
  *Applying the Hierarchy of Needs to the
    Family*
  *The Consumer Resource Exchange Model
    (CREM)*
  Categorization of Needs
  Measuring Satisfaction of Needs
Changing Perceptions of Needs
  Circumstances
  Personality
  Economic Status
  Technology
  Culture
  Life Span
  Gender Differences
Reality Check
Needs Assessment
In the News
Individual Needs Versus Societal Needs
Summary
Questions for Review and Discussion

Objectives

- Recognize the difference between needs and wants.

- Understand the hierarchy of needs and its application to family life.

- Be familiar with the consumer resource exchange model (CREM).

- Be aware of the categorization and changing perceptions of needs.

- Recognize the purpose of needs assessment.

- Explore the role of technological progress in meeting human needs.

All humans have the same basic needs . . . members of every society have the same basic physiological resources for satisfying their needs . . . humans everywhere develop a variety of derivative needs and desires that reflect their experiences as members of society.

—Lenski, Nolan, and Lenski (1995, pp. 27–29)

All families spend a great deal of time making decisions. On a daily basis, families must decide where to live, what to buy, and how to spend their leisure time. Other decisions may be life-changing, such as the decision to become parents or how to treat a life-threatening illness. The decision-making process is an essential tool for families. The first step in making any decision is to recognize existing needs.

NEEDS AND WANTS

Need: the psychological feature that arouses an organism to action toward a goal and the reason for the action, giving purpose and direction to behavior

Want: something desired, but not necessary

It is not uncommon to hear a phrase such as "I need a cup of coffee" or "I need a new car." Although someone may need a drink, or his or her car may be the only mode of transportation, the coffee or car may not actually be a need, but a want. What is the difference between a need and a want? A **need** can be described as a necessity such as food, clothing, or shelter. Needs are requirements for living. A **want** is something that you would like to have, but it is not essential.

The difference between needs and wants can be blurred by the contexts of our society. Time changes needs. At one time, owning a computer was considered a luxury. Today, the benefits of owning a computer have caused some to see it as a necessity. In fact, now you may not even consider the possibility of being without one. The context of place also affects wants and needs. It is dependent on where you live and the lifestyle you choose. For example, in a country like the United States, the standard of living is so high that even those who are considered poor may have more than the basic necessities of food, clothing, and shelter. Nielsen's "Television Audience 2009" report (2010) shows that while the average U.S. home has only 2.5 people, there is an average of 2.93 television sets in each home. Many people around the world would consider a TV a luxury, but in the United States, it is viewed as a necessity. The United Nations' Millennium Development Goals focus on global human needs, which include reducing hunger, increasing access to primary education, and addressing childhood mortality. Many of these human needs are taken for granted in industrialized countries such as the United States.

Even within the United States, the needs of one person may not match the needs of another. Those who live in a large city have different needs than do those who live in a rural area. Needs and wants are determined by personal choice. What is extremely important to one person may not be important to another. We choose between needs and wants every day. We are given hundreds of options, and we are influenced by the power of the media. Making the distinction between needs and wants can be relative to the individual making the choice.

Aaron, a college student, is planning a trip to New York City. Although he has visited New York before, he is excited to see it again and to take in some of the sights that he missed the first time he was there. He is especially looking forward to watching the Yankees play. Aaron needs a hotel room.

While looking online, he discovers a room for less than 20% of what even inexpensive hotels charge per night. Although the hotel is farther away from his destinations, there is a subway stop a few steps away. He also realizes that the location of this hotel may not be as safe as another area, and the hotel does not have many amenities. He decides to book the room. Aaron's need is to have an inexpensive place to lay his head after a long day of sightseeing, whereas another person may have a need to feel safe, require room service, or need alternative modes of transportation.

Hierarchy of Needs

According to Maslow (1954; Maslow & Frager, 1987), there is a common **hierarchy of needs** that individuals climb on the path to life satisfaction (see Figure 4.1). On the lowest level of this hierarchy are *physiological needs*, such as food and shelter. Individuals who are without these basic needs are motivated to meet these needs before looking ahead to fulfill other needs. The next level represents *safety needs*. These needs are also basic to living and include the need to be free from fear, danger, or deprivation. *Social needs* illustrate the need to relate to others in a meaningful way. According to Maslow, everyone seeks love and acceptance. *Esteem needs* include self-respect, status, and recognition. These needs are based on others' reactions to us and our own self-assessment. To fulfill this need, competence may be required. Maslow and Frager (1987) reveal that although all of these needs may be met, individuals may still feel unfulfilled, unless they believe that they are doing all they can to reach their potential— that is, they attain *self-actualization*. Although Maslow believes that few ever achieve self-actualization, the need for self-actualization is what motivates someone to be the greatest athlete, the finest novelist, or even the best parent.

Hierarchy of needs: Maslow's theory of motivation, which states that we must achieve lower-level needs, such as food, shelter, and safety, before we can achieve higher-level needs, such as belonging, esteem, and self-actualization

©iStockphoto.com/AvailableLight

▶ **Photo 4.1**
Homelessness illustrates survival at the physiological needs level.

Although Maslow is best known for his hierarchy of needs theory, his work on management should not be overlooked. Maslow, Stephens, and Heil (1998) suggest that applying the concepts of basic psychological needs to an organization provides an advantage.

The principles of Maslow's theory of needs apply not only to the individual, but to the group, "developing [the person] via the community, the team, the group,

Figure 4.1 Maslow's Pyramid

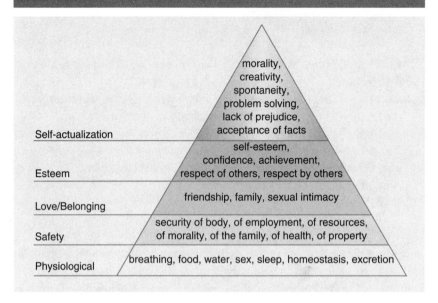

Self-actualization — morality, creativity, spontaneity, problem solving, lack of prejudice, acceptance of facts

Esteem — self-esteem, confidence, achievement, respect of others, respect by others

Love/Belonging — friendship, family, sexual intimacy

Safety — security of body, of employment, of resources, of morality, of the family, of health, of property

Physiological — breathing, food, water, sex, sleep, homeostasis, excretion

the organization—which is just as legitimate a path of personal growth as the autonomous paths" (Maslow et al., 1998, p. 4). In addition, Maslow suggests that any organization includes long-term relationships, loyalty, and communication. The family is such an organization. Family management depends on the identification of needs and progress in meeting those needs. Only then can family members begin to move toward realizing their potential as individuals. At the same time, family members love and care for each other in meaningful relationships over time. Let us examine more closely the hierarchy of needs as it applies to the family.

WORLDVIEW

In the book *Hungry Planet: What the World Eats* (2005), Peter Menzel and Faith D'Aluisio present photos of 30 families in 24 countries, including Bosnia, Chad, Egypt, Greenland, Japan, France, and the United States, and show what each family eats in one week. Each family has a different selection and amount of food based on their location, family size, and income.

Review the pictures on Menzel's website: http://menzelphoto.photoshelter.com/gallery/Hungry-Planet-Family-Food-Portraits/G0000zmg-WvU6SiKM/C0000k7JgEHhEq0w.

As you look through the pictures, notice the differences in food choices for each family. Together, the pictures highlight the similarities as well as the unique and sometimes extreme differences in the way people approach and eat food around the world. Recognize that the diet can be determined by outside influences, such as poverty, conflict, and globalization. Affluence does not necessarily guarantee healthy diet choices.

Applying the Hierarchy of Needs to the Family

All families have needs. Just as individuals identify needs specific to their own desires, the needs of families vary from family to family. Some things that are important to one family could be the least important to another. However, the lowest level of Maslow's hierarchy of needs, **physiological needs**, cannot be overlooked.

> *Emily is a single parent. She has struggled to make the best of her situation with her three children. Although Emily has a good job, recently her landlord threatened to kick out Emily's family if she doesn't pay the rent. There is never enough food, either. Emily is addicted to cocaine. Because Emily has determined that the need for cocaine will take precedence over the basic needs of the family, the physiological needs of her family go unmet. According to Maslow, not meeting these basic needs keeps the family from meeting higher-level needs, such as safety or social needs. Unless things change, Emily's children may risk shoplifting at the grocery store to meet their food needs.*

Safety needs are met as the family seeks to protect each other from danger or the fear of danger. Parents will take the steps necessary to ensure the safety of their children by building a fence, installing a security system, or fastening them into a car seat.

> *Mark and Debbie, a young couple in their early 20s, live in an urban setting. Although they were not impressed with the condition of their apartment, it was one of the only places they could afford, and it was near where they worked, eliminating the need for transportation. Shortly after moving in, they experienced several burglaries. Debbie was uneasy when she was home alone and often stayed late at work if she knew Mark would be late. Once home, they avoided going out with their friends, not wanting to risk another break-in. Eventually, Mark and Debbie decided to move to a safer area. Even though it cost them more, they decided that the need to feel safe was more important than other things they could do without.*

Ideally, the family is able to address the **social needs** of its members. Maslow suggests that this need is met when one has meaningful relationships. Family members who feel a sense of belonging create an atmosphere of love and acceptance that meets the social needs of the members.

Physiological needs: a person's most basic needs: food, shelter, and clothing

Safety needs: safety and security rank above all other desires and include physical security (safety from violence, delinquency, and aggressions), moral and physiological security, family security, security of health, and security of personal property against crime

Social needs: needs related to interaction with other people, including the need for friends, the need for belonging, and the need to give and receive love

©iStockphoto.com/CHBD

▶ **Photo 4.2**
Safety restraints meet parental needs for child safety and social mandates.

Matt and Jenny have been married for 18 years. Each of them has a high-profile career, and they have found it hard to spend time with their daughter, Angela. Jenny always made sure that Angela had the best of everything and was given the opportunities that some of her friends didn't have. Each summer she attended the best summer camp, and she took violin lessons from the finest teacher in the area. Angela knew that she was privileged, but she longed to have the kind of relationship that her best friend had with her parents—especially her dad. When Angela was 16, her parents learned that she was pregnant. As Angela's need for love and acceptance went unmet, she looked for it elsewhere.

Esteem needs: needs for being respected, having self-respect, and respecting others

Esteem needs are those that allow families to be the best they can be within their environment. Individually, family members look for self-respect, but as a family, they look for status and recognition within the community.

Cain and Beth wanted a big family. Early in their marriage, they talked about and planned for children. By their 10th anniversary, they were expecting their fifth child. Beth knew that not everyone approved, including her own mother. "How are you going to feed all these kids?" her mother would say. Beth was aware of the whispers as her family attended community functions or when she was shopping for school supplies. Cain noticed that there were fewer and fewer invitations to get together with other families. As a result, Cain and Beth decided to curtail their desire for more children. Their need for approval from the outside was greater than their need for a large family.

Self-actualization: a driving life force that will ultimately lead to maximizing one's abilities and determine the path of one's life

Although Maslow believes that individuals become **self-actualized** by reaching their potential, the family also benefits. Family members who are able to move ahead and realize their own potential are able to help other family members in their quest to be the best they can be.

Consider the lives of two brothers—Ned and Nick. Ned attended college right after high school, but he just couldn't seem to find a direction and soon dropped out. He went to work as a plumber's assistant. When he became disgruntled by the hours and hard work, he quit. Still living with his parents, he was able to be unemployed for months at a time, jumping from job to job. Nick's plan after high school was very different from Ned's plan. Nick sought the advice of his counselor to determine a career goal in physical therapy. Even while still in high school, he took classes that prepared him. Tragically, Ned and Nick's parents were killed in a car accident during Nick's senior year of college. Relatives were not surprised that Nick was able to make all the arrangements and handle the estate of his parents. Ned, on the other hand, could not seem to move ahead. Ned's physiological needs, safety needs, social needs, and esteem needs went unmet as a result of his parents' death. Until these needs are met, the potential for Ned's success will be limited.

Recently, Kenrick and colleagues (2010) have advanced Maslow's original ideas by suggesting the incorporation of evolutionary theory from biology, anthropology, and psychology to strengthen the understanding of human motivation. It is their belief that the concept of self-actualization is too broad in understanding the complexities of an experience that includes relationships such as marriage and parenting. They suggest that human motives are based not only on a person's internal needs, but on an interaction that includes needs that result from the threats and opportunities in the environment. In this way of thinking, a person may not become a parent for his or her own self-gratification; in fact, a parent often delays his or her own needs to fulfill the child's needs first.

The Consumer Resource Exchange Model (CREM)

Another useful model, the consumer resource exchange model (CREM), can be examined. Bristow and Mowen (1998) used the earlier human needs research to develop a model that is based on the concept that consumers manage resources to meet their needs. In the development of CREM, four basic assumptions are made and theoretically justified. The assumptions are as follows:

> Assumption 1: Consumers seek to manage resources that enable them to function more effectively in their world. Those resources include physical, social, informational, and financial resources.

> Assumption 2: Individual differences will exist in the level of importance consumers attach to each of the four resource types.

> Assumption 3: Resources exist as part of an interrelated/ interdependent system; each resource need type supports and is dependent on the others.

> Assumption 4: Time is a finite temporal space in which activities are performed. Time is not a consumer resource. (pp. 91–94)

Physical resource needs are those that maintain life, such as exercise and good nutrition. Social resource needs involve a person's relationships and interactions. They also involve the need to belong to a group. Financial resource needs focus on money. This need is satisfied by money or goods. Information resource needs are those that drive a person to satisfy intellectual curiosity. It is the need to know. Bristow and Mowen (1998) point out that these resources may not be all-inclusive. For example, the need for spiritual connection may be an additional need for someone. They also recognize that people will attempt to manipulate their resources to meet their needs. Finally, they propose that individual importance is placed on each resource.

The following example illustrates how the CREM is reflected in how a particular family meets their needs:

The Peterson family is getting ready for another vacation abroad. Although the family is not wealthy, Jack and Sharon feel that such experiences are valuable for their family, especially the children. They have been planning this trip for several weeks. Sharon has made sure that they will have access to the money they will need by checking the PIN numbers of their ATM and credit cards and has ordered the Euros they will take from their bank. Jack has carefully planned their itinerary to include plenty of exercise and has gone online to choose hotels that are close to a good variety of restaurants. He has also looked in several travel guides for local festivals that will be going on while they are there (assumption #1). The Petersons realize that many families do not place the same priority on travel as they do. Giving up cable TV and limiting the number of times they eat out has given them the resources to travel more. Jack and Sharon have been careful to solicit input from each of the family members about their preferences for how they will spend their time abroad (assumption #2). They cannot imagine not being able to see new sights, eat new foods, experience different cultures, and broaden their knowledge of the world (assumption #3). They only wish that they had more time to spend each day as they set off on their new adventure (assumption #4).

Categorization of Needs

Needs are met at different levels and for different reasons. Not all families have the same needs, nor are they met in the same way. For example, a family that lives on a ranch in western Texas would have different needs than would a family that lives in inner-city Los Angeles. At the lowest stages, needs are critical. Tomer (2001) describes the lower needs as cravings or strivings, whereas the needs in the higher stages can be described as aspirations. The needs of families can be divided into several categories.

Economic Needs

Of course, all families have economic needs that are met by adequate resources. Having enough money to buy the basic necessities is important for the well-being of the family. Family income may come from a variety of sources, such as employment, but may also come from gifts or inheritance. Successful management of income is a factor in meeting this need.

Physiological Needs

Physiological needs represent basic physical needs, such as nutrition and healthcare. While on Maslow's chart, physiological needs represent the first and most basic level of physical needs, which are met early in development, other physiological needs may come later in life, such as sexual satisfaction (Kenrick et al., 2010). Families need to be able to provide members with adequate food and the availability of a doctor when an illness arises. An individual's perception of good health may vary according to his or her desired quality of life.

Psychological Needs

Psychological needs involve intrinsic needs, such as self-esteem, autonomy, and competence. In their study of family caregivers, Irvin and Acton (1996) found that basic need satisfaction was directly related to high self-esteem. Timmerman and Acton (2001) later added to that by finding that individuals with higher levels of basic need satisfaction are also better able to deal with stress, resulting in healthier behaviors. Many studies have examined the relation between psychological needs satisfaction and well-being (Milyavskaya & Koestner, 2011). Those whose psychological needs are met have more satisfaction with their relationships (Patrick, Knee, Canevello, & Lonsbary, 2007) and are more likely to be content with where they live and feel a strong sense of community there (Molix & Nichols, 2013).

Social Needs

A family's social needs reflect their relatedness or affiliation within society. Some families have a difficult time recognizing their needs and may spend a great deal of time helping each other cope with situations caused by their inability to meet their needs. Other families are able to identify the needs and meet those needs in a short period of time. An alcoholic family member is using his paycheck to support his habit. Although he may need to get professional help for his addiction, the family may focus only on the need for the family to make more money.

Measuring Satisfaction of Needs

The ability to measure whether needs are being met is not universal. Doyal and Gough (1991) argue that it is difficult to measure need satisfaction. They point out that although the government has some indicators that show the health of our economy, such as the gross national product (GNP), human behavior is not considered and thus may not be a good way to measure whether people feel that their needs are being met. In addition, it may be easier to see whether people's basic needs are being met; however, the problem lies with the "intermediate" needs. Everyone needs food and clothing, but there are second-order goals or needs that build another layer within advanced societies. Some of these intermediate needs are

- Nutritional food and clean water
- Protective housing
- A nonhazardous work environment
- Appropriate healthcare
- Economic security
- Safe childbearing
- Security in childhood

Chris was transferred by his company to Pakistan. The company promised an increase in salary and extra benefits that included housing. When he arrived with his family, he was disappointed in the apartment that had been arranged. Although it provided the basic needs of shelter, security, and belonging, he and his family had other expectations. His children, Alison and Jacob, were used to their own rooms, and this apartment only had two bedrooms. The building was near a factory, so fine white ash formed on the family's furniture each day. In addition, the apartment faced a major street with lots of noisy traffic 24 hours a day. The family had "intermediate" needs that were not being met in this situation. Once the company realized the needs of Chris and his family, they were able to find other accommodations. Their intentions were then turned toward meeting their needs for safe food and clean water.

Measuring quality of life may be another way to evaluate whether needs are being met. Coverdill and colleagues (2011) suggest that although objective measures, such as income levels and education, can be easily measured, there are three common convictions among the literature that help identify the more subjective quality-of-life measures, such as happiness or satisfaction with life. First, it is agreed that there are multiple ways to assess quality of life. Second, quality of life is dependent on the person evaluating the situation, and people are generally capable of evaluating their own quality of life accurately. Third, quality of life is dependent on circumstances and is constantly changing.

Individually, people can evaluate whether their needs are being met by using measures of **relative deprivation** from a sociological perspective. Comparing what you have to what other people have is one way to evaluate where you stand in society. When a person believes that he or she is deprived of those things that society believes are necessary, it can be a beginning point for the person to act. It can be motivation for positive improvement. Relative deprivation may also cause some to overspend or to steal when they believe that they deserve the items they are obtaining.

Relative deprivation: a lack of resources to sustain socially expected levels of status or consumption

CHANGING PERCEPTIONS OF NEEDS

The way that individuals within families view their needs often changes over time. The needs of a family may change due to circumstances, personality, economic status, technology, culture, life span, and gender differences.

Circumstances

Circumstances: conditions, facts, or events accompanying, conditioning, or determining one another

Circumstances often change the perception of what a family needs. There are many situations that families face that will alter the needs that they have. Some situations may cause needs to be altered for a short time, and in other cases, people realize that their needs have changed permanently. For example, a child who has chicken pox may cause a family to have to change its schedule and sleeping arrangements for a short time, whereas a debilitating illness, such as a stroke that results in permanent disability, will cause the family to change indefinitely.

Situations such as illness, disability, death, and natural disaster all have an effect on the needs of individual families. Although it seems that monetary resources would be important in a crisis situation, research indicates that the most immediate need for those who are dealing with a critically ill family member is information and assurance (Bond, Mandleco, & Donnelly, 2003; Ward, 2001).

Social changes also require family needs to change. During the Great Depression of the 1930s, family needs were greater for basic survival. At this time in history, high unemployment, drought, and an unstable monetary system led many families to think differently about their needs (see Box 4.1).

BOX 4.1   MAIL FROM ELEANOR ROOSEVELT

During the Great Depression of the 1930s, First Lady Eleanor Roosevelt received more than 300,000 pieces of mail in her first year of office. Many of the letters pleaded for relief from the conditions of unemployment, poverty, and homelessness. Many of the letters were from children. Although most children are unaware of the financial situations of their parents, these children were fully aware of the struggles they and their parents were living. The following letters illustrate the differences in the needs of these children, as opposed to the "needs" that children might identify today.

Royse City, Texas
Sept. 6, 1934

Dear Friend:

Well I don't suppose you know who I am. But I'm a 16 year old motherless girl that has to work hard for all she gets. I have a brother and a sister and daddy. We are working as day labor for a living and don't get much of that to do. In the winter I could piece quilts if I had any scraps. We are trying to keep off the relief this winter so we are keeping every penny we can to buy groceries this winter. Whether we have sufficient clothes or not. We haven't even enough furniture. We haven't any bedsteads, a stove, or cabinet. Some of our neighbors are letting us use their stove, cabinet, & one bedstead. I thought you might have some old clothes, coats, and shoes, or any kind of clothing you

could sent to us. I have read so much about your kindness I know if you have any you will send them. I would send some money for postage but haven't any. Address to your loving friend Miss D. H.   (p. 48)

Gettysburg, S. Dak.
Jan 8, 193[4]

Dear Mrs. Roosevelt:

A young girl from a God forlorn country is writing to you. I will be 16 years old Jan 16. We are so poor we haven't hardly enough to eat. I have 2 sisters and 1 brother and father. Mother is dead over 5 years. She was killed in a railroad collision. I have to keep house. We haven't had a crop for 8 years. We get about ¼ can of cream in two weeks and that is only 10 cents so we can't buy anything. Eggs we haven't any. Would you be so very kind and send us a little money to buy a few necessary things. I suppose you get many letters like this but if you can please send a little I would thank you from the bottom of my heart.
     As ever your Friend.
A. N.   (p. 60)

L. B., an eighth-grade student from Illinois, to Eleanor Roosevelt
February 1934

I have a brother younger than I, and he's in the same grade with me. My mother would want both of us to go to school, and

(Continued)

Rationing: the controlled distribution of resources and scarce goods or services

During times of war, the United States experienced **rationing**, which also led to a reevaluation of needs for many families.

During World War II, people were encouraged to plant "victory gardens," and to conserve rubber, paper, aluminum, tin cans, toothpaste tubes, sugar, coffee, and even kitchen fats. Drivers were limited to three gallons of gas per week, leading to the formation of carpools or "car clubs" (Rauber, 2003, p. 32).

Personality

Personality: the consistent emotional, thought, and behavior patterns in a person

Personality differences play a role in the perception of needs. Personality measures point to differences in the need for closure or structure (Stalder, 2007), the need that introverts have to avoid communication (Opt & Loffrendo, 2000), and the need that risk takers have for variety, change, and excitement (Olsen, Tudoran, Honkanen, & Verplanken, 2015; Zuckerman, 2000). Individual desires, motivation, and behavior are assembled as a person grows and develops and have an influence on what is important to that person. For example, peer group pressures that someone experiences as an adolescent will influence his or her behaviors and motivations as an adult.

> *Sandy grew up in a family that stressed conservative values. She was not allowed to have many of the popular styles in clothing that her friends wore. As an adult, it is important to her that her daughter has the newest and most trendsetting clothes to help her fit in with her peer group.*

Economic Status

Socioeconomic status: the hierarchical distinctions between individuals or groups in societies or cultures based on social rank and monetary advantage

The **socioeconomic status** (SES) of a family will have an influence on its needs and how it meets those needs. For families with resources, the choices they make regarding their perceived needs will be different from those of a family that is barely surviving. Access to good education, healthcare, housing, and leisure facilities can assist in providing greater life chances that prove valuable throughout life. According to Gasana (2009), consumers' buying habits are influenced by those with similar socioeconomic status rather than based on their income.

For families that are struggling financially, basic needs such as healthcare, adequate housing, and healthy foods may not be met. Economic challenges often obstruct access to health and social services (Kurtz Landy, Sword, & Ciliska, 2008). Even the lack of educational experiences that children need becomes a disadvantage for some low-income families. Edwards and colleagues (2009) report that children from financially disadvantaged families have greater difficulty in being ready to begin school. Educational needs are critical to families' ability to rise out of poverty. The need for adequate education is important not only to the individual and his or her family, but to the nation as a whole.

Technology

Perhaps more than at any other time in history, technology plays a major role in the needs of families today. Technology is woven into the fabric of our lives in every way. Everything we see and do involves technology, from the media, the production and consumption of goods, and the workplace to reproduction and our physical quality of life.

To be on the right side of the **digital divide**, families need to be current with technology. Families who are more well off are three times more likely to have Internet access. Households with lower rates of Internet usage are those who are without jobs, are homeless, and may be in poor health and are at even more of a disadvantage (Shneiderman, 2010).

Culture

Cultural differences point out the variations in needs within families that have different priorities and structures. Meeting the needs of all racial and ethnic groups in the United States is a challenge. For example, the need for belonging takes on a different meaning between cultures. Some cultures place a great deal of emphasis on civic responsibility, whereas other cultures place more emphasis on family responsibility.

Doyal and Gough (1991) identified four preconditions that are necessary for needs to be met within any society: production, reproduction, cultural transmission, and authority. **Production** is necessary for goods to be made available for meeting basic needs, such as food and clothing. To continue, all societies must reproduce. In addition, **reproduction** involves caring for the young and their socialization. Another precondition involves the culture's ability to pass on cultural norms, rules, and values through communication among people. Whereas production and reproduction involve the physical environment, **cultural transmission** involves the human behavior necessary to cause the cultural group to move in a certain direction. **Authority** ensures that the cultural rules will be carried out.

It is difficult to identify needs that are common to all groups or cultures. Not all cultures agree on identifying basic needs. An American may see a car as a basic need, but in a Third World country, a car is a luxury or want. In addition, the range of need satisfiers varies greatly. Differences in food, clothing, and traditions magnify the differences in the way various cultures meet their needs.

Digital divide: the gap between those people and communities who can access and make effective use of information technology and those who cannot

Production: the making or creation of something; the process of manufacturing a product for sale

Reproduction: a copy of something in an earlier style; the act of reproducing something

Cultural transmission: how culture is passed on through learning from one generation to another

Authority: (a) a conclusive statement or set of statements (as an official decision of a court); (b) a decision taken as a precedent; (c) testimony; (d) an individual cited or appealed to as an expert

Donna is a registered dietitian in a large hospital; she is responsible for meeting the nutritional needs of the patients in that hospital. One of her patients is diagnosed with anemia. In visiting with the patient, Donna discovers that his religion does not allow him to eat any meat. The patient needs complete protein to regain his strength and red blood cells, but Donna helps him design a diet that also meets his need to practice his religion by introducing incomplete protein sources, such as beans, nuts, and other legumes. Although the foods available in the patient's native country met his dietary needs, once he moved to the United States, he was no longer getting the nutrition he needed.

These cultural differences can also involve the standards that are set within those cultures. The standards in the United States may differ from those in other countries. For example, the Occupational Safety and Health Administration (OSHA) sets minimum standards to ensure safe and healthy workplaces. Standards are also set for education, childcare, buildings, and other areas that affect families. Some standards are set by world organizations, such as the Convention on the Rights of the Child, adopted by the General Assembly of the United Nations in 1989.

Cultural rituals: practices that serve to unite a particular group by preserving cultural identity and heritage

Cultural rituals are another way that perception of needs differs among people. The importance that is placed on the rituals that families perform can vary greatly. One family may see burial as a ritual that has a high priority, and a good number of resources may be allocated to this ritual. Another family would view burial of their loved ones as a low priority in light of their other obligations. Some cultures place a high priority on specific rituals. In the Hispanic culture, a quinceañera is a celebration of a girl's 15th birthday. It is a special occasion because it is when a girl becomes a woman. Hispanic girls all over the world celebrate this occasion. Although a family may be struggling financially, this rite of passage cannot be overlooked, and a great deal of resources may be allocated to this event.

Life Span

Life span: the period or length of time in which a person lives

Changes throughout the life span can also bring changes for families as they go from being just a couple to a family and back again to being a couple. Each of these stages signals changes in their needs.

Infants have a way of letting us know that they have a need. Parents are often able to distinguish the different cries of their infants, because it is their only form of communication. Infants also have a need to bond or attach to their caregiver, which usually results in building trust that will follow them throughout life. Brazelton and Greenspan (2000) suggest that infants need loving relationships that offer encouragement and communication, and that can provide a stimulating environment for emotional and intellectual development. As children grow, they still need opportunities for physical development and exposure to language, as well as to have a sense of belonging in their family. Older children need encouragement for their accomplishments, consistency in the way that boundaries and limits are set, and to learn how to get along with others.

When a child becomes an adolescent, a new set of needs is identified. Hersch (1998) described the adolescent culture as a separate community: "More than a group of peers, it becomes in isolation a society with its own values, ethics, rules, worldview, rites of passage, worries, joy, and momentum" (p. 21). This social dependency creates needs that may not be identified within any other age group. In addition, many adolescents' risk-taking behaviors, such as drug and alcohol experimentation, risky sexual activity, and poor eating habits, require different healthcare needs.

Adults have different needs as well. According to Levinson (1978, 1990), both men and women follow a series of transitions as they progress into and through adulthood. Each transition represents changes that include separating from parents, forming meaningful relationships, and developing the ability to have control over their own lives.

> *Cyndi is spending her first holiday season away from her family. After finishing graduate school, she took a job several hundred miles away from her family. Her limited budget and the amount of time she could be away from work prevented her from going "home" for the holidays. Cyndi's mother knew that the holidays would be hard for Cyndi, so she decided to send several care packages. Although the packages were nice, Cyndi realized that her needs were changing. What she missed wasn't her mother's gifts or cookies but the chance to be with the people she loved. Over the next few weeks, she invited her new friends and coworkers to celebrate the holidays with her.*

As adults age, their needs often return to physical needs. Older adults need more help in carrying out their daily tasks. These needs may require them to seek shelter in assisted living facilities, choose foods that are more easily digested, or buy clothing that is easy to get on and off. Pandya and Coleman (2000) found that one in four American households is providing caregiving services for an older family member.

In addition to physical needs, Merriam, Cafferella, and Baumgartner (2007) have identified conditions of our current society that create the learning needs of the older adult. These researchers suggest that adults need information on changing demographics, the global economy, and information and technology. As adults live longer and more active lives than in the past, they must maintain their independence, competence, and connection to the world; these are essential needs for humans, especially as they age.

©iStockphoto.com/PeopleImages

▶ **Photo 4.3**
Female and male preferences and identification of needs differ.

Gender Differences

Despite the fact that the basic needs of families affect both males and females, men and women have different needs. Physically, there are differences that affect healthcare needs. DeLorey reports that "while women live longer than men, they

Communal traits: characteristics that are related to forming and maintaining social relationships with others, which are more common for women than for men

Agentic traits: characteristics that focus on independence, control, and completion of tasks, which are more associated with men than with women

are more likely to suffer from long-term activity limitations and chronic conditions such as osteoporosis, arthritis or migraine headaches" (2003, p. 1). Although men have been plagued by stress-related diseases such as heart attacks, strokes, and hypertension, more health professionals are beginning to recognize the danger of these ailments for women as well.

Personality differences between men and women also affect their needs. Bakan (1966) identified two groups of traits that describe these differences. **Communal traits**, more common for women than men, are related to forming and maintaining social relationships with others. Thus, women would be more likely to need companionship and social connection. **Agentic traits**, which are more associated with men, focus on independence, control, and completion of tasks, signaling more of a need for self-reliance and self-motivation.

> *Newlyweds Jim and Janet just bought their first house. Although they are satisfied with the structure and floorplan of the house, they plan to make some major improvements. They begin to make plans for a weekend where their friends and family can come and help them tear out the old paneling. Jim is looking forward to making progress on the house. Janet, on the other hand, is looking forward to the time they will spend with their friends and family members. Their needs for the workday are different.*

REALITY CHECK

In the age of information and communication, the needs of families have expanded as we learn more about the world and what it has to offer—news, advertising, movies, and technology. Is a cell phone a necessity or a luxury? Today, it is hard to imagine a world without cell phones. Adults recognize the need for cell phones in their daily lives, but parents have to make decisions about whether their kids need a cell phone and at what age. Many parents do not have a model of how their own parents handled such an issue, because this simply wasn't an issue in previous generations. Here are some of the arguments for why or why not kids would need a phone:

Reasons children need a cell phone:

1. Connection to parents: Children and parents have a constant ability to communicate with each other for practical planning and in emergency situations. Some phones have the capability for parents to use GPS to track the child at all times.

2. Connection to friends: A phone allows children to stay connected to their friends to socialize, work together on assignments, and make plans for events.

3. Lesson in responsibility: Having a phone gives children the opportunity to learn responsibility for the care of their device and to stay within their cell phone's plan if there are limitations for minutes used or other factors to consider.

4. Increased independence: Phones allow children more freedom to be away from their parents but add a measure of safety.

Reasons children should not have a cell phone:

1. Vulnerability: Being online increases the possibility of a child's being targeted. Cell phones also cause distraction that can lead to accident or injury.

2. Connection to friends: Unlimited time with friends may not be the best idea, especially without supervision.

3. Exposure to negative influences: Smartphones include access to the Internet, which cannot always be supervised when the child is away from his or her parents.

4. Expensiveness: Cell phones can be expensive, and extra charges can quickly add up.

5. Health issues: Some evidence has shown that heavy cell phone use may cause health problems.

In the end, parents may decide that the advantages outweigh the disadvantages, but there are some solutions to the potential issues. Parents can consider a prepaid plan with limits on what the phone can do. Limiting a child's time spent on the phone could also be beneficial. Parents should also have conversations with their children about the dangers associated with using a cell phone.

Source: Stavrinos, Byington, and Schwebel (2009).

NEEDS ASSESSMENT

Although accurate and timely reports provide demographic information about individuals and families, the real needs of those populations are not always known. Policymakers and human service providers often conduct needs assessments to determine the needs of those they serve. A needs assessment is an important tool used to communicate. Soriano (2013) suggests that the results of a needs assessment are important not only to identify needs and whether they are being met, but also to make decisions about resource allocations in the future. A needs assessment should be representative of the population, current, and used to meet the needs of the population for which it is intended.

A needs assessment that is representative of the population will provide accurate information about the population to be served. Thus, information about culture/ethnicity, family structure, age, education, employment, health, and so on will be included.

A needs assessment must also be current. Conducting a needs assessment that will be utilized years later is not acceptable when the needs of people are changing rapidly. A need that is important can become critical in a short period of time. It is also possible that what is considered a need today could no longer be needed tomorrow.

Several years ago, Community X conducted a needs assessment of low-income families and determined that they needed better jobs with higher wages and more family benefits. Community leaders began searching for a manufacturer that would consider relocating to their community. A beef-packing plant was soon built outside the city limits. After the first year, the plant was unable to staff all its shifts, and within three years, the plant closed. Later, it was discovered that a major problem for many potential workers was the lack of transportation to and from the plant. The community failed to assess the additional needs following the initial assessment and solution. As a result, the needs of the community were not met.

Finally, a needs assessment must be used to meet the needs of the population for which it is intended. To carry out this task, assessment must include a clear understanding of the perception of the problem(s), the barriers to accessibility, and who is responsible for the outcome(s). In addition, if new policy is set as a result of the assessment, there should be a good understanding about the implications that will result from the changes. Identifying and meeting the needs of individuals and families can be difficult, depending on the definition of their needs.

IN THE NEWS

Consumers and Daily Deals

Daily deals are big business on the Internet. Groupon and other companies like it have turned ecommerce business upside down. Since the beginning of the daily deal industry, skeptics have wondered whether these deal sites were here to stay. It appears they are not leaving anytime soon, and more and more are popping up every day. They operate with low overhead, no inventory, and good customer service, and consumers love them.

According to Amato (2011), there are several explanations for the popularity of daily deal sites:

1. Consumers will always want a deal.

Consumers are always looking for ways to save money. Daily deal sites are an easy way for consumers to find a good deal without having to search for it. Businesses are also happy to increase their customer base. It is a great way to increase sales efficiently, and it is not dependent on the economy.

2. Smart businesses will reap rewards, despite losing money on deals.

Although there have been stories about Groupon failures where local businesses were not able to accommodate the demands of their daily deals, most are successful. While a daily deal often causes a business to lose money initially, most should be able to see real long-term benefits following the initial deal by gaining new long-term customers. Businesses need to be savvy in creating a deal that results in repeat business or even "upsell" opportunities down the road.

3. The market is still maturing.

While daily deal sites have been around for a while, they are still relatively new. Both consumers and merchants are finding benefits, but the practice will continue to mature. Amato states, "Just a short year ago, a handful of players controlled 90% of the market in the daily deals space. While it's estimated some 200 daily deal sites exist, a handful of players still control that same share of the space" (2011).

Source: Adapted from Amato, J. (2011).

INDIVIDUAL NEEDS VERSUS SOCIETAL NEEDS

Planned obsolescence: the conscious decision on the part of a manufacturer to produce a consumer product that will become obsolete and/or nonfunctional in a defined timeframe

Meeting individual or family needs does not automatically mean that the needs of society are fulfilled. Meeting human needs, as we have discussed in this chapter, must combine socioeconomic and technical progress. Corporate America has manipulated consumers into believing that they need the products being sold through advertising. **Planned**, or **artificial**, **obsolescence**, a phenomenon that appeared early in the 20th century, came about to ease the fear that the economy would be slowed by a saturation of products. In the 1920s, the auto industry was facing a crisis; by the most accurate estimates at the time, everyone who could afford a car would own one by

1926, and sales would therefore decline. The president of General Motors, Alfred P. Sloan, suggested that the industry spur demand by creating dissatisfaction with past models as compared to new ones (Marling, 1994). In 1934, presenters at the Society of Automotive Engineers suggested that the life span of an automobile should be limited (Beder, 1998). Ethical concerns were raised about the responsibility of the manufacturers to provide quality products.

Artificial obsolescence also creates a new need for consumers. A good example comes from the fashion industry. Each season, "new" styles and colors replace those of the previous season. The need for change creates the need to buy the newest and latest fashions. Even when a style is repeated from a previous generation, superficial changes cause the consumer to buy the new product.

Not only are there ethical concerns involved in planned obsolescence; meeting human needs must also include the desire to conserve the earth's natural resources. The consequences of our "disposable" society will impact our world. The World Commission on Environment and Development has defined **sustainable development** as meeting the "needs of the present without compromising the ability of future generations to meet their own needs" (WCED, 1987, p. 43). Simply talking about a family's need for food will not ensure that the family's future will be bright. The societal need of producing food at a fair price, the guarantee of food safety, and the assurance that the soil used to grow that food will not be depleted are just as critical to that family's future.

In thinking about the needs of individuals and families, it is important to look at the larger picture. Societal needs influence and expand the family's decision-making process. As in any problem-solving process, asking questions that lead to an understanding of how decisions influence and impact those beyond ourselves is critical. It may be important to consider whether improving our lives *is* better. Siegel (2006) suggests that we are at the point in our society where we may have reached the limits of human needs. He suggests that we have moved from consuming necessities to consuming luxuries. This kind of consumerism creates problems when continued growth is a disadvantage socially and environmentally. Although his writings may be viewed as somewhat controversial, Illich (1978) stated more than 30 years ago that in our society the proliferation of commodities has turned wants into requirements. Eventually, these become needs on demand. What *are* the costs for getting what we need?

Artificial obsolescence: the phenomenon of industry's creating a new need for consumers that produces demand by creating dissatisfaction with past models

Sustainable development: any construction that can be maintained over time without damaging the environment; development that balances near-term interests with the protection of the interests of future generations

SUMMARY

It is critical that every family begin to recognize the difference between its needs and wants. Maslow's hierarchy of needs and the CREM are two ways to explain the needs of families. Each family has a different way of determining needs, and the way that a family perceives its needs changes over time. A needs assessment is used to determine needs and takes into account the culture/ethnicity, structure, age, education, employment, and health of the family. Needs assessments are important tools in determining policies. Technological progress and consumerism have changed human needs. In many cases, the media has influenced our perception of needs.

QUESTIONS FOR REVIEW AND DISCUSSION

1. What is the difference between needs and wants? Are they different for everyone? Why or why not?

2. Discuss the different levels of Maslow's hierarchy of needs. What kind of person is able to achieve the highest level of self-actualization? Apply these questions to a family.

3. Compare Maslow's hierarchy of needs with the CREM.

4. How do changing perceptions of needs affect a family?

5. When conducting a needs assessment, what should be included?

6. How do human needs affect societal needs? How do societal needs affect human needs?

CHAPTER FIVE

VALUES, ATTITUDES, AND BEHAVIORS
Understanding Family Choices

Objectives
Values
 Personal Values
 Family Values
Reality Check
 Values Across the Life Span
 Value Congruence Across Generations
Attitudes
Behaviors
Values, Attitudes, and Behaviors in the
 Decision-Making Framework
In the News
Values and Behaviors in Family Purchasing
 Decisions
 Brand Preference
 Quality Preference
 Price Preference
 Design Preference
Impact of Culture on Values, Attitudes, and
 Behaviors
Worldview
Impact of Socioeconomic Factors on Values,
 Attitudes, and Behaviors
Consistency Over Time and Situation
Summary
Questions for Review and Discussion

Objectives

- Understand the concepts of values, attitudes, and behaviors and how they impact family decision making.

- Become familiar with the factors that impact the development, maintenance, and changing of personal and family value sets over time.

- Become aware of how external forces impact value expression in the identification of needs and alternatives and in the decision-making process.

- Be able to apply understanding of values, attitudes, and behaviors to the critical analysis of family decisions and behaviors in society.

> **We are what we pretend to be, so we must be careful about what we pretend to be.**
>
> **—Kurt Vonnegut**

Individuals and families discover, rank, and create evaluative meanings for their needs. Every step of the decision-making process is impacted by one's values, attitudes, and behaviors. When family members are contemplating or discovering needs, they rely on these subjective measures to rank order or prioritize the multiple needs. For instance, family members need clothing. When that new clothing is required is a function of existing resources and environmental conditions. Beyond that, in American society, new clothing purchases are motivated primarily by social expectations and how deeply the family unit is persuaded to follow fashion and social pressure. A bride needs a wedding dress, right? Well, actually, legal marriage ceremonies do not mandate participants' dress. If a traditional wedding dress is perceived as a real need, it is processed as such. From that point, values and resources are weighed to determine what type of dress is obtained and how it is secured. Will it be borrowed? Purchased? Created? To understand the impact of values, attitudes, and behaviors on family resource management, we must understand the definitions of many terms that are often used loosely.

VALUES

Value: worth in usefulness or importance to the possessor; a principle, standard, or quality considered worthwhile or desirable

Value is a term used often in the discussion of human behavior from two unique perspectives. When discussing economics and consumer behavior, the term *value* is used as a measurement of exchange. If you spend money on goods or services, you expect satisfaction from that exchange of resources. It is determined to be a good value if the person exchanging resources feels that he or she has received a fair return. This determination of fairness is subjective. A baseball card collector may feel that one single card is worth several hundred dollars. Someone who is not involved in this hobby may feel that such a purchase would be a waste of monetary resources. A grandmother's collection of photographs may be priceless to one grandchild, but of little perceived value to another.

Another common use of the term *value* is perhaps even more subjective and personal in nature. Guiding principles of thought and behavior are often referred to as one's values. It is believed that these principles develop slowly over time as part of the individual's social and psychological development. Researchers have focused on these dispositions in numerous scientific studies in an attempt to measure, predict, and understand how values guide thought and action.

Universal values: beliefs existent or operative everywhere or under all conditions

Human rights: the rights one has because one is a human being; the right to life, freedom, and human dignity

A search for **universal values** has been troublesome to theorists. **Human rights** are discussed and presented as universal values, yet some of these rights are not embraced by all groups. The practice of female genital mutilation, or female circumcision, is one such debated violation of human rights. Senator John McCain (2010) states that human rights are "the right to life and liberty, to the protection of property, and to rule by the consent of the governed" (p. 11). Moyn (2010) purports that human rights are violated every time they are interpreted because they promise everything to everyone. While an ambiguous concept, human rights continue to surface as focal points when social groups believe they are uniting to make human conditions better for all. The Tea Party Movement of the past decade claimed that it, too, was a human rights movement based in the U.S. Constitution (Moyn, 2010, p. 37). Universal values may be difficult to define, but cultural or social values are not. When a group of people embraces a set of understood values, members operate within those beliefs and are judged accordingly. The discussion of worldview in Chapter 1 illustrates this concept. Simon (2010) connects culture and human rights: "Membership in a culture is predicated on membership in humanity" (p. 77).

In the United States, especially in business and educational institutions, punctuality is highly valued. Teachers expect students to be in class when that class is scheduled to begin. Not every American accepts that one particular value, but being late is generally unacceptable and carries consequences. Being late for a commercial airplane flight may result in the loss of the price of that ticket and the loss of travel via that medium. Being late for a meeting may result in missed leadership opportunities or, in some cases, unwanted responsibilities.

Personal Values

Values, when framed within a religious or spiritual framework, are often referred to as **morals**. Using morals in decision making is placing value judgments on a continuum of right and wrong. Kohlberg (1984) proposes that humans develop a set of morals as they mature, both socially and intellectually (see Table 5.1). One's sense of justice and how he or she makes judgments about what are good and bad decisions evolve over time, primarily due to changes in cognitive abilities. Young, school-age children think concretely. Something is always right or always wrong; there are no shades of gray. Adolescents, who are capable of abstract thinking, will begin to contemplate each **situation** in terms of context, alternatives, and impact of actions on self and others. Some adults, according to Kohlberg's sequence, will consider universal moral principles, even at the risk of breaking their own civil laws. One example frequently used to explain this concept is the husband who would break into a pharmacy to steal a medication that would keep his wife alive, rather than let her die because he couldn't pay for it.

Although this model of moral development assumes a progression through stages, it does not assume that every individual moves through each and every

Morals: ethics, codes, values, principles, and customs of a person or society

Situation: the general conditions that prevail in a place or society; the circumstances that somebody is in at a particular moment

Table 5.1 Kohlberg's Sequence of Moral Reasoning

Level	Stage
Pre-conventional	1. Obedience and punishment 2. Individualism, instrumentalism, and exchange
Conventional	3. "Good boy/girl" 4. Law and order
Post-conventional	5. Social contract 6. Principled conscience

stage. Thus, any group of adults may have individuals functioning at different phases of Kohlberg's model. Obviously, a multigenerational family will also have members operating at different levels. Adults in family units are most often the final decision makers, but that does not mean that family decisions will then reflect the higher moral levels. If those adults are functioning at lower levels, decisions will reflect that.

▶ **Photo 5.1**
When controversial values are expressed as attitudes, protesting becomes a possible behavior.

Mr. and Mrs. Jones set aside an entire day each February to prepare their income tax returns. They read the directions carefully and report both their earnings and their deductions honestly.

Mr. and Mrs. Smith wait until the last day to file taxes. They claim only the income they have received that can be traced through federal reporting forms and exaggerate many deduction amounts to reduce their final tax payment.

The Joneses are functioning at a moral level that reflects their beliefs in what is right and what is wrong and their sense of obligation to the government. The Smiths may feel that the government is misusing funds collected through taxation or may rationalize their behavior in other ways.

Moral beliefs that are held strongly enough within a group may ultimately become laws with punitive legal consequences. Accurate reporting of information on tax reports has legal consequences, but only when discovered.

When faced with decisions that impact society, but aren't mandated by law, family members responsible for making decisions regarding resource management must rely on their values, morals, and past experiences to reach decisions that they are comfortable making. One purchase decision faced by many families is the procurement of a vehicle for transportation. This decision has personal, family, and social ramifications.

When contemplating the purchase of automobiles in the United States, consumers have many options. The selection includes many sizes, configurations, materials, and fuel sources. Some vehicles are fuel efficient, whereas others are gas guzzlers. A conscientious consumer may forgo some size capacity and styling options because he or she wants to reduce the pollution and consumption of gasoline. Another may be determined to buy larger, less efficient vehicles because he or she needs the ability to transport others or materials. Neither is breaking a law. Both are expressing their consumer rights. Both may value the need to reduce air pollution and fossil fuel consumption. The second owner, however, is rationalizing his or her purchase by prioritizing existing needs (hauling capacity) above environmental concerns.

Family Values

Because families consist of more than one individual, the probability that family members' values will clash with one another on occasion is quite high. Gender has been shown to impact decision making. Traut-Mattausch, Jonas, Frey, and Zanna (2011) found that females are more likely to seek information about how they can make decisions that positively impact others in their lives than are males. Females are more likely to seek out multiple sources of information when making decisions that will affect their families. Males are less likely to consider the impact on others above the possible impact to themselves. Beyond gender differences, it

REALITY CHECK

Jeremiah was born and raised in a conservative Catholic community in the Midwest. He was the oldest of five children in a family that struggled to stay at the poverty line. He is approaching retirement age and reflects on the choices he has made over his adult life that were directly related to his inability to operate within the values and attitudes of his hometown.

> At 22, I hitchhiked across four states to the East Coast. I had completed a college degree in journalism, but knew that I wouldn't be happy in the geographical area I had grown up in for many reasons. One major reason—I was gay. In the sexual revolution of the 1960s, that wasn't such a radical thing, but in my home community, it was unacceptable. I went to Woodstock and hung out in New York City for a while and really enjoyed the lifestyle there. I met my life partner shortly after arriving. Eventually we moved to a small coastal community between New York and Washington, D.C.

Jeremiah physically separated himself from a value set that had discounted him and his sexual orientation, which resulted in a physical and emotional separation from his family of origin.

> My younger sister knew why I had moved away. My parents and extended family probably knew, but never acknowledged that, even now, 40 years later. I sent cards and letters home occasionally. My siblings, and even my mother, made short visits to Virginia and spent time with me, in my home, where my partner was also living. He was always referred to as my friend and roommate by family members. I was always upfront about our joint ownership of property and our growing investment portfolio. Eventually, I think they saw him as a "business partner" of sorts.

> I missed some important family gatherings, but always traveled back for anniversaries and weddings. Holidays were usually spent with my partner and our large extended family of friends and neighbors in our neighborhood. As I get older, I visit home more often. My partner has never gone back to the Midwest with me. It wouldn't be comfortable for him. Recently, his father died, and I was included in the obituary as his "life partner." That was a very emotional event for me. He was not acknowledged in that way in my parents' obituaries. But I do think my siblings and their families are okay with it now. They address cards to both of us and include my partner in invitations. We recently attended a nephew's wedding in my home state and felt very welcome.

Values, attitudes, and behaviors are slow to change. Jeremiah's family journey spanned almost half a century.

is also important to understand how the total membership within a family may impact the decision-making process. To understand how values in the context of multiple members impact family decisions, group dynamics must be explored. Do families develop unique value systems over time that might differentiate one family from another?

Homogamy: purposeful selection of a mate who has similar characteristics to your own

Homogamy is a term used to describe the purposeful selection of mates from a pool that has similar characteristics to our own. Homogamy is most visible in terms of race, religion, and social class. Although many contemporary thinkers may claim that this practice is fading, what do statistics indicate? Curtis and Ellison (2002) report that marriages remain largely homogamous, in both the United States and around the world. Data from 2002 indicated that 78% of marriages in the United States consisted of partners from the same or very similar religious groups. Educational similarity has been increasing within marriages over the last three decades as well (Shafer & Qian, 2010).

In terms of interracial marriages, the U.S. Census of 2010 reported that about 8% of the adult population is in an interracial or interethnic marriage. A record 12% of newlyweds in 2013 married across racial lines (Wang, 2015). That does not include marriages between Hispanics and non-Hispanics, which are considered to be interethnic. Although laws forbidding interracial marriages are no longer legal or enforceable, the rate of interracial unions is much lower than would be expected if mates were selected without regard to race. The number of interracial couples has increased in the United States since 1970—just 1% in that census. However, they remain a small percentage of all marriages.

Attitudes toward interracial marriage are changing. Survey results of college students by Bonilla-Silva and Forman (2000) found that only 30% approved of marriages between whites and African Americans. Wang (2015) reported that 37% of respondents viewed interracial marriage as a "good thing for society" in a large survey conducted in 2014. Johnson and Jacobsen (2005) suggest that for whites, educational and religious institutions provide social arenas for positive attitudes about interracial marriage, whereas work sites and neighborhood contacts do not.

In North America, the marital homogamous rate implies a purposeful search for a partner with similar religious, racial, and ethnic morals and values. Educational levels may be even more important in mate selection than religious affiliation. Blackwell and Lichter (2004) report that married and cohabiting couples are highly homogamous with respect to education. Another possibly confounding variable is the strong interrelationship between religion and race. American Mormons are overwhelmingly white, and African Americans are predominantly Protestant. Determining which factor—race or religion—guides mate selection becomes problematic.

Homogamy, in terms of social class affiliation, has been a factor in mate selection in all known societies. Although there is probably more mixed-class marriage in the United States than in many other countries, intra-class pairings are the norm. A pattern of finding mates whose parents have similar occupations to one's own parents is also firmly entrenched in U.S. courtship and marriage. Even geographical location impacts this type of homogamy. Neighborhoods are often delineated by income level and social class. Although transportation and career mobility have changed the opportunities for mate selection across geographical distances, most couples still find each other in relatively narrow geographical areas—community or state of origin.

> Peggy was born and raised in an affluent suburb of Washington, D.C. Her family was white, upper-middle-class, and Catholic. She attended private religious schools from K–12 and then attended an Ivy League college. Rarely was Peggy in a social situation where there were children or adults from minority groups. Her pool of dating partners reflected little diversity.

> Jolie grew up in Harlem, New York City. Her mother was African American, and her father was of Cuban descent. Her neighborhood, schools, and church were culturally and racially mixed, with the exception of whites. Few white children attended her schools, and even fewer participated in her religious and social activities. Although her pool of dating partners was more diverse than Peggy's, it still reflected a segregated sample.

Odds are that both of these women will select mates who are similar to them in terms of socioeconomic class and race. This is not necessarily purposeful homogamy, but more likely experiential in nature. As diverse families live and interact together, the rate of interracial relationships should be higher. Statistics in such cases, however, still indicate that purposeful selection of mates is impacted by race and ethnic preferences.

According to the data and theory on homogamy, it appears that couples forming new households and family units bring similar backgrounds with them in terms of race, religion, and social class factors, which would suggest that they have similar value and moral bases. Although probably true in the majority of cases, it is still essential that compromise and negotiation take place initially in newly formed families, thus resulting in a unique blending of values and approaches to decision making. These sets of **family values** will guide family resource management over time. As with all social memberships, family members may deviate from established family values, but there will be consequences for them in doing so.

Family values: values, especially of a traditional or conservative kind, that are held to promote the sound functioning of the family and strengthen the fabric of society

> Patrick and Katria are both college students in the central region of the United States. Although they have both grown to adulthood in different states, their educational, religious, and social experiences have been quite similar. When they decided to marry, there were minor differences between the families in terms of wedding details and living arrangements, but nothing extremely out of the ordinary. With a baby on the way, religious differences may present some problems.

> Derrick and Charlene are both Hispanic. Derrick has been raised in the Midwest in a foster home with a Euro-American family and middle-class social and educational experiences. He moved to the Southwest for employment and met Charlene. Charlene has grown up in a border town with language

and economic challenges. Although by all outward appearances, the marriage of these two young people would appear homogamous, they have many more obstacles and much more intense negotiation to work through as a new family unit.

Changing immigration patterns in recent decades have had a major influence on family and household behaviors in the United States (Taylor, 2002). As previously presented in Chapter 1, worldviews shape the values and behaviors of newly immigrated families and individuals. Over time, these families may **assimilate** to the value system of the majority, or they may create a unique blending of the two. Since early in the 1900s, the largest wave of immigrants has been from Latin America, Asia, and other Third World countries. Although studies have varied greatly in reporting structural differences in the family unit that are culturally derived, it is important to remember that the family unit is essential within all minority communities. Differences among these groups in family practices and living arrangements are the result of "unique demographic and ancestral backgrounds, cultural histories, ecological processes, and economic origins and statuses" (Wilkinson, 1987, p. 204).

Food consumption choices are deeply embedded in values—personal and cultural. Choosing to be a **vegetarian** is a conscious decision of many Americans. This choice is often in opposition to that of other family members. The main reasons for choosing a vegetarian diet today are health, animal ethics, and environmental issues (Bryant, De Walt, Courtney, & Schwartz, 2003). All of these reasons reflect certain values held by individuals and their social groups.

When one or more family members practice vegetarianism and other family members do not, meal planning, food procurement, and food preparation increase in complexity. Restrictive diets of any kind require advance planning and continual monitoring. Thus, family resources—time, effort, and finances—must be expended to enable family members to follow specific dietary regimes.

Religious commitments often impact food selection and consumption in the United States and across the globe. Hinduism promotes a strong tradition of vegetarianism rooted in more than 2,000 years of history (Bryant et al., 2003). Vegetarianism is widespread in Buddhism and Jainism, which promote nonviolent treatment of all beings and so prohibit the killing of animals for consumption (Whorton, 2000). Hunger fasts and product boycotting are also expressions of values held by individuals and social groups.

Economic values are also expressed in food consumption. When families purchase food in bulk, stockpile, or devote time and energy to the growing of raw foodstuffs, they are expressing their values or beliefs about materialism and the efficient use of family resources. When families depend on fast food and restaurant catering to meet their food needs, they are expressing their values of time and financial expenditures. Purposefully selecting foods and planning meals to meet nutritional requirements is also an expression of values—health, longevity, and self-discipline.

Assimilate: to take into the mind and thoroughly comprehend; to make similar; to absorb into the culture or mores of a population or group

Vegetarian: one who subsists on a diet composed primarily or wholly of vegetables, grains, fruits, nuts, and seeds, with or without eggs and dairy products

The phrase family values also has been used to discuss socioeconomic concepts pertaining to the family as a social institution. Folbre (2001) offers a simple definition of this concept—love, obligation, and reciprocity. Members of a family care about other members' welfare and happiness. They devote a certain amount of mental, physical, and spiritual resources to those other individuals to maintain both the group and the members. In turn, it is expected that other family members will do the same.

Within the family, values are expressed through behaviors toward one another. Folbre (2001) warns that the "work" within the family is unpaid and, thus, devalued by society. She notes a trend toward transferring economic activities from family and kin-based systems to the larger, less personal institutional levels, such as government and service industries. The movement away from family-based care for aging adults and toward the institutionalization of frail elderly family members would be a reflection of this concept. The same could be said for the reliance of working parents on daycare and educational facilities for childcare.

Politicians often expound on the negative changes they perceive within families as declining family values. Although touted as important parts of a candidate's platform, family values are not always clearly defined. Often the phrase is used in the discussion of the "breakdown" of the family unit, which is then illustrated through a series of examples highlighting the diversity of family structures operating in contemporary society. Correlations are then made between these diverse structures and the success or failure of family members. The phrase family values also is used to express an external concept. The value and expectations that the larger social system places on the family seem to have shifted through recent history. As discussed previously, the increase in cohabitation challenges the social importance of traditional marriage. In recent years, tax deduction discrepancies for single and married citizens suggest that the federal government has a bias for one or the other. Availability and quality of childcare have been identified as important national issues. The importance of, or the value placed on, families in the United States continues to reflect the level of attention devoted by the media.

Values Across the Life Span

Do our values change over time and across the life span? When psychological constructs are developed slowly and over long periods of time, as are values, they become deeply ingrained in individuals and family units. Experiences, cognitive development, and moral maturity can force one to reconsider current values and, with enough justification, can move one to actually change previously held convictions and beliefs. When microwaves were first introduced for household use, many families were reluctant to use a new technology that they did not understand. Over time, the perceived value of time spent preparing food became more important than perceived risks or fears, and now the majority of households in the United States own at least one microwave. New inventions and discoveries force us to revisit our values and behaviors and bring both into alignment or balance.

Through shared experiences, cohorts or **generations** develop. People born within a few years of one another are likely to experience similar economic,

Generations:
groups born in
different time
periods

▶ **Photo 5.2**
Traditions often include special foods and rituals.

political, historical, and technological changes through the life course. Baby Boomers, born between 1947 and 1964, have experienced the rise of computerization, the fall of major world powers, and the increasing influence of media on consumption. They can remember how things were before September 11, 2001, and before the assassinations of John F. Kennedy, Robert Kennedy, and Martin Luther King, Jr. They experienced hours standing in line to register for college courses or to change college schedules. They can remember when gasoline was less than 25 cents per gallon. These shared memories have an impact on how those between the ages of 50 and 70 process and evaluate new products, situations, and proposed changes. They may value security differently because they can reflect on how it *was* in previous decades. Those born after 2001 will not have a memory of when airline travel did not require extensive security checks, so they will not be as disturbed or as grateful (depending on the individual's disposition) for this process as their grandparents might be.

Travel, domestic and international, is another example of how values may change over the life course. Less than a century ago, traveling 100 miles was a daylong event for most families. With the increasing availability and affordability of airline travel, people are developing an expectation of distant travel in their lifetimes. College students are encouraged to take advantage of international study opportunities. International travel experiences have been shown to impact attitudes, and ultimately behaviors (Asay, Younes, & Moore, 2006). Exposure to different ways of thinking and living may encourage individuals to consider some alternatives when problem solving that they might not have before. Newly married couples are expected to travel to exotic places for a honeymoon if they can afford it. Retired adults have come to expect and plan for travel opportunities once they have time to devote to such activities. The value of travel, as an entire concept, has changed during the last decades. Personally, individuals value travel experiences differently as they age and participate in the workforce.

Value Congruence Across Generations

Is there a generation gap in terms of values? A great deal of research has been devoted to the study of adolescent values and the impact of peers on values and behaviors. From that research emerged insights on how parental value systems impact adolescent decision making. Bjornholt's study (2010) of fathers and sons suggests that patterns of values, beliefs, and behaviors in one generation do not necessarily transfer to the next generation. Edgar-Smith and Wozniak (2010) found, however, that parent–adolescent relational values agreement patterns have high levels of **value congruence** between generations. Their affluent

Value congruence: the degree to which all members of the group agree on values about group processes and group work

subjects demonstrated a highly shared and distinctive pattern of values and ideals about how family life should operate. Values change slowly among all generations, but eventually an alignment may be achieved.

Studies support the idea that children look toward adult values expressed within their families for guidance in decision making. In a nationwide survey funded by the Henry Kaiser Family Foundation (Blum, 2002), researchers found that 64% of teens between the ages of 15 and 17 who had decided not to engage in sexual activity attributed their decisions to fear of what their parents might think of them. Miller (2002) found that parent–child closeness or connectedness and parental supervision or regulation of children, in combination with parents' values against teen intercourse (or unprotected intercourse), decrease the risk of adolescent pregnancy.

▶ **Photo 5.3**
Family celebrations reinforce attitudes and beliefs across generations.

©iStockphoto.com/Shmulitk

Decision making regarding adolescent educational participation has also been linked to central family value systems. Featherman (1980) reports that the vocational aspirations of adolescents are strongly correlated with their parents' jobs. Parent–child similarity emerges as a function of educational attainment. Read (1991) found that one reason female high school students cite when asked why they purposefully drop out of gifted programs and select a less academically challenged track in school is that they were discouraged by their parents from continuing rigorous subjects. Hence, not all adults have embraced the idea of female financial independence through vocational accomplishments in their parenting practices. Seabald (1986) found that peers are more influential in short-term, day-to-day matters, such as appearance management, but parents have more impact on the basic life values and educational plans of their adolescent children.

Parents and other adults within the family are the first teachers of values and morals in a child's experience. Their value systems will guide and support the developing value foundation of younger family members. Although later experiences and education may bring about changes to that initial set of values, past research suggests that a core set of values created early in life and supported over time will likely endure.

ATTITUDES

Values are abstract constructs. Feather (1990) suggests that values affect behavior by influencing one's evaluation of possible consequences of his or her actions. **Attitudes** are expressions of how we feel about any given thing, reflections of the values we hold. An attitude is a learned predisposition to respond in a consistently favorable or unfavorable manner to any given object (Fishbein & Ajzen, 1975, 1980, 2010). Attitudes are values couched within social situations. Sherif

Attitude: a mental position with regard to a fact or state; a feeling or emotion toward a fact or state

and Sherif believed that attitudes are expressions of how individuals conceive "their ways of life, their ways of doing things, their stands on the family and on social, religious, economic, and political issues, and how they conceive the ways and stands of others" (1967, p. 1). Thus, the focus is on how people expect their expressed beliefs to be judged by others. Allport (1935) defined attitudes in cognitive terms. He proposed that an attitude is a state of readiness that will impact an individual's response to any situation.

Fishbein and Ajzen (1975, 2010) studied the formation and expression of attitudes and proposed that attitudes are learned, and therefore are dynamic (see Figure 5.1). They can and do change with experience and education. These **predispositions** are assumed to also incline one to certain actions and behaviors. If one believes that human life begins at conception and is to be protected, he or she may purchase pro-life T-shirts and bumper stickers. The attitude is expressed or communicated to others in this way. Statements could also be made to express this attitude. Attitudes are values couched within context. If this person were consistent in his or her attitudes, abortion would be wrong in any case. Humans aren't always consistent, however. Under certain circumstances, such as rape or severe malformations, this same person may believe that abortion is an acceptable option.

Theorists have long held the belief that attitudes are created and maintained through interactions over time with parents, family members, and other socially significant individuals in a child's realm. The field of behavioral genetics has begun to address a possible genetic component within attitude formation. Arvey, Segal, Bouchard, and Abraham (1989) reported that approximately 30% of the observed variance in job satisfaction in a twin study conducted by that research group was

Predispositions: inclinations beforehand to interpret statements in a particular way; dispositions in advance to react in a particular way

Figure 5.1   Fishbein-Ajzen Theory of Reasoned Action

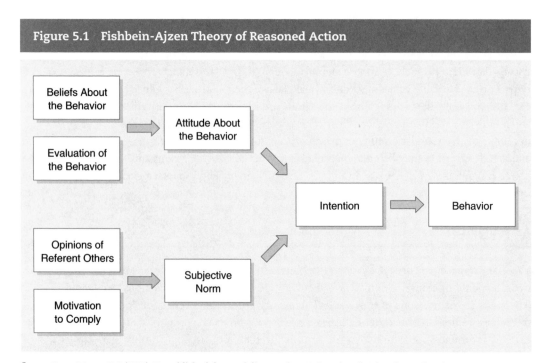

Source: From Moore, T. J. (1995). Unpublished doctoral dissertation, University of Nebraska at Lincoln.

attributable to genetic factors. Other studies (Eaves, Eysenck, & Martin, 1989; Tesser, 1992) support the idea that some attitudes are more resistant to change, perhaps because they have psychological protection mechanisms around them exhibited by biological discomfort when faced with change. For example, when an attitude is an expression of a core value, such as a religious belief, and evidence is presented that questions that belief, a religious person is faced with high levels of stress. Because the existing belief, and attitude attached to it, is strongly connected to many other dimensions of one's life, even a small change would have an enormous ripple effect in that individual's life.

Attitudes have an important impact on one's judgment of the world around him or her. These value judgments can impact every part of the decision-making process, especially when information must be gathered and processed. Selective interpretation is illustrated in the efforts of cigarette smokers who rationalize their addictive behavior, claiming that research reporting negative health findings are biased and unfounded. Selective memory is one of the oldest ideas in attitude research. People find information supporting their attitudes easier to accept than information that contradicts their existing attitudes (Olson & Zanna, 1993).

Where adults turn for the information that influences their attitudes and behaviors is evolving. The impact of social media on the 2016 presidential election has been the focus of much research. Isaac and Ember (2016) report that Twitter was perceived as a source of disinformation, intimidation, and harassment on Election Day. Young voters are especially impacted by information presented on Facebook and Twitter. The Pew Research Center (2016) found that social media was the preferred source of news for those between 18 and 29 years of age. Voters over the age of 50 still depend on television and traditional news outlets for election information, but some argue that politics skew the news reported by many of those channels. As consumers increase their dependence on social media for information about products, services, and political candidates, the issue of fact finding and the monitoring of truth become even more important to the safety and well-being of individuals and families.

Selective interpretation: purposeful dissemination of certain information in ways advantageous to the individual

Selective memory: purposeful retrieval of certain information while ignoring other information stored in memory

BEHAVIORS

Choices made and actions taken by individuals and families are the behaviors that become important in the family decision-making process. After a century of research on attitude and behavior, predicting behavior based on attitudes assessed is still problematic. There are several reasons that the two are not perfectly matched.

Fishbein and Ajzen (1975) propose that the connection between attitude and behavior is multitiered:

- One's behavior can be predicted from intention.

- Intentions can be predicted from one's attitude toward the behavior and one's perception of what others think one should do.

- Attitude is a function of how one perceives the action's outcome will be received by others.

Behavior: the manner of conducting oneself; anything that an organism does involving action and response to stimulation; the response of an individual, group, or species to its environment

Research conducted using this set of beliefs has included cigarette smoking, seat belt use, self-monitoring of health, and selection of career behaviors. Those applications have been successful in predicting intentions and behaviors.

As discussed in Chapter 4, individual and family needs are important triggers in the family decision-making process. Dupont (1994) included the dimension of needs in the explanation for behavior. He believed that all of our actions are motivated by our needs and values. Kurtines and Gewirtz (1991) added situation into the mix of factors that impact the connection between attitude and behavior.

Studies in the field of social psychology have provided insight into the impact of behavior on attitudes, the reverse of previous studies. Bem (1972) proposed the self-perception theory, where individuals attempt to bring their attitudes into alignment with their behaviors without losing face among others who observe those behaviors.

> Jed is daydreaming in class. When his teacher calls attention to his distraction and assigns a detention penalty for it, he focuses on how the situation might negatively impact his social situation within his peer group. After class, while walking with friends to another classroom, Jed comments on how dull and boring that last class had been. He insists that his inability to attend to the situation was not his fault, but the teacher's.

The cognitive dissonance theory (Vinski & Tryon, 2009) internalizes the same types of situations. If Jed has consistently been an attentive student during his school years and he prides himself on that personal attribute, daydreaming and the act of being caught in that activity causes him personal discomfort or internal dissonance. Jed is uncomfortable and needs to bring this current behavior into alignment with his long-held attitude.

Just as individuals develop tendencies to behave or react across situations in fairly consistent ways, families exhibit similar characteristics. Some family behaviors may be purely reactionary, especially when the unit or individuals within the family are threatened in any way. When a family member is diagnosed with a terminal disease, the family may pull inward initially. As the unit works through the process of handling immediate needs, there is little energy focused on doing what others outside of the family would expect them to do. However, most behaviors occur on a more conscious level and are actually the result of a complex thought process. The way family members choose to present the family group to others in the larger social environment guides much of the decision-making process. For instance, when a family member dies, members will initially react in instinctual ways, focusing on self and the immediate needs of other family members. Eventually they will turn time and attention to planning the funeral for the deceased. Acceptable practices are firmly embedded in religious, cultural, and social layers. Choices will be made by family members based on their perception of "how it should be done." The focus often shifts from the deceased to the social expectations of those outside the family circle—friends, neighbors, and community members.

At a higher level, membership within a social group and an identified cultural group depends on a person's acceptance and demonstration of certain values, often referred to as ethics. **Ethics** presents a framework that can be adopted by a family or any group of people to guide the behavior of group members. A **code of ethics** consists of a set of moral principles that exist in formal or unwritten modes. Professional organizations often create, publish, and encourage members to follow a set of behaviors based on unwritten values embraced by that profession. Family units rarely have such formal value and behavioral structures in place, but their values and behaviors may be consistent with such structures.

Ethics: the discipline dealing with what is good and bad and with moral duty and obligation

Code of ethics: a set of moral principles to guide group behavior

VALUES, ATTITUDES, AND BEHAVIORS IN THE DECISION-MAKING FRAMEWORK

When used as a verb, *to value* implies that individuals develop a ranking order of what is important to them. Based on that unspoken ranking, resources are expended to a higher degree to protect or build certain other resources. As discussed in relation to the culture of poverty (Payne, 1998), when monetary resources are limited, families tend to judge their success or status based on relationships within the family and throughout the community. Time and energy are devoted to further developing personal relationships and maintaining interpersonal connections between and among group members. When money is readily available or when one desires to be accepted by others who have monetary resources, material goods take on increased importance.

IN THE NEWS

Does Leadership Require High Moral Character?

What do all of these powerful political leaders have in common?

    Donald Trump

    William Jefferson Clinton

    Arnold Schwarzenegger

Perhaps many things, but most Americans would be quick to acknowledge that all of these men were the subject of very public infidelity scandals. While politicians, and voters alike, profess to care about family values, does morality really matter when it comes to selecting public leaders?

What do voters want from a candidate in terms of marriage and family values? According to a Pew Research Center poll (2011), Americans are much more forgiving of a divorced politician than a cheating one. Only 11% reported that they would be less likely to support a divorced candidate; however, 85% said it wouldn't matter. Republicans are more likely than Democrats to discount a candidate because he or she has been divorced. When it comes to cheaters, though, 46% say a candidate who's had an affair would be difficult to support. It doesn't seem to matter if the infidelity is proven; accusations alone can derail a campaign. Herman Cain, who surged to the top of the Republican ticket for 2012, announced his departure from the race shortly after a female acquaintance claimed to

(Continued)

have been his partner in a long-standing sexual affair. Previous accusations of sexual harassment were quickly denied, but advisors felt that suspicions of infidelity were insurmountable.

Larson (2011) suggests that the demands of being president of the United States are just not compatible with being a model husband and father—the hours, the travel, and the stress. So character may count, but the kind of character required to be president may not be what Americans view as the same kind of character that makes for a good husband and father. Voters want a man or woman willing to put family second and nation first, someone who is able to wear a poker face during negotiations with difficult national leaders threatening global security, and a leader who can wield that slick, phony surface in times when diplomacy matters. These are not the kinds of character traits or behaviors listed when one is asked to describe good parents and spouses.

And perhaps there is a gender difference in the application of these expectations. Sarah Palin supporters embraced her "family values" in the 2008 campaign but did not seem comfortable balancing her personal ambition with her family crises. Hillary Clinton became a polarizing figure early in her political career when she implied a criticism of women who didn't work—those who stayed home and baked cookies, as she put it. Her focus on women's rights during her time as first lady and secretary of state aligned with her aspiration to be the first female U.S. president. However, her ultimate loss may be viewed as either a setback to female equality or as a reset for the women's political movement. So, do "values" have a place in politics?

Research shows over time that Americans tend to elect politicians with a healthy family life, or at least the appearance of one (Dubner & Levitt, 2009). Much of the popularity of former President Barack Obama was based on the public displays of affection between him and his wife and his obvious devotion to his daughters.

Values are beliefs that guide behavior of family members and the decision-making process. They must be expressed through words or actions to bring about decisions within a group. Some beliefs are so central to the family unit's functioning that they are assumed in almost all decision-making activities. After several decisions are reached, basic values and beliefs may move to the subconscious level of family members. Only when their decisions are challenged by outsiders will they recognize the importance of those values.

> *Mr. and Mrs. McCallister were both college athletes. During training they were encouraged to eat high-protein, low-fat foods. Breakfast, for them, consisted of skim milk, juice, and cereal or a bagel. Years later, their daughter has a friend spend the night. At breakfast, this friend is distraught because the McCallisters do not have bacon, sausage, or eggs, which she is used to having at her house. For the first time, these parents have to explain their dietary choices to their daughter.*

VALUES AND BEHAVIORS IN FAMILY PURCHASING DECISIONS

Marketing and advertising specialists have devoted a great deal of time and energy to studying family buying patterns and motivations. Manning and Reece (2001) describe product buying **motives** as reasons consumers purchase one product in preference to another. They propose that consumers operate on one of four possible sets of motives: brand preference, quality preference, price preference, or design preference.

Brand Preference

Long-standing, well-established manufacturing companies have the opportunity to develop positive product images of quality and performance in the minds of prospective buyers. *Brandweek*, a former weekly publication serving media and marketing professionals, was actively involved in surveying consumer brand loyalty using the Brand Keys Customer Loyalty Index. This information was gathered through phone interviews with 16,000 active brand users twice per year. Participants rated brands that they used regularly based on categories of products. The results of these surveys were published in *Brandweek* and a multitude of other media sources interested in consumer behavior. Survey results have indicated that consumers are less loyal to brand names than they have been in the past.

Companies providing products and services for families continue to spend a great deal of money to convince these buyers that name-brand products have benefits beyond the obvious. Consumers are encouraged to consider the benefits of established company guarantees and histories of customer satisfaction when weighing the choices available in the marketplace. When comparing similar products, these intangible attributes may convince buyers to pay more for the peace of mind that well-known brands give them. Habibi, Laroche, and Richard (2016) suggest that social media give increased power to customers to share their experiences with products with their entire social network. They can also give tips on how to maximize product usage.

Another aspect of brand loyalty stems from the desire for families to present themselves in specific ways to the larger social groups in which they function. Orth and Kahle (2008) found that reference groups do influence consumer choice for products such as wine. They found that as the level of internal values of an individual increases, that individual's susceptibility to social branding of products decreases. For less internally driven individuals and family units, visually presented identifying logos, obvious or subtle, imply a level of discrimination in their purchasing decisions. This behavior may also be a reflection of perceived quality preference.

Quality Preference

Manning and Reece (2001) suggest that the contemporary consumer exhibits higher levels of quality standards than did past generations of buyers. When product and service competition is high, quality is one of the factors that differentiate one from the other. Quality can be the result of better materials, workmanship, or quality control, or quality can be a perception of higher standards. Consumers may believe that products with higher price tags indicate higher quality, they may equate name brands with higher quality because they have had positive experiences in the past with those brands, or they may have been exposed to promotional information aimed at setting that brand apart from competitors.

Large-ticket purchases, such as automobiles and appliances, include an expectation of performance for multiple years. Quality may be perceived as an indicator of such performance. Although the competition among and the number of models within automobile manufacturing firms have increased over time, the selection available to consumers could be considered somewhat limited when other types of products are considered. Factors cited as obstacles to new producers include development and production expenses, but another important hurdle to entering the automobile industry is the perception of quality and the sense of security buyers perceive when dealing with the same number of well-established companies.

Price Preference

Family resources are used in exchange for goods and services. Even when a family is resource rich, product selection usually factors price differences into the decision-making process. For many products, especially electronics, technological advancements and creative product development have created a "wait for the price to come down" expectation among consumers. Tabletop calculators sold for as much as $1,000 in 1975. Smaller calculators with several more features are now available in handheld versions for under $50. Many calculator features are also available on consumer smartphones and other personal electronic devices.

When two products that both meet the criteria set by a family have noticeable price differences, price increases in importance in the selection process. Price can also be used in the initial phases of decision making if an acceptable price range is established before exploring all available options. That range may screen out several options, thus making the decision less time consuming. Generic prescription drugs are a good example of how price can become the primary discriminating factor among competitive products. Generic equivalencies of certain drugs have been identified by insurance companies and physicians. FDA requirements imply that all approved drugs are safe and effective. Because generics use the same active ingredients and are shown to work the same way in the body, they should have the same risks and benefits as their brand-name counterparts. Once generic drugs are approved, there is greater competition, which drives the price down. Many insurance companies provide limited coverage of name-brand equivalencies, forcing patients to pay more out-of-pocket expenses if they select these drugs. When faced with that trade-off, most patients select the generic equivalents.

Design Preference

A lawnmower cuts grass. A riding mower provides wheels, a seat, and blades. How many variations of this product can there be? Thousands. Once a family's needs move beyond the level of security, preferences for style, size, color, and comfort begin to emerge. These preferences reflect personal and group values that have evolved over time. Producers invest a great deal of money in product design and development and in redesign and redevelopment to position their products among competitors' offerings. The level of technology within automobiles is another example of how consumer demand is impacted by new developments. Within this decade, manufacturers will likely find that buyers will expect their automobiles to interface easily with their smartphones and personal computers. Auxiliary products, such as speakers, wires, headsets, and dash-mounted phone pads, will be rendered obsolete.

IMPACT OF CULTURE ON VALUES, ATTITUDES, AND BEHAVIORS

Individuals operating within social or cultural systems learn the important values of a particular group. If they accept and live by those values the majority of the time, they will be able to exist in that group and depend on group membership when seeking necessary resources. If they do not accept or display the majority of these values, they risk being cast out and cannot depend on group support when needed. To maintain a cultural group, this important set of values must be transmitted to future generations and new members. The cultural environment and social interaction have tremendous influence on an individual's set of values. Theorists propose that children are encouraged to accept existing value sets within their culture.

Individuals may affiliate simultaneously with more than one social group. They must then balance their value systems and behaviors carefully to retain membership in both groups. Within the United States, there are several different religious and professional groups. The U.S. legal system and governmental body operate within a code of ethics or system of values that reflects the beliefs of some of these subgroups more readily than others. For instance, federal offices and services build working calendars around the Christian holiday of Christmas. Workweeks are generally scheduled with Sunday, or the Sabbath, as a nonworking day. Those seeking to observe other religious holidays must negotiate within the existing framework of employer expectations. Even higher education is wrapped around a system of beliefs that may inconvenience citizens exercising their right to participate in religious practices.

WORLDVIEW

In many cultures, there are practices and beliefs about the interdependence of individuals: "Do unto others . . ." "You scratch my back, I'll scratch your back," "Quid pro quo." China has a similar concept—*guanxi* (pronounced "gwon-see"), a personal relationship between any two individuals with long-term benefits for both (Yu, Chan, & Ireland, 2006). Imagine a spider web of personal connections, cultivated over one's life span, functioning as a network of favors and obligations. In a society with rigid social hierarchies, those who have power are easily distinguished from those who do not. To survive, the powerless recognize the importance of *guanxi*, and those with power realize the benefits of maintaining connections with those in the lower levels.

As China emerges as an attractive global market for exportation of goods and services, *guanxi*

(Continued)

(Continued)

is an important tradition for business analysis. Although China's younger generations are shedding many ancient traditional behaviors, *guanxi* holds steadfast, although slightly altered by modern technology. The Internet expands networking opportunities exponentially. Moving from personal, face-to-face contact, Chinese young people can build networks without such personal investment.

Cynthia needs concert tickets. She instant messages 20 of her network friends using a sophisticated social network site. The probability of someone in her network with connections to either ticket holders or ticketing offices is 20 times more powerful than her personal resources. Cynthia has a lot of "face," Chinese for status.

Lam and Graham (2007) stress the highly contextual aspects of doing business in China. Contracts and business deals are sealed in social settings, such as restaurants and karaoke establishments. Business relationships, within and between companies, include a complex system of gift exchange. Yu et al. (2006) present this system as an art form—it's not the thought; it's the brand and cost of the gift that secure *guanxi*.

Social networks like Facebook, LinkedIn, and eHarmony provide global platforms for the exchange of information and the creation of personal and professional networking opportunities. The very definition of relationships must evolve to maintain pace with this contemporary communication phenomena.

Sam is an adolescent who has been raised within the Mormon religious community. Upon graduation from high school, it may be expected of him to spend 2 years as a missionary of his faith. Because the insurance industry in the United States adopts the idea that students graduating from high school should move directly on to postsecondary educational programs, health insurance coverage of family members pursuing college degrees may be terminated at a certain age, regardless of degree completion. If Sam follows his desire to be a missionary for a few years, he may be covered by his parents' insurance only through 4 to 6 years of college study. His peers who enter college immediately after graduation may be covered through their graduate or professional programs. Scholarship opportunities may also differ for him because he will be viewed as a nontraditional student when he enrolls. Recent legislation has extended insurance benefits to nonworking children up to age 26, allowing parents to cover such children through their own employment benefits. However, this was in response to rising unemployment rates, not religious inequity.

IMPACT OF SOCIOECONOMIC FACTORS ON VALUES, ATTITUDES, AND BEHAVIORS

Old money: families that have been wealthy for several generations

Do families with immense pools of resources approach the decision-making process differently than those with limited resources do? Contemporary literature implies that they do. Aldrich (1996) devoted an entire book to the subject of **old money**. His premise is that America's upper class has significantly different values toward and meanings of wealth. These values differ from those of the marketplace and the newly emerging rich. Other authors explore the unwritten code of family preservation among the families that have held wealth over several generations. From selection of potential marital mates to the simplicity and elegance of clothing, home, and automobile selections, this concept of old money continues to intrigue those aspiring to acquire wealth or those frustrated with what they view to be unfair advantage.

Stein and Brier (2002) provide guidelines for raising responsible children of wealth. They suggest that parents introduce their children to the attorneys, accountants, and financial planners that manage the family's wealth. Another piece of advice given to parents with large inheritances to pass on to their children includes how to teach those young people important tenets inherent to their social and economic positions:

- Children must be taught to share their good fortune with others.

- **Philanthropy** is a key factor in teaching children to be responsible managers of their money.

- Wealth is not an entitlement. (pp. 2–3)

New money, or large accumulations of wealth within the current generation, is also explored by many theorists and social science authors. Brown (2000) presents the idea of "the sudden wealth syndrome" as experienced by new millionaires in Silicon Valley. Rapid technological changes and the making of large fortunes at an early age may have serious consequences for those families. The term **affluenza** has made its way into books and the media as a way to describe the increasing value placed on money and the materialistic side of American society. Underlying the emergence of new syndromes and maladies associated with money is the suggestion of an out-of-control society with success defined as acquisition of money and the power that is inherent to that commodity. This desire to get ahead, fast and furiously, seems to overshadow the values most often associated with the family unit—love, obligation, and reciprocity.

CONSISTENCY OVER TIME AND SITUATION

Capitalism, by its nature, results in a dynamic environment where one can rise and fall financially in short periods of time. The 2008–2009 U.S. economic recession illustrated this quite clearly. Are values, attitudes, and behaviors impacted by changes in economic conditions? When needs are analyzed simultaneously with values and attitudes, one must remember that survival needs will always be more important than higher-order needs. A middle-class family that finds itself suddenly in the throes of extreme poverty due to unemployment, disease, or accident will focus first on food and shelter. Only when a relative level of comfort and safety has been reached can the individuals within that family focus attention on evaluative dimensions of the choices they have available to them. Existing value systems will remain intact until they are challenged sufficiently enough to consider changing and reforming those core beliefs.

Philanthropy: the act of donating money, goods, time, or effort to support a charitable cause, usually over an extended period of time and in regard to a defined objective

Affluenza: an extreme form of materialism resulting from the excessive desire for material goods

Capitalism: an economic system characterized by private or corporate ownership of capital goods, by investments that are determined by private decision, and by prices, production, and the distribution of goods that are determined mainly by competition in a free market

SUMMARY

Values impact family decision making at every phase. They determine what and how needs will be determined and, once determined, how important each need is relative to all other needs. Once the need has been determined, the alternatives available to fulfill that need are processed in terms of values and attitudes of family members, especially those most responsible for the consequences of the decision to be made. The post-decision evaluation is based almost entirely on the value and attitude structures that lead the decision and implementation processes. Families consist of multiple human beings, inherently social beings. Outsiders will never fully understand the unique unfolding of this value-laden process, but the understanding and acceptance of the fact that families create, display, and maintain value systems allow all family service providers the opportunity to be as objective as possible.

QUESTIONS FOR REVIEW AND DISCUSSION

1. How do values and attitudes differ?

2. Why might the same family come to entirely different conclusions on two separate occasions, when the decision to be made is essentially the same in each situation?

3. How does brand loyalty reflect consumer values and attitudes?

4. How are family values used politically?

UNDERSTANDING RESOURCES

The Decision-Making Process

- Recognize existing needs
- Identify alternatives to fulfill needs

Chapter 6. Identification of Family Resources

- Evaluate identified alternatives

Chapter 7. Families Within the Economic Environment

Chapter 8. The Impact of Society on Family Decisions

- Select and implement alternatives
- Reflect on and evaluate the alternatives selected

CHAPTER SIX

IDENTIFICATION OF FAMILY RESOURCES

Objectives
Resource Availability
Worldview
Resource Theory
Human Resources
Economic Resources
Reality Check
Environmental Resources
Social Resources
In the News
Measurement of Resources
Resource Allocation and Use
Summary
Questions for Review and Discussion

Objectives

- Be aware of the nature and characteristics of a resource.

- Be familiar with resource theory.

- Recognize the different types of resources.

- Be familiar with how resources are measured and managed.

- Be acquainted with the way that resources are used and allocated.

My mother's menu consisted of two choices:
Take it or leave it.

—Buddy Hackett

From the moment that humans inhabited the earth, they set about to learn and expand ways to use its resources. Hamilton (1992) defines a resource as "anything people use or might want to use to achieve an end" (p. 10). Foa (1993) defines a resource as "any item, concrete or symbolic, which can become the object of exchange among people" (p. 2). Zimmerman (1964) defines resources not in terms of substances, but as a "living phenomenon, expanding and contracting in response to human effort and behavior" (p. 7). Howitt (2001) expands on Zimmerman's definition to explain that resources are a "matter of relationships not things" (p. 4). In this definition, resources have more to do with the relationship or transactions between people and their cultures.

Resources: commodities and human resources used in the production of goods and services; anything identified to meet an existing or future need

RESOURCE AVAILABILITY

The lowest level of Maslow's hierarchy of needs, as discussed in Chapter 4, relies on the idea that people use resources to meet their physical needs of food, clothing, and shelter. There are certain conditions that cause resources to change. The industrialized world that we know today was created by uncovering and using new resources. However, nothing becomes a resource unless there is a use for it or unless someone determines that it has value, no matter how much of that

WORLDVIEW

The Real Price of Coffee

Do our purchasing habits have a real impact on people in faraway lands? The answer is yes, and few products are better evidence of this than coffee.

The little red fruit that produces coffee is the base of something far wider-reaching than a drink: In many cultures, it is a social act. It is also a lucrative business: Coffee is the most consumed brew in the world and is a trade that is worth $71 billion annually, according to Fairtrade España.

Unlike other crops for export, most of coffee's production corresponds to small farmers: 25 million farmers produce 80% of coffee consumed in the world. The coffee plant employs 100 million people and is, for some countries, the main source of foreign trade.

Coffee is also a metaphor for the inequality that causes the international division in a global capitalist system. As Eduardo Galeano wrote in his book *Open Veins of Latin America*, "coffee benefits those who consume it a lot more than those who produce it. In the United States and Europe, it generates income and jobs and shifts large capital; in Latin America, it pays starvation wages."

The truth is that the chain of production, distribution, and commercialization of coffee shows a radical inequality between the negotiating power of countries who cultivate and export it and those who distribute, commercialize, and consume it.

A study by the International Assessment of Agricultural Knowledge, Science and Technology for Development (IAASTD) shows that coffee for which a producer in Uganda is paid $0.14 costs $42 to an English café. The price is multiplied 300 times and, according to the same study, the large leap is seen in the distribution phase: It goes from costing $2 when it leaves from the factory, already processed, to more than $25 in the supermarket. The result: Millions of small farmers are left in misery, while the industry remains under the control of large multinationals like Sara Lee (Marcilla), Nestlé (Bonka) and Kraft/Philip Morris (Saimaza).

Apart from the pressure to cheapen their costs, the small coffee farmers are plagued by the unpredictability of international coffee prices, which rise and fall depending not on demand, but on market speculation. If this situation affects all commodities, the consequences are particularly serious in the case of coffee, because cultivation takes between two and four years to bear the first fruits and, once it does, guarantees the harvest for twenty years.

The injustice of this model is, in large part, due to the disconnect between producers and consumers, which leaves the oligopolistic distribution sector with great bargaining power and, therefore, the bulk of the profits.

The good news? It is easy to access fair trade networks who work on the ground with small producers and ensure that they get a fair price.

Source: Castro, Nazaret. "The real price of coffee." Translated from www.carrodecombate.com. Creative Commons, 2013.

substance exists. A good example of this is the diamond. Diamonds are mined in great quantity for industrial uses because of their hardness. Until people began to equate the diamond with a symbol of marriage, the value of the diamond was much different. Although the raw value of a diamond was not that lavish, the value of the diamond ring to romantic Americans is high.

Resources have certain characteristics that make them useable. A resource must have a purpose or **utility**. In the past few years, the penny has come to have less utility. Buying "penny candy" or feeding a parking meter with pennies is no longer possible. People may walk over pennies laying on the street all day without stopping to pick them up because they have less purpose or utility in our society.

Utility: the quality or condition of being useful; usefulness

Most believe that having money is all that is important for accessing what is needed. However, a resource must also be available before it can be used, no matter how much money you have. As a result, **accessibility** is an important characteristic. For example, a person who needs a specialized type of surgery cannot access that service if he or she is not able to get to the hospital where it can be performed, even if he or she has enough money to cover the operation.

Accessibility: the ability to obtain something when needed

Resources must also be transferable. **Transferability** allows consumers to move assets to where they are needed the most. Some resources are more transferable than others. For example, real estate may be a good investment and over time may increase in value, but it may not be able to be liquidated and transferred as quickly as cash or stocks can be.

Transferability: the quality of being exchangeable

Resources are **interchangeable**. Money can be exchanged for goods or services. We can go to the grocery store and exchange cash for food that we can take home to prepare, or we can go to a restaurant and exchange our cash for the service of having a meal cooked and served. Any resource can be substituted as a means to gain assets. For example, someone might work to help tend a neighbor's garden in exchange for tomatoes and green beans, or those green beans might be exchanged for tulip bulbs from another neighbor.

Interchangeable: resources that can be exchanged or substituted as a means to gain assets

Manageability of resources is a characteristic that allows consumers to make decisions about how resources are used, transferred, or exchanged. The ability to manage resources leads to more efficiency and maximum use of resources.

Manageability: something that is capable of being managed or controlled

RESOURCE THEORY

Resource theory was first created by Foa (1971). The idea behind this theory has its roots in social psychology and maintains that people attempt to meet their needs in the context of social interaction. According to the theory, it is through relationships that people gather resources. The theory identifies six types of resources:

Love: an expression of affectionate regard, warmth, or comfort

Status: an expression of evaluative judgment that conveys high or low prestige, regard, or esteem

Information: advice, opinions, instruction, or enlightenment

Money: any coin, currency, or token that has some standard unit of value

Goods: tangible products, objects, or materials

Services: activities on the body or belongings of a person that constitute labor for another

These resources are those that are exchanged in relationships. For example, groceries are usually exchanged for money, and services are performed in exchange for money. In school, information is exchanged for status (a high school diploma or college degree).

Particularistic: the exclusive devotion to the interests of one's own group

The theory also identifies resources as particularistic, as well as their degree of concreteness. A resource that is particularistic is one in which the person is selective in choosing. A good example of this is love. Usually we are careful about those with whom we give and receive love. In contrast, money is the least particularistic resource because we don't usually care about with whom we exchange money. The degree of concreteness also helps us understand resources. When we sell a car, the car is gone. Exchanging goods has a high degree of concreteness, in that a possession can be gained or lost. However, some resources are symbolic, as in the case of information. We may "give away" information, but after the transaction, we still possess the information. We may use our skills to perform a service, but in the end we still possess that skill. Around the circle on the diagram of resource theory, the different types of resources are arranged by similarity. For example, money is next to goods, but opposite of love. Foa believed that this order predicts that people prefer to exchange resources that are similar. For example, most people would exchange money for goods or information more readily than they would exchange money for love or status.

Concreteness: characterized by or belonging to the immediate experience of actual things or events

Although resource theory does explain a lot about human behavior and economics, it is not without weaknesses. Because the meaning of the exchange is more important than the exchange itself, it represents something different from pure economic behavior. For example, the relationship between the two who are exchanging can range from strangers to intimate partners. Therefore, the meaning of the exchange is different. Other factors may involve the intensity of communication between the exchangers, the self-esteem of the exchangers, or the nature of previous exchanges.

HUMAN RESOURCES

Human resources: human wisdom, experience, skill, labor, and enterprise

Human resources are those that are unique to people. People bring a variety of assets that enrich their lives and those around them. Cognitive or mental resources are the most common of the human resources and the most flexible. These resources include experience that has been gained from the past, the know-how that results from learning, the skills that are acquired, and inherent creativity.

Davenport and Prusak (1998) identified the components of human capital as ability, behavior, effort, and time. *Ability* involves a person's knowledge and skills, but also his or her inborn talent. Most employers desire education. Although education may add to a person's ability to produce goods and services, it is also a signal of intellect, determination, and discipline. It may also signal motivation or the individual's ability to set goals and make plans to meet those goals. *Behavior* consists of observable ways that someone does things that contribute to accomplishing a task, including ethics, values, and beliefs. *Effort* is the component that activates or applies ability. It is the motivation to get things done.

Although time is not a resource within the person, it is the most fundamental resource that is under their control. From an economic perspective, Beblo (2001) observed that time is allocated into three basic economic categories: paid labor (workplace or market), unpaid labor (household), and leisure. The concept of time from an ecological perspective must be considered at multiple levels, including historical time, social time, family time, and individual time. This perspective provides a basis for considering the complexity of time within the family system (Perry-Jenkins, Newkirk, & Ghunney, 2013). Family members gauge their time or pace themselves by using the time they are given. Each person is given a limited amount of time each day. Choices are made that determine the use of time. People may choose to go to work, collect a paycheck, and use that money to buy goods and services. They may also choose to use the time for their own leisure or to spend time with their family. The value of that time can be viewed differently among individuals.

> *Shannon recently gave birth to her first baby. Before the birth, Shannon and her husband decided that she would stay home with the baby for the first few years rather than work outside the home.*
>
> *Shannon's friend, Julie, is in a similar situation. Julie has called several times to ask Shannon to have lunch, go shopping together, or just visit over the phone. Shannon almost always declines.*
>
> *Shannon tells her husband, "I feel that it is a waste of time to spend the day with Julie. When will I do the laundry, prepare meals, and keep up with the housework?" Julie, in contrast, values the time that she can get out of the house and interact with other adults. Both Shannon and Julie value the resource of time, but in different ways.*

As a resource, time may be more valuable than money. The busy working parent may choose to buy partially or fully prepared foods. This food may be less expensive for the family than the loss of more expensive work time. Although most workers cannot exchange work time for home time, buying convenience foods does afford parents more time to spend with the family at the end of a long day.

Rosa (2003) suggested that Western societies have become acceleration societies where less time is needed to carry out production, communication, and other daily tasks. The Internet and other similar technologies, designed to improve and ease our lives, have in some ways served to complicate them. Instead of saving time, technology may have just changed the way we work as well as created new activities and practices (Chelsey, Siibak, & Wajcman, 2013). Those operating from a different worldview may not see time as a manageable commodity. Their perception of time, as a resource, may not be to see time as "limited," but rather to see it as "renewable." Each new day has boundless potential.

©iStockphoto.com/Viktorcvetkovic

▶ **Photo 6.1**
Multitasking
is an effort to
manage time more
efficiently.

Another human resource is energy. People possess the ability to use their bodies—legs, hands, and muscles—to accomplish tasks. These psychomotor skills allow people to create as well as maintain resources. For example, someone can take raw materials such as wood and create a beautiful cabinet. After the cabinet is finished, that person can use his or her energy to keep the cabinet polished and clean, which helps maintain the investment. Personal energy is used in working and in leisure. These activities are central to living.

ECONOMIC RESOURCES

Economic resources: the basic inputs or component parts of an economy, such as land, labor, and capital

Family **economic resources** are gained by either acquisition or inheritance. Family members earn economic resources by working. Workers are compensated by a wage or salary. Employees who earn wages are paid by the hour. The government sets minimum wage levels according to the Fair Labor Standards Act (FLSA). Several states have raised their minimum wage above the federal minimum. Debates over the minimum wage continue as full-time minimum wage employees hover close to the poverty level. Although proponents of raising the minimum wage argue for the need to increase employees' earnings for low-income families, those against this idea argue that raising minimum wages would benefit only teenagers in middle-class families. Others fear that raising the minimum wage will encourage an underground economy where lower wages are paid to those having trouble getting a job without reporting to the government. The Federal Reserve Bank also points to evidence of jobs being lost since the minimum wage was increased, but the bank argues that this should be weighed against higher wages for workers who are already employed (Neumark, 2015).

Living wage: the minimum hourly wage necessary for a person to achieve some specific standard of living

The term **living wage** has been used to describe a wage rate that would allow wage earners to provide for their families above the poverty level. The living wage movement began in Baltimore in 1994. Many cities have some form of living wage law in place. New laws are scheduled to take effect in the near future, with even more slated to appear on the ballot in cities and states around the United States (National Employment Law Project, 2015). Controversy around the living wage centers on the definition of *poverty* and the wide range of wage rates and benefits standards that have been set across the country. Current debate has focused more on the need to create jobs and raise the quality of jobs during times of economic crisis rather than funding business assistance for living wages.

In contrast to wage earners, employees who are paid a salary are usually those who have spent time preparing for lifelong work in a particular field or profession. These workers have engaged in training or education that allows them to move into careers that require specific skills. Although it is not uncommon to find an hourly wage earner who brings home more money than the person who is in an entry-level position on a salary, statistics show that the salaried person will probably move up the pay scale more quickly over time. Although the cost of a college education continues to rise, it is still a good investment over a lifetime for most. A recent Pew Research Center report found that 86% of college graduates consider the cost of their college education to be worth it. According to the report, college graduates with a bachelor's degree earned an average of $17,500 more per year than did those with only a high school education, which adds up significantly over a lifetime (Pew Research Center, 2014b).

Resources also come in the form of **benefit packages** that workers receive as part of their earnings. Benefits all have a significant impact on the total resources of the worker and their family. Some benefits are required by the government (see Chapter 8 for more information on Social Security), whereas others are voluntarily provided by employers. Employers must contribute to their workers' Social Security, Medicare, and unemployment insurance funds. Beyond those basic requirements, employers may decide to offer paid vacations, sick leave, health insurance, life insurance, disability insurance, and retirement savings plans. Benefits account for more than 30% of labor costs of U.S. employers (U.S. Bureau of Labor Statistics, 2016). When the demand for employees exceeds the supply of laborers seeking employment, companies use voluntary benefits to attract and keep their labor forces. When unemployment figures exceed the number of job openings, employers may not need the incentives provided by benefit packages to fill empty positions.

It is crucial that working adults understand the benefits packages available to them before they accept a job and when they are considering changing jobs. A job with a lower salary may actually provide more resources when benefits are considered. One should be especially careful in reviewing optional benefits available with certain positions. These options are often referred to as **cafeteria plans** because employees can pick and choose from among several different kinds of benefits, meeting their unique current and forecasted needs. Employers may provide workers with a set number of benefit dollars and a menu of possible benefits priced individually. Employees can select what they want from this menu. Thus, if Employee A is single, he or she may select the $150 single health plan and a $50 disability insurance plan, whereas his or her married colleague may select the family health plan for $200 and forego the disability plan. If the company offered a straight health insurance option to all employees, Employee A would actually be receiving $50 less per month because of his or her single status.

> *Job A has an annual salary of $25,000, with a 3% contribution to the employee's retirement savings plan, and a contribution of $350 per month toward the employee's $450 health insurance premium. Job B has an annual salary of $28,000, no retirement contribution, and $150 toward the health insurance premium. Which job actually pays out more to the employee?*

Gender may also have an impact on earning potential. Wage differences between men and women historically have favored men. Reasons given for this difference have included the types of jobs held, longevity and commitment to

Benefit packages: services an insurer, a government agency, a health plan, or an employer offers under the terms of a contract

Cafeteria plans: employee benefit plans that allow employees to select among various group programs to best meet their specific needs

the job, and other factors. The U.S. Bureau of Labor Statistics (2016) reports that between 1979 and 2014, women's wages rose, peaking at 83% of the wages earned by their male counterparts, up from 62%, thus reducing the gap between pay differentials. Conversely, Blau and Kahn (2016) argue that the pay gap may not be interpreted correctly. They suggest that the jobs of men and women in the comparison are not the same, and when that is taken into account, the ratio of women's pay is closer to 92% to that of men. Employment patterns of lower-paying occupations and less experience make up the major differences. One of the major reasons why women have less experience in the workplace may be mother-hood. Baumle (2009) found that women pay a penalty for being mothers. Women may place more emphasis on how their job will affect their family life (Heckert et al., 2002), and they differ on what their role of being a mother and a worker means (Hagelskamp, Hughes, Yoshikawa, & Chaudry, 2011).

The other way that family economic resources are gained is by inheritance. The history of inheritance can be found in antiquity, with various cultures establishing their own way of distributing assets after the death of a family member. In the United States, inheritance practices followed the early settlers from their native country. In colonial times, if someone didn't make a will, the state would decide how the assets would be divided. Because many settlers owned their own businesses or farms, dividing the resources was difficult if it meant jeopardizing the operation. Deciding who would get the family business was complex. In addition, they were reluctant to adopt the English laws that so many were fleeing. *Primogeniture*, the English law whereby the eldest son inherited everything, was rejected by most of the colonies. However, male children continued to receive more of the inheritance.

Following the Revolutionary War, most states passed laws to give children equal shares. Also, unlike English inheritance laws, which bypassed widows, a woman could inherit provisions for her lifetime. Not until the late 19th century did states pass the Women's Property Acts, which allowed wives to inherit estates from their husbands. This act allowed women to keep ownership and control and to decide inheritance among their children after their husband's death. Today parents are living longer, and many are more concerned about retirement resources than inheritance for their children. When someone dies, the assets are usually given to the surviving spouse. When both spouses are gone, the assets are often liquidated and divided among the descendants. Although it sounds simple, there are two factors that often complicate inheritance. First, the emotions and expectations of the family members may make dividing resources more difficult. Families may find themselves faced with disagreements about fairness.

> Dan has never considered any other profession than farming. Since he was a child, he enjoyed being outside with his father on the family farm. Although he attended and graduated from college, he always knew he would come back to the farm. When he married his wife, Sandy, they both assumed that they would continue to work the land together and grow old on the farm that they both loved.
>
> Dan and his father had continued to work together until 2 years ago, when his father suffered a stroke that left him unable to do much of the work. This year,

Dan's father passed away from another stroke. While working with a lawyer, Dan found out that the farm assets would be divided equally among himself and his three sisters. In order to continue to farm, he would either have to rent the land or buy the land from his sisters.

Although the farm had provided enough income for Dan and his parents, the new expenses would make it impossible to continue to farm. When he came home from the meeting with the lawyer, he said, "I can't believe that I have given my life for this farm and my sisters don't care about it at all, yet they still get their share!"

Disagreements over family heirlooms sometimes erupt when one person feels that he or she is entitled because of special circumstances or relationships. In addition, the value of some assets may be in dispute. For example, one brother may value a particular set of dishes because of the memories they hold of family time, whereas the other brother may value the dishes because of their retail value. Which brother should have the dishes? Or should only a daughter have dishes and a brother get tools? These questions are at the heart of the emotional side of inheritance.

The other factor that complicates inheritance is the set of tax laws that applies to a situation. In 1916, Congress enacted for the first time a tax on the transfer of estates. This estate tax was joined in 1935 by the Revenue Act, which allowed for inheritance tax to be collected. An inheritance tax is imposed on those who receive property, and estate taxes are imposed on the deceased's estate. Today the federal government collects estate taxes, and some states impose inheritance taxes. Sometimes these taxes force people to sell property to meet obligations to the government. Considering the prior example of the farmer, if the father and mother had not done any estate planning, the farm assets may have had to be sold to pay the taxes, regardless of who inherited the land. Many people attempt to avoid these taxes by setting up trusts or other legal methods to bypass the tax system. Those who have the financial means and can afford legal advice are most often the ones who benefit from these legal loopholes. Even in death, those with the most resources have the advantage.

REALITY CHECK

What Is the Value of an Education?

Today, more than at any other time in history, an education is directly related to economic success. Although there are many ways to define education, most agree that more education means higher wages. According to data from the U.S. Bureau of Labor Statistics (Torpey & Terrell, 2015), the financial difference between a bachelor's and master's degree is nearly $12,000 per year.

(Continued)

(Continued)

Median Usual Weekly Earnings of Full-Time Wage and Salary Workers Age 25 or Older

    Doctoral degree: $1,623

    Professional degree: $1,730

    Master's degree: $1,341

    Bachelor's degree: $1,137

    Associate's degree: $798

    Some college, no degree: $738

    High school diploma, no degree: $678

    Less than a high school diploma: $493

While earning potential with education is higher, the cost must also be taken into account. Patton (2015) predicts that, accounting for inflation, the total cost of tuition and fees for a student at a public university totals $40,000, and the costs would top $135,000 for a private institution, not including the additional costs of housing and books. While scholarships and grants are important in lowering those out-of-pocket costs, many students depend on student loans to cover costs. The average student will leave college with $35,000 in student debt (Kantrowitz, 2016). What are the rewards and costs of education over 40 years of work life?

ENVIRONMENTAL RESOURCES

Environmental resources: anything an organism needs that can be taken from the environment

Renewable resources: resources that can be used and will not be depleted, or those that can be used over and over again

Nonrenewable resources: resources such as coal, oil, and other fossil fuels that are finite in supply and replaced so slowly that they are soon depleted

Environmental resources include those resources in the physical environment around us that are provided by nature. Families all over the world depend on the earth's resources to live and work. As environmental resources are used, they may be depleted and eventually exhausted.

Environmental resources are either renewable or nonrenewable. **Renewable resources** are those that can be used and will not be depleted, or those that can be used over and over again. *Flow resources* are those that are available on a continual basis. Good examples of these are the sun and wind. Other renewable resources are renewed by the biological process, such as plants, animals, and fish. Although we consider renewable resources to have unlimited potential for use, misuse or overuse will eventually deplete the supply. For example, although trees continue to reseed and grow voluntarily in the biological process, aggressive logging can remove enough trees in one area to prevent them from being given a chance to replenish. **Nonrenewable resources** are those that are available in limited quantity. Once the resource is used, it is not replaced. Examples of these types of resources would include minerals and fossil fuels. Much of the physical environment is nonrenewable and needs to be protected for the generations that will live on the earth in the future. There are several ways to think about how natural resources should be used. Some view the use of resources in terms of restricting consumption. Conservationists want to educate people and effect policies that will recognize and protect resources. Some generations have been more aware of and willing to protect the environment. Whenever a natural resource is threatened, there are those who rise up and call for more protection. Others advocate for new technologies that will allow more efficient use of resources or create alternative resources. A good example is the research being done on alternative power for automobiles, such as electricity and hydrogen.

Environmentalists and economists (Gerlagh & Sterner, 2013; Sterner, 2003) suggest that environmental resources are in danger for various reasons. An increase in population has caused depletion of and shortages in natural resources. These can include the increased demands for natural goods, such as lumber and water, and the added chemicals associated with the production of goods. Another danger comes from inadequate environmental policies that lack timely plans for sustainability. Politics are often in the middle of the debate over how to protect the environment. Environmentalists argue that nothing should allow the environment to be compromised, whereas industry pushes for less restriction to increase production and profits.

SOCIAL RESOURCES

The previous types of resources discussed have been tangible (those that can be seen), whereas social resources are those that are felt. McDermott (2004) suggests that in the past, the economic community largely treated social resources as something that only individuals could acquire. He suggests that social resources instead should be brought to the social level. Putnam (2000) describes social capital or resources as "connections among individuals—social networks and the norms of reciprocity and trustworthiness that arise from them" (p. 19). In addition, human and economic resources can be owned individually, whereas social resources are collectively owned.

Social resources: resources that are felt and collectively owned

Social resources are both those that are found inside the family and those that come from outside the family but affect the family. Social resources found inside the family include the functions of caring for and meeting the needs of the family members. Family social resources also include relationships skills. One of the most important family social resources is the ability to effectively communicate with each other. This social resource prepares children for future relationships.

> Bernard and Jenny are newlyweds. They met and married after a short courtship. Even though Bernard was a quiet man, Jenny was convinced that he was the perfect mate. Jenny's family had always been very open and honest with each other, and they were able to resolve any conflict fairly. It was a surprise to her that when she and Bernard disagreed, he would clam up and often disappear for a few hours. When he returned, he acted as if nothing had happened.
>
> At first Jenny let it go, but over the next year, she became frustrated that the same disagreements kept coming up and Bernard would never stay and talk it out with her. When Jenny threatened to leave him if they didn't go to counseling, Bernard finally agreed to talk. Jenny soon discovered that Bernard's family had never been able to resolve conflict. Bernard did not have the resource skills to effectively communicate or effectively resolve a conflict.

Another social resource within the family is an archival family function. Families that pass on their history pass on an important social resource, whether it is through photographs, stories, or heirlooms. Although it is pleasant to reminisce

about the past and to hear interesting stories of ancestors, the past is an important part of the future. Family members must come to realize that it is important to understand the past as a historical process that shapes the future. Passing on family history gives us a sense of belonging and attachment to the family that cannot be accomplished with any other social group.

▶ **Photo 6.2**
Passing on family history through photographs is an archival family function.

Travis was in his third year of college. One night he and his friends were talking about their family histories. Although most of them didn't really know much about their families' histories, Travis was able to talk about how his great grandparents had emigrated from Scotland and settled in Ohio. He had read in a family diary about the hardships and challenges that they faced over those early years—financial difficulties and harsh climate. The other young men were intrigued by how much Travis's own perseverance at school reflected that of his ancestors' determination generations earlier.

Collective socialization: a process by which children within a community social network are influenced by common behavioral expectations

Social resources are also found within the community or environment outside the family, including the family's ability to connect to and utilize the social resources available in the community. In addition, **collective socialization** refers to how the community as a whole engages in family life (e.g., how adults look out for the children of the community and whether parents appreciate this or isolate themselves from their community).

The Lewis family is active in their children's school. Mrs. Lewis attends all the parent advisory meetings and often helps out at school fundraising events. In the summer, the Lewis children participate in recreation activities sponsored by the city. Mr. Lewis has volunteered as a soccer coach and helps with Little League tryouts.

The Miller family views their community quite differently. The Millers work long hours to provide for their family and have little time or money to participate in social activities. Mr. and Mrs. Miller are not active in their children's education and rarely interact with other families outside of their own family and extended family. They do not take advantage of the educational or sports opportunities that are offered through their community and rarely leave their children with anyone other than grandparents.

In contrast to the Miller family, the behavior of the Lewis family is an example of collective socialization.

There are advantages to social resources. Communities in which people band together to improve and maintain a good quality of life have many advantages. Wickrama and Bryant (2003) found that, in addition to the previous literature that has shown that a lack of community resources leads to community adversity, such as dropouts and substance abuse, the presence of community resources leads to effective parent–child relationships and less adolescent depression. Torquati (2002) stated that social support, whether formal or informal, is associated with positive parenting.

Local, state, and federal benefit programs are social resources that are available to families. Local governments provide services for families in the form of public libraries and public parks. State governments provide other opportunities, such as state parks and state museums. Some examples of federal programs are Cooperative Extension System (CES), the Federal Emergency Management Agency (FEMA), the Veterans Health Administration (VHA), and the National Endowment for the Arts (NEA).

Economic social support is available through Social Security. The Social Security Administration began in 1934 to assist families that could not provide basic needs during the depression. One of the major purposes of Social Security is to provide a safety net for families that need social assistance. It was originally designed to be a short-term resource, however, and the idea of generational welfare is a challenge for the program today. Although most people support the idea of Social Security, many have doubts about its effectiveness. Reforms such as the recent replacement of Aid for Families with Dependent Children (AFDC) program with the Temporary Assistance to Needy Families (TANF) are working for change. Social Security is discussed more in Chapter 8.

Today, as social media and technology continue to influence family members as their connection to the outside would, some believe that social capital in the form of volunteerism may be changing. Several years ago, Putnam (2000) observed in his book *Bowling Alone* that the previous four decades had experienced declining **volunteerism** and participation in civic organizations, political apathy, and a rising distrust among cultural groups, which signaled serious problems ahead. Others argued that belonging to a particular group or political party didn't automatically ensure social resource benefits and might actually be detrimental to society if groups became closed and self-serving (Stolle, 2003) and that people were more likely to join in a cause without a formalized group both at home and abroad in the globalized community (Thomson, 2005). According to the 2015 Millennial Impact Report (Feldman, Wall, Hosea, Banker, & Ponce, 2015), 70% of millennials volunteer their time, and 84% make charitable donations. Unlike their parents and grandparents, their motivations are different. Previous generations volunteered as a result of involvement in their workplace or a social group, often for a predetermined cause. **Millennials** are more likely to participate because they believe in the cause or at the urging of a friend or someone they admire. They are also more likely to use social capital, such as skills and expertise, rather than just time and money, so that they can see how their contribution helps the cause.

Volunteerism: contributing one's time or talents for charitable, educational, social, political, or other worthwhile purposes, usually in one's community, freely and without regard to compensation

Millennials: the generation born in the 1980s and 1990s

Regardless of the purpose and future of volunteerism, the family may be most instrumental in raising awareness of societal needs by teaching children the value of social capital. It is parents who model the value of performing civic duty, who show the value of cooperation with others, and who teach their children about trusting or mistrusting others (Stolle, 2003). Lewton and Nievar (2012) suggest that family volunteering can advance family development and expand family members' knowledge of available resources.

IN THE NEWS

The Majority of the World Lives With Light-Polluted Skies

Most of us have looked up at the stars and observed the wonders of the night sky. According to Engelking (2016), that ability is going to change. Fabio Felchi, a researcher at the Light Pollution Science and Technology Institute in Thiene, Italy, created the first atlas of night sky brightness more than 10 years ago.

Recently, Felchi updated the atlas and added new, more powerful tools to make the latest version even more accurate. Felchi and his team combined high-resolution satellite data and on-the-ground sky brightness measurements to quantify what they call "global glow." There are some areas, called "red zones," that are so bright at night that people never experience true night.

The new atlas revealed that more than 80% of the world lives under light-polluted skies. The night sky is slowly disappearing above the glow of artificial light. One-third of viewers can no longer see the Milky Way.

Canada and Australia are the best areas to experience the night sky. The American West and parts of Scotland, Sweden, and Norway also have some unspoiled skies.

We should want to preserve night skies not only for our own viewing, but also because too much light hinders ground-based astronomical observations. It also disturbs migrations of birds, turtles, and other species.

Felchi's team hopes the new map will be a valuable tool for researchers as they explore the environmental effects of light pollution. This issue needs to be examined before it changes the future forever.

Source: Adapted from Engelking, C. (2016, June 10). Goodbye to night: 80 percent of humanity lives under light polluted skies. *Discover: Science for the Curious.*

MEASUREMENT OF RESOURCES

When an exchange of resources is made, most people prefer to have an equitable exchange. In other words, we want to receive something equal to what we give, as in the case of paying a fair price for a gallon of milk at the supermarket. However, resources and the value of those resources can be measured in various ways. When giving something to a friend or family member, many would not expect something in return. There may be other times when you expect a better rate of exchange, such as getting a good deal on a swimsuit because it is the end of the season. To a child, $100 is perhaps more valuable than it is to a wealthy person. The value of an exchange may depend on the nature of the interaction and the relationship of those involved.

In relationships, the theory of relative resources (Blood & Wolfe, 1960) assumes that the balance of power in that relationship will be on the side of the partner who has the most resources. In the past, the balance had traditionally favored the male partner, whose contributions of earning power and status outweighed the value of homemaking and childrearing. As women entered the workforce and relationships became more egalitarian, the balance changed. This theory tends to view resources from the cultural context of the United States. However, Rodman (1967) argues that in traditional cultural settings, where the husband has all the authority, marital power is not associated with the resources of each partner.

> *Mahavir and Sashi have been married for 5 years. They were both raised in New York City, but they continue to follow the customs of their native India. Sashi and Mahavir both have professional careers as attorneys, with Sashi's salary actually exceeding her husband's salary. Still, because of their cultural traditions, Mahavir has all the authority in their relationship.*

The most effective way to measure resources involves improving people's lives while weighing the effects of culture, environment, and equity. Every culture has different meanings and places different values on resources. At the same time, the physical environment must be considered and guarded. Economic equity must also be considered. A society where gross economic inequities exist—with extreme poverty existing side by side with extreme wealth—will face many future problems.

Family resources are used to meet basic needs. For some families, resources that are plentiful are used to satisfy wants as well. Unfortunately, most families have only a limited number of resources and must find ways to effectively manage what they have to meet their needs. Effectively managing resources can help families. The family's ability to manage resources may come as a result of the combination of resources available to them. For example, when a family needs to make decisions about the care of an elderly member, they may draw on their own resources, such as other family members' willingness to help and financial resources, as well as social resources, such as hospice or home health services.

Resources can affect the family directly by providing economic stability or indirectly by helping the family cope. When families are worried about how they will use their resources or whether they will not have enough resources, stress can result. These stresses can come from expected events, such as marriage, or unexpected events, such as divorce. They may also be temporary, as in the case of an illness, or long term, as when dealing with a chronic condition like diabetes. Individuals and families who implement adequate financial planning can diminish the vulnerability that leads to economic stress. Monetary resources help the family in tangible ways when there are doctor's bills to pay, but often other resources are needed when money cannot be used to "fix" the problem, and those resources then become more valuable. Coping resources that are in place before stressful events occur are those that can be drawn upon when an event occurs. These resources, such as support from the community, counseling, or effective coping skills, may be needed. Commitment to marriage, strong family relationships, good problem-solving skills, and higher levels of education contribute to successfully coping with financial stresses (Fox & Bartholomae, 2000; Matheny & Curlette, 2010).

©iStockphoto.com/shapecharge

▶ **Photo 6.3**
Careful planning and shared decision making make resource management more positive for families.

Regulating the flow of resources is important in managing resources and helps the family plan for the future. Of course, when someone continues to work, resources continue to come into the household. However, job loss, crises, or unexpected events can interrupt the flow of resources. Careful management of resources can prepare the family in the event that resources stop.

In a family, the way that resources are measured may be influenced by a variety of factors. Traditions or celebrations that are yearly or milestone events will affect resources. Some families choose to use their resources for future events, such as college or weddings, because those are highly valued. Family roles may also affect resources. If both the husband and wife work outside the home, they may value and use their resources differently than a couple that chooses different work patterns would.

RESOURCE ALLOCATION AND USE

Resources are used in a variety of ways. In the discussion of resource theory, the idea of exchanging resources is presented. Giving up one resource in exchange for another is the most common use of resources. Other uses include producing and consuming. Many resources are produced today in mass quantity. Factories turn out millions of goods each day that are distributed to stores for consumers to buy. Consumers buy the goods to consume. Most families consume goods, and some families also produce goods.

In addition to being exchanged, resources can also be saved or invested. Saving resources will allow someone to have a reserve to be used in case of emergency or to be used for a later purpose.

> *The Smiths live in the panhandle of Florida. During the hurricane season each fall, they aim to be prepared by making sure that they have plenty of bottled water, ready-to-eat foods, and plywood for their windows. In September, the panhandle experienced a major hurricane. Because of the erratic behavior of the hurricane, the stores were not prepared to sell enough supplies, so prices were much higher. Planning ahead for the eventuality of a hurricane by storing up and saving resources was an effective strategy for the Smiths to avoid paying these higher prices.*

Saving resources can also be a way to increase resources. Over time, antiques and real estate may become more valuable. Saving money yields interest at a bank or savings institution. Investing can also be a good use of resources. Families may choose to not use all their income as it comes in, and may choose to invest some money in hopes of increasing their resources over time. Investing may include stocks, bonds, mutual funds, and annuities. Investments are discussed in detail in a later chapter.

Most people want to protect their resources. Some resources are protected by insurance. Lenders who hold mortgages and car loans require insurance to protect against something happening to the property before the buyer pays it in full. Banks assure customers that their money is federally insured by the FDIC in case something happens to the bank. Others protect their resources by taking precautions. Locks, security systems, and even zippers on purses are all ways that people protect their resources.

Resourcefulness is the ability to identify and use resources to meet needs effectively. The resourcefulness of families or how they use their resources is not the same in all families. According to Lauer and Yodanis (2011), most married couples "pool" their money and use their resources, including income, equally, but that is not always the case. Changing family structures, previous relationship experiences, a need for autonomy, and other reasons lead couples to use and distribute resources in various ways (Bennett, 2013).

As discussed in Chapter 2, exchange theory explains how resources are balanced within relationships, depending on income, status, skills, and other assets. That balance does not always come easily, and there is often conflict over how those resources will be distributed and used. Although some family members may cooperate to get the most out of the available resources, others may compete for the resources. One aspect of relationships that makes decision making about resources difficult is that there is a certain amount of power associated with deciding how resources will be used. Safilios-Rothschild (1976) uses the terms **orchestration power** and **implementation power** to describe the types of decision-making power within many relationships. Those who have orchestration power are given power to make major decisions that often determine the lifestyle of the family. Yet they often use that power to pass minor decision making to someone else (usually the other spouse) for day-to-day management. That person then realizes a certain amount of implementation power when they are given the responsibility of the day-to-day decisions. Woolley (2003) found that women are more involved than men in managing the money within a relationship; however, those with higher incomes have more control over the money. Bertocchi, Brunetti, and Torricelli (2012) later added that other factors, such as age differences, previous economic knowledge, and even the husband's characteristics, can influence who controls the household finances.

The way that families allocate their resources is also related to the conditions in which they are making those decisions. Langholtz, Marty, Ball, and Nolan (2003) suggest that the conditions of certainty, risk, and uncertainty have an effect on how resources are used. It is less complicated when the decisions about use of resources are made under the conditions of **certainty**. For example, a family

Resourcefulness: having inner resources; being skillful or imaginative

Orchestration power: responsibility for major decisions that often determine the lifestyle of the family

Implementation power: responsibility for day-to-day decisions

Certainty: the quality or state of being certain, especially on the basis of evidence

with a stable income, substantial savings and investments, and adequate life and health insurance will find the decision to buy a new car fairly simple. Even the daily decisions are made easy under the certainty of a set number of resources from a monthly paycheck. However, under the conditions of **uncertainty**, such as unstable work conditions or poor health, the decisions would be more difficult. Although a family has the stability of a regular paycheck each month, it may have the uncertainty of a family member who has a chronic illness. If that family member has to be hospitalized, they may not be able to bring resources in, and more resources will have to be used for the hospital bills, medicine, and other expenses. Under the conditions of **risk,** the family doesn't know what resources will be available and has to make decisions under assumptions that the resources will be there. These conditions make it difficult to make decisions about allocation of resources.

> Robert and Lisa have been married 14 years and have two children, ages 8 and 10. Due to a series of mergers in Robert's company, Robert's job description has changed over the past 6 months, and he has become increasingly unhappy with his work situation. In his mind, either the job will have to change or he will have to leave. Last week, the 15-year-old family car began having problems. Both Robert and Lisa knew that it meant that they would have to buy a new car. The decision would be made under the condition of risk, knowing that Robert's job was questionable. He could stay and negotiate his present job, he could quit and be unemployed, or he could find a new job that would pay more than he is making now. Because they need a car, it is a risk they will have to take.

Research on **resource-allocation behavior** (Langholtz et al., 2003) has examined possible strategies that people use when they make decisions about how to use their resources. Resource-allocation problems are different from common problem solving because the decisions are often multilayered. At first glance, there is usually not one obvious solution when deciding on how to use resources. Sources of resources, the way resources are valued, and multiple ways to allocate resources contribute to the complexity of decisions.

> Carol loves to cook. After a long day at work, she finds it relaxing to spend several hours each evening creating a wonderful gourmet dinner for her family. Her coworker, Rose, would rather spend her evening hours reading or watching television with her family. Rose wants to spend as little time cooking as possible, so she often buys time-saving precooked meals or orders takeout. The relative number of resources may be the same for both Carol and Rose, but the allocation is different.

Langholtz et al. (2003) found that many people tend to use resources without thinking about the future outcome. They tend not to think about whether using their resources would have either a gain or a loss and instead adopt an "assume-no-loss strategy," where they don't worry about the outcome until a loss actually occurs. However, those with fewer resources and more uncertainty tend to plan more for losses. In addition, people tend to use more of their resources early in the time period, using fewer toward the end. Most people save between 10% and 25% of their resources at the end. For example, at the beginning of the month, someone might spend more money on groceries than at the end of the month, making sure that there is money left before the next pay period for emergencies. Another strategy that people use is to make adjustments in how they use resources along the way. If necessary, people will change the way they allocate their resources midstream if it means the outcome will be more efficient and improve their results.

Deutch (2005) identified three principles of **distributive justice** to determine how resources are distributed and to guide the use of resources. The principle of equity can be based on fairness, where distribution is contingent on contributions to the system—for example, the idea that those who pay taxes are the most deserving of public services. In contrast, equity can also be determined by how much someone deserves a particular resource—for example, a person who has contributed to the system in the past, but now finds that he or she needs help after becoming homeless. The principle of equality is purely based on equal distribution. Dividing resources equally among the group or family members certainly helps create cooperation and harmony, but does not always address everyone's needs. The principle of need is also a way to distribute resources. This principle is what drives some programs, such as Social Security, or some organizations to give grants or scholarships. This principle is used especially when resources are limited.

Distributive justice: justice dispensed in the community to confer maximum value to those in need through the notions of fairness and consistency

> *The Sandoz family has four children ranging in age from 2 to 15. Maria Sandoz has always been sensitive about treating her children equally. She makes sure that she shows an equal amount of love and attention to all her children. When it comes to dividing their resources, however, distributing them equally is not the best solution. Fifteen-year-old Jose needs more than twice as much food as 2-year-old Rosa does. As school starts, Jose will also need new athletic shoes for football and a special type of calculator for his math class. At this time in their family life, the number of resources needed by Jose outweighs what is needed by the other children.*

The concept of voluntary simplicity may affect the way that resources are used in some families. Although this concept may or may not be attached to political or religious organizations, it is rooted in a rejection of the ideas behind consumerism and is practiced by those who choose not to live a life where the main objective is to "buy" the good life in favor of simple living. Although some fear that consumerism has led to an insatiable desire for more "stuff," living a simple life is less about the number of purchases than the underlying values that cause people to make those purchases. Examples of voluntary simplicity for families may include living with less technology, buying only biofriendly products, cutting down on work hours to spend more time at home, and downsizing living space and possessions.

How and why people use resources is often complex. Looking at the context of the situation in which decisions are made may be as important as the decisions themselves. How the need is presented, the values of the person making the allocation, past history, and even the practicality of using resources in a particular way are all factors that need to be taken into consideration.

SUMMARY

Individuals and families utilizing the decision-making process first determine needs. Once needs have been identified, possible alternatives must be explored that could fulfill or meet those needs. Identification and evaluation of resources available to families provide choices and determine the success or failure of the process. Resources are tangible and intangible, bountiful and limited. Decisions based on solid understanding of alternatives available have a greater chance of satisfying and enriching family existence, presently and in the future.

QUESTIONS FOR REVIEW AND DISCUSSION

1. How does someone's culture or family background affect the use of resources?

2. Considering resource theory, how is the exchange of love different from the exchange of money? How can status be exchanged?

3. Looking at the reasons why we invest our resources, how would the reasons be different for work and the family?

4. Why do gender differences continue to exist for paid work?

5. With parents participating more in paid work, does this limit the time they have to model the value of social capital in our society? If so, what will be the consequences?

6. Explain why families have differences in their definition of resourcefulness.

CHAPTER SEVEN

FAMILIES WITHIN THE ECONOMIC ENVIRONMENT

Objectives
Beginnings of Consumerism
Economic Principles
In the News
  Supply and Demand
  Pricing
  Income Fluctuations
  Changes in Preference
  Employment
  Money
Reality Check
  Exchanging Nonmonetary Resources
Families in the Economy
Worldview
Summary
Questions for Review and Discussion

Objectives

- Understand the basic concepts of economic theory.

- Explore the interdependency of the economic system and families.

- Comprehend the impact of the economic system on the family decision-making process.

- Understand how a family's economic status impacts quality of life.

The quickest way to double your money is to fold it in half and put it in your back pocket.

—Will Rogers

As discussed in Chapter 2, family systems theory explains how families impact their environments and are simultaneously impacted by changes in those same environments. Each family, individually, and all families, collectively, impact the economic systems locally, regionally, nationally, and globally, while they are impacted by those same systems. Individuals within families exchange human resources in the production and distribution of goods and services. They pool the money they earn within the family and consume goods and services, thus stimulating the entire economic exchange process. The resources available to families determine how deeply they are involved in the marketplace.

BEGINNINGS OF CONSUMERISM

Services: the nonmaterial equivalent of a good

How did families become so enmeshed in such a system? The exchange of goods and **services** is evident throughout recorded history. Artifacts found in ancient Egyptian tombs were created by skilled craftspeople who were commissioned by the ruling class to exchange their time and talents for protection or for the prestige that accompanied such assignments. Pioneer families in the United States were self-sustaining in terms of food, safety, and shelter. Eventually, however, these families produced more foodstuffs than they personally required and began participating in trade among other families in the area, eventually becoming an integral part of the economic system in nearby communities.

> Early settlers in the Great Plains states left Midwestern travel centers like Chicago and St. Louis to carve out a place of their own in the land opened to settlement by the movement of the transcontinental railway. Their provisions on departure included basic farming tools, a few livestock, and food staples for the trip. These pioneers knew that their survival would depend on raising their own food, building their own shelter, and a great deal of luck. Although there were a few small towns already in existence at strategic points along the major trails westward, the availability of goods and services was limited. Farmsteads were regularly miles from these rudimentary marketplaces, anyway, so self-sufficiency was crucial.
>
> Crops were planted, tended, and harvested. Food gathered during harvest was dried, pickled, salted, canned, and stored for use until the next harvest could be expected. Livestock were bred, raised, and slaughtered as needed. Meat was used fresh, dried, salted, and stored as best it could be. Game, such as birds, squirrels, deer, and other local fauna, was used when possible. All family members were actively engaged in sustaining their existence. Living and working was a family affair, with people of all ages toiling side by side from daylight to dusk. Recreation was unplanned but a natural part of daily life. Their existence was quite different from that of relatives who stayed behind in the established cities with expanding retailing opportunities.
>
> When these pioneer families depleted the monetary stores they had brought with them, they needed to participate fully in the trading network available to them. Extra foodstuffs, animals, and seed were carted to the nearest town and traded for supplies or cash, depending on the needs and resources present at the time and location of the exchange. Once the transportation system of the railroad became the steady supplier of goods across the country, these

farm families found better markets and prices for the goods they produced. Wholesale and retail businesses in these small towns grew to accommodate the exchange.

Over time, farm families became less self-sufficient. Crops and livestock were raised primarily for exchange in the marketplace. Gardens still provided some foodstuffs, and the occasional animal was butchered for meat, but canned goods, frozen foods, and prepackaged foods were available through exchange of money received from crops and livestock. Farms evolved into full-fledged businesses. Farm families became dependent on the economy, and their success or failure is now rooted in global economics.

The American economic system is rooted in the European economic developments prior to the Revolutionary War. Much of the motivation for a separation of the colonies from England came from dissatisfaction with economic exchange between these two societies. McCracken (1988) explores how **consumerism** shaped the European economy of past centuries and suggests that the relationship between individuals and their economic system depends on the willingness of individuals and families to engage in the process of conspicuous consumption. He traces this phenomenon back to the royal court of Queen Elizabeth I of England in the late 16th century.

Consumerism: the promotion of the consumer's interests

Queen Elizabeth I insisted that the nobility visit her personally at court. Until that time, these landholders and titled families could receive royal goods and favors through intermediaries who traveled to and from London. Elizabeth insisted that nobility plead their cases directly to her. Traveling to London and taking part in the lavish proceedings of the court were quite expensive. Payments for the required finery and privileges fed the royal coffers, thus allowing Elizabeth to maintain the opulent court system at their expense. These noble men and women, while at the top of the system back at their estates, found that they had to compete for the queen's attention among other nobles at court. This need for competitiveness forced them to acquire magnificent wardrobes, larger and more elaborate townhouses in the city, and rarer and more noteworthy royal gifts, as well as to give bigger and better parties than their noble peers. McCracken (1988) called this "a riot of consumption" (p. 12).

This engagement in conspicuous consumption had an impact on both the function of the family unit and the purpose of family in society. The concept of acquiring material goods and financial wealth that would be passed to and enhanced by future generations was challenged by the need to spend large sums from the current family holdings to maintain family status at court. Spending shifted from a need to build future holdings for the entire family to a need to be fashionable. The increased demand for fashionable goods and services fueled the local community's production of both. What had once been an economy based mainly on sustainability evolved into an economy focused on an early version of mass production, marketing, and distribution (McCracken, 1988).

Industrialization: the adoption of industrial methods of production and manufacturing by a country or group, with all the associated changes in lifestyle, transport, and other aspects of society

Another historical era that further increased the participation of U.S. families in the economic system was the capitalistic **industrialization** in both Europe and America during the 1800s. Before the Civil War, the U.S. economy was primarily centered on agricultural production and distribution. Production was usually done at or near the home, and trade was primarily within local market areas (Welch & Welch, 2004). Railroad transportation, telegraph and telephone lines, mechanical and electrical inventions, and mass production in large factory settings opened new markets and provided new goods and services. These developments greatly influenced American families. As presented in the last chapter, many adults, primarily male, began working in the production and distribution sectors of the economy. Instead of trading products from their home base, these adults now used their monetary wages to trade for goods and services. Mass production made goods readily accessible and affordable, so families increased their consumption.

©iStockphoto.com/y_carfan

▶ **Photo 7.1**
Luxury cars and travel are expressions of conspicuous consumption.

The stock market crash of 1929 devastated the U.S. economy and sent companies, workers, and families into the Great Depression, which lasted for more than a decade. The economy eventually pulled out of the downward spiral, mainly due to the end of World War II. At that time, the U.S. government spent massive amounts of money, fueling a rebounding economy (Collinge & Ayers, 2000). Passage of the Employment Act of 1946 cemented the participation of families in the economic system by providing expectations of full employment, full production, and stable prices. Congress was given the authority to manipulate taxes and government spending to bring the economy to a desired level of activity (Welch & Welch, 2004).

The more recent U.S. recession employed these same governmental actions to try to turn a failing economy around. With the passage of the American Recovery and Reinvestment Act in 2009, a safety net of increased unemployment insurance lessened the impact of the rising unemployment rates. The Federal Reserve lowered the interest rates for banks to zero. The stock market ultimately turned around, and increased government spending and targeted tax cuts jumpstarted the unstable economy. These solutions were the result of intensive, thoughtful planning that relied on the basic principles from the field of economics.

American families are an integral part of the U.S. economy for several reasons. First, families spend their resources on products that they believe will meet their needs. Together, families represent one of the largest markets for goods and services, driving the production of goods and services with their choices of what to consume (Bade & Parkin, 2015). Other large consumer groups include the government, institutions, and industry. Second, families provide the labor force necessary to maintain business operations. To better understand the **symbiotic** relationship between families and the economy, one must understand the economic process.

Symbiotic: any interdependent or mutually beneficial relationship between two persons, groups

ECONOMIC PRINCIPLES

Economics, like the decision-making process, is all about making choices. Families must meet their needs and wants by selecting from limited resources. Regardless of income, a family establishes limitations on how much of its available resources will be traded for any particular need. Producers must decide what they will produce, and service providers must focus their supply of human resources to meet demand. Economics exists because the resources we need to fulfill our wants and needs are limited.

Economics is the study of how resources are expended to fulfill the needs and wants of individuals, families, and social groups. Resources are inherently limited, and needs and wants are rarely limited, so decisions must be made continually to balance the two. Most often the focus centers on material needs, such as food, clothing, housing, transportation, entertainment, and other things that consumers believe they need to live satisfying lives. However, essential to the cycle of production and consumption are **intangible** resources, such as time, energy, and human knowledge and skill. Contemporary American economics is fueled by money. Money is obtained through the exchange of these intangible human resources, the promise of future exchange (credit), or through inheritance or chance.

Is purchasing a lottery ticket every week your idea of retirement planning? How would a huge check change your life? Nguyen (2010) interviewed five lucky winners and compiled some sound advice, gained through both positive and negative experiences.

Good financial advice is essential. Although the winning amounts are very large, taxes are pulled long before winners receive an actual check they can deposit. Those deductions can reduce winnings by up to 75% in some situations. A knowledgeable tax advisor can reduce that impact. Dramatic changes in lifestyle can drain new bank accounts quickly—real estate taxes, property taxes, utilities, and upkeep. Privacy can be impacted when winners are publicly acknowledged. This also increases the chance of criminal attacks and targeting by charities and nonprofit foundations. And of course, the tax agencies at the local, state, and federal levels will increase scrutiny of all tax-related transactions. Personal, family, and community relationships can be negatively impacted by dramatic shifts in finances. A lot can be "lost" when you "win" the lottery.

Economics:
a social science concerned chiefly with description and analysis of the production, distribution, and consumption of goods and services

Intangible:
without material qualities, and so not able to be touched or seen

IN THE NEWS

Are the Rich Getting Richer at the Expense of the Poor?

The economy of the United States is experiencing a dilemma of widening proportions. The gap between the richest Americans and the poorest is broadening, making the national economy and the individual experience vulnerable. Roughly 20% of the U.S. population receive 50% of the total national income (U.S. Census Bureau, 2015). The 20%

(Continued)

(Continued)

with the lowest incomes receive just 3% of the total income.

Where has the middle class fallen in this readjustment? In the last 30 years, about 5% of the annual national income has shifted from the middle class to the nation's richest citizens. That translates to more than $650 billion, or $100 million per capita (of those already affluent). That is a large chunk out of the middle-class sector (Lynch, Smith, Harper, Hillemeier, Ross, Kaplan, & Wolfson, 2004).

How does this impact the near future? In times of recession, those with cash can take advantage of foreclosed property and commodities ravaged by instability. The opportunity increases to get even richer. Those saddled with debt and devalued properties (the middle class) do not have the liquid resources to do the same.

The gap widens further between these two groups. When unemployment is high, the poor or "working-wage" population is impacted first. They move into survival mode. The balance shifts. Even when the economy is relatively stable, the impact of inflation and proposed tax changes can have a disproportionate negative impact on the poorest citizens.

Questions and unrest over what constitutes economic fairness are moving citizens to demonstrate, to vocalize, and to challenge the morality of high unemployment during times of record corporate profits. The term *class warfare* has infiltrated news reports and talk shows. Can capitalism and social equality coexist? The presidential election of 2016 created great division between and within political parties over this debate.

Supply and Demand

Supply: a quantity of something on hand or available, as for use

Demand: the quantity of a commodity or service wanted at a specified price and time

At the center of the study of economics are the concepts of supply and demand. Buyers and sellers are key players in an economic system. When buyers are willing to exchange resources for a particular good or service, this is referred to as *demand* for that good or service. When sellers make the decision to produce or provide goods and services, this is referred to as *supply* of that good or service. A common example of this relationship is the demand and supply of greeting cards. Individuals purchase paper or e-mail cards to send, thus remembering or celebrating important days, events, and milestones of family members, friends, neighbors, or colleagues. The demand for Christmas cards exists only because of the holiday celebrated at that time of the year. Many families and individuals send greeting cards in December—demand. Manufacturers of greeting cards produce the anticipated number of cards many months before the actual season to make sure these cards are available in stores and online—supply. Which comes first, supply or demand? This is much like the chicken-and-egg controversy. Years ago, there was no Administrative Professionals' Day. Did the desire to honor these assistants create a demand that was then met by the manufacturing companies? Or did the official designation of Administrative Professionals' Day and the production of cards for this occasion (the supply) spawn the consumer demand?

Surplus: something that remains above what is used or needed

Shortage: when there is excess demand and limited supply

Demand is a complex concept. Consumer demand fluctuates over time; if producers fail to predict these changes adequately, they may be stuck with goods and services that are no longer in demand. When product inventory increases against a decreasing demand, a surplus of unwanted products will result. When fewer products are produced than are demanded, a shortage exists. How can buyers and sellers work within this uncertainty?

Pricing

In an economy such as the United States, goods and services are often offered at various prices. How do providers determine these amounts through pricing, and how do consumers decide whether those goods and services are worth the price attached? Both are complex processes, and both are dependent on the decision-making process.

Pricing: the manual or automatic process of applying prices to purchase and sales orders

Producers or providers of goods and services must cover the cost of providing those goods and services. The price of a hamburger at a fast-food restaurant must cover the cost of the burger, bread, condiments, wrappings, and labor to flip and prepare the burger. There must also be some money included to cover the overhead of the company (management, utilities, facilities, advertising, etc.). A business will exist only if there is profit to be made through its exchanges. So, after covering all of these costs, there must be a bit more money in the price to provide that profit.

As the price of something increases, the demand typically decreases. There are several reasons for this. Milk is a fundamental part of many American families' shopping list. When the price of milk remains stable, the amount purchased by families across the country stabilizes. If the price of milk increases slightly, there may be little or no impact on the amount purchased because consumers will tolerate small increases before they will change something that is considered both healthful and integral to their diets. However, when the price increases dramatically, by more than 10%, families may reevaluate their need for milk.

Supply and demand work in predictable ways as long as consumers do not find other ways to satisfy their needs. However, consumers react in diverse ways to changes in the price of goods they want. They may accommodate a price change by drinking less milk, or they may substitute other liquids like water or juice where milk had been the drink of choice. They may change brands if other brands or generic brands are available at lower prices, or they may use canned or powdered milk products if they can be purchased for less and family members will accept these different products as substitutes. Another contemporary example of how consumers adjust to changes in supply and pricing is reflected in the fluctuating gasoline prices of the last few years. Because the U.S. population has become accustomed to mobility, few consumers have actually lowered their miles traveled or traded gas-guzzling models for more efficient vehicles to accommodate price increases. Some have turned to public transportation as a substitute travel method to lower their costs. Many merely have adjusted other expenditures to enable them to continue traveling as they had before. As prices have fallen, consumer motivation for purchasing vehicles with better fuel economy has reflected their desire to lessen the impact of pollution on the environment more than their reaction to price.

Accommodate: to make fit, suitable, or congruous; to bring into agreement or concord

Substitute: to replace something with another similar product or good

When producers find that they have more products than consumers want, a surplus emerges. By lowering the price, producers may be able to stimulate consumer demand. The lure of a sale may convince a buyer that the purchase is necessary. Consumers may purchase larger quantities of something if they feel there will be a future need for that product and the current reduced price is lower than it will be at that future time.

Functional value: having a practical application or serving a useful purpose

Preference: a real or imagined "choice" between alternatives and the possibility of rank ordering these alternatives, based on the happiness, satisfaction, gratification, enjoyment, and utility they provide

When consumers want something, but producers have not anticipated that demand and there are not enough products to meet demand, there is a shortage situation, and the price may increase. Buyers are willing to spend more money to get something that has a higher value, regardless of whether that value is obvious. That value may be linked to its level of scarcity. For instance, pieces of artwork have been known to increase in value when the artist dies. Because there will be no more works by that person, past works may be considered to be collectibles or to be rare. Owning them creates an aura of prestige and privilege.

Prices do not always reflect the **functional value** of a product. **Preferences**, real or imaginary, may create a situation where the price of a product can be increased and consumers will still buy. Wine is a liquid that could be used to quench one's thirst. What is the difference between a $5 bottle and a $500 bottle? Quantity could be the same, but if the consumer believes that the more expensive bottle tastes better or that owning that bottle will increase her social value due to its rarity, the extra money may be rationalized, and the decision to purchase the more expensive bottle may be made.

SUPPLY AND DEMAND INTERRUPTED: THE HEALTHCARE SYSTEM

As you are sitting in the doctor's office waiting for your appointment time, or when your physician can work you in regardless of your appointment time, do you notice a pricing board with fees and procedure charges posted for consumer viewing? Probably not. In the U.S. healthcare marketplace, prices are not determined by supply and demand, and competition is not the driving force. Actually, prices are usually set by the service providers, and the consumer would have a difficult time evaluating the quality of services consumed. You can have your appendix removed only once. If you are not satisfied or you feel the charge was too much, what can you do? The medical staff won't put it back so that you can try another doctor or hospital. Most providers and consumers of healthcare view these goods and services as priceless. Americans with health insurance are determined to optimize their personal health and that of family members. Health insurance makes services accessible by providing a safety net to subscribers.

For a monthly premium or fee, the insurance company agrees to pick up your medical bill once it reaches the point where you would not consider it an option if you were paying directly out of your pocket. In 2011, out-of-pocket payment by consumers of medical services was approximately 12%, while insurance companies and governmental programs paid the other 88% (Young, 2013). With this kind of parachute, consumers do little comparison shopping for healthcare procedures they feel are necessary. In essence, the consumer depends on the provider for advice on what treatments are needed. Although it may seem like a conflict of interest, those providing the advice are also setting the price for those treatments. Even selection of the hospital or treatment facility is made from relatively few possible choices. Location and doctor affiliation most often determine the facility used. When supply is greater than demand, prices should fall. The medical field is different, however, because the providers are actually creating the demand for their own services. Studies show that the number of hospital beds used by members of any community is closely linked to the number of beds available in that community (Rosenbaum, 1993).

Income Fluctuations

Individuals and families participating in the American economy have the opportunity to improve their financial position through additional education, job promotion, inheritance, and investment gains. They also face the possibility of losing their current position and falling to a lower socioeconomic level when crises occur—unemployment, loss of health, and loss of family providers. Adjusting to these changes in available resources is a complex process. Families will need to continue to meet the basic survival needs of family members, regardless of financial position; however, their consumption patterns will change to accommodate rising or falling income situations.

Research reveals that expenditures by families can be analyzed using the following categories:

- Housing

- Utilities

- Food

- Transportation

- Medical care

- Insurance

- Clothing and personal care

- Education

Although not all-encompassing, these categories allow analysis of family expenditures that cross all socioeconomic levels and address basic survival and social needs of contemporary families. There are several groups that depend on information gathered about these categorical expenditures—marketers, producers, financial institutions, social scientists, and governmental agencies. The data gathered also provide insight on how changes in economic position affect family purchasing.

Food, while essential for survival, also has social implications. One person can comfortably consume only a limited amount of food. However, the type and cost of that food can vary greatly. A fast-food hamburger may be less than $2, but a steak or lobster tail may cost a great deal more. As families move up and down in income levels, the percentage of income spent on food is relatively stable, with slight differences among income levels. Households spend more money on food as incomes increase, but a smaller share of their overall income. The poorest segments of the U.S. population spend between 28% and 43% of their income on food (Tuttle & Kuhns, 2017). Those with the highest incomes spend between 7% and 9%. Middle-income families spend about 13% of their pretax income on food products. While the difference between what is spent on in-home cooking and dining out also differs among income levels, the relatively inexpensive prepared foods available to lower-income budgets do account for a gap in healthfulness.

Access to and use of fresh and wholesome foods is higher among higher-income segments. Housing costs across income levels indicate a steady 25% to 35% expenditure. Families in the lower-income group must spend a slightly larger percentage on housing to meet minimum standards. Those on the other end of the income scale adjust size, materials, and location preferences to maintain their expenses at that level.

> *Bo and Cher have been married for 5 years. They have been living in an apartment that is located close to both of their jobs. Currently their rent and utilities consume about 30% of their combined incomes. Both have just received promotions in their companies and find that their total income has jumped by more than 25%. Although their apartment is still functional for their needs, they feel social pressure to move to a location that reflects their new socioeconomic status. They will be entertaining more. Homeownership is expected of middle management in their social circle. They decide to purchase a home in the suburbs, increasing their housing costs to 35% of their new income and adding commuting expenses on top of that. Getting ahead can often translate into running even faster to maintain expectations.*

Other studies have reported that certain expenditures have marked differences between family income levels. Gambling is one of those choices. Of the families studied, those from low-income groups spent about 10% on recreation and gambling, whereas those in the higher-income groups spent only 4%. However, that 4% was considerably higher in terms of actual dollars. Another expenditure showing differences by income level was tobacco. Households in the middle-income groups spent almost twice as much per week on tobacco as did those in the lower income groups, and they spent more than one-third more than did those in the highest income groups.

So, do families functioning at extreme ends of the socioeconomic scale behave that much differently in the consumption of goods and services in the economic system? Probably not. Families must meet the same basic needs of members. The number of resources available determines which possible choices are attainable— the 75-cent can of generic soda or the $5,000 glass of wine. The selection is then made from the value base of the decision maker.

Thomas J. Stanley (2004) has written some interesting pieces on the spending habits of self-made millionaires. He conducted interviews and gathered survey data from people who had made their own millions, rather than inheriting or winning their fortunes. He found that these subjects live relatively simple lives. They often drive used cars, use coupons when purchasing goods, and reside in middle-class housing. Many even refuse to use debit and credit cards.

Stanley found a marked difference between these self-made men and women. He focused an entire book on these differences (2004). After surveying 1,165 affluent women, he reported that they were more generous, more frugal, and harder working than men in similar situations. They donated an average of 7% to charity, more than three times the amount average families report. These women often mended their own clothing and reported being value-driven purchasers.

Changes in Preference

Economic theory can provide guidelines for both producers and consumers. However, consumers are human and have been known to be fickle. Other than price, there are three less visible factors that impact buying behavior—taste, fashion, and innovation. Individuals express unique preferences when presented with choices. The color of the refrigerator will not impact its performance, yet manufacturers offer several color and material options to customers. The concept of **taste** is an important part of the decision-making process in product selection. Taste is related to sensory response before, during, and after product consumption. Families, over time and when resources are available, develop preferences for brand names, recipes, furniture styles, and even types of toilet paper. The flavor, feel, smell, and aesthetic aspects of products draw different responses from different people. Over time, purchasing these favored products becomes ingrained in personal and family behavior. Price changes may have some impact on families' favorite products, but if a preference is strong enough, they will accommodate price fluctuation.

> **Taste:** a personal preference or liking

Fashion is another deciding factor in product selection that reflects preference; however, fashion is an expression of preference on a much larger scale. Social groups develop preferences that become part of their membership criteria. Clothing is an obvious example of this concept. Skirt length, allowable skin exposure, and width of pant legs are all subject to acceptance or rejection of the social group. Although perfectly functional, pieces of clothing will be thrown away or donated to charity if they no longer reflect the tastes of the group. Seeking acceptance, individuals and families judge their current material possessions and future purchases based on choices made by the majority of their social group.

> **Fashion:** a distinctive or peculiar and often habitual manner or way; mode of action or operation

New products that can function as a replacement of currently preferred products may enter the marketplace. These new choices may be innovative, such as the pop-top aluminum can that replaced the bottle cap, or they may be new flavors, new formulations, or merely packaged differently. Soda producers had to adjust to the emerging popularity of sports drinks to maintain market share. Most introduced their own fortified drinks and even entered the bottled water market to compete in the health-conscious market. Flat-screen TVs have replaced the square or rectangular sets that had been staples in American households.

©iStockphoto.com/Paolo_Toffanin

▶ **Photo 7.2**
Preferences for small, portable pets have increased in metropolitan centers.

Smartphones have infiltrated the everyday lives of Americans across all socioeconomic levels. Portable telephones have been available to U.S. consumers since 1960 but were slow to sell during the end of the last century. Not so anymore. The question has shifted from "Do I need a smartphone?" to "Which smartphone features can't I live without?" Borrowing from the futuristic cartoon *The Jetsons*, one of the most popular uses of the smartphone unit is the visual component. How could this market get any sweeter? Don't forget smartphone accessories! Entire stores are popping up all over the country to help consumers personalize their newest must-have communication tool. Designer cases, antennas, and programmable video games are just a few popular postpurchase options. And entire websites are devoted to the coveted "apps," or applications, that can be purchased or downloaded free of charge to facilitate activities, such as shopping for bargains, finding directions, monitoring the weather, and playing games. The ability to compare product prices, download "coupons," and facilitate point-of-purchase transactions has made the smartphone part of the marketplace, not just a product itself. It is impacting product pricing and availability. Much like the TV set of decades past, the smartphone has moved out of the luxury, want-to-have category into the everyone-needs-to-have level as a staple communication device. This is just one more example of how inventions change both the marketplace and the decision-making processes of consumers.

Smartphones also provide interesting possibilities for social scientists who are interested in how this movement toward constant and convenient communication within families will impact relationships. One area of importance in this type of research is the dependence/independence aspect of adolescent decision making. Now that parents are always just a second away, will adolescents have less motivation to make independent decisions?

Employment

Human labor and skills, when traded for money, fuel the financial stream of an economy. Money available is then spent, saved, loaned, or lost, depending on the behavior of the participant. Companies that determine their products will be in demand will hire employees and maintain production. When their products are no longer in demand, they will cut their workforce, resulting in unemployed family members.

Employment opportunities exist only because there is a demand for labor in the market. This demand for labor is determined by the demand for goods and services. So, families participate on both sides of this equation. Family members provide labor and create demand for goods and services by spending the income their jobs provide. Unemployment of family members results in a reversal of that process. When money is unavailable to exchange for goods and services, families must seek other resources and limit their spending at all levels.

The U.S. labor force consists of all people over the age of 16 who are seeking work or who are already employed, including both men and women and those past the typical retirement age. The labor force is defined and calculated to understand the impact of employment on the economy. On the production side, if people are not employed, they cannot be producing goods and services. On the consumption side, if paychecks are not available, goods and services cannot be purchased. The unemployment rate, or the percentage of people seeking employment but without work at the current time, is another important measure to economists.

Labor force: people ages 16 years or older who are employed or looking for work

Unemployment rate: the percentage of people seeking employment but without work at the current time

Although the goal may be full employment of all those seeking jobs, it is not in the best interest of an economy to be at that point. A desired point supported by most economists and labor analysts is 4% unemployment. With that cushion of unemployed workers, the system can accommodate workers moving in and out of jobs while moderating employment costs.

Unemployment

Unemployment is often categorized into one of three types: frictional, cyclical, or structural. Frictional unemployment includes those workers who have decided to leave one job and look for another. Typically frictionally unemployed workers are out of the labor market for short periods of time. They may be seeking positions of higher status or may be returning to school to enhance their employable skills.

Cyclical unemployment is involuntary and is the result of production lags, recessions, or business restructuring. Some business sectors are more likely to contribute to cyclical unemployment because their success is closely tied to general economic conditions. Examples include automobile production, building construction, and manufacturing. When the economy slumps and money becomes tight, consumers do not buy large-ticket items like homes, cars, appliances, and furniture. Employee layoffs are the result of this drop in demand. Another group highly impacted by cyclical unemployment is young workers with little seniority and those preferring part-time schedules. They are most often the first to be fired and the last to be rehired.

Structural unemployment is also involuntary. It occurs when changes in the economy result in a loss of demand for certain types of jobs. Most common in contemporary America is the restructuring of jobs due to changing technological requirements. Current employees may no longer have adequate skills to operate new computerized systems or may be unwilling to be retrained to accommodate the change. Occasionally, a technological advancement results in the elimination of certain positions or even entire divisions. One computerized software program can accomplish in a matter of seconds what might have taken several payroll managers to enter and calculate manually. Automated telephone answering systems have eliminated the need for humans in many transactions.

Unemployment, regardless of the cause, creates individual and family hardships. Loss of income intensifies the scarcity of family resources, forcing adjustments in expenditures and eliminating many choices available in the decision-making process. Families may need to make severe changes to survive periods of unemployment, such as moving to more affordable housing, selling or giving up existing possessions, and relying on governmental services or the support of other family members. These decisions impact personal self-esteem and strain relationships. Psychologically and physically, unemployment has been shown to be closely related to higher likelihood of cardiovascular disease, psychosomatic disorders, depression, anxiety, and lower life satisfaction (Griep, Hyde, Vantilborgh, Bidee, DeWitte, & Pepermans, 2014).

Frictional unemployment: workers who have decided to leave one job and look for another; typically, frictionally unemployed workers are out of the labor market for short periods of time

Cyclical unemployment: the increase in unemployment that occurs as the economy goes into a slowdown or recession

Structural unemployment: unemployment caused by basic changes in the overall economy, as in demographics, technology, or industrial organization

Seth, 45 years old, had been working in middle management for a large distribution company for more than 20 years. As purchasing over the Internet became the preferred method of product access for most of the consumers in this market, Seth's company lost several large accounts. He was told that his job had been eliminated early last year. Since that time, Seth has been actively seeking other jobs, but he finds that both his age and lack of marketable skills are obstacles. He finds that he has lost much more than his job. He no longer has a routine schedule and finds it difficult to self-manage his activities. His motivation to seek another job is falling with each rejection. His role as provider to his family is gone, and he feels devalued and resentful as his wife and children depend on him more and more for household chores. His circle of friends has disappeared. Colleagues from his previous job have either moved on or have become frustrated with their own situations. Neighbors and family friends are busy working during the day and aren't available when Seth needs their company. Although his wife and children try to be supportive, the changes and restrictions brought on them by his loss of wages have negatively impacted their social status. Seth's depression and mood swings are driving his family further away. Even a new job won't heal all of these wounds.

Unemployment insurance (UI) is a nationwide program created by the Social Security Act of 1935 to provide partial wage replacement to unemployed workers while they conduct an active search for new work. UI is a federal–state program, based on federal law, but executed through state law. Employers finance the UI program through tax contributions. The UI program benefits the individual and the local community. Payments made directly to the individual ensure that at least some of life's necessities, such as food, shelter, and clothing, can be met while looking for work. For the most part, UI benefits are spent in the local community, which helps sustain the economic well-being of local businesses. It is not a 100% replacement program, however, so families must still adjust spending and reevaluate previous budgeting practices.

To receive UI benefits, an individual must meet certain qualifying criteria, including previous earnings guidelines. Once qualified, he must show continued effort to secure a job through documentation of applications and rejections. Because states administer this program, benefits and qualifiers will vary from state to state. All states have maximum time limits for which benefits will be dispersed. The program was designed to be a temporary safety net, not a permanent replacement for earnings.

Other programs, both public and private, are available to displaced workers. Many provide educational and skill-building opportunities while the worker is unemployed.

Women in the Labor Force

While the labor force includes only those actively working or seeking work, participation of women complicates the calculation. In the United States, there is an expectation of choice that is available to females, but not to males. Adult males are generally expected to provide for themselves and their families. Adult females, if they can afford to do so, are allowed to stay home and devote their energies to maintaining the household and participating in the social volunteer network, or to choose to work for a wage in their homes or outside of their homes.

Historically, women have always participated in the work of the family and in the economic system. Their role before the 19th century was often viewed as one of support and team player. Agricultural families survived with cooperative participation of all family members. Women also participated in trade in both production and management capacities long before the women's movement of the mid-1900s. Pre-industrialized Europe relied heavily on female craftswomen and entrepreneurs, depending on the social gender norms of the times. Industrialization and mass production reframed women's participation in the economy, however, and the roles of females have been publicly and privately debated over the last century.

In the United States, relatively few married women worked outside of the home for a wage between the Civil War and World War I. As the social climate changed after the turn of the 20th century, young women who did not choose to marry directly after completing high school in their mid-teens were encouraged to attend business schools, medical schools, and teachers' colleges to become secretaries, nurses, and K–12 teachers. An understood social expectation was for these young women to work in these positions for a few years and then leave the workforce, marry, and raise their families.

During the 1940s, when huge numbers of working men left their jobs to join the armed forces to fight in World War II, women, young and old, were the only pool available to fill empty production and management positions. As the 1950s unfolded, many women left these wage-paying jobs and returned to the home. However, the percentage of women in the labor force in 1947 dropped only 4% from the participation rate during the war. From 1950 to 2001, women have slowly continued to increase in both numbers and percentage points within the U.S. workforce. Currently, 47% of all American wage earners are female. Seven out of 10 mothers are actively employed (U.S. Census Bureau, 2015).

Mary Harshfield finished public school in 1907 at age 16. She entered a local college, or "normal school," to complete training required at that time to teach at both the elementary and high school levels. In 1908, she took her exams, received her teaching certificate, and started teaching at her hometown's rural one-room K–12 school. Three years later, Mary stopped teaching, married a local farmer, and gave birth to 10 children over the next 18 years.

Of Mary's three daughters, one farmed with her husband and raised a family of two daughters. The other two women married and had children, but worked for a wage outside of the home for most of their adult lives. Mary's 16 granddaughters all worked before marriage, and 10 held full-time jobs outside of the home. Of her 25 great-granddaughters, only two did not work full time after their youngest child entered public school. All four generations of women have lived or are living in America's middle class, some in rural areas, others in large cities. This last century has brought about great changes in both the expectations and participation of women in the workplace and their place in the economic system.

Women cite the same two reasons for working outside of the home as their male counterparts: to gain personal satisfaction and to obtain financial resources to support their families. Enrollments and diplomas from colleges and universities indicate that females are just as likely to seek professional training for career development as males. Gender differences within and between certain fields are also narrowing. Males are entering the fields of nursing and education in record numbers, and females are pursuing careers in engineering and technology.

Because it is a choice available to many women, understanding why some wives and mothers work while others don't can be explored using an economic framework (Becker, 1991). The employment decision of a mother is based on a comparison of the value of her work (wage rate, childcare expenses, education capital) with the value of her time at home. The **opportunity cost** of not working is the loss of advancement potential and job skills. The opportunity cost of working is the loss of investment in the home and children. The cost–benefit analysis in this decision depends on several factors: the quality of childcare available, the participation of the father in parenting and housekeeping, personal and social values, and the type of position the mother holds. Professional women, such as lawyers, physicians, and business executives, may face severe setbacks in future advancement possibilities if they choose to leave their positions for any extended period of time. Those employed in other types of jobs may require additional education and training to reenter the job market to ensure that their skill levels are appropriate to the changing technological environments in many fields.

Opportunity cost: an opportunity forgone; what is lost because a decision is made

Women are definitely a key part of the employment picture in the United States. Should the trend of female participation reverse itself, serious implications in production and consumption would result. Should women continue toward full participation, the issues of wage gaps and glass ceilings will magnify in scope. Workplace environments and policy could face dramatic changes to accommodate female preferences and needs.

When the labor force participation rate for women with infants dropped slightly between 1998 and 2000, the media rushed to publish articles and headlines focused on women's innate desire to leave their careers and stay at home with their babies. In reality, the choice to participate in the labor market or not is a reality for all women in the United States. However, it is much more difficult for some than for others to be unemployed. The media's attention at that time was focused on white, married, middle-class, professional women leaving their jobs behind to focus on their families and children. Unless many working women are willing to rely on governmental subsidies, they do not have the choice to leave their paying jobs. Single women have little or no other financial support available to them. Those married to men working in middle- to lower-income-producing jobs face drastic reductions in living standards should they quit working.

Dickson (2004) stated that the media's report on women's desire to leave the rat race of the business world was oversimplified. A survey of senior female executives in large U.S. companies revealed that these women want the top job just as much as their male counterparts. Both men and women in this survey reported problems with balancing their professional and personal lives. Contemporary men are more involved with their families and household management than those of decades ago. These findings diffuse the belief that women will be leaving the workforce in significant numbers in the near future.

Adolescents on the Job

> Brock works evenings and weekends at a local supermarket to help his single mother pay the bills. Sharon works afternoons at a local bank through a vocational program at her high school. The money she makes is added to her personal college fund. Tyson works in fast food whenever possible and fills in other free time with various jobs—lawn care, childcare, errands, and deliveries. His money goes toward maintenance of and improvements on a sports car he purchased earlier this year. All three teens are juggling work and school demands for different reasons. They are part of the powerful adolescent job force and consumer movement in the economic system.

Another labor pool and consumer group is increasing in importance in the U.S. economy. Adolescents are holding down part- and even full-time jobs while completing high school requirements. More than one-half of American adolescents are employed—a much larger percentage than in any other developed country (U.S. Bureau of Labor Statistics, 2015). U.S. teens spent $155 billion in 2000. Their participation in the marketplace has earned them the label *skippies*, or school kids with purchasing power (Quart, 2003). Teens in middle- and upper-class families work for spending money to increase their material possessions and to build savings for the anticipated expenses of higher education. Those from families struggling financially often work to contribute to the family income. A relatively small percentage of teen workers are seeking enhancement of future career skills. Regardless of the motivation, adolescents are participating in the workforce in rapidly growing numbers.

The jobs that adolescents typically hold are usually limited to lower-paying, lower-skill positions in production, sales, and services. They are usually the first to be fired when demand drops and the last to be rehired. Teen participation in the workforce is therefore a complex concept. National teen unemployment rates are reported in much the same way general rates are gathered and analyzed. Although many teens work around the calendar, the greatest surge of teens in the workforce is seen during the summer months. Their paychecks continue to play an important part in the overall economic picture of the United States as they buy goods and services and participate in the tax and financial bases of the national economy.

Experts disagree with regard to perceived risks and benefits for working teens. Some believe that working modestly, or for just a few hours weekly, teaches responsibility and social skills and occupies idle time that might be spent in less productive activities. Managing their time and money earned is also cited as a positive benefit for adolescent employees. Job experience during high school may also provide a teen with valuable work experience and insight into possible future vocations.

Others argue that working during high school undermines a teenager's educational and emotional development. Studies have found that teenagers working more than 20 hours per week were more likely to have lower grades, higher alcohol use, and inadequate relationships with parents and families (Greenhouse, 2001). Others report that students who work long hours often lack time and energy for homework and miss out on social and intellectual skill development through participation in school extracurricular activities.

Money

Money: a good or token that functions as a medium of exchange that is socially and legally accepted in payment for goods and services and settlement of debts

Money is anything that can be used for exchange. In the United States, buyers and sellers agree that **currency**—bills and coins—have inherent value and can be used in the exchange of goods and services. Some people believe that this currency must be supported by a cache of precious metals, such as gold and silver. The true value of paper and coin currency lies within its value of exchange. If you were suddenly transported to another planet carrying $1,000 in U.S. currency, you would find it impossible to use that money. Even traveling to other countries makes this concept

---

REALITY CHECK

Women's Weight in Economic Recovery

A major difference in the unfolding of the 2008 recession from previous experiences is the role that working women played before and during the meltdown, and their position in the recovery process. Forecasts and reports did not always acknowledge these unique impacts. For instance, households with two adult earners were less severely distressed by unemployment than those dependent on one income. If one partner in a dual-earning relationship lost his or her job, resulting unemployment benefits were combined with the remaining partner's income, softening the overall loss of money. Even if both earners faced unemployment, two unemployment checks were better than one.

Male-centered employment, such as in building and manufacturing, saw heavier job losses than did jobs typically held by women, like those in education, healthcare, and other services. Working women stabilized their family economic situations and were poised to pull the country forward as jobs slowly returned. More educated and more highly represented in the fields projected to grow most rapidly, women have been flipping the balance of financial power within their family units.

Dual-earning families, however, also have suffered because of their initial earning position. Many had purchased homes and used credit based on the income of both adults. Overall, this presented higher debt loads and heavier losses in real estate value of mortgaged properties.

The economy of the United States and other developed countries is increasingly dependent on the labor and spending of working wives and mothers. The next generations may no longer view female employment as secondary or optional to family functioning.

apparent. Countries participating in the European Union have agreed on the euro as their accepted currency. Few vendors in those countries will accept American or even British money for purchases. You must exchange foreign currency for domestic currency to participate in trade of any kind. Even if you use your debit or credit card for purchases in a country that does not use your country's currency, a conversion will be made through the card company to enable the transaction to be completed. Although Ireland and Scotland embraced the euro currency even though England did not, now that Great Britain, as a whole, voted to leave the European Union in 2016, Ireland and Scotland face a return to using the British pound sterling as currency.

Currency: something (e.g., coins, treasury notes, banknotes) that is in circulation as a medium of exchange

Considering the vast numbers of different currencies across the globe and the fact that even something like a pack of cigarettes can be used as exchange currency if the two people involved in the trade agree on it, how can we determine what the value of money actually is?

A $5 bill is worth whatever you can trade it for in any given circumstance. A currency's value is measured by the goods and services it will purchase in the marketplace. Economists define money in terms of its function. Money is used as a medium of exchange, a store of value, and a unit of account. Families are involved with all three monetary functions.

Throughout recorded history, there is evidence that once a society formed its general basis, a method to facilitate the exchange of goods and services emerged. Originally, it took the form of **barter**, where one good is directly exchanged for another. For instance, Neighbor A helps fix a fence for Neighbor B and is repaid when Neighbor B helps fix Neighbor A's broken axle. Or a chicken is traded for a sack of seed. The problem with this type of exchange system is that it works only when individuals have simultaneous, seemingly equal needs and resources. Monetary currency eliminates the need for the perfect time and situation. It serves as a medium of exchange that is accepted in all transactions, by all those involved, regardless of time, place, or need.

Barter: to trade by exchanging one commodity for another; to trade or exchange

To function as a medium of exchange, currency must hold value over time; that is, it must be a store of value. Other assets function in the same way, but are not as **liquid**, or as easily converted. For instance, a family may possess a home that is of value over time. That home could even increase in value, but until it is sold or borrowed against, there is nothing to exchange in transactions. Money is always liquid, although its value decreases with inflation and increases with appreciation, so there is some fluctuation to consider.

Liquidity: an asset's ability to *quickly* be liquidated or converted through an action of buying or selling without causing a significant movement in the price and with minimum loss of value

When money is supported by a tangible resource, like gold or silver, the economy is on a commodity standard. The United States used to back its money with gold but now operates on a paper standard. U.S. money is backed by the people's willingness to accept it and by the strength of the nation's economy. Across the globe, the strength of the U.S. dollar is calculated against all other foreign currencies and markets. One U.S. dollar may be equal to 1.0 euro on one day and fall to an exchange of 0.8 the next week. If a dozen silk sweaters were priced at 4,600 euros and a U.S. buyer placed the order in the second week instead of the first, his or her company would pay $1,128 more (in U.S. currency) because of this change in the exchange rate. That would translate into a probable increase in the price of each sweater to the U.S. consumer of almost 25%.

Money, in the form of currency or electronic transfer, provides a common measure of the value of goods and services being exchanged. Countries express this measure of value using a base unit. In the United States, the base unit is the dollar. In Japan, the base unit is the yen. With a base unit, the value of everything can be expressed in terms of that unit (e.g., a car might be worth 40,000 times a dollar unit). Having this base unit makes it easy to create comparisons among the values of goods and services. Being aware of the value or price of something, in terms of money, gives both the seller and the buyer a basis for decision making. It provides a common denominator for both sides. This function of money, however, can be manipulated and misleading. Higher prices create the aura of higher quality and value, when that is not always the case.

To participate in the national economy as consumers, families must understand the banking system, even if they do not have checking and saving accounts. Money circulates through the banking system, thus providing storage and distribution functions. A bank receives deposits from individuals, families, and other groups. Banks store money and even pay interest to depositors for certain types of accounts. Banks then put those monetary deposits back into the economic system through loans to individuals and groups. The financial institution must keep some of the deposit available for depositors, should they want to make a withdrawal, but most of the deposited money is recirculated into the economy. Banks also provide a method for storing and growing wealth.

> Jess has $25 directly deposited from his paycheck each week into a savings plan that earns 5% interest annually. At the end of a month, he has $100 in that account. At the end of a year, he will have approximately $1,200, plus the interest his deposits have earned over time.
>
> Jade buys a bracelet for $1,200 on credit at the beginning of the year. She pays $100 per month, plus 8% interest.
>
> Who made the wiser decision in terms of using that extra $25 per week? The answer isn't that obvious. Jess will have approximately $1,350. Jade will have a bracelet with no debt attached. If the value of that bracelet has increased to more than $1,350, her investment, should she agree to sell the jewelry, would have been more profitable. Participating in the investment realm requires an understanding of inflation and utility.

Inflation: an increase in the supply of currency or credit relative to the availability of goods and services, resulting in higher prices

Inflation occurs when there is an increase in the general level of prices. Inflation of prices has become an expected phenomenon in our economy. An automobile that sold for $5,000 30 years ago may cost $25,000 today. That looks like a tremendous leap, but when distributed over that many years, it lessens in intensity. An economy with an inflation rate of 2% to 3% per year doesn't have a serious inflation problem. However, when prices jump across the board, by 7% to 10% or more, an economy can fall apart.

Inflation impacts some income groups more drastically than others. Individuals and families living on fixed incomes, such as Social Security payments, must cut their buying because their income will not rise as prices do when inflation is active. Over time, this will result in dramatic declines in their standard of living. For this reason, cost of living adjustments (COLAs) are usually instituted each year for Social Security recipients. However, those adjustments have not kept pace with the inflation rates, and a general decline in purchasing power has resulted for this group of citizens. Another group with similar concerns is that of employees who contract for wages and salaries over long periods of time. They, too, will be negatively impacted in times of inflation. If a service union agrees to an annual wage increase of 3% over the next 5 years and inflation averages 4%, those workers will experience a decline in buying power each and every year under that contract.

Much like a typical faucet/drain arrangement, money flows into the economic system in the form of wages, salaries, winnings, and inheritance, and flows out into the marketplace through purchases made. The economy may become unbalanced if both the faucet and the drain are not in equal use. The growing dependence on credit has impacted this balance already and threatens to cripple the economy if unchecked. The growing reluctance to invest and save money when interest rates are low also impacts the balance of money flow through the overall system.

> The Martin family is thinking about buying a new 3-D TV set. They are thinking about either taking the money needed to purchase this item from their savings account or buying the TV on a 1-year, interest-free loan promotion that the store is offering. If the interest being paid on their current savings account is less than the inflation rate of the coming year, it would probably be a better decision to withdraw the price from savings and buy the TV. The TV will cost more next year than the money would have made in the bank, and there is no accurate way to judge whether the family's income can support the new loan, even interest free.

When interest being paid on savings is lower than anticipated inflation, consumers are enticed into spending more and saving less. This trend would boost the economy in terms of production, employment, sales tax collected, and standard of living, but reduce the amount of money banks could loan to companies and individuals.

Exchanging Nonmonetary Resources

Not all exchanges of human resources take a financial form. Some family members may exchange childcare with other families in a cooperative arrangement. Other family members may exchange favors with neighbors or extended family that would otherwise require an exchange of money.

> Grace belongs to a group of 20 adult women in her neighborhood. Each woman shops for and cooks one large meal for 20 families, packaging and freezing

these meals in individual family-size portions. Once per month, these meals are exchanged, and each family ultimately has dinner for every working day for an entire month. Instead of 20 individual families preparing meals every evening after a long day at work, each family is involved in only one large-scale preparation at a convenient time. This arrangement saves time and energy when both may be at their lowest availability. However, this effort requires great coordination and cooperation.

A more common cooperative arrangement among families is that of carpooling children to school and activities. By sharing the responsibility, time, and automotive costs, more time is available for other tasks. This, however, is reflective of a worldview (see Chapter 1) that sees time as "manageable." It would not make sense to someone who views time as uncontrollable.

These types of exchanges are impossible to calculate because there is no common unit involved for comparison of value. A family with rich connections to other family and community nonmonetary forms of exchange will have more resources available in their decision-making process and may accomplish more over time than a family that depends wholly on goods and services purchased through the marketplace. A young working couple with a relative or friend who is willing to care for their young children without pay may translate into thousands of dollars more in annual net income for that couple. However, this type of nonmonetary service will usually require the exchange of other resources, such as time, energy, and emotional support. The value and costs of these types of exchanges cannot be calculated in an economic system that is dependent on the dollar as a unit of exchange. These intangible resources may really be priceless.

We have explored the interconnections and interdependency of families and the economic system. They are inseparable in the context of family resource management and of major importance in family decision making. But to understand the connection between these two entities, it is important to understand how family decisions, collectively, impact something as complex and worldly as the global economy.

FAMILIES IN THE ECONOMY

Household: a group of individuals occupying a house, apartment, group of rooms, or a single room that is considered a housing unit

Households constitute the largest spending group in the nation's economy, purchasing more goods and services than businesses, government, and foreign consumers combined (Welch & Welch, 2004). The United States had 126,000,000 households in 2016 (U.S. Census Bureau, 2015). The census categorizes a household as one or more people occupying a housing unit, such as a house or an apartment. These individuals do not need to be related to be grouped into the same household, so these data are not pure family data. As of 2016, the average household size was 2.6 people, slightly lower than in previous decades.

Data are gathered concerning the income within these households to analyze the impact of household financial management on the national economy and public services provided. Most of these existing households are operating on earned

WORLDVIEW

Tanshin Funin

Almost half a million married employees in Japan live separately from their families because they have been transferred by their employers in an expected system of worker development. Many Japanese firms follow a practice of developing employee skills by rotating workers from one job to another, from one department to another, and eventually from one office to another. This process provides economic benefits for the employee moving up in the company, but has substantial social ramifications. Single posting, or *tanshin funin*, is especially common among employees between the ages of 35 and 55. They establish small living quarters, often provided by the company, and live there during the workweek. If possible, they travel to their family's home on weekends and company holidays.

Employees involved in this practice accept it because it involves promotion. They are unable to move their families with them for several reasons. The housing market in Japan is tight, and finding appropriate housing for spouses and children is difficult. It is also common for workers in this age group to be living with and partially supporting their aging parents. Relocation of these elderly family members would involve medical and social difficulties.

Education, however, is an even bigger obstacle to family relocation. Admission to middle and high schools is based on test performance. Once students are admitted, leaving and finding comparable schooling opportunities would be virtually impossible. Living with both parents must be weighed against the opportunity costs of disrupting the children's educational opportunities and possibly limiting their future access to prestigious universities. Thus, mothers and children most often stay behind. This situation has been created by employment practices, housing shortages, and an inflexible educational system. Choices available in the family decision-making process have been greatly limited by the economic environment (Sugimoto, 1997).

and investment income. The remaining households are receiving Social Security or transfer payments from federal and state aid programs. There has been a growing reliance on transfer payments over the last few decades. These include old-age, survivor, and disability insurance provided by the Social Security Act; unemployment and disability benefits to workers; public employee retirement benefits and veteran's benefits; and public assistance. The forecast is for even greater dependence on transfer payments as the Baby Boomers enter retirement.

Household incomes differ greatly from one unit to another. Households of married couples report much higher average incomes than do those headed by a single female—almost twice as high. Other factors that seem to impact household income are the age of family members, the education level of family adults, and the geographical location of the household.

Economists are, of course, interested in how households spend their incomes. Often, this is analyzed in terms of purchases of **durable goods, nondurable goods,** and services. Durable goods are expected to be used for more than a year. Automobiles, homes, furniture, and appliances are typical durable goods

Durable goods: goods that have a life span of 3 or more years

Nondurable goods: items that generally last for only a short time (3 years or less)

purchases. Things with shorter useful life spans, or nondurable purchases, include gasoline, food, and hygiene products. Services, especially medical services, have increased in total expenditures dramatically over the last few years.

Household spending habits and trends help economists predict future economic developments and anticipate changes in the production of, distribution of, and demand for goods and services. This analysis is predicated on the belief that individuals and families make economic decisions based on their desire to maximize their economic well-being. This balancing process is evident in the family decision-making process central to this textbook. This balance requires weighing advantages, benefits, disadvantages, costs, satisfaction, and impact of goals with each important decision regarding resource allocation within families.

SUMMARY

Individuals and families interact with the national and global economies on a daily basis. This relationship is interdependent, as the economy relies on family members as both consumers and workers. Singly, one family's decisions will have little, if any, impact on even the local economy. Together, however, family households drive the U.S. economy. Buying, selling, working, and exchanging nonmonetary resources are all integral actions within the overall economic system. Family decision making, in terms of resource acquisition and expenditures, results in better choices and long-term planning when basic economic principles are understood and managed.

QUESTIONS FOR REVIEW AND DISCUSSION

1. How does the concept of conspicuous consumption impact your choices of clothing? Career? Housing?

2. There is great debate across U.S. college campuses about students working more and devoting less time and energy to study. How would your experience differ if you were not allowed to make the choice to work or were not permitted to work while you attend college classes?

3. How would your life change if you were to suddenly inherit a large sum of money?

Would this change your basic goals and aspirations?

4. Many people propose that contemporary consumers are becoming immune to the lure of sale prices in marketing. How do you and your friends and family view price reductions, and how does anticipation of sale prices impact your purchasing decisions?

5. How might wages in your community be impacted by the closure of a major employer and a surge of unemployed workers?

CHAPTER EIGHT

THE IMPACT OF SOCIETY ON FAMILY DECISIONS

Objectives
Individuals and the Tax System
   Federal Taxes
   State and Local Taxes
   Social Security
   Medicare
   Unemployment Insurance
Government-Supported Assistance
   Programs
Worldview
   Health and Human Services
   The Department of Agriculture
   The Food and Drug Administration
In the News
   Consumer Protection
Reality Check
Privately Funded Programs
Compulsory Education
   History
   The Federal Level
   The State Level
   The Community Level
   Family Involvement
   Alternatives to Public Education
   Making Educational Choices
Supply and Demand: An Application in
   Education
Summary
Questions for Review and Discussion

Objectives

- Understand the impact of legislated consumer protection laws on the choices that families have available in the decision-making process.

- Understand, contrast, and compare educational alternatives available in the United States.

- Be aware of individual and family tax liabilities.

- Be able to identify resources provided through governmental funding.

- Understand the importance of linking assistance available and existing family needs.

I am proud to be paying taxes in the United States. The only thing is I could be just as proud for half of the money.

—Arthur Godfrey

Families living in the United States work within specific legal parameters and social expectations that have evolved over the last two centuries. Understanding the obligations and benefits of living in such a society is a complex process. In this chapter, we explore four primary connections between families and the local, regional, and national social systems they contribute to and benefit from. These social constructions have tremendous impact on the choices available to decision makers as they struggle to meet needs with limited resources. These constructions include tax obligations, compulsory education, government-supported resource programs, and consumer protection legislation.

INDIVIDUALS AND THE TAX SYSTEM

Most employees remember the shock they experienced when they opened the envelope holding their very first paycheck. Although many realize that taxes will be taken out of their earnings, the realization of just how much those taxes will reduce the check is usually disheartening. Americans realize many benefits in exchange for the taxes they pay. Some argue the disparity of the tax system, feeling that people within other groups receive more than their fair share of these benefits. Regardless, the informed taxpayer has the ability to plan effectively for payment of his or her tax liability.

Federal Taxes

Income tax, Social Security, and Medicare are the three primary types of federal taxes that wage earners pay. Employees working for wages and salaries rarely have to manage the regular payment of these taxes. Employers are required to deduct employee tax liabilities during the payroll process and to deposit those deductions directly into government accounts. The employee, however, provides the information necessary to ensure that the proper amount is deducted regularly by completing and submitting a W-4 Form (www.irs.gov/pub/irs-pdf/fw4.pdf). By answering questions concerning family situation and obligation, a worker completing this form provides a number of dependents that should be used in the tax calculation each pay period. That number is used to determine how much income tax should be deposited.

> *Carlos is a single accountant with no dependents. He will have a higher tax liability than his friend Jonathan, who has a family of four. The American tax system considers the additional needs of children and dependents and utilizes that implicit value in calculating tax liability. Both men make the same amount of money, so they would seemingly have the same tax liability. However, Jonathan's cost of living is higher due to the needs of his family. When filing yearly income taxes, Carlos and Jonathan will enter their income and then calculate their deductions to determine their actual liability. Assuming that Carlos will have a higher liability, it is important that he deposit more each month to meet that liability. Otherwise*

he may need to come up with a large amount of money at that point to fulfill his obligation, and he may be penalized for not depositing more each month.

The government will refund any prepaid taxes that are overpaid; however, it will not pay interest on that amount. The Internal Revenue Service (IRS) will, however, charge the taxpayer interest and penalties for unpaid taxes. It is in the best interest of all taxpayers to be aware of their obligations and to be honest in each calculation. The IRS of the federal government receives quarterly and annual reports on employee earnings from employers. Those figures are used to substantiate employees' liability and deposits.

Self-employed people must also pay income taxes. Their rates are identical to those working for others, but they must handle the deposits and reporting themselves. Because employers match their employee federal tax deposits, the self-employed may seem unfairly taxed because they must pay the entire amount. There is an adjustment within the tax-figuring process to compensate for this, but income tax liability is often seen as an obstacle to self-employment.

Taxpayers receive goods and services in exchange for their tax dollars. Money collected by the federal government is used to fund a multitude of public benefits, as illustrated in Figure 8.1. During times of war and terrorist alerts, a larger portion

Figure 8.1 Federal Expenditures of Tax Dollars

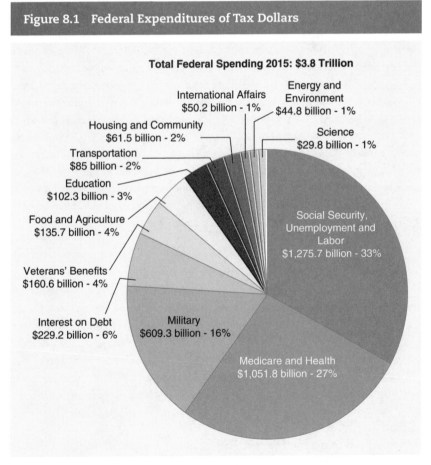

Total Federal Spending 2015: $3.8 Trillion

International Affairs $50.2 billion - 1%
Energy and Environment $44.8 billion - 1%
Science $29.8 billion - 1%
Housing and Community $61.5 billion - 2%
Transportation $85 billion - 2%
Education $102.3 billion - 3%
Food and Agriculture $135.7 billion - 4%
Veterans' Benefits $160.6 billion - 4%
Interest on Debt $229.2 billion - 6%
Military $609.3 billion - 16%
Social Security, Unemployment and Labor $1,275.7 billion - 33%
Medicare and Health $1,051.8 billion - 27%

Source: Used with permission of the National Priorities Project, 2015, nationalpriorities.org.

of tax dollars is channeled to military spending. Federally funded programs directly impacting families include education, job training, employment, health, justice, environmental protection, transportation, and community development. Other programs with broader impact, but less specific to families, include veterans' benefits and services, international affairs, science, space, technology, and the general costs of running governmental offices and programs. Agricultural support, energy programs, and housing programs are also funded with tax dollars.

State and Local Taxes

Individual states have the right to tax residents' income, although not all do so. Some states have no income tax liabilities or assess state income tax only on dividends and interest received during the year. All other states have individual formulas for calculating a resident's income tax liability (see http://taxfoundation.org for yearly updated state individual income tax rates and brackets). Funds collected through state income tax are used to support a variety of public programs and services. State and local taxes are used to support community programs, parks, and other public resources.

Individuals residing in and/or working in states that levy an income tax also must prepay their liability. Based on the information provided by the employee on Form W-4, state tax rates are used to calculate a probable tax liability. Money is deducted from each paycheck and is deposited in the state's account to ensure that the employee meets his or her year-end liability. If the taxpayer owes even more than he or she deposited over the year, that difference must be paid on or before the tax-filing deadline. There may be late payment penalties on underpayments.

Communities may levy taxes on real estate, automobiles, and other personal property of citizens. This tax money is utilized for local and community purposes, such as street and road improvements, school funding, and protective services. These taxes are usually figured on an annual basis, with payment due at the beginning of the tax year, in installments during the year, or it may be collected in the year following the actual assessed year. Owners are responsible for payment of these taxes. However, many mortgage companies will pay the yearly real estate tax and collect that money with mortgage payments to ensure that the property is current on the tax rolls.

> *Jasmine is considering purchasing a townhome and moving from her rental apartment. She thinks it would be a good time to start investing for the long-term. As she is working with a bank mortgage officer, she realizes that the monthly loan payment for this townhome would be just $850. Currently she pays $1,000 per month to rent her apartment. She is excited to buy! However, she would also need to purchase home owners' insurance and pay local property taxes if she owns the townhome. With the loan payment, she would need almost $1,500 per month. In addition, Jasmine would be responsible for all exterior maintenance of her townhome and pay a monthly fee for yard care. Ownership would increase her monthly housing expense by more than 50%.*

States and communities also have the right to impose sales tax on consumer purchases. These taxes impact all citizens equally and have a direct impact on family financial resources. The location of the actual purchase determines which tax rate applies. For instance, if the city closest to you has a 5% state sales tax rate and a 1% city rate, qualifying purchases made by you in that city will have an additional 6% added to their price. A $1.00 pen costs you $1.06. However, if you buy that same pen at a convenience store just outside the city limit, you would only pay the state rate; thus, the final cost would be $1.05. That difference may not seem large, but when you are buying larger-ticket items, such as furniture and automobiles, it can make a large difference. For instance, 1% of a $2,000 sofa is $20. On a $30,000 automobile purchase, you would pay $300 more if purchased in a city with that 1% sales tax.

When a consumer is traveling, local taxes can have a substantial impact on the travel budget. Many cities collect a tourism tax on hotel, travel, and recreational purchases of visitors. For instance, San Antonio has a hotel tax rate of 16.75%. A hotel room priced at $100 per night would actually cost a traveler $116.75 for each night's stay. Communities often use these types of taxes to fund construction and maintenance of facilities that both draw the travelers into their city and provide those visitors with access to things like sports, cultural events, and meeting facilities.

Social Security

Federal tax liability is somewhat proportional. If you make more money, you will probably pay a higher percentage in taxes. Social Security is a uniform rate for all. Employees currently pay 6.2% of their gross income into the Social Security fund. Employers match that amount, for a total of 12.4% of earnings. The total Social Security tax liability is capped, however, because individuals only pay this amount on the first $127,200 (2017 level) of labor earnings.

> *Employee A makes $30,000 annually and pays $1,860 into the Social Security fund. Employee B makes $60,000, and $3,720 is her Social Security liability. Both have contributed 6.2% of their wages. If Employee C makes $150,000, his or her liability stops at $127,200, so he or she pays $7,886.40 into Social Security. That translates into 5.3% of total wages. Those in the higher earnings bracket ultimately pay a lower percentage of their income to Social Security tax.*

In exchange for the money paid into the Social Security fund, taxpayers receive many benefits, although usually deferred. The Social Security Administration pays retirement, disability, and family and survivor benefits. The most well-known benefit is the retirement income provided. Wage earners who have paid into the Social Security fund for at least the minimum length of time (determined by a point system) and reach the official age of retirement are eligible for monthly income payments as determined by benefit calculations. Currently employees earn "credits"—up to four each year. In 2017, one credit was earned for each $1,300 of wages or self-employment income. Most people need 40 credits, earned over their working lifetime, to receive retirement benefits. Once enough credits have been accumulated, benefit amounts are determined using the average earnings over the entire working lifetime. Theoretically, if you made more than your spouse, you will collect a higher monthly amount. The amount possible, however, is capped.

The age of retirement will also impact the amount you will receive in Social Security benefits. Currently, if you were born before 1938, your full retirement age will be 65. This age increases gradually to 67 for people born in 1960 or later. Some people retire before their full retirement age—if you do so, you will receive a reduced rate of payments. If you continue working after your full retirement age, you can receive higher benefits because of additional earnings and special credits for delayed retirement. Individuals must consider health, earning potential, and life expectancy when contemplating retirement before they reach the full retirement age.

> Sal has just turned 62. If he retires now, he will receive a monthly check for $1,108. If he waits until his 65th birthday, he will receive $1,573 each month, a difference of $465 monthly. Assume that he does retire at age 62. When Sal reaches 75 years of age, he will have received approximately $173,000 (with no adjustment for increases). Assume also that his twin brother, Ed, waits to retire until he is 65 years of age. When Ed turns 75, he will have collected approximately $188,000. So, even though Ed will have been receiving benefits for only 10 years and Sal will have been retired for 13 years, Ed will surpass his brother in benefits received from Social Security.

This scenario impacts the decision-making process dramatically if all other variables are equal—personal health, health of spouse, and goals and objectives. If Sal's decision to retire early reflects his concern that his wife's health is failing, he may be willing to forgo the chance to collect more money for the opportunity to spend 3 more years with her while she is still able to enjoy their time together.

The concept of longevity has negatively impacted the Social Security program. When the program was originally introduced in 1935, the average life expectancy of working men (few women were considered in this plan) was not much over 65 years of age. The program was intended to provide a stable cushion of income to the elderly during the last few years of their life. Today's life expectancy for both men and women is approaching 80 years of age. On the average, then, retirees can be expected to draw from Social Security funds for at least 10 years, many for much longer. Today's retiree may well take out of the system more than he or she paid into it over his or her working life. That focuses partial weight for supporting this program onto payments made into the system by current wage earners. How will the pool grow large enough to support the current workforce when they reach retirement age if their funds are being used and not invested? It is forecasted by the Social Security Administration (2016) that by 2034, the Social Security Trust Fund will be entirely depleted. By then, the number of Americans at retirement age will have doubled. There will not be enough younger people working to pay all of the benefits owed. Social Security, a compact between generations, is facing serious future problems.

Many current retirees are finding that Social Security benefits are not enough to cover their necessary expenses. Retirees can continue to work and draw their full benefits at the same time if they retire after age 65. If they opt for retirement earlier, there is a limit on how much can be earned without negatively impacting the monthly payment received.

Because the Social Security legislation was passed during a time when relatively few married females were in the workforce, a provision for wives who had not earned their own qualifying points was created. Although previously assumed that the nonworking spouse would be the woman, the terminology is "spouse," so the same provisions and regulations apply to all spouses, male or female. A spouse will receive 50% of the retired worker's full (age 65) benefit unless the spouse begins collecting benefits before reaching full retirement age. In that case, the amount of the spouse's benefit is permanently reduced by a percentage based on the number of months before he or she reaches age 65. If the spouse begins receiving benefits at age 62, the benefit amount would be 37.5%.

▶ **Photo 8.1** The future of Social Security is questionable.

If the spouse has worked and accumulated enough points, she is eligible to receive the full amount calculated. If that amount is less than 50% of his or her spouse's benefit, the larger amount will be provided.

> *Marjorie did not work for a wage outside of her home. When her husband retired, he qualified for a monthly Social Security payment of $900. She is entitled to collect a payment of $450 based on 50% of his benefit. Joan did work for a long enough period of time to accumulate the necessary points to qualify for her own Social Security benefit. Her earnings history resulted in an initial monthly check of $750. Her husband collects $1,600 each month from Social Security. His record entitles Joan to a payment of $800 each month. She will forego the payment based on her own earnings to collect the larger check. She cannot receive both.*

The term *spouse* also refers to an ex-wife or ex-husband in many cases. If you are divorced (even if you have remarried), your ex-spouse may qualify for benefits on your record if you are age 62 or older. To qualify on your record, your ex-spouse must

- Have been married to you for at least 10 years

- Be at least 62 years old

- Be unmarried

- Not be eligible for an equal or higher benefit on his or her own or someone else's Social Security record

If your former spouse continues to work while receiving benefits, the same earning limits apply to him or her as apply to you. The amount of benefits your divorced spouse gets has no effect on the amount of benefits you or your current spouse may receive.

Social Security also has a **disability benefit** available to those with qualifying point accumulation (currently 40 credits, 20 of which were earned in the last 10 years, ending with the year you became disabled; younger workers may qualify with fewer credits). Once disabled, a qualified worker must wait for 6 months to receive disability benefits. At that point, it must be determined and documented that the worker has a physical or mental impairment that is expected to keep him or her from doing "substantial" work for a year or more or is expected to die. The financial support provided through this benefit is not expected to fully replace one's prior earnings, but rather is treated as a supplement, much like disability insurance plans.

Much like Social Security retirement, spouses and children may qualify for disability payments under the primary wage earner's account. Current or divorced spouses, minor children, or adult children disabled before age 22 may receive benefit payments. Each may qualify for up to 50% of the worker's benefit amount. The total amount disbursed depends on how many family members qualify.

Paulette, age 42, was diagnosed with a degenerative bone disease. Her monthly income averaged about $4,000. Although in pain, she continued to work full time until it became impossible for her to make the trip from her home to the workplace. She tried working from a home office, but that also became impossible. Six months ago, she applied for government disability benefits. She has met all necessary criteria and will begin receiving a check for about $1,400 each month from the Social Security Administration. This payment will help her meet expenses, but other sources of support will be necessary to sustain her current standard of living. Although she did not choose to do it, she could have also opted for disability insurance through her employer as part of her benefits package. That extra money monthly would help balance her previous income.

Survivor benefits are also provided to qualifying workers through the Social Security Administration. Once a person is dead, certain members of the deceased's family may be eligible for monthly payments:

- Spouses age 60 or older, or 50 or older if disabled (including divorced spouses, if the marriage lasted at least 10 years)

- Spouses of any age, if caring for their children under the age of 16

- Unmarried children under 18 (including stepchildren, grandchildren, step-grandchildren, or adopted children) who are still in school (or up to age 19 if still in school)

- Adult children who become disabled before the age of 22

There is also a one-time death benefit paid to the surviving spouse of all qualified workers. Currently this benefit is $255.

Employees currently in the workforce can view the amount taken out of their paycheck to fund Social Security payments in two ways. First, it allows them to eventually qualify for retirement, disability, and survivor benefits—a type of insurance. Second, it provides the money necessary to fund these benefits for friends and family members who have already met qualifying criteria—social responsibility. The question looming over the system is whether money will be available to fund benefits when current workers fulfill their own qualifying criteria in decades to come.

Medicare

Like Social Security deposits, employee wages are subject to Medicare taxes through a straight percentage calculation (1.45%). Employers match employee contributions, so the pool of funds to support this benefit is 2.9% of employee income. Unlike Social Security, there is no annual wage limit. Thus, Medicare liability is calculated evenly among the poor, middle class, and wealthy. The money collected is used to fund the Medicare health insurance program available to qualifying workers 65 years of age or older. There are certain disabilities that qualify individuals under the age of 65, including permanent kidney failure requiring dialysis or a kidney transplant.

WHAT INDIVIDUALS PAY WHEN PARTICIPATING IN THE ORIGINAL MEDICARE PLAN

Qualifying individuals select doctors, specialists, and medical facilities that accept Medicare patients. Generally, a fee is charged each time a service is provided.

Covered Expenses:

Hospital Stays
Semiprivate room, meals, general nursing, services, and supplies.

Skilled Nursing Facility Care
Semiprivate room, meals, skilled nursing, and rehabilitative services (only after related 3-day inpatient hospital stays).

Home Health Care
Part-time or intermittent skilled nursing care and home health aide services, physical therapy, occupational therapy, speech-language therapy, medical social services, durable medical equipment, medical supplies, and other services.

Hospice Care
Drugs for symptom control and pain relief, medical and support services from a Medicare-approved hospice, and other services not otherwise covered by Medicare.

Blood
Pints of blood received during a hospital or skilled nursing facility stay.

Participant Co-Pay or Deductibles

Like private health insurance programs, participants are expected to pay a base amount each benefit period. A benefit period begins the day one enters the hospital or skilled nursing facility and ends when one hasn't received any hospital care for 60 days in a row. If someone enters a hospital after one benefit period has ended, a new benefit period begins, triggering a new deductible.

Unemployment Insurance

In general, states and the federal government work together to provide unemployment benefits to eligible workers who are unemployed through no fault of their own. States, under federal guidelines, set eligibility criteria and collect payroll taxes from employers to manage this program. In most states, employees do not pay into this fund. Although utilized as an important part of a family's coping strategy during times of unemployment, this fund is not intended to provide full compensation and is limited in scope.

Base period: a period of time that is used as a measurement yardstick for economic data; a base period may be a month, a year, or an average of years

To be eligible for unemployment benefits, the worker must have established at least a 1-year period of time, or a base period, to qualify for compensation. Most states use the first four out of the last five completed calendar quarters prior to filing of the claim. It must be established that the worker was not responsible for his or her situation. Newly unemployed workers must contact the state unemployment insurance agency as soon as possible to file a claim for benefits. There is a lag time of about 3 weeks between filing and the receipt of the first check.

Those receiving benefits must continue to file regular claims to support continued eligibility. These reports include progress information about the claimant's efforts to find another job. It is a general expectation that unemployment benefits will not continue after 26 weeks unless special chronic unemployment situations are determined by the state.

Families are connected to the tax system through both funding and usage. Members pay money into the various accounts, and they withdraw payments when they are deemed eligible. The concept of equity often fuels debates between and among the different socioeconomic groups. Are Americans getting what they pay for? Are some groups benefiting more than others? These questions provide dialogue for political campaigns and policy discussions. Another concept that triggers debate is the administration of the funding within these tax-based programs. Wasteful spending and unnecessary overhead costs are concerns of all taxpayers.

GOVERNMENT-SUPPORTED ASSISTANCE PROGRAMS

Public programs: publicly funded assistance programs

Private programs: privately funded assistance programs

Individuals and families have both private and public programs available to supplement or replace resources lost through crises or acute circumstances. This assistance may take the form of money, vouchers, food, or actual services. Public programs are financed and/or supported by tax dollars. Private programs are financed through charitable contributions. Both public and private programs require some justification or qualifications for families to qualify for assistance. Public funds must have higher levels of accountability in terms of equity, fairness, and distribution. Private funds can be more or less discriminatory depending on the goals of the source of funding.

WORLDVIEW

In Chapter 1, the concept of Worldview was explained to understand how people facing the same decision can make very different decisions. Globally, worldview is especially helpful in understanding the issue of healthcare.

Feeling stressed out? If you have a certain type of insurance coverage in Germany, you may be able to indulge in a stress-relieving spa vacation. The German culture believes that a healthy, restful routine lessens the impact of stress on one's overall health. You could get a doctor to prescribe a couple days at the spa, and insurance would cover the cost. The "spa" experience would include exercise, rest, and meditation, not facials and body waxing. Why isn't this part of the U.S. system? The U.S. culture focuses on medical interventions when stress brings headaches and other physical symptoms.

Citizens of Taiwan are issued a small plastic card upon which all of their medical history is stored and updated with each visit and treatment provided by a healthcare worker. With one electronic swipe, an attending physician has the information necessary to begin treatment. What a great idea, right? Well, the U.S. culture believes strongly in the right to individual privacy. Such information could make you vulnerable if someone wanted to use it against you. Such a "smart card" could violate your rights.

Want to move somewhere to ensure that you will live as long as possible? Monaco, a small country near France, has the longest life expectancy (almost 90 years of age) in the world. Chad, a populous country in central Africa, has the shortest life expectancy (50 years of age). The number of medical facilities and professionals per capita is a major factor in the discrepancy between these two nations. Lifestyles, resource availability, and expectations of these two countries reflect vast differences in worldviews and practices.

Where are doctors most affordable and readily available? Cuba. Because the income of physicians is held to a consistent level and medical schooling is free to the qualifying public, doctors are abundant and are dispersed throughout the country—urban and rural communities. In the United States, the low supply and high demand of physicians and the high value placed on the profession and specialties drive the fees for physician care. Medical professionals expect to make higher salaries, and the areas that pay the most are the highly populated urban cities.

Healthcare and the use of such goods and services vary greatly across the globe. Cultural practices and worldview determine both availability and ultimate consumption of both.

Source: Carver, C. (2015, October 16). *6 things you didn't know about health care around the world.* https://www.globalcitizen.org/en/content/6-things-you-didnt-know-about-health-care-around-t/.

Health and Human Services

One of the most recognized U.S. agencies that provides assistance programs is the Department of Health and Human Services, which administers more than 100 separate such programs (see www.hhs.gov). Of nearly $1.145 billion budgeted for 2017, more than one-half will be paid out in the Medicare benefits described earlier in this chapter. Medicaid, the state-level programs supported by these funds, will require the next largest amount. The remaining money in the budget is used to finance many other programs focusing on disease, safety, disasters, child and family services, and aging services (see Figure 8.2).

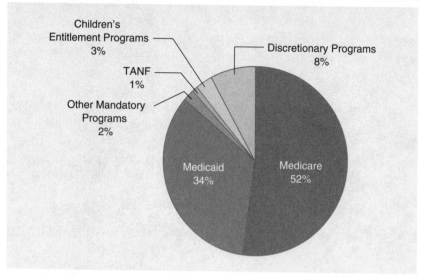

Figure 8.2   Health and Human Services 2017 Budget

Children's Entitlement Programs 3%

TANF 1%

Other Mandatory Programs 2%

Discretionary Programs 8%

Medicaid 34%

Medicare 52%

Source: U.S. Department of Health and Human Services. "HHS FY 2017 Budget." *HHS.gov.* https://www.hhs.gov/about/budget/fy2017/budget-in-brief.

For nearly 50 years, the Administration on Aging has provided home- and community-based services to millions of older persons through the programs funded under the Older Americans Act. These services include home-delivered meals (e.g., Meals on Wheels) and food and nutrition services in congregate settings. Other services made available by funding in this HHS-based agency include transportation, adult daycare, legal assistance, and health-promotion programs. Ombudsmen are provided for nursing homes, providing an ongoing presence in long-term care facilities, monitoring care and conditions, and also providing a voice for those who are unable to speak for themselves. The National Family Caregiver Support Program provides a variety of services to help people who are caring for family members who are chronically ill or who have disabilities.

The Department of Agriculture

The U.S. Department of Agriculture (USDA) provides food assistance programs to citizens. The Supplemental Nutrition Assistance Program (SNAP, otherwise known as the food stamp program) serves as the base of federal food assistance, providing crucial support to low-income households and individuals transitioning from welfare to work. It provides families with electronic benefits transfer (EBT) cards, which can be used to buy eligible food in authorized retail food stores. The SNAP program helped put food on the table for some 21.9 million households each day in fiscal year 2004. Commodity food resources are also made available to qualifying families when the USDA purchases such foodstuffs from agricultural producers in an effort to support the food-producing segments of the country's population. Food safety, nutrition education, and research are also supported by this agency.

The National School Lunch Program, initiated in 1946, is another USDA program. It provides free, reduced, and low-cost lunches to school children in public and nonprofit schools and in qualifying residential childcare institutions. A similar program, the School Breakfast Program, provides nutritious morning meals to children. Both of these programs have income eligibility guidelines that are adjusted periodically to reflect changes in the economy and wage base of participants. Other programs address the needs of elderly, pregnant, and breastfeeding women, as well as provide disaster relief.

In addition to the food and nutrition programs, the USDA provides programs and services to farmers and rural communities throughout the country. These include funding for issues such as rural development, disaster relief, land conservation, and marketing agricultural products as well as education and research. These programs are provided through the Farm Bill funding.

The Food and Drug Administration

The Food and Drug Administration (FDA) is dedicated to promoting and protecting the public health through monitoring the safety and effectiveness of certain types of products on the market. Products such as new drugs and medical devices must be proved safe and effective before the FDA will allow producing companies to sell them to private and public consumers. Other potentially harmful products, such as microwave ovens and over-the-counter drugs, are also under the FDA's jurisdiction.

To ultimately determine the safety of new products, the FDA requires science-based testing and research and diligent decision-making efforts concerning the risk versus benefit of such products in terms of consumer health and safety. These requirements keep many new products off the market for long periods of time. Occasionally, other countries will allow the marketing of such products before the United States.

©iStockphoto.com/asiseeit

▶ **Photo 8.2**
Assuring the safety of medications is an important charge for the FDA.

Drug companies were working on an emergency contraceptive drug alternative for many years. One such product was approved for distribution in Europe long before it was legal to distribute the same medication from U.S. pharmacies. The FDA was not convinced of the drug's safety and effectiveness. In the meantime, the drug's availability through the Internet market became controversial. After further testing and deliberations, this drug is now legally available in the United States and is even being considered for over-the-counter distribution. However, deaths associated with this drug are forcing the FDA to reevaluate that decision.

The FDA safeguards the nation's food supply by ensuring that all ingredients are safe and uncontaminated. It must also approve any new food additive before it can be used in food products available for sale in the United States. Infant formulas and dietary supplements are also under its jurisdiction, although standards for supplements are much less rigorous than for pharmaceuticals that may be sold for similar needs. Because a supplement is consumed by the purchaser, it must be safe and uncontaminated. The FDA does not, however, require these substances to verify the claims made by distributors (weight loss, improved sexual performance, etc.). Meat products, however, are regulated by the USDA.

Medical products under the FDA's regulations include medicines, biologics (vaccines, blood products, biotechnology products, and gene therapy), and medical devices. The devices regulated include tongue depressors, thermometers, heart pacemakers, and dialysis machines. Only the most complex new devices are reviewed, however, before marketing. The FDA even regulates drugs and devices for animals. Cosmetics are monitored for safety and accuracy in labeling, but are not reviewed or approved by this administration.

Labels on medications and food products must be accurate and informative. The FDA monitors existing labeling practices and institutes changes when they are determined to be necessary. The FDA's current role is still evolving, but it continues to blend law and science in an effort to protect consumers.

An ordinary trip to the grocery store is relatively free from worry about the safety of products available there because of the FDA—a tremendous service to American consumers, but not without a cost. The administration is funded through public tax dollars. The process for approving products and withdrawing products from the marketplace is time-consuming, however, and consumers get caught in the flow. Some medical patients will not have access to new drugs that may improve their condition because of the lag time between discovery and approval. Other consumers may suffer from the use of dangerous products during the time it takes to test the products, gather data about problems, and ultimately order these things off the market.

There are numerous other governmental programs providing services to the public. Families do have other sources of assistance from private organizations that provide goods and services to members or to the general public. The United States has a long tradition of neighbors helping neighbors and philanthropic activity.

IN THE NEWS

EpiPen Controversy Fuels Concerns Over Generic Drug Approval Backlog

September 6, 2016
By Sydney Lupkin, Kaiser Health News

Consumers and Congress members pushing for cheaper alternatives to the EpiPen and other high-priced drugs are seeking answers about a stubborn backlog of generic drug applications at the Food and Drug Administration that still stretches almost four years.

As of July 1, the FDA had 4,036 generic drug applications awaiting approval, and the median time it takes for the FDA to approve a generic is now 47 months, according to the Generic Pharmaceutical Association, or GPhA. The FDA has approved more generics the past few years, but a flood of new applications has steadily added to the demand.

By comparison, the European Medicines Agency, Europe's version of the FDA, has just 24 generics or biologically-based "biosimilars" awaiting approval. (The FDA's count does not include biosimilars.) And the EMA along with the European Commission, which handles approval of marketing materials, are approving generics and brand name drugs in about a year on average, according to the EMA.

Critics say getting generic alternatives to the U.S. market for products like EpiPen is still taking far too long.

"We are concerned that Mylan (maker of the EpiPen) has not faced much competition for its product," five U.S. senators wrote in August to FDA Commissioner Dr. Robert Califf, adding that one of EpiPen's non-generic competitors, Auvi-Q was recalled in October, granting Mylan a near monopoly. "News reports indicate that generic versions of the EpiPen have been subject to additional questioning by the FDA and have yet to be approved."

Last week, three members of the House Committee on Energy and Commerce wrote a similar letter to the FDA, seeking information about the EpiPen generic applications it has received and how they've been prioritized.

When asked whether the FDA holds any responsibility for the lack of EpiPen competition, FDA spokesman Kristofer Baumgartner said he couldn't comment on pending applications or confirm their existence, citing confidentiality rules. But he stressed that the FDA pushes pending applications for drugs with no current generics to the front of the line and approved a record number of generics in 2015.

"The FDA is confident that the overall trend in actions on generic drug applications will be one of continuing improvement," Baumgartner said.

In March, Teva Pharmaceuticals told investors that its generic version of EpiPen—the life-saving allergy treatment—was rejected by the FDA, and that it wouldn't be able to launch the generic until at least 2017. Adamis

Pharmaceuticals reported a similar rejection from the FDA for its EpiPen generic in June.

Mylan has said it will offer a $300 generic in the coming weeks. Because Mylan also makes the brand name product, it will not have to wait in line behind other pending generics. And Dr. James Baker, the CEO and chief medical officer of the advocacy group Food Allergy and Research Education, said this may deter other generic manufacturers from seeking approval.

Adrenaclick is the only other epinephrine auto-injector on the market, but it is not a generic for EpiPen and cannot be swapped out at the pharmacy if a doctor has written a prescription for EpiPen. It's also not widely available, Baker said.

"You call up 100 pharmacies, and maybe 10 have the device, from what we gather," Baker said of Adrenaclick, adding that several factors have allowed EpiPen's price tag to swell over the years. "Is Mylan doing anything illegal? No. It's taking advantage of all these things to take the market and basically push it to an extreme."

Efforts to Speed the Approval Process

The FDA's generic backlog isn't a new problem. In 2012, it was so large that it prompted the government to start charging user fees to generic manufacturers to provide the funds for the FDA to speed the process. The fees built on the 20-year-old Prescription Drug User Fee Act, which required brand name drug manufacturers to pay fees to increase FDA efficiency. In the first three years, the FDA collected $1 billion from generic drug manufacturers.

The fees were used to hire an additional 1,000 employees, and put the Office of Generic Drugs on par with the Office of New Drugs by re-organizing it, and moving it to the FDA's main campus from four buildings in Rockville, Maryland. The funds were also used to replace the office's information technology system and implement a few other changes.

As the FDA notes on its website, "Additional resources will enable the Agency to reduce a current backlog of pending applications, cut the

(Continued)

(Continued)

average time required to review generic drug applications for safety, and increase risk-based inspections."

In October 2012, there was a backlog of 2,868 generic drugs awaiting approval, and the FDA said it would take a "first action" on 90% of these drugs by 2017. This summer, the agency met its goal a year early, but a first action isn't an approval. Only 1,551 generics have been approved since the fees were initiated, and that includes some extras that weren't considered part of the official backlog. So the agency has only approved about half of the backlogged generics that were awaiting approval in 2012.

"Most applications from the backlog will need to come back to FDA for additional review due to deficiencies in the submissions, before approval is possible," the agency said in a statement in responses to questions.

The GPhA argues that the agency has declared applications to be "of 'poor quality'

because they don't meet new, more recent standards updated while these applications sit in the backlog."

The applications for generic drugs have continued to pile up even as the FDA approved a record number of generics in 2015 and again in the first seven months of 2016. The number of generic drug applications tripled from 2002 to 2012, according to January congressional testimony from Janet Woodcock, who directs the FDA's Center for Drug Evaluation and Research.

Still, some observers are hopeful.

"I think that it is an optimistic picture overall . . . at the FDA, there's been a lot of progress, and I think there is more to be made," said Dr. Aaron Kesselheim, who leads a research program at Harvard Medical School and Brigham and Women's Hospital. "This is not something that people should think has been solved at this point. It's totally an ongoing process."

Source: Sydney Lupkin, Kaiser Health News. Kaiser Health News (KHN) is a national health policy news service. It is an editorially independent program of the Henry J. Kaiser Family Foundation. http://khn.org/news/epipen-controversy-fuels-concerns-over-generic-drug-approval-backlog.

Consumer Protection

Although U.S. citizens have many protected rights that allow multiple choices during the decision-making process, some alternatives are regulated by laws designed to protect the consumer. Focusing on just the lowest-level needs from Maslow's hierarchy, it is evident that regulation of food, housing, and water safety impacts choices. A family member may be able to hunt for game during restricted seasons and only with a legal permit. Food resulting from that activity can be consumed by the family; however, it cannot be sold to others without passing through a series of regulated processes. These processes will increase the final price of that meat. Family adults may be able to construct a dwelling that meets their basic needs, but often that structure must meet local, regional, and even national codes before an occupancy permit is issued. Meeting those standards will ultimately increase the cost of that dwelling. Parents of young children are restricted in terms of size and features when selecting an automobile. Child restraints are required by all states, and these devices require minimum seat space and seatbelt capabilities.

Consumer protection is a reflection of cultural beliefs that producers of goods and services cannot be fully entrusted to protect the safety of those who consume their goods and services. The Bureau of Consumer Protection's (BCP's) mandate is to protect consumers from possible unfair, deceptive, or fraudulent practices.

Consumer protection: government regulation to protect the interests of consumers, for example, by requiring businesses to disclose detailed information about products

The BCP enforces a variety of consumer protection laws enacted by Congress, as well as trade regulation rules issued by the Federal Trade Commission (FTC). Its actions include individual company and industry-wide investigations, administrative and federal court litigation, rulemaking proceedings, and consumer and business education. In addition, the BCP contributes to the FTC's ongoing efforts to inform Congress and other government entities of the impact that proposed actions could have on consumers. Specific areas of enforcement fall into seven categories—advertising, enforcement, financial practices, marketing practices, planning and information, international issues, and consumer and business education.

The Division of Advertising Practices protects consumers from deceptive and unsubstantiated advertising. Its law enforcement activities focus on

- Tobacco and alcohol advertising, including monitoring for unfair practices or deceptive claims, and reporting to Congress on cigarette and smokeless tobacco labeling, advertising, and promotion

- Advertising claims for food and over-the-counter drugs, particularly those relating to nutritional or health benefits of foods and the safety and effectiveness of drugs or medical devices

- Performance and energy-savings claims made for energy-related household and automotive products

- Environmental performance claims made for consumer products, including claims that products are environmentally safe, ozone-friendly, or biodegradable

- Infomercials—long-form (30-minute) broadcast advertising—to ensure that both the format and content of such programs are not deceptive

- General advertising at the national and regional levels, particularly advertising making objective claims that are difficult for consumers to evaluate

The Division of Enforcement conducts a wide variety of law enforcement activities to protect consumers, including (a) ensuring compliance with administrative and federal court orders entered in consumer protection cases; (b) conducting investigations and prosecuting civil actions to stop fraudulent, unfair, or deceptive marketing and advertising practices; and (c) enforcing consumer protection laws, rules, and guidelines.

The Division of Financial Practices enforces many of the nation's consumer credit statutes, including

- *The Consumer Leasing Act:* This law requires leasers to give consumers information on lease costs and terms. Products most often leased are cars, housing, business facilities, tools, and equipment, and even such intangibles as airspace and trailer pads.

- *The Credit Practices Rule:* Americans are actively involved in the use of credit. Often consumers overextend themselves, and the Bureau of

Consumer Protection must ensure that creditors cannot unduly harm the welfare of debtors. This law prohibits certain security interests and collection remedies in consumer credit contracts, confessions of judgment, wage assignments, waivers of exemption, and security interests in certain household goods. It is responsible for the protection of an individual's personal information gathered by creditors and for ensuring that all terms and conditions within credit contracts are presented fully and understandably to those seeking to borrow.

- *The Equal Credit Opportunity Act:* The focus of this law is protecting consumers from credit discrimination on the basis of sex, race, marital status, religion, national origin, age, or receipt of public assistance.

- *The Fair Credit Billing Act and the Electronic Fund Transfer Act:* These acts have been instituted to address the contemporary problems associated with the exchange of goods and payment using electronic methods. One important component of these laws is the establishment of procedures for resolving mistakes on credit card and electronic fund transfer accounts.

- *The Fair Credit Reporting Act:* Lenders require accurate information when determining whether a borrower is a good credit risk. Borrowers can be negatively impacted if inaccurate, negative information about their credit and payment practices is publicized. This law ensures the accuracy and privacy of information kept by credit bureaus and consumer reporting agencies. It gives consumers the right to know what information credit bureaus and consumer reporting agencies are distributing about them to creditors, insurance companies, and employers.

- *The Fair Debt Collection Practices Act:* Creditors have tremendous power in the lending process; because they have a stronger interest in collecting what is due them than in considering the welfare of their debtors, this law was created to prohibit debt collectors from engaging in unfair, deceptive, or abusive practices, including overcharging, harassment, and disclosing consumers' debt to third parties.

- *Gramm–Leach–Bliley Act:* Information about a consumer's financial standing may increase that person's vulnerability to identity theft and unlawful manipulation. This act provides the FTC's Privacy and Safeguards Rules, which require financial institutions to maintain the privacy and security of consumer information.

- *The Holder-in-Due-Course Rule:* When a consumer purchases goods using credit, his or her debt is often passed to a third party. If the goods purchased are faulty or substandard, the issue of liability surfaces. Is it the original seller or creditor who is responsible for product performance? This law provides certain protections to consumers when the goods they buy on credit are not satisfactory.

- *The Truth in Lending Act:* This act safeguards the consumer from creditor manipulation at the onset of a credit contract. Terms and phrases used in contracts may be difficult for average consumers to understand. Creditors are required to disclose in writing certain cost information, such as the annual percentage rate (APR), before consumers enter into credit transactions.

The Division of Marketing Practices responds quickly and decisively to the rapidly changing world of fraudulent marketing practices. It enforces federal consumer protection laws by filing actions in federal district court on behalf of the FTC to stop scams, prevent scam artists from repeating their fraudulent schemes in the future, freeze their assets, and obtain compensation for scam victims. The priorities of this division include

- Shutting down high-tech Internet and telephone scams that bilk consumers out of hundreds of millions of dollars annually

- Halting deceptive telemarketing or direct mail marketing schemes that use false and misleading information to take consumers' money

- Stopping pyramid schemes and other fraudulent investment scams

Telemarketing: solicitation of business using the phone or Internet conferencing

The Division of Planning and Information collects and analyzes data to target law enforcement and education efforts and measure the impact of activities related to the FTC's consumer protection mission. The division is responsible for various projects and functions, including

Direct mail marketing schemes: misleading marketing programs using advertising that is distributed via the mail system

- *The Consumer Response Center:* Counselors respond to consumer complaints and inquiries received by telephone, mail, and e-mail.

- *The Identity Theft Program:* The division coordinates the FTC's Identity Theft Program. The agency has been directed by statute to serve as a central clearinghouse for identity theft complaints. Consumers can call or visit www.consumer.gov/idtheft.

Pyramid schemes: schemes where participants make money only by recruiting more members

- *The Consumer Sentinel:* This binational, multistate computerized consumer fraud database uses the Internet to provide secure access to more than 200,000 consumer complaints for more than 150 law enforcement organizations across the United States and Canada. The site offers law enforcement access to telemarketing, direct mail, and Internet complaints from the FTC's Consumer Information System database and from various law enforcement and private sector partners. The site also provides other information useful for investigations and prosecutions.

Investment scams: illegal programs designed to entice individuals to invest large sums of money in fraudulent funds

- *The International Coordination:* The division coordinates the FTC's international consumer protection work and helps facilitate international information sharing among consumer protection law enforcers.

- *Operations*: The division administers the core financial, administrative, and litigation support activities of the FTC. It manages the agency's consumer protection redress activities and coordinates strategic planning and performance measurement.

The International Division of Consumer Protection seeks to promote consumer confidence in the international marketplace. Its activities focus on expanding international cooperation and information sharing through

- Negotiating and implementing bilateral consumer protection cooperation agreements. Agreements exist with consumer protection agencies in Canada, Australia, and the United Kingdom.

- Coordinating participation in the International Marketing Supervision Network (IMSN), an international network of consumer protection law enforcers in 30 countries.

- Coordinating and managing econsumer.gov, a website where consumers can file cross-border e-commerce complaints, which can be accessed by consumer protection law enforcers in 15 countries.

- Providing litigation support for enforcement actions with an international component—where wrongdoers, their assets, or their victims are abroad.

- Developing international consumer protection and e-commerce policies that promote consumer confidence while minimizing regulatory burden and promoting growth of the international B2C marketplace.

- Offering international technical assistance to developing countries in building consumer protection frameworks.

The Office of Consumer and Business Education (OCBE) plans and implements public education campaigns for consumers and industry on topics such as fraud, deception, and unfair practices. The OCBE also produces, promotes, and disseminates educational messages and materials to the widest possible audience through multifaceted communications and outreach programs. These efforts involve the use of print, broadcast, and electronic media, the World Wide Web (the OCBE maintains the webpages of the Bureau of Consumer Protection and the consumer.gov website), special events, and partnerships with government agencies, consumer groups, trade organizations, businesses, and other organizations.

While the government provides consumer protection and offers education to citizens on how they can protect themselves, ultimately it is the consumers' responsibility to be aware of what they are buying and consuming. Watchdog groups offer information for consumers in addition to what the government provides. Ralph Nader is one of the most influential figures in consumer protection. His decades of activism have led to legislation for consumer protection.

REALITY CHECK

Regulations and Affordable Housing

A great deal of attention has been focused on why affordable housing is such a problem for many families in the United States. One impact on housing costs is the set of building regulations created and enforced by local governments. Examples of how these rules, codes, and standards impact housing costs include the following:

- Local regulations determine minimum lot sizes or how much ground must support a new structure. Even slight increases to these minimums reduce the number of houses possible in new developments. If the total cost that developers charge for their financial needs is set and the number of lots within that piece of ground drops from 12 to 10 because of lot size restrictions, each lot will be priced more than 16% higher, pushing the total cost of the house up that much.

- Many communities enforce impact fees and regulatory costs on each new home built in that municipality. Some studies show that such fees in some California communities add up to more than $100,000 per home built.

- New energy codes enforce a nationwide aim to increase energy efficiency in American homes. Although this goal is a long-range benefit to home buyers through reduced heating and cooling bills, initially these regulations can increase the cost of building, and thus the price of housing for consumers.

- Rising real estate taxes to support local governments and schools positively increase the cost of homeownership for families. Issues of equity surface when families without children feel they should not be burdened with the cost of providing schools to those who choose to have children. This issue is of increasing concern in communities with large retirement populations.

- The costs of securing and maintaining public utilities are passed from municipal governments to homeowners and general consumers. As regulations are enforced to alleviate the problems of garbage dumps and sanitation services, consumer prices for such services increase. Access to municipal water sources is impacted by the costs of increasing sanitation methods.

Consider this illustration of governmental and other legal costs and their impact on the cost of housing:

Cost of building a home: $170,000, including materials, labor, and lot

Real estate broker fee: $12,000

Local permits and fees: $8,000

Profit to the builder: $10,000

Purchase price of the home: $200,000

Down payment: $20,000, for a 30-year mortgage at 7% interest

Amount financed: $180,000

Mortgage payment without taxes and insurance: $1,200 monthly

Annual real estate taxes: $200 monthly

Home insurance required by lender: $100 monthly

Total monthly payment: $1,500

If building codes required 5% less material, if labor costs and lot size restrictions weren't imposed that originally added 16% to the lot cost, and if local permits and fees were reduced by 50%, the purchase price could drop to $175,000. Even keeping real estate broker fees and builder profits at the same percentages, the cost of building and selling the home is reduced enough to lower the price more than 12%. The monthly mortgage payment could be reduced to $1,100. Real estate taxes would be lower because the purchase price impacts tax valuation, and insurance fees would be lower because of the replacement cost of the home. Essentially, the homeowner could choose to either buy a larger home or allocate the mortgage savings to other family resource needs. Higher energy costs due to the reduced building requirements would need to be at least $300 per month to justify the original monthly mortgage payment.

PRIVATELY FUNDED PROGRAMS

In addition to government funded programs, privately funded programs provide valuable services. A nongovernmental organization (NGO) is nonprofit and engaged in activities for a specific purpose, such as a social or religious goal. NGO activities may include issues such as human rights, the environment, or health and can take a local, national, or international scope. Privately funded programs may be able to respond more quickly to emerging needs, can focus on specific populations, and can be more flexible in how funds are used. On the other hand, funding for privately funded programs may mean smaller amounts of funding, and continued funding can be difficult to anticipate.

Privately funded assistance programs are often faith-based, funded through donations channeled through religious organizations. Many private hospitals have foundations that seek funding from donor sources and then provide financial assistance to patients who could not afford them otherwise. St. Jude's Children's Hospital provides care to all patients, regardless of ability to pay. It also funds research and health education programs. Habitat for Humanity has been addressing the need for family housing since its inception in 1976, building more than 1 million homes for low-income people all over the world. Food pantries and clothing donation centers operate from local and regional centers. Many other needs are met through private assistance programs at local, state, regional, national, and international levels.

The challenge for professionals serving families is to identify needs and link people to these existing resources. The Internet has provided access to information and application procedures. Ironically, those most in need of these programs are the least likely to have access to computers or to have the training necessary to search, understand, and complete application procedures.

COMPULSORY EDUCATION

This nationally held value has its roots in the belief that an educated citizenry is necessary to maintain a democratic government. Although not specified in the U.S. Constitution, public education was an expectation of the early leaders of this country. What that educational system will look like is left to the individual states, but federal policy and funding link these schools by providing guiding goals, objectives, and policies. Education provides opportunities to individuals and a knowledgeable workforce for employers. Families are impacted at many levels by the availability, quality, and choice of school systems for their children.

History

As early as the 1640s, inhabitants of what is now Massachusetts allocated some of their meager resources to publicly creating and supporting schools. Schooling at this time in American history resembled the private school patterns of today. Often they were part of local churches and included religious curriculum. In 1827, the Commonwealth of Massachusetts became the first state to make elementary instruction free to all citizens. By 1929, all 50 states, the District of Columbia, and Puerto

Rico had enacted some form of compulsory school attendance laws. This form of public education is based on state-level efforts, so the exact requirements for attendance vary between and among states. Nonattendance is often presented as *truancy*, with legal punishment for a child within the age limits of expected attendance who does not meet minimum attendance requirements. Most often the legal ramifications are imposed on the parent or responsible adults as fines and/or imprisonment.

▶ **Photo 8.3**
Education is a national value rooted in local delivery.

Many argue that the real basis of our contemporary compulsory school expectations stems from the Industrial Revolution. This movement created a high demand for an educated workforce, the reduction of family-centered production, and the emergence of childhood and adolescent protection from unhealthy employment participation. By the 1950s, a common, standardized educational experience became the rule, or the norm. Recent efforts to further standardize curriculum and assessment further illustrate this expectation.

The Federal Level

Although only about 8% of funding for public education comes from federal money, this financial support is essential for local school systems to operate. At the federal level, there are three important departments interfacing with public schools—the Department of Education, the Department of Health and Human Services, and the Department of Agriculture.

Head Start and Early Head Start are comprehensive child development programs that serve children from birth to age 5, pregnant women, and their families. They are child-focused programs and have the overall goal of increasing the school readiness of young children in low-income families. The Head Start program is administered by the Head Start Bureau, the Administration on Children, Youth and Families (ACYF), the Administration for Children and Families (ACF), and the Department of Health and Human Services (DHHS). Grants are awarded by the ACF Regional Offices and the Head Start Bureau's American Indian–Alaska Native and Migrant and Seasonal Program Branches directly to local public agencies, private organizations, Native American tribes, and school systems for the purpose of operating Head Start programs at the community level.

The Head Start program has a long tradition of delivering comprehensive and high-quality services designed to foster healthy development in low-income children. Head Start grantee and delegate agencies provide a range of individualized services in the areas of education and early childhood development: medical, dental, and mental health; nutrition; and parent involvement. In addition, the entire range of Head Start services is responsive and appropriate to each child and family's developmental, ethnic, cultural, and linguistic heritage and experience.

All Head Start programs must adhere to program performance standards. The *Head Start Program Performance Standards* define the services that Head Start programs are to provide to the children and families they serve. They constitute the expectations and requirements that Head Start grantees must meet. They are designed to ensure that the Head Start goals and objectives are implemented successfully, that the Head Start philosophy continues to thrive, and that all grantee and delegate agencies maintain the highest possible quality in the provision of Head Start services. The Head Start program has enrolled more than 32 million children since it began in 1965.

The State Level

Because public education is not addressed specifically in the Constitution, education of citizens falls within the realm of state governments. Control and coordination of public education within each state usually falls under the jurisdiction of state-level departments of education. These units centralize curriculum, teaching licensure and training, and special education expectations for public school sites across their states. Budgets of these departments are devoted to enhancement of school performance. The connection between federal programs and funds and state schools is also part of the mission of these departments. State taxes also support budgets for these schools, as determined by their legislators and voting constituents.

The burden of funding education at the state level is often problematic, especially during times of recession. Although each state is different, approximately 50% of school funding comes from state funds. When state revenue is strained, budget cuts at the state level force school districts to offer fewer services and raise more local revenue, usually through property taxes.

The Community Level

Public education in the United States operates at the local level. Daily operations, budgeting and financial management, and policymaking begin at this level under the state guidelines. Free attendance for all children in each school district is a right. Administrators, teachers, staff, and parents deliver, monitor, and assess the education of children in their communities. Local school boards create policy and budgets for schools within their jurisdiction. Thus, public education is delivered locally, is coordinated at the state level, and has historically been marginally supported at the federal level.

Because most schools are funded at the local level by property taxes, there can be differences in the amount of funding available. Problems are created when this inequality results in an education gap caused by poor quality and lack of resources for some school districts.

Family Involvement

Parents in the United States do not have a choice about whether to educate their children. They do have options, however. These options are discussed later in this chapter. Parental involvement in education has been the subject of much debate.

Some parents choose not to be involved in the educational system and have been accused of "dropping their children off for kindergarten and picking them up at high school graduation." Essentially, parents cannot avoid participation in the process. They are legally obligated to enforce compulsory attendance. Minimally, this would require efforts necessary to get their children to and from the school site as required. It also involves expenditures for necessary clothing, supplies, and fees required for school participation. Realistically, most parents are involved at a much higher level in the education of their children.

In early colonial education, parents were expected to be involved in curriculum selection and monitoring and teacher evaluation. During the early 1900s, schools became more bureaucratized, and school personnel became more professionally organized. This change led to a division of home life and school life, where parents were expected to support what was provided at school in their homes, while leaving the curriculum and teaching decisions to the staff and administrators (Barge & Loges, 2003). The role of parents in the education of their children has made a concentrated swing back toward fuller participation with state and federal laws and as a reflection of the national frustration with school and student performances. Parental involvement, while increasing, still differs between and among social groups. Several studies indicate that low-income minority parents are less involved than higher-income nonminority parents. Others dispute those findings by reporting that minority parents have higher levels of participation in some areas, and older and more educated parents are more involved in other areas and what they believe their roles should be in the educational process (Bornstein, Cote, Haynes, Hahn, & Park, 2010; Desimone, 1999). When parents choose to be involved, resources necessary to facilitate that decision include time, knowledge, and energy. The perceived return of the investment of those resources must be positive.

Age is shown to be a factor in parents' involvement with their children's education (Hornby & Lafaele, 2011). Cordry and Wilson (2004) reported that approximately 77.4% of parents are actively involved in their children's education during grades K–5. This involvement decreases to an average of 67.4% of middle school parents and 56.8% of high school families. These authors also report that active parental involvement has a positive effect on student morale, attitudes, and academic achievement. What, then, accounts for the "dropping out" of parents through the educational process?

There are often barriers to parental involvement. Low levels of education, socioeconomic status (SES), family structure, and cultural differences are identified as factors (Jafarov, 2015). Teacher attitudes also negatively impact participation of parents (Hornby & Lafaele, 2011). More than 80% of Americans attend public schools. However, some parents are not convinced that public education is providing their children with appropriate teaching, curriculum, values, or morals. There are alternative routes to meeting their states' compulsory laws.

Alternatives to Public Education

All children in the United States have the right to public education. Citizens paying taxes at both the federal and state levels are funding these services and facilities.

When public education is perceived as less than desired, alternatives are explored. Three categories of alternative schooling are charter schools, homeschooling, and private schools.

Charter Schools

The first charter schools were originally public school facilities. Parents and/or other organized groups proposed new, creative alternative curricula and administration for existing schools that were struggling. Some states agreed to fund these alternative schools with per-student payments, whereas other states did not acknowledge or fund charter schools. Additional funding necessary was obtained through fundraising of the sponsoring parent or community group. States participating in this alternative process continued to monitor and support these schools. Essentially, the state is outsourcing education of some students to the charter school sponsor groups. Some charter schools have been successful, whereas others have found the funding too difficult to manage.

Homeschooling

The practice of providing education in the home setting has roots in the U.S. pioneer experience. Until enough families settled in any one area and/or transportation methods improved, creating and maintaining common educational facilities did not make sense at any level. Parents assumed the responsibility of teaching basic literacy skills to their children within their homes. Arguably, parental control of their children's education is greatest in this form of instruction. Because U.S. lawmakers acknowledge a certain level of privacy within parental rights, states do allow parents to provide state-required curriculum in the home setting. The U.S. Department of Education reports that 3% of children were being homeschooled in the 2011–2012 school year, and this alternative to public education continues to grow. The majority of homeschooling parents report that their concerns about the environment of other schools was the reason for choosing this option.

The institution responsible for coordination of state schools oversees and grants permission for homeschooling. Parents, or whoever is responsible for presenting curriculum, must be approved, and curriculum guidelines and materials are either supplied or approved by this body. This approach to education of children requires high levels of resource dedication, including time, energy, knowledge, space, and materials.

Private Schools

More than 10% of U.S. school-age children attend private schools. These schools do not receive public tax funding for general operations or faculty and staff payrolls. The financial base of these schools is a combination of pupil tuition and foundation funds. Some autonomy exists in private schooling in terms of curriculum and teacher expectations; however, to meet compulsory education requirements, these schools must follow state curriculum and teaching guidelines to some measure. Most private schools are religion-based. Other sponsoring institutions include military, boarding, and prep schools. Beyond the mandated curriculum, these schools are free to include instruction and expectations set forth by their funding sources.

Making Educational Choices

Families must ensure that children attend state-approved educational institutions or receive instruction in the home setting. The need has been created by the compulsory education laws. Alternatives to meet that need include public education, private education, charter schools, or homeschooling. A few states also offer parents another choice through **school vouchers**. Some states allow families to choose alternatives to public education and will allow public funds to be diverted to these alternatives in the form of a voucher to be used for the educational program of their choice. As families evaluate these alternatives, their values, past experiences, and future goals will direct them to the type of education they provide for their children. That decision creates opportunity costs, but also results in educational experiences for the children involved. Parents and their school-age children should continually evaluate this decision and the results of their selection to ensure that the needs of family members are being satisfied. Once such a decision has been made, parents are free to change their minds and move their students to other acceptable educational settings.

Knowledge and skills are essential resources that each member of a family contributes to the welfare of the entire group. The expectation of education is to provide and enhance the ability of family members to make good decisions. As children grow physically and cognitively, their ability to contribute to functions within family living increases. Individual families must decide how these new, expanding resources can contribute to overall functioning.

Time, and the management of family time, is greatly impacted by schooling decisions. All formal, out-of-home schooling works within a structured schedule. Many operate on a 9-month annual format, although several utilize a year-round calendar. Weekly and daily schedules resemble workplaces in many ways. Most schools operate on a Monday-through-Friday format and have a 6- to 7-hour class day.

School voucher: a certificate by which parents are given the ability to pay for the education of their children at a school of their choice, rather than the public school to which they were assigned

SUPPLY AND DEMAND: AN APPLICATION IN EDUCATION

Compulsory education in the United States creates a large market for education. Public education is available to all children. Private education is accessible only to those who can pay for it or those who qualify for tuition waivers. Core curriculum, guided by the state, is generally similar in both. The quality of the education provided by any two school systems is rarely equal. Even within the public school network, there is disparity between and among publicly funded school sites. As recently as two decades ago, the public school available to children was determined by their place of residence. In many communities, that is still the deciding factor. If a neighborhood school was substandard in the parents' estimation, their choice was to accept the situation or pay tuition for their children to attend private schools.

Compulsory education: schooling required by law

The demand was guaranteed by law, and the supply of schools was determined by funding available through taxes collected. Quality was the unknown factor; because choices and resources are limited, ensuring equality across all public school sites was impossible. Many economists and others have proposed that parental choice would ultimately raise the level of quality across the board by adding an element of competition to the mix.

SUMMARY

Families living in the United States have many freedoms. Societies, however, strive to protect members, and U.S. citizens must operate within several constraints intended to enhance their quality of life. Funding for large-scale programs and governmental expenses comes from collection of taxes. These tax obligations reduce the number of monetary resources available to families, but provide other resources important to social goals and family survival. Consumer protection efforts and educational programs directly impact resource acquisition and expenditure of both individuals and families. Family professionals seek to understand and match existing resources to existing needs, while also managing tax obligations and personal accountability.

QUESTIONS FOR REVIEW AND DISCUSSION

1. The U.S. income tax system is criticized for being too complicated and for disproportional assessment—the wealthy seem to pay less. How do income, sales, Social Security, and Medicare taxes differ in that respect?

2. The FDA has a delicate balancing act to handle, meeting consumer needs for new, improved medications and foods and ensuring the safety of these new products. Identify three new products currently making news headlines and discuss how the FDA is managing that balance.

3. Who is ultimately responsible for consumer safety—the consumer or the government? Discuss.

4. How are public schools and the business model interdependent? Schedules? Curriculum?

5. What resources do public schools provide families? What resource needs do they create for families?

MAKING CHOICES

The Decision-Making Process

- Recognize existing needs
- Identify alternatives to fulfill needs
- Evaluate identified alternatives
- Select and implement alternatives

Chapter 9. Managing the Future

Chapter 10. Communication Within the Decision-Making Process

Chapter 11. The Individual Within Family Decision Making

- Reflect on and evaluate the alternatives selected

CHAPTER NINE

MANAGING THE FUTURE

Objectives
Goals, Objectives, and Standards
The Planning Process
   Types of Plans
Worldview
   Schedules
   Budgeting
Family Financial Planning
Reality Check
Creating the Financial Plan
In the News
Emergency Action Plans
How Plans Emerge
Summary
Questions for Review and Discussion

Objectives

- Understand the planning process.

- Explore goal setting and the creation of implementation plans.

- Differentiate between long- and short-term goals and objectives.

- Understand the budgeting process.

- Explore the objectives of financial planning.

- Appreciate the need for family planning for emergencies/crises.

By failing to prepare, you are preparing to fail.

—Benjamin Franklin

Decisions are worthless unless they are implemented. Once a decision is made, individuals or family units must complete a new series of operations and choices. They must develop a plan of action.

The Omega family has decided that their credit card debt is too large. They have reached an agreement that involves paying off current debt and reducing their dependence on the use of credit from now on. This type of decision requires long-term commitment and a strong plan designed to change their behavior.

Caren Bellows, a college senior, has decided that she needs to strengthen her résumé before she begins looking for a job after graduation. Her advisor met with her, and together they decided that increasing Caren's campus activities would help prepare her for social expectations in her field of marketing. Caren plans to join two student organizations this semester and contribute 2 to 3 hours per week to a local soup kitchen. This plan is short term and focused.

Everyone is involved in the short-term planning process. This behavior is essential to human survival—that is, meeting basic needs. Long-term planning is a universal trait across cultures and generations. However, cultural differences in how an individual believes he or she controls the future impact his or her willingness to engage in long-term planning and implementation of those types of strategies (see Chapter 1). Family resource management, as a process, is highly dependent on the planning process.

GOALS, OBJECTIVES, AND STANDARDS

Goal: something that somebody wants to achieve

Objectives: specific and measurable means for accomplishing goals

A **goal** is an end that one tries to attain. It is something that one wishes to reach or accomplish within a timeframe determined by the individual. **Objectives** are subsets of goals (Palomba & Banta, 1999). For instance, if the goal is to increase healthfulness to enhance quality of life, objectives within that goal may include weight management, exercise expectations, and nutritional changes. Objectives are more specific and measurable than the overall goal, acting as checkpoints to enable one to measure progress toward goal achievement.

Setting, pursuing, and achieving goals contribute to personal growth and satisfaction with life (Griffith & Graham, 2004). Goals help individuals guide and direct their behavior toward completion of tasks and objectives. Within the process of goal attainment are other tasks, such as self-regulation and problem-solving skills. Goals reflect basic values, attitudes, and beliefs. Goals are also bound by an individual's understanding and experience. Education is often cited as a goal of new immigrants. For parents from backgrounds of poverty and illiteracy, this may be structured elementary and high school opportunities for their children. For parents who are graduates of higher education institutions, a bachelor's degree may be part (an objective) of a larger goal—graduate degrees for their children. This does not mean that both sets of parents do not have high goals and expectations. It merely reflects the reality that each family has available based on their knowledge of options and experience in the educational system.

Short-term goals: goals that will be achieved in the near future

Intermediate goals: goals that will be accomplished in less than 1 year

Long-range goals: goals that usually require more than 1 year to complete

There are many ways to categorize goals. **Short-term goals** generally can be accomplished in less than 3 months. **Intermediate goals** will be accomplished in less than 1 year, and **long-range goals** usually require more than 1 year to complete.

Pamela agreed to work 3 extra hours per week between Thanksgiving and Christmas to make enough money to buy holiday presents for her family and friends (short-term goal). She is also spending more time studying to raise her

final GPA before graduation in May (intermediate goal). After graduation, she will begin specialized study to become a radiologist (long-range goal). She has many goals of different duration operating at the same time.

Societal goals are reflected in rules and expectations within larger social groups. Reducing the dependence of Americans on foreign oil is a goal expressed by the government and ecologists alike. **Family goals** provide motivation for family members to work together to bring about positive changes for individuals within the group and for the family unit as a whole. **Personal goals** are specific to the individual. When goals are categorized by source, there will always be some overlap.

Societal goals: goals that are reflected in rules and expectations within larger social groups

Family goals: broad statements of ideal future conditions that are desired by a family

Personal goals: goals that are specific to the individual

Sergio is a first-generation college graduate with several good job offers. He has reached an important personal goal. His entire family shares this success; however, his parents and siblings have sacrificed along the way to support this process. His promising career also meets the criteria of a societal goal, as he will move out of poverty and will be prepared to help his family do the same.

Recognizing that individuals juggle several goals simultaneously, it is important to understand how they manage to focus, prioritize, and endure. Goals must be reasonable, understood, measurable, and specific.

Kim wants to advance in her place of employment. Specifically, she wants to become an assistant manager and move up on the pay scale. A reasonable goal would be to focus on the next, logical position in the existing chain of command. She will want to involve her superiors in the process, so all that will be impacted by her goal are aware of her ambitions and how they may be able to assist her efforts, as well as how her personal goal might impact their positions. A couple of progressive steps should be agreed on— quarterly reviews and professional development opportunities. She will know she accomplished this goal when she is awarded the promotion and pay increase.

Family members responsible for or impacted by goals should be included in the creation of those goals. The level of acceptance and shared responsibility for achieving group goals increases when the individuals involved feel that their voices were heard in the decision-making process and that their needs were considered by those ultimately setting the goals. Goals, and the objectives within them, provide direction, an element of control, and a shared understanding of where a family is currently operating, where it desires to be in the future, and how members of that family can contribute to the unit's success. Attainment of goals provides satisfaction and a sense of accomplishment, enhancing the life experience of family members and encouraging the successful completion of other goals.

Standards: a degree or level of requirement, excellence, or attainment

Standards, or perceived acceptable levels of adequacy within a family, will also impact goals. For some students, a passing grade is sufficient. For others, only excellent grades are acceptable. Standards develop slowly over time, and family standards reflect a multigenerational developmental process. Young adults often face the task of realigning their standards of living, moving from an established home, fully furnished and functional, into their first independent apartments or shared housing. As the standard of living for middle-class Americans has continued to rise over the last three generations, young adults in those households have grown accustomed to high levels of comfort and even excess. Televisions, microwaves, and climate control are expectations, instead of options. Young adults will experience discomfort when their own resources cannot support that level of living. Often this leads to overdependence on credit and the pledging of huge sums of future earnings for immediate gratification and enjoyment.

THE PLANNING PROCESS

Planning process: a process that begins with a decision and includes identification of a situation that requires action, a formulation of a plan, and the implementation of that plan

Many decisions are complex in nature, requiring focused planning to fully implement. The decision to stop smoking requires both goal setting and a plan of action. Whether the method employed to accomplish that goal is to cease smoking immediately or approach it slowly and methodically, deliberate action is necessary. The **planning process** begins with a decision. This decision must be analyzed in terms of the activities necessary to fulfill the inherent goal. The objectives, or key events, are plotted in terms of time and difficulty, and tasks are assigned and agreed on by those involved in the process. Some decisions are completely under the control of one individual, but in many family decisions, there is a need to delegate or assign specific tasks to certain members to complete the entire process. Those decisions and development of a time framework result in a plan—formal or informal. Implementation and eventual evaluation of the plan, regardless of whether it is completed, complete the planning process.

The Planning Process

- Identification of a situation that requires action
- Formulation of a plan
- Implementation of that plan
- Evaluation of the plan's success or failure

Plan: a proposed or intended method of getting from one set of circumstances to another

Schedule: a plan for carrying out a process or procedure, giving lists of intended events and times

A **plan** is a course of action created to move a decision forward—toward goal accomplishment. Each plan is actually a set of multiple decisions and actions arranged in sequence or steps. As plans formalize, **schedules** emerge. Examples of schedules include lists, timetables, calendars, electronic scheduling devices, and computer programs, all used to plot the way from the beginning to the end of tasks and appointments. Schedules depend on **sequencing**, or a mental process of laying out activities and resources needed to complete any particular task or goal. The complexity of these activities determines how much time, energy, and thought are required. Preparing a meal requires gathering of foodstuffs and equipment and a purposeful sequencing of tasks. Vegetables must be cleaned and often cut into edible pieces before they are cooked. Water must be drained from pasta before sauces are added. An electric coffee maker must be filled with water and ground coffee beans, and then the button to begin brewing can be activated. Doing any of these steps out of sequence may result in failure. Writing a research paper involves gathering sources, organizing ideas, and then the actual writing or word processing of the paper. Sequencing is key to the planning process, whether deliberate and conscious or habitual and subconscious.

Some actions require complete dedication and concentration. Completing a high-level algebraic equation or properly aligning a domino display are examples of such activities. Other activities may require less concentration but limit the types of other activities you can be involved in simultaneously. Many activities require such low levels of attention that they can be done at the same time. **Independent activities** are unrelated to one another. In the morning, you can brush your teeth, comb your hair, and dress in any order you prefer. None of these activities is dependent on the other. **Interdependent activities** are more time and sequence specific. One activity within a series of activities must be completed before another in interdependent situations. You must obtain the title to an automobile before you can license and insure it. You must license and insure it to drive it legally. Ownership, licensing, and insuring are interdependent activities in that situation.

Many daily activities require little focus and allow us to **multitask**. You may do your homework with the TV and radio turned on and in the presence of friends and family. You might drive your car through traffic while conversing on your cell phone and eating fast food. The ability to multitask does increase our ability to accomplish more in less time. The quality of the end result and the safety of such behavior are questionable, however. Rubinstein, Meyer, and Evans (2001) found that, in all types of tasks, participants in their research lost time when they had to switch from one task to another. These time costs increased with the complexity of the tasks. They suggest that individuals go through two distinct stages when switching between tasks. *Goal shifting* involves the decision and action necessary to switch, and *rule activation* is the process needed to switch from the rules of the first task to the rules of the second.

Laws banning texting while driving indicate that multitasking is a serious concern to safety on the roads. Some situations require multitasking, such as in hospital emergency room centers. Walter, Raban, Dunsmuir, Douglas, and Westbrook (2016) found that the medical professionals in their study were able to adjust their attention and necessary actions in spite of interruptions. Physicians in the emergency departments of hospitals are constantly in a state of multitasking under high stress and dangerous situations. This study illustrated the importance of strong communication strategies and preparedness to minimize the possible negative results of multitasking.

Sequencing: doing things in a logical, predictable order

Independent activities: activities that are unrelated to each other

Interdependent activities: activities that are dependent on each other and are sequence-specific

Multitasking: a human being's simultaneous handling of multiple tasks

Josh is watching his 2-year-old niece, talking to his girlfriend on the phone, and playing computer Solitaire. He is focused on explaining to his girlfriend why he will be late picking her up this evening when he hits a snag on the game. He deliberately shifts his focus to the game (goal shifting) and pulls up the rules and past strategies he has stored in his memory (rule activation). This half-second of time lost to task switching can be critical if his niece has discovered an unprotected wall socket at the same time.

Intuition:
understanding without apparent effort; quick and ready insight seemingly independent of previous experiences or empirical knowledge

Brainstorming:
a group problem-solving technique that involves the spontaneous contribution of ideas from all members of the group; the mulling over of ideas by one or more individuals in an attempt to devise or find a solution to a problem

Decisions that have been repeated many times or those with little risk or investment involved are often implemented by one individual's using **intuition** and past experience. The household is running low on toilet paper. Any of the family members capable of purchasing supplies can implement the decision to purchase more. Toilet paper is a frequent purchase, so preferences do not need to be examined each and every time. It is a low-expense purchase, so pricing is not a high-level concern, especially in cases of emergency.

In group situations, such as families, **brainstorming** may be implemented to create a plan of action. Multiple members are asked to generate possible courses of action to address the decision. This approach to planning ensures diverse possibilities and creative options, but it is not an efficient approach. A large number of possible plans will need to be sorted, evaluated, ranked, and then decided on. When risk is high and time is available, families may find brainstorming to be both useful and effective.

Abbie has always wanted to travel internationally. As a senior in high school, she is eligible for the student exchange program in her district. She has an opportunity to spend the next semester in Spain. Because Abbie's mother is a single parent with two other children, Abbie's absence for that length of time will disrupt three other family members' lives. The family sits down to discuss how Abbie's dream can be realized with the least disruption to everyone else.

One issue is how to transport her brother Jackson from middle school to home. Abbie has been able to pick him up in the family car each day and stay with him until their mother returns from work. Jackson suggests that he walk or ride his bike the 10 blocks from school each day.

Mom's idea is to use the school's after-hours program, allowing Jackson to stay at school an extra 2 hours to work on assignments and participate in scheduled activities. Tenille, the oldest sister, offers to postpone her next semester of cosmetology coursework and work part-time instead to allow her to cover the late-afternoon needs. While Mom's idea would probably rise to the top by itself, this process of brainstorming illuminates important information about both Jackson's and Tenille's needs. Jackson is seeking ways to become more independent and supportive within his family. Tenille is possibly not convinced that she is pursuing the right professional program of study. In the end, Abbie's absence will be handled, all family members are able to show support of Abbie's opportunity through offers of sacrifice, and important individual needs are expressed.

Obviously, brainstorming has advantages and disadvantages. It requires time, discussion, and teamwork. Not all ideas generated will be useful or practical. However, by allowing more members of the group to participate in the decision-making process, a higher level of agreement and commitment will exist when the final decision is made. This approach to decision making also provides a higher level of creativity and originality.

▸ **Photo 9.1** Research suggests that multitasking is not as efficient as once thought.

Types of Plans

Many plans never reach a formalized, written state. They are merely stored in our mind or shared verbally with others. The probability of success, or completion of the goals and objectives within a plan, increases with the degree of formality of the plan. When a plan is made public, it is more likely to succeed than if it is held in secrecy. Once the specifics are announced to others, a level of accountability emerges. Informal or ad hoc plans are created by individuals in all of their pursuits. Any purposeful action requires some level of planning. Structured and formal plans are most often used by multiple people who are working together to achieve a common goal. Examples include military strategies, career planning, and estate planning. It is common for less formal plans to be created as abstract ideas and remain in that form as they are maintained and put to use. More formal plans, although initially created with and as an abstract thought, are likely to be written down, drawn up, or otherwise stored in a form that is accessible to multiple people across time and space. This allows more reliable collaboration in the execution of the plan.

Jaime is going to the theater with friends. All four individuals are traveling from different parts of the city to meet at the theater prior to the curtain call. Jaime has never taken the subway system from his place of work to the theater district, so he accesses the navigation program on his cell phone and programs his destination into the prompt, informs his boss that he will be leaving a few minutes early, and sets off. While making a connection, he grabs a snack from a vending machine. His travel plans are more formal than his eating plan, but both are successfully achieved.

A **directional plan** moves an individual or group along a path toward completion of a goal. Career management is one example. To become an architect, you must first complete secondary school. Then you must complete an undergraduate

Directional plan: a strategic plan that guides the future of decision making

degree that is compatible to a graduate degree in architecture. After receiving the graduate degree, you must complete supervised work experience for a certain period of time, take and pass licensing tests, and eventually present yourself to the public as a fully licensed professional.

WORLDVIEW

THE PUSH AND PULL OF IMMIGRATION

There are many reasons why people choose to immigrate to the United States. Push and pull factors include economic, social, and political motivations. *Push factors* are those that cause people in other countries to feel that they would be better off to leave the country because of low pay, lack of employment, underemployment, or the absence of family members who have chosen to leave before them. Exposure to endemic violence, persecution, and oppression are also push factors. *Pull factors* are those that give the immigrant the sense that the new country is pulling the individual away from his or her original country and may include the possibility of higher earnings, securing employment, joining family members, and a hope that the person will have a better future than he or she envisions in the current situation.

Scanning newspapers and analyzing political speeches illuminates three common myths about immigrants from Mexico and Central America: (1) These immigrants plan to stay in the United States permanently; (2) Latino immigrants drain public benefits and make little, if any, economic contributions; and (3) Spanish-speaking immigrants refuse to learn English and are determined not to assimilate into U.S. culture.

Schaefer (2008) found that Latino immigrants send a great deal of their earnings back to family members in their country of origin. He estimates that this equates to billions of dollars of earnings; however, he suggests that even those amounts are not necessarily a drain to the U.S. economy when the human capital represented in those wages is considered. The production of goods and services by these workers is fueling the exchange within the U.S. economy. This investment in family members still in their native country implies a continued commitment to their country of origin, suggesting a temporary mind-set, rather than a permanent change of residence. Many surveys have indicated that at least half of Mexican immigrants hope to return to Mexico at some future point (Lacy, 2006). Moving to another country to meet basic needs of their families does not necessarily equate to the abandonment of generations of history and personal investment in their native countries. Many Americans have moved to Europe and the Middle East to capitalize on high-paying, temporary kinds of employment without intending to permanently migrate to those locations.

Immigrants working in the United States are contributing to the economic base through labor and the tax system. Employers are required to collect and submit income tax to the Internal Revenue Service during the payroll process. If a worker is using a fraudulent identification number, the money is still deposited into the government's coffers. To draw public assistance, individuals must provide necessary documentation for qualification. Illegal workers and their families cannot readily access these types of programs (Lacy, 2006).

The use of English by newly immigrated workers is a much discussed and highly debated topic. Survival in the workplace and marketplace requires at least a rudimentary knowledge of the prevailing language. Lacy (2006) found that the majority of immigrants in her survey were actively working to improve their English-speaking skills.

The findings dispelled these three common myths about Latino immigrants.

As presented in Chapter 1, within the discussion of worldview, groups of people differ in their beliefs about social relationships, management of their futures, and behaviors that are important to their groups. U.S. citizens are quick to attribute their cultural beliefs about job/career goals and materialistic acquisition to those who immigrate into their communities. Ties to and feelings for one's homeland are central to one's identity. Extended family relationships do not dissolve over geographical distances. Immigrating, whether legal or illegal in nature, is a decision that requires intense planning and complex family decision making. Priorities, goals, and objectives are driving forces. The demand to meet basic family needs, not necessarily to improve personal standards of living, is a strong motivational force.

Experienced planners know that plans must be **adaptive** to succeed. Rarely does an individual or family operate in a climate of complete control. Unexpected and uncontrollable events can make the original plan unworkable. These disruptions may be minor and require moderate changes, or they may be so dramatic that they require complete abandonment of the plan. **Contingency plans** are alternative plans created simultaneously with the original plan, anticipating the possibility of problems. The degree of risk and the importance of successful goal achievement determine whether contingency plans will be part of the planning process.

> *Melia is 16 and is looking for a summer job. She applies at a fast-food restaurant, a dog daycare site, and the local library. The fast-food job would allow her to work flexible hours, but if the restaurant doesn't offer her a job, her friend's mother owns the dog daycare, and her aunt works at the library. With two backup plans, Melia will probably have a summer job.*

Proactive plans purposefully strive to avoid surprises and crises. They are designed with forethought and consideration of anticipated events. Proactive planners are controlling a situation by causing something to happen, rather than waiting to respond to it after it happens. Anticipating financial needs in retirement, a working adult may decide to contribute to an employer's retirement plan to supplement the Social Security payment expected. Although there is no way to know how much the person will actually need to sustain the standard of living expected after retirement, having more money is obviously a better situation than not having enough.

> *A manager in a fast-food restaurant has noticed that employees are taking shortcuts and risks to their personal safety in the area near the large oil fryer equipment. She arranges a safety meeting for the next day and creates an educational, short-term training plan for all employees on fryer safety. The manager has anticipated a possible problem and has decided to be proactive to prevent possible injury.*

Reactive plans are spontaneous, without forethought. These types of plans are almost always created quickly in response to an unwelcome

Adaptive: showing or having a capacity for or tendency toward adaptation

Contingency plan: a plan designed to deal with a particular problem, emergency, or state of affairs if it should occur

Proactive plans: plans that are designed with forethought and consideration of anticipated events

Reactive plans: plans that are spontaneous and without forethought

event. A family living from one paycheck to another will be forced to react quickly to loss of employment or housing. They will have to lower their standards because they have no resources to draw on. They may decide to seek aid from other family members or friends or to access public programs designed to help in such emergencies. A sudden total lack of income will force immediate action.

> The McGraw family from New York City decides to take a quick trip to a Canadian mountain park. A neighbor asks if they all have the necessary documentation to cross the border between the United States and Canada. They had not thought about that requirement. It would take several days to get all of those travel papers in order, so they have to readjust their plans. When they try to make a reservation at a northern New York mountain resort, they find that there is no availability. They decide to simply set out driving south to see if they can find a vacation spot somewhere along the coast. Frustration and disappointment are risks within the reactive approach.

Strategic plan: a tool used to outline a group's priorities and future goals

When a family engages in directional, purposeful planning processes in proactive ways, they are practicing **strategic planning** methods. Strategic planning often incorporates contingency planning and continual problem solving, too. Using a strategy is necessary in high-risk situations, such as military combat, medical treatment for chronic and life-threatening diseases, and severe social crises. The increasing use of technology to create databases of healthcare information about individuals provides both promise and concern. Families and physicians need as much information as possible to create strategic health plans. That need for information must be weighed against the possible negative impact of making such information available and the difficulty of protecting the individual's rights (Marvin, 2017).

> Don has just had a mild heart attack. His physicians determine that there is severe blockage in two of his arteries. One form of treatment is less invasive than the other proposed, but possibly not as effective. Don's family has had little experience with such an illness, and no family members are medical professionals. Because the family's medical insurance provides monetary support, the family seeks a second opinion from another medical specialist. She proposes that Don undergo the less invasive procedure at a leading medical facility. If, in her opinion and those of her colleagues, that procedure is not completely successful, Don will have the second procedure while still on the original operating table. In essence, she has proposed a contingency plan. Prior to the surgery, Don will be participating in drug therapy to enhance his chances of survival and recovery. After surgery he will begin a regimen of medications, exercise, and behavior modification to further enhance the medical procedure. This plan includes elements of high risk, contingency planning, and proactive behaviors—all essential in this strategic planning process.

Schedules

A plan may involve formal delineation of who, what, when, and where in a scheduled format. Families typically juggle multiple schedules of members as efficiently and effectively as possible. Using lists, calendars with manual entry systems, and electronic scheduling devices, parents manage to get children to school, activities, and other social obligations. Adults work out ways to divide transportation and supervision duties while maintaining employment schedules and household management tasks.

This type of schedule is a written, detailed plan of activities, locations, and timeframes necessary to facilitate the completion of tasks. Schedules may also be in electronic or even mental format when an individual is capable of planning and remembering information effectively. The level of complexity and the number of people and activities requiring coordination will determine how formal a schedule will need to be in order to facilitate completion of all tasks desired.

Computer and Internet use has revolutionized the scheduling process. Smartphones and portable computers can be programmed to record appointments, remind the user of upcoming appointments, and maintain records of standing appointments across large time spans. Regularly scheduled credit payments, such as mortgage and utility bills, can be handled electronically by scheduling and authorizing them through a bank's computer network. Paychecks and payments from government programs can be scheduled to automatically be deposited from the payment source into your checking account.

Before leaving this discussion about the scheduling process, it is important to address a contemporary problem among American families—overscheduling. Parental work schedules, children's school schedules, extracurricular activities, and afterschool lessons all must be coordinated for busy families. Dunn, Kinney, and Hofferth (2001) report that preadolescent children are spending more and more time in structured activities, such as organized sports, private lessons, and paid leisure activities. Their parents encourage and support this participation in extracurricular activities because they believe it provides their children with opportunities to discover and enhance important lifelong skills.

Anderson and Doherty (2005) found that problems related to overscheduling of family members create opportunities for family professionals to research the impact of this issue and to create solutions for busy families. Lareau (2007) found that working mothers were those largely responsible for scheduling and chauffeuring their children's activities. Hofferth (2003) found that the mother's education level is positively related to the number of activities her children juggle. If overscheduling of children is determined by researchers to be a problem, college-educated women will have to be the first to set the limits (Lareau, 2007).

Budgeting

A budget is another form of planning useful to families. It is a statement of monetary planning that defines income expected and expenses anticipated over a period of time. Most families with adult wage earners focus on budgeting one month at a time. When used in conjunction with accurate recordkeeping, budgets

Overscheduling: family activities where members are too busy; a contemporary problem for many families

Budget: a plan for the coordination of resources and expenditures; the amount of money that is available for, required for, or assigned to a particular purpose

enable families to identify unnecessary spending and adjust expenses to better meet family goals and objectives. The initial creation of a budget requires gathering information about past income and expenses. Records, receipts, bank drafts, and other paper and electronic trails provide historical information important to budget creation.

Budgets are usually divided into two large categories: income and expenses. **Income** includes the salary or wages family members collect on a regular basis. Salaries are most often paid to professionals and managers. Wages are determined for workers who earn a certain amount for each hour or part of an hour they work.

Income: the amount of money received over a period of time as payment for work, goods, or services, or as profit on capital

> *Allison is a nurse. She earns $22 per hour at the local hospital. Her weekly gross pay is $880, or approximately $3,520 each month. She is limited to 40 hours each week unless her employer is willing to pay her overtime compensation—$33 per hour (time and a half).*
>
> *Stacia is the human resources manager at the same hospital. She is on a salary schedule, earning $4,000 per month. There are no automatic overtime requirements for a salaried position. Allison may actually earn more per month if she works overtime occasionally.*

When creating a family budget, it is necessary to gather income information from all working members who are expected to contribute to the budget plan. Weekly budgets can be created, but monthly budgets are more practical and less redundant. After adding all expected income, the **gross family income** is entered onto a budget form (a paper or computer version). Gross income is money earned before taxes and other scheduled deductions are subtracted. Refer back to Chapter 7 for more information on payroll taxes. Because these deductions will be made and the liability already exists, that money will not be available to spend. The amount of money available to spend after all deductions have been made is referred to as the **net income**. Other income that may be added to this section of the budget would include interest payments from savings accounts, payments received from federal programs such as Social Security survivor benefits, and qualifying payments from governmental sources for food stamps and other support programs. After all probable income amounts are determined and added together, the expendable income for a family has been determined.

Gross family income: family income before taxes are removed

Net income: the money available after tax liability is removed from gross income

Expenses: payments disbursed to secure a benefit or bring about a result

Expenses must be determined to compare with the income calculated. There are two distinctive categories of expenses: variable and fixed. **Variable expenses** will not be exactly the same from one period to another. They include automobile expenses such as gasoline, clothing purchases, food, entertainment, gifts, medical bills, and utilities. **Fixed expenses** do not vary remarkably from one payment period to the next. They include mortgage payments or rent, automobile loans, childcare, insurance, and some taxes. Together, these expenses represent the outflow of money from the household for each budgeted period. Fixed expenses are easier to determine, but reviewing past expenditures in the variable category can provide a dependable way to estimate future payments for similar products and services.

Variable expenses: costs that are not always consistent and that change due to circumstances within and external to the family

Fixed expenses: those expenses that remain the same regardless of circumstances

When the total income is compared to the total anticipated expenses, a budget **surplus** or **deficit** will result. When there is a surplus, or more money available than required, the family will decide how to allocate the excess. It can be used to pay down large debts, support wish lists of family members, or be invested for future use. It is important to plan how surplus money will be allocated. Without a formalized plan known to key players in the family, this money may be used in ways that could eventually harm the family.

If a family has a surplus, it is important to consider the following:

- Have any expenses been underestimated?

- Has income been overestimated?

- Could this extra money be used to strengthen the family's economic position?

If a deficit emerges, consider these possibilities:

- Have any expenses been overestimated?

- Has income been underestimated?

- Are family goals and standards of living too high?

- Have all possible sources of income been identified?

Budgeting is a process, not a one-time event. Many families find budgeting tedious and constraining. Others practice quasi-budgeting, recording income in their checkbooks or constantly monitoring bank balances electronically, and then using reactive management as the money is depleted before expenses have all been paid or making unplanned purchases if a surplus appears toward the end of the payroll period.

A great deal of research has been conducted on family budgets and expenditures. Johnson, Rogers, and Tan (2001) reviewed 100 years of family budgeting in the United States. The information collected revealed that the purpose of collecting these data has changed over time. In the first decade of the 20th century, family living conditions, including income and expenses, were explored to investigate the condition of women and child workers. Standards of living—minimum and fair—were determined at that time. After World War I, information was gathered to determine the impact of rapidly rising prices on working families. Terms such as sufficiency of food, respectable clothing, sanitary housing, and minimum essential sundries were new standards set.

Surplus: something that remains above what is used or needed

Deficit: an excess of expenditure over revenue; a loss in business operations

Budgeting: allocating funds; planning or providing for the use of funds in detail

©iStockphoto.com/andresr

▶ **Photo 9.2**
Including children in family budgeting develops lifelong skills.

In response to the devastation to the American economy brought about by the depression period of the 1930s, two budget types were proposed. A maintenance budget met minimum need, but below standard conditions. The emergency budget was proposed as a way to cut the maintenance budget with the least amount of harm to family functioning. By the end of World War II, the economy was rebounding. Maintenance and subsistence levels were no longer the issue. Tax issues surfaced as money was raised to pay for the war. Congress was concerned that low-income families were being unfairly tapped for tax revenue. Efforts were made to determine a cost-of-living scale for analysis. From that time forward, the government has collected data periodically and has reported these findings as descriptive budgets of average households. The information gathered provides contemporary families with guidelines to compare their expenditures, lending important insights into their personal spending habits in relation to others (see Table 9.1).

Williams, Rosen, Hudman, and O'Malley (2004) focused attention on the challenges for low-income family budgets in recent years. Family interviews were conducted in three U.S. cities exploring work, spending patterns, financial challenges, priorities, and healthcare. They report that nationally, low-income families spend 7 out of 10 dollars on basic living expenses, including housing, transportation, and food. Income declined during 2003 due to a lagging economy. Family members reported working overtime and multiple jobs to make ends meet. One strategy identified was that of rotating bills, paying the most important first and paying portions of bills instead of complete balances if necessary. Many families, even those with insurance, reported large unpaid medical bills. These bills eventually result in bad credit ratings and insurance problems. Families struggling financially are more likely to lack health insurance, and thus seek healthcare only

Table 9.1	Major Budget Categories and Average Expenditures by Families	
Expenditure Category	**Amount**	**Percentage Share, 2015**
Total family budget	$69,629	
Food in home and away from home	$7,023	10.1
Housing	$18,409	26.4
Apparel and services	$1,846	2.7
Transportation	$9,503	13.6
Healthcare	$4,342	6.2
Entertainment	$2,842	4.1
Education	$1,315	1.9
Personal insurance and pensions	$6,349	9.1

Source: U.S. Department of Labor (2015), *Consumer Expenditure Survey,* www.bls.gov/cex.

in emergency situations. The more recent recession changed family dynamics, especially among two-career families (Hanes, 2009). Unemployment impacted a larger percentage of males. That new gender imbalance may have changed the employment dynamic in American families for generations to come.

FAMILY FINANCIAL PLANNING

Chances are that most of your future goals will, in some way, involve monetary resources. American social ideals revolve around many materialistic acquisitions—cars, homes, and possessions. As we become an increasingly mobile population, with travel and leisure opportunities more of an expectation than a luxury for middle- and upper-income groups, it is important for adults to realize the importance of financial planning from an early age. In an environment of spending and credit usage, the value of saving money may be blurred for many. Although good financial management is important at any age, it is essential that it begin early.

Family needs change over the life course. Although a discussion of typical families across the life course is problematic due to the diversity of family compositions in contemporary society, there are periods of time where certain types of purchases and financial planning commonly occur (see Table 9.2). During the first three decades of adulthood, two primary goals are explored and implemented: personal career or working-life expectations and family formation.

Young adults are expected to be productive in American society, so career preparation and immediate employment after completing school are expectations.

Table 9.2   Family Financial Life Cycle
Stage One: Early Adulthood to Middle Age
• Choose to remain single, marry, or form an alternative family structure
• Initiate long-term savings for future goals
• Determine and fulfill insurance needs
• Purchase a home
• Plan a career
Stage Two: Preretirement
• Adjust retirement planning if necessary
• Create an estate plan
• Adjust insurance to meet evolving needs
• Establish a retirement living plan
Stage Three: Retirement
• Reap retirement finances accumulated
• Adjust to family changes (widowhood, medical crises, blended families)

▶ **Photo 9.3**
Moving a child into his next life stage is hard, even when parents have planned for years.

©iStockphoto.com/fstop123

Education is an objective for many, intended to prepare people for initial employment and advancement opportunities in the future. The economy, health, family obligations, and other uncontrollable factors can have positive or negative effects on one's progress. From ages 20 to 50, adults typically accumulate a base of wealth to support their current needs and plan for future needs. At the same time, many individuals create their own family units and become independent of their original family group. This experience in the United States often includes cohabitation, marriage, divorce, and remarriage. Occasionally, widowhood is an unexpected experience. The number of dependents or children, partners, and parents one must provide for may vary greatly during these decades, or an individual may choose to remain single and independent.

Careers typically peak after the mid-50s are reached. In the past, this time was focused on approaching retirement, disengaging from the workplace, and developing plans for leisure activities. With increasing life expectancy, it may be unrealistic to continue this pattern. A female retiring at age 65 can expect to live for at least 15 more years. The fastest growing segment of the population is 80 years of age and older. Can the economy maintain positive growth if employees continue to be encouraged to retire before age 70? Do citizens want to leave businesses and careers they have worked to establish while they are still vital and healthy?

The acquisition of material goods (assets) follows patterns across a family life course as well. During family formation, housing, transportation, and the expenses of raising children place a large burden on income providers. Those choosing to parent may face the financial burden of college just as their careers peak and stabilize. Financial support also may be required for aging parents. Downsizing housing at or near retirement age is a trend identified in recent decades, as is the purchase of secondary housing in retirement communities or resort areas. The concept of "active adults" is driving the housing market into new areas of development to meet the expected needs of those adults between retirement age and the new old age.

Financial planning in terms of investment savings has also followed patterns across the family life course. Many employers offer retirement savings plans to their workforce. This creates a large pool of young workers with early savings patterns. Those without employee-sponsored plans can purposefully invest in independent saving plans, but that group is much less likely to actually begin saving early in their careers. Tax and estate planning (see Chapter 12) has usually emerged between 40 and 60 years of age.

Although the life course just discussed is a firmly held concept, it is not as common as believed. Poverty, chronic health conditions, and economic uncertainty wreak havoc on the lives of many Americans. Financial planning and budgeting are time and energy intensive, and many adults fail to set or follow original plans once they are created. When this happens, their financial future is dependent on life circumstances. To avoid this type of uncontrolled dependency, individuals and families need to be committed to financial planning and implementation.

REALITY CHECK

Eileen left her small hometown at the age of 19. It was during World War II, and she found employment as an office manager with a national brewery in the Pacific Northwest. She secured housing in a relatively safe neighborhood.

I found a one-bedroom flat on the third floor of a newer apartment building, just eight bus stops away from my office. I didn't need a car, and my weekly paychecks more than covered my living expenses. It was a crazy time. Young men were rare, most in the service, but all of us working girls liked to party, and we had a great time!

Eileen remained single for her entire life. She had a few steady male friends, but never felt the need to marry. At the age of 36, she met a man who had just lost his wife to cancer. They became a couple, but never married, and both maintained separate living quarters.

I lived in the same apartment for 55 years! The landlord wasn't very happy with me the last 20 years, because rent caps were instituted and he couldn't raise my rent as high as the market would allow. I worked for 25 years at the brewery and then for 35 years at the airplane factory—both nice office-type jobs. My bank account and retirement savings grew. Finally, at 79, I decided to retire and enjoy what was left of my life. Barton's health had gotten very poor, and his children wanted to move him 500 miles away into a care home. That would have broken my heart and his, so I moved into his house to take care of him.

My nieces and nephews helped me move my things from that old apartment. I had so much junk to get rid of!

Eileen took care of Barton for 3 years. One day, when a niece hadn't heard from her in a while, a family friend was asked to check up on the two of them. He found Eileen in a diabetic coma and Barton in a state of shock. Important care decisions had to be made by both families. Because they were never married, Eileen could not make decisions for Barton's healthcare. His daughter moved him to Southern California to be in a care home near her. Eileen's niece moved her back to that small town Eileen had fled so many years before.

I planned and saved for my retirement, but when it came down to it, I couldn't take care of myself, after all. I miss my friends out there, and I really miss Barton. I don't regret any of my life, though. It was a crazy time, and I really lived it up good!

Retirement planning is an important activity for everyone. Although it is impossible to predict which relationships will continue in one's late adulthood, many adults plan for retirement and aging with certain family members and friends as expected sources of support. Choosing to remain single, or to marry and not to have children, eliminates spouses or children as possible sources of assistance in later life. Quality of life is not necessarily sacrificed with those decisions, however. Financial planning and solid legal documentation can ensure that one's personal needs will be fulfilled regardless.

CREATING THE FINANCIAL PLAN

Individuals or couples need to start the planning process with a fresh perspective and an understanding of the **flexibility** required in long-term planning. One inherent goal of financial planning is management for worst-case scenarios. To expect the unexpected is a difficult concept for many to grasp. The odds that crises will occur in any family across a long period of time are high. Illness, unemployment, death, and economic crises are common experiences across generations. A plan creates alternatives and available financial resources to enable a family to work through these crises and move forward.

Expected expenses, such as college, travel, long-term care, and home buying, require the accumulation of wealth or savings over time. Meeting these anticipated needs requires strategic planning approaches and contingency arrangements. Retirement needs may seem too distant to motivate young families to plan, but everyone is encouraged to be proactive. Even if Social Security funds are available several years from now, they are intended only as a supplement, not as full replacement of income. Actively managing the tax liability over a family's life course is also essential. Families need to keep as much of the assets they accumulate over time as possible to meet future needs while balancing their tax responsibilities.

A general understanding of financial investment and insurance management is necessary for all participating in long-term financial planning. It is important to recognize when savings and investments require professional guidance; however, it is important to remain actively involved in your family's savings plan. No one cares more about your money than you do! Be aware and alert.

As with all plans, it is best to begin by identifying goals. These goals may be primarily long term, short term, or a mixture. Common financial goals for families include

- Accumulation of an emergency fund

- Eliminating current debt

- Saving money for a down payment on a home

- Creating a college fund

- Funding home improvements

- Financing a pregnancy and birth

- Setting aside money for retirement

It is not uncommon for a single family to have multiple goals. It is important to keep the goals separate in nature, however, because certain types of investments are better for long-term than for short-term goals. It is also essential to realize and appreciate the fact that as goals are met, new ones will replace them. The life course is always presenting new challenges and redefining family needs.

Goals require plans of action. Each individual and family plan will be unique, reflecting the values and motivation associated with the particular goal. If creating the goal seems overwhelming, it may be helpful to employ a professional financial planner. The trade-off between the time spent studying and gathering data and the fees paid to such professionals must be carefully considered. Whether professionally developed or personally crafted, there are characteristics of good **financial plans**. These include flexibility, liquidity, **protection**, and **tax efficiency**.

The plan must be flexible enough to respond to changes in family needs and unforeseen crises. Gresham's law of planning states that short-term emergencies rise in priority, taking attention away from long-term goals.

> *Gerard and Petra have a special fund set aside for the eventual purchase of a condominium in a trendy part of the city. Every month they contribute $500 to that fund. This month Gerard accidentally breaks the sliding glass door of their apartment. The couple decides to apply next month's contribution toward the door replacement.*

Life is unpredictable, and families must remain flexible to deal with the curves they are thrown. Plans that are too rigid are not conducive to real-life experience and, thus, are doomed to fail.

Although it may seem responsible to secure savings, to avoid the temptation of wasting money on unnecessary purchases, every family needs access to extra funds in times of emergency or temporary adjustments. **Liquidity** refers to the accessibility of funds when they are needed.

> *Troy was serious about buying a new car when he finished his initial job training in 2 years. He put $500 in 6-month certificates of deposit from every monthly paycheck. When his roommate left abruptly, Troy was stuck paying the entire monthly rent for 3 months while he searched for another roommate. He had already put away $2,000 for the car, but the first CD would not mature for another 2 months. If he withdrew that $500, he would lose up to $50 as a penalty for early withdrawal. He had to borrow $1,000 to meet his rental obligation.*

Individuals and families need a certain level of emergency funding available, either in cash or easily liquidated savings plans. Once that fund is large enough to provide security, longer-term savings and riskier investments can be explored.

Although catastrophes are rarer than TV and movie scripts lead us to believe, they do happen. Risk management is fully discussed in Chapter 12, but it is important to include mention of insurance in this discussion of financial planning. Beyond the emergency funds available, individuals and families should have insurance protection in cases of large disastrous events, such as fire, major illness or disability, and death. Premium costs for these types of insurance must be budgeted carefully, and the rate of premiums must be considered in terms of affordability and risk minimization.

> *Rocky and Maddie are purchasing an engagement ring. The retailer offers insurance coverage in the event of loss. The annual premium for this*

Financial plan: a budgetary planning document reflecting the way an organization plans to use its financial and human resources in a given year

Protection: the act of preventing somebody or something from being harmed or damaged

Tax efficiency: financial planning that involves consideration of tax liability

Liquidity: an asset's ability to *quickly* be liquidated or converted through an action of buying or selling without causing a significant movement in the price and with minimum loss of value

insurance is $100. The young couple is on a tight budget. That amount of money would require cutting other expenses. Is it necessary? Would that $100 be better spent on renter's insurance or enhancement of a life insurance policy?

Tax liability is an essential part of citizenship. It is also an important consideration in financial planning. Many types of interest earned on investments are taxable. Some are not taxable. Investors need to ensure that their money is earning the maximum amount after taxes and inflation are accounted for. There may be certain times and circumstances where saving money is less profitable than spending it.

You have $10,000 from an inheritance. Your TV is not working anymore. If you invest that money in a savings account that yields less than 5% annually and you are in a high tax bracket, you may pay 30% of the interest in income taxes [$500 − $150 (tax) = $350 (real earnings)]. If, after a year, the cost of replacing that TV has risen from $1,000 to $1,500, you would have made a better decision to buy the TV, rather than investing the total inheritance.

Mortgage insurance is deductible in personal income tax formulas. When interest rates are low, it may be more financially sound to invest in real estate than in stocks, bonds, or certificates of deposit. Gains in those types of venues are taxable. Money paid on the real estate mortgage interest is deductible, and the real estate may have appreciated in value.

Financial planning is crucial to the fulfillment of long-term goals. Because an important characteristic of families is sustaining the unit over time, financial preparation is essential for all families. General knowledge of personal finance premises is basic to the successful creation and implementation of these plans.

IN THE NEWS

Planning to Avoid Future Tragedy in the Wake of Earthquake Destruction

In 2010, an earthquake struck one of the poorest and least developed countries in the world—Haiti. Following the earthquake, an estimate in *The New York Times* (Archibold, 2011) reported more than 316,000 deaths. Six years later, Hurricane Matthew caused catastrophic flooding, killing more than 1,300 people and leaving more than 35,000 homeless. These two natural disasters hitting the same country beg the question: What positive action can be done to prevent such situations in the future?

Proactive planning is very useful when catastrophe is predictable. A country with constant political upheaval, health crises, and frequent hurricanes can be sure of the need for disaster planning. The challenge is finding the resources needed to create such plans and then securing the resources necessary to implement those plans.

When Haiti's capital, Port-au-Prince, was leveled by the earthquake, a few planners and visionaries recognized an opportunity to fix chronic structural problems. Ultimately, these experts proposed shrinking the size of the city and revitalizing the surrounding rural area's agricultural potential. Goals included job creation, food production, stronger building standards, and lessening the overcrowded living conditions. The time seemed ripe to implement these ideas, as the infrastructure would need to be rebuilt anyway.

The challenges, however, seemed insurmountable. Irrigation was problematic, and distribution chains for crop sales and food processing were almost nonexistent. Foreign aid ebbed and flowed after and between crises, ultimately ending as the crises faded into memories. The Interim Haiti Recovery Commission closed in October 2011. The mandate had expired, and the momentum of foreign giving had waned. The envisioned growth of manufacturing jobs also faded. Without an obvious strengthening of political stability, foreign investors and aid providers were reluctant to provide the resources and guidance needed. Had the effort to strengthen the infrastructure after the earthquake been successful, would it have mitigated some of the damage from the hurricane? Probably.

The opportunity to rebuild and strengthen an entire country presents similar challenges that often prevent families from rebounding from adversity. Goals must be understandable and must be viewed as possible in order for those involved to want to devote time, energy, and resources to their implementation.

EMERGENCY ACTION PLANS

The global experiences of the last decade have highlighted the importance of preparation and planning for disasters. Despite the obvious importance of crisis planning, a recent Red Cross survey indicated that 67% of Americans believe such preparation is important, but only 16% are actually ready with plans in place (Pagan, 2006).

A good strategy for emergency planning is to identify all possible disasters the family might face. Conducting family discussion sessions about how everyone might respond in the situations identified will illuminate strengths and weaknesses that currently exist in plans and family communication channels. The weaknesses can be discussed, and better plans can be created to better prepare all family members for crisis action. Important questions to consider include the following:

- Where would we/I go if . . . ?

- Who would we/I be responsible for if . . . ?

- What possessions are important to take with us/me if . . . ?

One important lesson learned in recent disasters is that of supplies acquisition. In large-scale disasters, supplies of all kinds may be inaccessible. Pagan (2006) recommends that families have a safety stash of food and water, a first-aid kit, and necessary medications. She also recommends that families have basic financial resources available in times of emergency—cash, checkbook, and credit cards. Important documentation, such as birth certificates, Social Security cards, financial statements, and insurance identification cards, should be stored in a waterproof or fireproof container that could be easily carried away from the disaster. Don't forget pets when creating this emergency plan. Their safety is often out of their own control.

HOW PLANS EMERGE

Chapter 10 delves into the importance of communication in family decision making. Communication patterns determine who and what will be involved in the planning process that emerges from decisions requiring action of family members. Chapter 11 discusses how leadership within families brings about implementation of plans and delegation of roles within those constructions. Communication and leadership are both important core concepts in the management of family resources.

SUMMARY

Planning is a natural process for humans. The planning process enables individuals and families to focus current energies on future goals, leading to the long-term success of the family unit. Different approaches and strategies are necessary for different goals, and family members responsible for such decisions must be informed and prepared or aided by professionals in the field to be effective and efficient in maintaining the welfare of all members. Financial and emergency planning are two major types of plans instituted by families to prepare for the future.

QUESTIONS FOR REVIEW AND DISCUSSION

1. What are important steps in financial planning?

2. Why do some plans fail?

3. How do goals and financial needs change over the life course of any family?

4. How does planning impact your daily life?

5. List five long-term goals you have for your future (over the next 20 years). What kinds of planning activities might you use to ensure that you will reach these goals?

CHAPTER TEN

COMMUNICATION WITHIN THE DECISION-MAKING PROCESS

Objectives
Communication Theory
    Family Communication
In the News
    Communication and Conflict
Worldview
Communication and Information Technology
    Radio and Audio Streaming
    Television and Online Media
    Telephones and Mobile Devices
Reality Check
    Computers and the Internet
Application to Family Decision Making
Summary
Questions for Review and Discussion

Objectives

- Describe the communication process.

- Apply the communication process to family decision making.

- Explain family communication patterns.

- Explore power and conflict within family communication.

- Understand the impact of technology on family communication and decision making.

Half the world is composed of people who have something to say and can't, and the other half who have nothing to say and keep on saying it.

—Robert Frost

The decision-making process that guides families in identification of needs and selection of alternatives to meet those needs is heavily dependent on another process—the communication process. Galvin, Bylund, and Brommel (2012) view **communication** as a "symbolic, transactional process of creating and sharing meanings" (p. 24). Family communication illustrates this process of creating and sharing meanings as it unfolds to identify needs, alternatives, and ultimately the completion of the decision-making process.

Communication: a process by which information is exchanged between individuals through a common system of symbols, signs, or behavior

Family systems theory refers to these shared understandings as family rules. Strong, DeVault, and Sayad (2008) explain *family rules* as patterned or characteristic responses, generally unwritten, that are formed over time and are difficult to change. These rules fall within a hierarchy and are ranked in order of significance to the family unit. They are created consensually or through conscious and unconscious power struggles among family members. These rules may operate at overt levels (visible to family members) or at covert levels (hidden and unrecognized).

COMMUNICATION THEORY

The communication process operates within a framework (see Figure 10.1). Communication involves multiple senders, receivers, and messages, and is thus a complex process. Multiple points exist for noise to impact the message. *Noise* is anything that detracts from the pure, intentional message. It could be static on a telephone line (channel) or the bad mood of your friend (channel) who is taking a message to your teacher.

Family Communication

The communication process is continuous and always changing. It is transactional, in that when people communicate, they have a mutual impact on each other. This impact can be intrapersonal, interpersonal, within the group, or out to the external world. Communication can be oral or written, formal or informal, verbal or nonverbal.

Because communication plays a central role in the family, Koerner and Fitzpatrick (2002) suggest that any theory of family communication must include both intersubjectivity and interactivity. **Intersubjectivity** is the element of communication that involves shared meanings. When multiple members are interacting in the communication process, the understood meanings within messages are key to the successful outcome of the process. Individuals within the family system bring uniqueness to their encoding and decoding activities. However, family units have shared vocabularies and archived histories that serve as reference points

Intersubjectivity: communicating shared meanings

Figure 10.1 The Communication Process

Message—encoded by the Sender

Channel—Sender selects and loads

Message sent through the channel to Receiver

Receiver gets message and decodes

Feedback is given by the Receiver to the Sender

Sender processes feedback

Source: Adapted from Schermerhorn, Naumes, Naumes, and Schermerhorn (1996).

for encoding and decoding messages. **Interactivity** is the way in which a family communicates. How family members interact with each other to get messages across is the focus of interactivity. Both are necessary to understand because they take place at the same time within a family.

Interactivity: the way in which a family communicates

Communication is at the center of family functioning because it is through communication that members are able to establish social reality (Baxter & Braithwaite, 2002). In addition, family members participate in the process because the focus is on relationship building and maintenance, rather than on the individual participants.

The encoding or decoding process is impacted by a variety of factors, and there are many variables that cause the message to be misunderstood. These misunderstandings are found in filters and distorters. **Filters** convince the sender and receiver that the message was not intended in its true form. *He really did not mean it like that.* **Distorters** convince the sender and/or the receiver that the message has a hidden meaning. What did he mean by that tone or that choice of words? Common filters are culture and wishful thinking. If a woman receives an e-mail with sexual overtones from her male boss, she and others may brush it off as something men say, but don't actually intend. If a parent receives a note from a child away at camp saying, "I hate it here," he or she may interpret it as a case where the child simply hasn't adjusted yet, but it couldn't be that bad. An example of wishful thinking is common among young adolescents. *He pushed me because that is his way of showing that he likes me.*

Filter: a way to convince the sender and receiver that the message wasn't intended in its true form

Distorter: an element of communication that convinces the sender and/or the receiver that a message has a hidden meaning

Common distorters may result from the differences found between the two genders. Expectations and responses of men and women differ in regard to communication. Tannen (1990) argues that men typically use **report talk**, which is meant to convey information, and that women use **rapport talk**, which is meant to strengthen intimacy. Using Tannen's model, Edwards and Hamilton (2004) did not find that gender was the cause of difficulty in communication, but that differences between males and females are reconciled by the gender roles of dominance and nurturance. In contrast to Tannen's earlier work, they believe that the characteristic of nurturance leads to cooperation, which actually reduces difficulty in communication between the sexes. Strong, DeVault, and Sayad (2008) report that in conversations where conflict is present, wives tend to send clearer messages to their husbands than their husbands send to them. Women are often more sensitive and responsive to messages received from their partners. Husbands tend to either give neutral messages or withdraw from the conversation. In arguments, wives set the emotional tone, escalating conflict with negative verbal and nonverbal messages and deescalating argument with an atmosphere of agreement. Wives tend to use emotional appeals and threats more than husbands, who tend to seek conciliation and try to postpone or end an argument.

Report talk: conversations meant to convey information; typically used by men

Rapport talk: conversation meant to strengthen intimacy; typically used by women

Differing worldviews may also be a common distorter in communication. Cultures differ in terms of high and low context. The United States tends to operate in a low context, where words carry most of the meaning in a conversation. A high-context country allows body language and other behaviors to have equal, if not higher, meanings than the actual words used.

> *Jasmine wants to convert the basement storage room into a private room of her own. When she approaches her parents about this, her father utilizes a low-context response. "If you are willing to clean it out and fix it up, it's all yours." Jasmine's mother most often utilizes high context in her communication. "Jasmine, go for it." Her eyes roll upward as she says these four words, and her shoulders and hand gestures imply that she is sure Jasmine will never follow through on her promise, so the private room will never become a reality. Her words and mannerisms say two very different things. Jasmine knows from experience that her mother's implied messages are much more accurate. She can anticipate little, if any, support from her mother in her efforts to convert the storage room.*

Families are the purveyors of culture. Members learn culture of the larger group through interaction with older family members. In reality, families have unique cultural frameworks within their own units. These shared understandings increase the complexity of the communication process when it functions within family decision-making situations.

Family Communication Patterns

Conformity orientation: parental assertion of power and control of communication in the family

Conversation orientation: a situation where family members of all ages have the freedom to express their opinions openly and freely

Consensual families: families that stress both the socio- and concept-orientation dimensions of communication, with the result that children are encouraged to explore the world about them, but to do so without disrupting the family's established social harmony

Families usually follow two types of communication orientation: conformity and conversation (Koerner & Fitzpatrick, 1997). Although the family usually fits one or the other type of orientation, some families have a mix of orientations within the same family. A family that has a conformity orientation is one where common attitudes, beliefs, and values are expected. This family opposes conflict and stresses compliance to the decisions made by parents or older family members. Conversation orientation allows the family members of all ages the freedom to express their opinions openly and freely. From these two orientations, four family communication patterns emerge (see Table 10.1; Fitzpatrick & Ritchie, 1994). Consensual families are high in conversation and conformity. A consensual family is able to communicate with each other and desires to have agreement.

Table 10.1 Family Communication Patterns Versus Family Types		
	Family Types	
Family Communication Patterns	**High-Conversation Orientation**	**Low-Conversation Orientation**
High-Conformity Orientation	Consensual	Protective
Low-Conformity Orientation	Pluralistic	Laissez-faire

Sources: Fitzpatrick and Ritchie (1994); Galvin, Bylund, and Brommel (2004); Koerner and Fitzpatrick (1997).

Bob and Judy are in the process of deciding where to go for their family vacation. Although they have suggested some things to each other, they decide to ask their three teenage children for their suggestions. Judy tells them, "We want you to help make the decision because we want everyone to be happy and enjoy this vacation." Everyone made suggestions, and a vacation spot is determined.

The **pluralistic family** is one that is high in conversation, but low on conformity. These families are good at communication, but do not expect that everyone will agree.

Although the Phillips family had always attended church together, Paul, the oldest of the children, announced that he would not be going to church anymore. His parents were upset at first, but then sat down with him and had a conversation about his announcement. He explained that he wasn't sure that his beliefs matched those of the church and he didn't get anything out of the service. His parents listened and then talked about how faith was important to them. In the end, they said, "Paul, you know where we stand on this, but we will leave this decision up to you."

The **protective family** is low in conversation and high on conformity. This family expects everyone to follow the rules, and there is no need for communication about them.

Amanda just turned 16. The day she got her driver's license, she planned to go out with her friends. She was having so much fun that she completely forgot about the time. When she realized it was past her curfew, she immediately called her parents. When her dad answered the phone, he informed her that she would no longer have driving privileges for 2 weeks. He ended with, "You know the rules—now you will have to suffer the consequences. I don't care what excuse you have!"

The **laissez-faire family** is low in both conversation and conformity. This family does not communicate very much, and family members often carry on with their own lives outside the family.

Tim and Diane are high school friends. After they attended a friend's birthday party the night before, Diane noticed that Tim was wearing the same clothes the next day at school. When she asked about it, Tim told her that he had car trouble and spent the night at a friend's house. When Diane asked if his parents were worried, he said, "My parents don't even know. I don't have a curfew, and they are usually gone for work before I get up for school. I guess I don't know if they would be worried or not—we've never talked about it."

► **Photo 10.1**
Instant video chatting is the next best thing to being there in person.

Family Communication Standards

Individuals often have a set of standards or beliefs about what the ideal relationship should include. Many of these standards involve communication. Someone may believe that a good relationship includes full disclosure and would be concerned if his or her partner ever held anything back. Others may believe that it is necessary to withhold information that could potentially hurt their partner. Communication varies greatly across families because all families are different. Differences between generations and between cultures, and even the degree of closeness within the family can alter the way a family communicates. Some grow up in families that talk very little, and others are raised in households where conversation takes place continuously. These differences can cause problems for couples as they form a new family. Caughlin (2003) identified 10 distinct communication standards of family communication (see Table 10.2).

Power is a subtle yet important element in family communication. The ability that one family member has to exercise power over another family member can be expressed in various ways.

Power can be verbalized as the following:

- Withdrawal
  - "I'm not speaking to you."

- Guilt induction
  - "How could you ask me to do this?"

- Positive coercion
  - "Kiss me and help me move this sofa."

- Negotiation
  - "I'll do that if you do this."

- Deception
  - "I'll just charge it to the credit card and he'll never notice."

- Blackmail
  - "If you do that, I'll tell them about. . . ."

- Physical/verbal abuse
  - "Watch your back."

Where does power within a family unit originate? Szinovacz (1987) developed a view of family power and describes it as a dynamic, multidimensional process

Table 10.2 Caughlin Family Communication Standards (in Order of Frequency)

Communication Standard	Description
Intimate disclosure	The ability to discuss intimate topics, such as one's feelings, drugs, and sex
Negativity/conflict	A family's tendency to engage in certain conflict behaviors, such as criticism, yelling, and swearing
Respect	Showing respect for other family members by not being rude, swearing, or talking back
Routine contact	Chatting/keeping up with other family members; the importance of checking with others the importance of asking others what they mean, rather than having the ability to mind-read
Creating/demonstrating cohesion	The importance of the family being close or communicating to bond
Treating each other with equality	Everybody gets a say; parents talk to children as equals (vs. kids not being supposed to talk); children get input in important decisions
Openness about problems	Expectations about whether family members should talk openly about potentially troublesome issues, problems, or disagreements
Politeness	The extent to which a family's communication is seen as proper and formal (rather than relaxed)
Discipline	Rule setting; dealing with rule violations, curfews, groundings, etc.; this includes both rules that parents set for children and rules for the parents' behavior
Emotional/instrumental support	The manner or extent to which family members provide each other with social support or acceptance when there is a difficulty

Source: From Caughlin, John P., "Family Communication Standards. What Counts as Excellent Family Communication and How Are Such Standards Associated With Family Satisfaction?" (2003). *Human Communication Research*. Blackwell Publishing, Ltd. Reprinted with permission of Blackwell Publishing, Ltd.

with **power bases** that are linked to individual family members. Adult members of families have the ability to reward, coerce, and ignore younger members when making decisions that impact all family members. Other than age and financial resources, expertise is another important power base. Children with higher technological skills may hold more power in situations involving computerization than parents. Newly immigrated parents often find themselves reliant on their children's ability to translate and communicate in the new language.

Power bases: positions where individual family members have power when making decisions that impact other family members

The balance of power within families is also reflective of the relationships between and among family members. Blood and Wolfe (1960) developed a resource theory of family power in their classic study. More power is given to the spouse or the family member with the most resources. In turn, the person gaining the most from the relationship at any given time will be most dependent on other family members. Such is the case of young children. Their survival depends on the actions of older family members. Adolescents sense lessening dependence as they mature, thus shifting the power balance in certain decision-making situations.

Family members may use resources to increase control within the family. McDonald (1980) identified five types of resources that are used as bases of family power:

1. **Normative resources** are those where culture or society identifies who should have the power in the family. For example, in a society where the traditional family is valued, the father will have more overall power, with the mother having power over the children.

2. **Economic resources** refer to monetary resources. Those who bring the money into the family will have more power and will probably make more of the financial decisions.

3. **Affective resources** are those that are more relational. An example would be a wife who withholds affection from her husband because she doesn't approve of his behavior.

4. **Personal resources** are inherent in the personality or appearance of the family member. The person who has an outgoing personality is much more likely to garner power within the family. Another example would be the youngest child, who may charm the others into getting them to do anything for him or her.

5. **Cognitive resources** allow a family member to gain power because of his or her intelligence. This often includes the person who logically reasons strategies to gain power from the other family members. An example of this is the child who learns how to get what he or she wants by working his or her parents against each other.

Waller and Hill (1951) discuss the impact of the **principle of least interest**. In marriages and cohabitation situations, the partner with the least interest in continuing a relationship has the most power in it. The changing dynamics of male/female dependency over the last several decades has presented increased complexity in family decision making and communication. Some family theorists challenge the idea that women participating in the workforce have shifted the power balance within the family from one of subservience to one of equality.

> If power is defined as the ability to change the behavior of others intentionally, women, in fact, have a great deal of power. It is rooted in their role as nurturers and kin-keepers, and flows out of their capacity to support and direct the growth of others. (Kranichfeld, 1987, pp. 42–56)

Normative resources: family power that is given to those within the family who are identified by culture or society as having a particular type of authority

Economic resources: the basic inputs or component parts of an economy, such as land, labor, and capital

Affective resources: resources that relate to feelings, preferences, and values

Personal resources: resources that are inherent in the personality or appearance of a family member

Cognitive resources: mental-skill abilities, such as concentration, memory, problem solving, and reasoning

Principle of least interest: a phenomenon where the partner with the least interest in continuing the relationship has the most power in that relationship

Fitzpatrick (1988) views power dynamics and communication within the interactions of adult partners as either symmetrical or complementary. **Symmetrical conversations** occur when partners send similar messages that impact how the relationship is defined. Both individuals adopt the same tactics, but utilize different approaches within the communication process. **Competitive symmetry** occurs when both partners view the situation as a competition, where both aim to defeat the other. This creates a win/lose situation that results in escalating hostilities. Ammunition in this conversation is open to everything that has ever transpired between the two individuals. **Submissive symmetry** results when neither individual will accept responsibility for making a decision and taking action. The eventual goal is win/lose, to outlast the other in the process of passing the responsibility back and forth. **Neutralized symmetry** reflects the desire for a win/win outcome. Both individuals respect each other and seek to avoid assuming control over the other. Each gives a little, and both gain. A **complementary interaction** results when both individuals adopt different tactics. One must accept the dominant position, and the other must accept the submissive position. This action is not to be confused with exertion of power, but rather with a give-and-take relationship where individuals work together for mutual enhancement of the unit.

The Everett family must decide what to do for Christmas this year. We assume that other members of the family are too young to participate fully in the decision:

Competitive Symmetry:

> **Mother:** *I don't want to go to your family's celebration; it's too far to travel.*
>
> **Father:** *It's not much farther than your family. You just don't like my mother.*
>
> **Mother:** *I don't like your mother; she's bossy, and she can't cook.*
>
> **Father:** *My mother's bossy. What about your mother?*

Submissive Symmetry:

> **Mother:** *I don't care where we go; I just don't want to have it at our house.*
>
> **Father:** *I don't care, either. My family won't be unhappy.*
>
> **Mother:** *My family won't be unhappy, either. Maybe you should call your sister.*
>
> **Father:** *Why don't you call your brother?*

Neutralized Symmetry:

> **Father:** *Where did we go last year?*
>
> **Mother:** *We went to my family for Christmas Eve and yours for Christmas Day.*
>
> **Father:** *That worked for me. How about you?*
>
> **Mother:** *I think it might be good to switch this year.*
>
> **Father:** *That sounds fine.*

Symmetrical conversations: conversations that are balanced in regard to dominance

Competitive symmetry: an interaction between two people where both want to define the interaction or dominate

Submissive symmetry: an interaction where each person accepts the other's definition of interaction or submits

Neutralized symmetry: a situation in which neither person in a conversation seeks to be dominant

Complementary interaction: when each person in an interaction adopts a different tactic of conversation, with one being dominant and the other submissive

Complementary Interaction:

Mother: *My mother really wants us to come there this year.*

Father: *My parents will be disappointed, but they'll understand.*

Mother: *We'll find a way to make it up to them.*

IN THE NEWS

Parent-Child Relationship in the Digital Era

Perhaps the greatest change in parent-child relationship has occurred in the past two decades, with the advent of the digital age. This change is most noticeable in the relationship between an adolescent child and the parent. The knee-jerk reaction is to believe that the digital age has deteriorated the relationship between the parent and adolescent child. But, a more rational approach shows that such stressors have always existed in different avatars and technology has in fact improved the relationship between the parent and adolescent child. The digital age has altered the hierarchial [sic] nature of conventional parent-child relationship into a form that is more equal, intimate, and egalitarian than it has been in the past.

Four integral features of digital communication have influenced the parent-child relationship in the past decade-

- Persistence: "Forgive and forget", the maxim of traditional communication, has morphed into "forgive but persist" in digital communication.

- Changeability: Technology, as some claim half in jest, is perpetually in beta stage. The high turnover rate of technology tools, and the ease with which the digital native adolescent adapts to it, leaves the parent often in a state of lag.

- Scalability: When I was an adolescent, my social circle was well within the grasp of my parents because of geographic limits. The expanse of social media makes this more difficult.

- Access to data: While mortification was limited in the past at being dropped by a mother at the movie theatre or such like, now the easy access to data and information can sway the relationship between child and parent.

It is undeniable that in terms of parenting and parent-child relationships, the digital era is vastly different from the one that preceded it, but it must also be acknowledged that digital tools have indeed benefitted parenting in that the village that takes to raise a child is now a global village. Parents themselves are different today and as it has always been, parents have to adapt and mesh their parenting attitudes and activities with the digitally rich environment that their children are born into. It takes conscious effort and constant course correction to bypass the pitfalls of digital tools and enhance the riches that these tools bring into the parent-child bond.

Source: **Used with the permission of Mobicip.**

Communication and Conflict

Not all communication in the family is positive. Some communication patterns incorporate negative tactics of manipulation through guilt or power. These communication habits are difficult to break and may cycle into tremendous problems and extraordinary circumstances for a family. Anticipation and prevention of conflict within the communication process are helpful, but conflicts will occur. **Conflict** is a state of disagreement or disharmony. It creates a stressful situation that is uncomfortable to one or to all parties involved. **Conflict resolution** is the negotiation of conflict toward a positive goal. This negotiation may involve a generation of consensus among participants or a majority rules process.

It is inevitable that there will be conflict in a family. Relationships are intimate, and an internal struggle of roles and expectations plays out over time. Each new family member creates more complexity in relationship building and maintenance. Each family member who leaves creates a chasm or a hole that needs bridging or filling. Our communication patterns evolve from our interaction with parents, caregivers, and siblings.

The most harmful conflicts within a family are interpersonal—those that exist between and among individual members. These conflicts shake the foundation of the family unit. Especially destructive communication in these situations includes direct verbal attacks on an individual. Things can be said and retrieved from past situations that damage the individual's perception of self and ultimately split families into opposing sides. This type of destructive communication has been associated with lower relationship satisfaction and higher divorce rates (Gottman & Notarius, 2000). Gottman (1995) identifies four specific communication behaviors in conflict that are predictors of a failed relationship. Known as the "Four Horsemen of the Apocalypse," these behaviors are criticism (attacking the person's character or personality), contempt (communicating disgust with the other person), defensiveness (believing the other person is responsible for the entire conflict), and stonewalling (turning away from the conflict and the relationship).

Money is a major source of marital conflict. Who makes it? Who decides how it will be allocated? Who sets priorities? Who enforces priorities? Another mitigating factor in money-based family conflict is the difficulty inherent in talking about money matters. People can be both secretive and defensive in such discussions. In addition, decisions about money affect everyone in the family, and power and control issues may come into play for those making the decisions (Jenkins, 2002). Olson, DeFrain, and Skogrand (2014) suggest other reasons why finances cause problems for families. These include the inability to create and stick with a budget, heavy reliance on credit, differences in spending and saving habits, and family members' different meanings for money.

Some conflict within a family unit, or any group, is necessary and healthy. When communication focuses on the problem, not the individual, positive problem solving can occur. Kranichfeld (1987) suggests that resolution of family resource conflicts can result in three outcomes:

1. **Agreement.** Members agree without coercion or threats, giving freely without resentment. This agreement is based on perceived reciprocation at a later time.

©iStockphoto.com/keeweeboy

▸ **Photo 10.2**
All families have conflict.

Conflict: the opposition of persons or forces that gives rise to the dramatic action in a drama or fiction; a state of disagreement or disharmony

Conflict resolution: the process of consensus arrived at after discussion of a disagreement between people

Agreement: the act or fact of agreeing; harmony of opinion, action, or character

Bargaining: to negotiate over the terms of a purchase, agreement, or contract; to haggle; to come to terms

Coexistence: to exist together or at the same time; to live in peace with each other, especially as a matter of policy

2. **Bargaining.** Within relationships, equity is a goal. During the discussion, family goals and relationships are focus points.

3. **Coexistence.** When differences can't be resolved, they will be accepted. Discourse is absorbed within the family relationship without jeopardizing individual relationships.

WORLDVIEW

Cultural Impact on Communication

How does the culture of individuals engaged in communication affect the communication process?

1. *Different communication styles:* Across cultures, some words and phrases are used in different ways. Nonverbal communication is also different across cultures. Facial expressions, gestures, personal distance, and sense of time can communicate different ideas across cultures. One family may see an increase in volume as a sign of exciting conversation, whereas another family might react with alarm.

2. *Different attitudes toward conflict:* Some cultures view conflict as a positive, whereas others view it as something to be avoided. Some families may see conflict as necessary and are encouraged to deal directly with conflicts that arise. Other cultures would find open conflict embarrassing.

3. *Different decision-making styles:* The roles that individuals play in decision making vary widely from culture to culture. Although some cultures value individual decision making, others prefer consensus.

4. *Different attitudes toward disclosure:* In some cultures, it is not appropriate to be frank about emotions, the reasons behind a conflict or misunderstanding, or personal information. Other cultures would have no problem in sharing these kinds of details.

5. *Different approaches to completing tasks:* People across cultures have different ways to complete tasks based on the resources available, beliefs about what is important, and their orientations to work. Even how cultures view relationships as they work together can impact how a task will be accomplished.

6. *Different approaches to knowing:* How people come to know things represents cultural differences. European cultures gather information based on measurement of facts. Other cultures may base their information on symbols or stories that have been passed down from generation to generation.

How would these differences affect an interracial marriage?

How would these differences affect an international couple living in the United States?

Source: Adapted from DuPraw, Marcelle E., and Marya Axner. (1997). "Working on Common Cross-Cultural Communication Challenges." *The Public Broadcasting Service.*

COMMUNICATION AND
INFORMATION TECHNOLOGY

Although radio, TV, the Internet, and smartphones are all means of communication common to American families, they also represent a large consumer market. What originally represented a way to connect to the outside world and a form of entertainment for families has developed into a multimillion-dollar industry that has had an effect on the family. The media now plays a role in the maintenance of family relationships and in their connection to society. Although the family has always been the center of socialization in preparing children to live in society, one aspect of the media is its socialization role. It is through media that we learn about the world and ourselves.

Radio and Audio Streaming

Originally used as a means of communication for the military, the radio began to appear in American homes in the 1920s. As the first electronic medium in the home, the radio was seen as an important window to the world. For the first time, Americans were able to have information in real time. At the same time, there were parents who were concerned about the effects of adult radio programming on their children.

Although the radio and other audio streaming is still a popular form of media, it has changed dramatically over the last decade. Public radio stations compete with private stations for audience share. Digital television radio (DTR) and satellite radio, widely available and very reliable, are commercial free and subscriber supported. Unlike the early years of radio, families do not gather together to listen to the radio. Individuals choose to listen on their own. Younger listeners are turning to portable electronic devices and downloaded copies of preferred music, avoiding the social, political, and economic implications of radio broadcasting. Purchase of these electronics, accessories, copy permission fees, and subscriptions to private radio broadcasting channels have added to the financial costs of audio entertainment.

Television and Online Media

When the TV was first introduced in the 1950s, families placed this "appliance" in the living room or the most prominent place in the home. All members of the family had access and usually watched together. Wartella and Jennings (2001) report that, in the early days of TV, people believed it would benefit the family by keeping the family together, solving marital problems, and keeping problem children off of the streets.

TV viewing today is different from watching TV in the past. As wealth increased, so did not only the size of homes, but also the number of TVs in each home. In the United States, 99% of households have a television (Steuer & Hustedt, 2002). The Nielsen Company (2010) reports that 31% of American households have four or more TV sets. The cable and satellite industry provides the consumer with a multitude of options for specialized viewing. In addition, the opportunity to aggregate or stream video using services such as Hulu and Netflix serve to marry the TV with computer technology, which establishes individual viewing from a variety of devices.

In the late 1970s, the government began to investigate the effects of TV on the family. Pearl, Bouthilet, and Lazar (1982) conducted research that looked at children's aggressive and antisocial behavior, which was believed to be associated with TV viewing. Recent research has found other negative effects associated with television viewing, including obesity (Hands et al., 2011; Harris, Schwartz, & Speers, 2011), isolation (Bickham & Rich, 2006; Sisson, Broyles, Newton, Baker, & Chermausek, 2011), and cardiovascular disease (Taylor, 2011). Although most acknowledged that TV had some negative influence, it was generally considered the responsibility of the family to educate and instill morals. Not until the 1990s did parents organize to campaign for controls such as the V-chip or content labeling in addition to demanding antidrug commercials (Andreasen, 2001). Researchers have proposed that there may be a shift away from the idea that television affects viewers negatively or positively to the ideas associated with cultivation theory (Gerbner, Gross, Signorielli, & Shanahan, 2002). This theory suggests that television, or all media for that matter, is part of a process of constructing meaning from what a person watches or hears over time that influences their understanding of the world in which they live. As such, the continual and ever changing stream of information and entertainment a person interacts with on a daily basis can combine with the contexts of their situation to affect their worldview, assumptions, and beliefs.

Whatever position is taken on the value of TV and other online media within the family home, the messages received through this media format have had an impact on the social climate and social learning of the current generation. Signorielli and Morgan (2001) suggest that "television is one of the major players in the socialization process" (p. 333) and is more likely to portray family life as it already exists, rather than to affect changes in future family life. This position is likely to be argued and debated for some time.

Telephones and Mobile Devices

The introduction of the telephone into the family represented a major change in communication. Although most were excited about the possibilities of being connected to the outside, some worried about the intrusion into the home and the loss of information out of the home that could weaken family relationships or compromise privacy. The technology of the mobile or cell phone was even more of a change in family communication and represents the fastest growing technology in history. Mobile phones and other mobile devices such as tablets or wearable computers continue to evolve. Ninety percent of American adults have a cell phone, with 58% having a smartphone, and 42% own a tablet computer (Pew

Research Center, 2014a). Smart watches and glasses are on the market now and will no doubt change the way we communicate once again.

The original intention of the cell phone was for use in work-related situations and for safety or security. In time, the advantages of cell phones expanded to include social interactions. Families now use smartphones as a way to connect children, parents, and extended family members. Smartphones improve efficiency in time by providing immediate information, such as being able to quickly ask someone a question, and by coordinating events, such as meeting at a restaurant. Smith (2011) reports that people use smartphones not only for communication, but for information retrieval via the Internet, for entertainment, and to avoid interacting with people around them. Research suggests that text messaging may be a way to improve family relationships because of the immediacy of the way communications are answered (Crosswhite, Rice, & Asay, 2014).

Ling and Yttri (1999) found that teenagers have created new forms of communication and interaction. Microcoordination is when social groups make plans over their smartphones to meet somewhere and activities are coordinated. Hypercoordination is when smartphones are used not only to coordinate activities, but also to develop group norms through emotional and social communication. Brown (2011) suggests that rather than this form of communication working toward cross-cultural communication that encourages diversity, a "digital tribalism" is emerging where people use technology to connect with those who share the same beliefs and values.

Microcoordination: when smartphones are used only to coordinate activities

Hypercoordination: when smartphones are used for coordination of activities and the development of group norms through emotional and social communication

Along with their advantages, smartphones have also created some disadvantages. Most notable is the lack of boundaries between public and private space. Users are connected between home and work at all times, not allowing for a break between being at work and being at home. Smartphone disruptions in business meetings, classes, and public gatherings have prompted the need for phone etiquette (see the Reality Check feature [Mobile Phone Etiquette: Dos and Don'ts]). Concerns continue in terms of privacy, safety, health effects, and environmental impact. Almost all states have laws in place to prevent texting while driving. The Technical Advisory Council for the Federal Communications Commission reported that at least one-tenth of all thefts and robberies committed in the United States are associated with the theft of a mobile device (FCC, 2014).

©iStockphoto.com/gpointstudio

▶ **Photo 10.3**
Smartphones have appeal to all ages.

REALITY CHECK

Mobile Phone Etiquette: Dos and Don'ts

By Pamela Eyring

The Sydney Morning Herald, July 23, 2013

Mobile phones are ubiquitous and research shows that although most users think they have good mobile manners, many people report being irritated or annoyed by the use of the phones in public places.

Clearly there's a lack of understanding of what is and isn't acceptable in terms of mobile etiquette. Following is a list of dos and don'ts:

- Do respect those who are with you. When you're engaged face-to-face with others, either in a meeting or a conversation, give them your complete and undivided attention. Avoid texting or taking calls. If a call is important, apologize and ask permission before accepting it.

- Don't yell. The average person talks three times louder on a mobile phone than they do in a face-to-face conversation. Always be mindful of your volume.

- Do be a good dining companion. No one wants to be a captive audience to a third-party phone conversation, or to sit in silence while their dining companion texts with someone. Always silence and store your phone before being seated. Never put your phone on the table.

- Don't ignore universal quiet zones such as the theatre, church, the library, your daughter's dance recital and funerals.

- Do let voicemail do its job. When you're in the company of others, let voicemail handle non-urgent calls.

- Don't make wait staff wait. Whether it's your turn in line or time to order at the table, always make yourself available to the waiter. Making waiters and other patrons wait for you to finish a personal phone call is never acceptable. If the call is important, step away from the table or get out of line.

- Don't text and drive. There is no message that is so important.

- Do keep arguments under wraps. Nobody can hear the person on the other end. All they are aware of is a one-sided screaming match a few feet away.

- Don't forget to filter your language. A rule of thumb: If you wouldn't walk through a busy public place with a particular word or comment printed on your T-shirt, don't use it in phone conversations.

- Do respect the personal space of others. When you must use your phone in public, try to keep at least three meters between you and others.

- Do exercise good international calling behavior. The rules of phone etiquette vary from country to country.

Good mobile phone etiquette is similar to common courtesy. Conversations and text exchanges have a tendency to distract people from what's happening in front of them. Mobile users should be thoughtful, courteous and respect the people around them.

Pamela Eyring is the president of The Protocol School of Washington, which provides professional business etiquette and international protocol training. Founded in 1988, PSOW is the only school of its kind in the US to become accredited. Any opinions expressed are her own.

Source: Used with the permission of Pamela Eyring, President of the Protocol School of Washington.

Computers and the Internet

The computer was originally used in the home as a time-saving device. Word-processing and recordkeeping capabilities were the reasons that Americans bought personal computers when they became available. Because families with children were more likely to own computers, marketing strategies for home computers focused on fear as a motivator for parents to provide their children with what they needed to compete in the digital world (Wartella & Jennings, 2001). Although the computer was originally meant to be used for educational purposes, children use the computer more for entertainment and, according to Giacquinta, Bauer, and Levin (1993), game playing.

The Internet also has had an impact on the family. Family life has changed dramatically since the Internet appeared—the way we communicate, pay bills, shop, and live on a daily basis. Ninety-one percent of Americans have access to wired broadband, and 81% have access to mobile wireless broadband, with 500 million devices that are Internet connected (National Telecommunications and Information Administration, 2013).

Although some studies have established that children's primary use of the Internet is in searching for school-related information, few studies have been able to record actual usage rather than self-reported usage. In reality, more studies have found that communication with friends consumes more Internet time, especially among older children and adolescents (Jackson et al., 2006). More than half of teens go online several times a day, with 71% belonging to more than one social network site (Lenhart, 2015).

Access to information, guidance, and material goods has grown exponentially with the continued growth of the computer industry and computer marketing services. This can be beneficial to families during the decision-making process if the increase in available information is not overwhelming. Time spent using the computer cannot be regained or redirected. It depletes certain kinds of family resources.

> *Tory was anxious to plan a vacation for herself and her two school-age children. She wanted to travel to the Florida area, so that the kids' paternal grandparents could join them for a day or two. When she googled family Florida vacations, she received thousands of possible webpages devoted to that topic. She continued to narrow her search by limiting the city, type of activity, and desired cost, but she still had hundreds of options. Her initial search had taken seconds to find the information, but hours to process it. Individuals must weigh the value of time with the increased value of options generated to meet their needs.*

What makes the Internet different from the other forms of media is its interactivity. The ability to connect with others in real time makes this technology different from the one-sided media of radio and TV. As more people spend time online, the way we connect and develop relationships with others also changes.

Dating sites, which were once thought to be outside of the normal way to meet a potential partner, have grown in popularity and represent a billion-dollar industry. Dating in virtual space can save time, provide flexibility, and can be a safe way to meet others (Brown, 2011). Hertlein (2012) has suggested that new technology has redefined how relationships are structured and carried out. The rules, boundaries, and roles are different than they were in the past. For example, forming a new relationship online can be problematic in terms of reading social cues, sharing information, and allowing uninhibited behavior that would not be acceptable in a face-to-face interaction.

Although more people have become connected to the Internet and others through e-mail, interactive websites, and chat rooms, it has also provided for more commercial activity. Advertising and selling products online represents a whole new industry. This form of technology has opened many new opportunities to the outside world, but at the same time it can change the way that families interact with each other. Although the Internet has the capacity to strengthen family relationships through communication, it also has the capacity to isolate family members for long periods of time in individual activity. Parents and children may have more conflicts over access time. In addition, the constant availability of goods also creates tensions between what kids see and want and what parents are able and willing to buy.

By the end of the 20th century, people, especially parents, became more aware of the risks as well as advantages of being online. Hughes and Campbell (1998) identified six parental concerns for Internet use and children: (1) distribution of pornography, (2) sexual predators, (3) misinformation and hidden messages, (4) loss of privacy, (5) unscrupulous vendors, and (6) development of childhood behavior disorders, including social isolation and Internet addiction disorder. In 1998, Congress responded to these concerns by passing the Children's Online Privacy Protection Act (COPPA), which regulated data collection for children under age 13.

Digital divide: the gap between those people and communities who can access and make effective use of information technology and those who cannot

Family structure, race, and income influence computer ownership, which contributes to what has been known as the **digital divide**. Today, the digital divide has come to represent more than just access to the Internet but also keeping current with all technological changes (Graham, 2011) and whether people actually access the technology available to them (Warschauer, Matuchniak, Pinkard, & Gadsden, 2010). Goode (2010) suggests that students who do not access technology are at more of a disadvantage academically than those students who use new technologies.

Beginning with the radio, mass media has been a part of the home for almost a century. As each new technology was introduced into the family setting, a debate about the impact of that media on the family began. What can be done to ensure that the individual, the family, and business and industry not only benefit from the technology available, but are also realistic and safe while using technology as a communication tool? The Obama administration prioritized resources to address cybersecurity in an effort to ensure that programs are in place to protect Americans, business, and the government (The White House, Office of the Press Secretary, 2011). Until policies and laws are in place, there are safeguards to keep in mind. Users need to be aware of the network connections being made each time information is given and be safe about what they share. Personal information that is shared can end up in the hands of those who may use it against you. Ultimately, individuals are responsible for monitoring and protecting the technology being used. Realize that decisions to use technology are complex (multifaceted) and dynamic (ever changing).

APPLICATION TO FAMILY DECISION MAKING

For thousands of years, the family has been the primary organization for managing property, distributing resources, and setting the division of labor. An understanding of the basic communication process and mitigating problems prepares group members for stronger and more positive communication of needs and problem solving.

Communication plays a principal role in how families make decisions and solve problems. The verbal and nonverbal messages, the meaning of those messages, the use of power, and the process of conflict resolution all contribute to the family's ability to effectively manage the decisions of life.

Although the adults assume primary responsibility for family maintenance, children's voices and those of elderly members must be addressed. Empathy and patience are necessary. The ability to listen to other members is crucial. Miscommunication within the family can often be traced to

- Inability to listen
- Refusal to listen
- Unwillingness to share feelings
- Lack of understanding and multiple viewpoints
- Refusal to acknowledge the legitimacy of another's point
- Lack of time
- Existence of and reliance on assumptions
- Need for self above others (selfishness)
- Weak self-esteem of family members

Listening skills must be learned and practiced to facilitate a positive family communication process and good decision making.

SUMMARY

Communication is essential for good decision making and interaction within the family. The process of communication involves senders, receivers, and messages, which all have mutual impact on the members of the family. Family communication involves both intersubjectivity and interactivity. The way that messages are sent and received can lead to misunderstandings, as well as differences in gender and worldview. Families follow and develop unique communication patterns and standards. Within the process of family communication, power structures present challenges and opportunities. Communication can be both negative and positive. The negotiation of conflict resolution is necessary and healthy, moving the family toward a positive goal. Information technology can be an advantage and a disadvantage for families. Communication plays a major role in how families make decisions and solve problems.

QUESTIONS FOR REVIEW AND DISCUSSION

1. Describe the theoretical framework that explains the communication process.

2. What is the difference between the elements of intersubjectivity and interactivity in family communication?

3. What role do filters and distorters play in misunderstandings?

4. What are the two types of communication orientations that families follow?

5. How do communications standards affect family communication?

6. How does power affect family communication?

7. Why is conflict necessary?

8. Explain how information technology can be both positive and negative for families.

CHAPTER ELEVEN

THE INDIVIDUAL WITHIN FAMILY DECISION MAKING

Objectives
Group Dynamics
Groupthink
Reality Check
Leadership
Theories
Leadership and Parenting Styles
In the News
Worldview
Summary
Questions for Review and Discussion

Objectives

- Contemplate how group dynamics complicate family decision making.

- Understand the concept of leadership and how it applies to management of family resources.

- Explore how leadership impacts the family decision-making process.

> **If your actions inspire others to dream more, learn more, do more and become more, you are a leader.**
>
> **—John Quincy Adams**

Anytime more than one person is involved in the same decision-making process, the complexity of the process multiplies. Rarely will there be complete agreement and total participation of all family members in a group activity. Someone will emerge during the process as an obvious leader, depending on the situation, the intensity, and the ultimate impact that decision will have on him or her and the other individual members. The same person will not always assume leadership. Such a role requires personal investment; if a member of the family will not be positively or negatively impacted by the decision, he or she may choose not to invest personal resources necessary for leading the group at that time.

GROUP DYNAMICS

Most family decisions are impacted by the group process. Husbands and wives, parents and children, and even extended family work toward a decision that

▶ **Photo 11.1**

Individual choices affect families across generations.

impacts the family. The process of making decisions involves various dynamics of the group that play an important role in the outcome. There are factors that differentiate leadership in the workplace from leadership in the family. These factors also point to the difference between how families make decisions and how other organizations make decisions. Sorrels and Myers (1983) found that family groups are less affected than other outside groups by focusing on one problem too long, a dominating member, inflexible status levels, or avoiding the emotional or personal dimension of the task. Similarities between outside groups and family groups included members who do not feel competent, lack of tolerance for other ideas, criticisms, pressures to conform, and the hidden agendas of the members.

Love, attachment, and other affective characteristics present the family as a group with different dynamics than other organizations. Just as attachment, love, and loyalty provide powerful affective components, so do rebellion, anger, jealousy, and resentment. Barsade (2002) found that emotional contagion is an important factor in group dynamics. As such, a group member's mood can have an effect on the other group members' understanding, attitudes, and behaviors within the group. In addition, contagion for a positive mood was found to be just as powerful an influence as a negative mood (Eisenkraft & Elfenbein, 2010).

Mary Ann had always been a positive and upbeat person. As a wife, she made it a point to encourage her husband in whatever he did. She also set a positive tone for the children by looking for the good in every situation and praised them for their accomplishments, no matter how small. Her sister Ellen was just the opposite. She never failed to point out her husband's faults to him and corrected her children for their negative behaviors. She seemed to look only at the negative consequences for every circumstance, as if always knowing that something bad was about to happen. How does the mood of each sister affect their families? In any decision that these two sisters make, how will the outcome differ for each of their families?

Within the structure of the family, members also have a lifelong investment in the success of the group. At the same time, the long-term nature of the relationships may have a negative effect on the group because of unresolved issues or past history preventing them from being able to effectively solve problems or make decisions.

Emran and Cyan have struggled with issues of managing money since the beginning of their relationship. Emran is a saver, and Cyan is a spender. Now, decisions need to be made about how to finance the college education for their oldest daughter. Unable to rationally discuss whether to seek financial aid or take a second mortgage against their home, they cannot reach a decision without arguing and bringing up the past.

Merton and Kitt (1950) identified two types of groups to which people belong. People belong to a **membership group** by birth or life circumstance. This group membership is not voluntary. Membership is based on racial, ethnic, or sexual association. A **reference group** is a group to which members choose to belong. Families may belong to both types of groups. Within the family decision-making process, individuals bring a set of values, beliefs, and attitudes that, when combined with others in the family, produce unique dynamics.

Not all families make the same decisions, nor do the same decisions always produce the same outcomes. Factors such as social class, cultural or ethnic norms, communication styles, power structures, and previous family experience may also affect the dynamics of the family and the decisions they make. The socioeconomic status of the family may even have an influence on the family. For example, low-income families make decisions that may require them to select between two unfavorable choices, such as whether to buy medicine or food, or whether to take on a second job or apply for government assistance. An adolescent from a low-income family may not seek help from the family group to buy the sport shoes he needs because he knows it is not a possibility, whereas the adolescent from a family in a higher socioeconomic group may petition the family for this purchase.

Cultural or ethnic norms also influence family group dynamics. The worldview of individual cultures can shape the way decisions are made in the family. For example, cultures that value a collective identity believe that decisions should be made based on what is best for everyone. For such a society, every decision is a family decision. In contrast, those in an individualist society would make decisions based on what is best only for them. Other cultural orientations enter into the decision-making processes of many family issues, including parenting, gender roles, and interactions between generations.

> *Tomoko is struggling to make a decision about the medical care for her mother, who is suffering in the last stages of cancer. Although she has lived in the United States most of her life, she still abides by the traditional Japanese cultural orientation of filial piety, which gives a high degree of authority and respect to the elderly family member. Tomoko is torn by the desire to care for her mother in her home, yet understands how unequipped she is to handle the medications and procedures that will ease her mother's pain. She decides to leave the decision up to her mother.*
>
> *Down the hall of the hospital where Tomoko's mother is a patient, another family has to make the same kind of decision. Stefano and his brothers and sisters have all gathered in the waiting room to talk to the doctors about their father's condition. Once they learn he has a terminal illness, they all agree that their*

Membership group: a group where people belong as a result of birth or life circumstance

Reference group: a self-selected membership from which one receives feedback on his or her actions

father should not be told that he only has a few months to live. They are following a cultural norm designed to actively protect the patient as a function of love and respect. They decide to keep him as comfortable as possible and to continue to talk hopefully about his recovery.

One floor down, still another family has to make a decision about their elderly parent. This family makes their decision based on their personal needs. Jodi is married with a full-time job and a family. Vaughn is a busy accountant, a civic leader, and a father. Neither of them feels that they will be available to care for their father, so they make the decision to admit him to a nursing home, where he will get the attention he needs. How are the decisions that are made by all three families influenced by their culture?

The way the family communicates with each other impacts the dynamics of the group and their decisions. As in any group, there are members who are more vocal and those who express themselves very little. In addition, the family member who is able to articulate his or her message clearly and is able to quickly move the group to see his or her way of thinking has an advantage over the family member who cannot express him- or herself very well. Hsiung and Bagozzi (2003) found that influence and persuasion were important concepts within family decision making.

The dynamics in the family and the decisions that result are influenced by the power structures within the group. Family members who garner the most power within the family are likely to influence the decision-making process. In addition, when family members form coalitions, they may influence the decisions of the group by their majority representation.

Calvin and Melinda have three children. As the children have gotten older, family decisions have largely been made with input from the whole family. Calvin recently called a family meeting to discuss a promotion that he was offered at work. The promotion involved moving several states away. The family members weighed the pros and cons of the decision, noting the increase in salary and perks of the new position. They also realized that they would be leaving well-established friendships and discussed several other negative outcomes for taking the new position. In the end, the children's protest of being uprooted in their last years of high school outweighed any of the positive outcomes that they identified for the new position. Calvin declined the promotion. How would the outcome of the decision have been different if Calvin held complete authoritarian power within the family?

The decisions that a family makes as a group may be influenced by past experience or behavior of the group members. Some of these behaviors are cyclical in nature and may continue generation after generation. A good example of this would be parenting behaviors. Seldom do parents discuss their parenting choices with their children. However, unless you make a conscious choice to change, you will probably parent your children similarly to the way you were parented (Kerr,

Capaldi, & Pears, 2009). The model that you saw becomes the behavior that you use, and it may continue for generations.

Another example can be found in family violence. Martinez-Torteya, Bogat, Von Eye, and Levendosky (2009) found that children who are a witness to violence in the home are significantly and negatively affected by that experience. Children automatically observe and learn from their environment. Even parents who exhibit type-A personality traits (such as time consciousness, competitiveness, and control) tend to influence and pass those traits on to their children (Forgays, 1996). More controversy surrounds the influence of alcoholism or drug addiction on family members. Some believe that addictive behavior is genetic and, therefore, cannot be learned from others. Others suggest that the behavior is learned through the environment, by watching others. Most agree that some environmental influences play a role. The quality of the parental relationship (Miles, Silberg, & Pickens, 2005), the relationship to risk-taking within the family (Feldstein & Miller, 2006), and parental mental health (Molina, Donovan, & Belendiuk, 2010) are all environmental influences that have been found to affect the outcome of passing on alcoholic behavior from parent to child. The result of observing and learning from past experiences will have an impact on decision making both now and in the future.

How do family group dynamics evolve? Parents and other adult members of families create cultures of cooperation or resistance. Sensitive parenting that meets the needs of other family members, especially children, fosters the development of attachment, which encourages cooperation and compliance (Brooks, 2013). Because the majority of family resource management decisions are made by the adults within the family group, it is important to understand how adult relationships influence choices that ultimately impact all family members.

▶ **Photo 11.2**
Individuals may be more expressive in the middle of a crowd.

Conflict may not be pleasant, but it is necessary for change. For example, a married couple may not wish to have an argument over taking out the garbage, but it may be necessary for them to communicate about it so that a decision can be made and change can take place. Other paradoxes include the wishes of the individual versus the good of the group (a husband's desire to further his career vs. choosing what is best for his family), self-disclosure versus privacy (a daughter's need for help in a struggle with depression vs. her need to keep it private), and authority versus submissiveness (a son's need to parent an alcoholic father vs. his role as a child).

GROUPTHINK

Groupthink explores how group dynamics can interfere with effective decision making. Groupthink was a word coined by Irving Janis in the early 1970s

Groupthink:
conformity in thought and behavior among the members of a group, especially an unthinking acceptance of majority opinions

to describe what happens in groups when there is pressure to maintain unity and the group resists or ignores ideas that are contrary to the way the larger group is thinking. In his book *Victims of Groupthink*, Janis (1972) argues that a group that is influenced by groupthink may fall victim to an overestimation of success and can fail even though the group may consist of otherwise intelligent, thinking people. He describes eight symptoms of groupthink that prevent good decision making.

The first symptom of groupthink involves the illusion of invulnerability, where group members believe they are invincible and that whatever decision they make will be the right one. Second, group members want to discredit or explain away any thoughts that are contrary to their thinking. In a sense, they ignore the warnings that their way of thinking may be flawed. Third, groupthink involves the group members' belief that they are making decisions based on morality, but they often do not consider the consequences of their actions. They often believe they are doing something for the "good of all" and are proud that they are thinking of others, but really haven't stopped to think about how it will affect everyone. Fourth, the group relies on mutual stereotypes to validate their thinking. No matter how inaccurate the stereotypes, all group members perpetuate those same attitudes about people or ideas. Fifth, groupthink involves pressure to conform to and agree with the thinking of the group. Dissenters are targeted and viewed as disloyal. Along with this pressure is the sixth symptom of self-censorship. When a group member does question or express opposition, he or she is censored or made to feel uncomfortable enough to keep his or her thoughts to him- or herself. The seventh symptom of groupthink is when the group members believe that everyone else agrees with the decision being made. Individuals may have a feeling that "if everyone else believes this is a good decision, I don't need to question it." Silence within the group can add to this belief if no one speaks up. Finally, the eighth symptom is a group that includes what are known as "mindguards." These are self-appointed members who take on the role of protecting the group against anyone or anything that would cause disharmony. Janis (1982) further suggests that, to avoid groupthink, groups must employ vigilant decision-making practices, which includes encouraging group members to freely deliberate, allowing various points of view to emerge, gathering credible information to help make informed decisions, and having contingency plans in place once the decision is made. He warns that leaders of groups need to be impartial and open.

Although groupthink was developed within the arena of politics, family decision making can also find application.

> *Thomas and Marisol are part of a large extended family. Every Sunday night, they gather together for dinner. Over the course of the evening, various topics are discussed, including local events, national and international politics, and family issues. Although the discussions can sometimes become heated, everyone tends to agree. When Thomas first became a part of Marisol's family, he was thrilled to be a part of such a large and close group. His own family was not very close as a result of his parents' divorce early in his adolescence. However, now there are times when he feels that Marisol's family is so close*

and connected that they don't always see other points of view. For example, here is the conversation that transpired last Sunday night:

> **Marisol's brother:** *"Did anyone see the article in the paper about that new strip mall they are proposing? I can't believe that the city would let them build that thing so close to our neighborhood. What's next, a big Walmart next to the church?!"*
>
> **Marisol's dad:** *"Yeah, I saw it. Those rich people think they can do whatever they want and the city just looks the other way."*
>
> **Marisol's uncle:** *"Somebody should tell them that we don't want their big money around here! Nobody wants it."*
>
> **Marisol's aunt:** *"I heard there's going to be a Starbucks. Who needs it—why would anyone pay four bucks for a cup of coffee?"*
>
> **Thomas:** *"They might be trying to keep the younger generation around."*
>
> **Marisol's brother:** *"We have gotten along just fine without them all these years, and we will continue to do business as usual without them for years to come."*
>
> **Marisol's mother:** *"Oh, come on now—we all want the same things, don't we? We are all alike in this neighborhood!"*

No one said anything for a few seconds, and then Marisol said, "Who made that salad with the red peppers? I really like it—can I get that recipe?"

What are the symptoms of groupthink for this family? What role does Thomas play in the family? What role does Marisol's mother play? What are the dangers of groupthink for this family?

Janis (1982) also identifies antecedent conditions or existing characteristics that are likely to promote groupthink. These conditions include the insulation of the group from outside ideas, high cohesiveness within the group, impartial leadership, little knowledge of effective decision-making processes, homogeneous members, stress from external threats, and low self-esteem. These characteristics are found within families and make them vulnerable to groupthink. In the prior example, Marisol's family is cohesive and shares similar cultural and socioeconomic beliefs. They speak about the past and the need to stay the same, which may indicate that they are unaware of or unwilling to investigate the reasons and need for change within the decision-making processes taking place in their community. It also appears that the leadership or strong personalities within the family do not want to consider outside opinions or other ways of looking at the situation. These are all reasons why it may be easy for this family to have fallen victim to groupthink.

Groups need to guard against falling into groupthink by developing strategies for preventing this type of faulty thinking. Such strategies include establishing an environment where alternatives and other ideas are welcomed and valued. In addition, the leader must not only take the lead in maintaining this open environment; he or she must also work more as a facilitator than as a dictator, including accepting criticism (Janis & Mann, 1977). These strategies need to be considered within a family. Within an open-environment, family members should be allowed to voice their divergent opinions toward a solution while maintaining respect for the leader. The transformational leadership style mentioned later in the chapter lends itself more to this strategy and works against the groupthink model.

REALITY CHECK

Cults and Family Parallels

One of the consequences of cult involvement is in breaking through the bonds created to form "fictive families" that parallel commitments people often make to dysfunctional and abusive families in our society. The controlling leaders often demand loyalty by asking that they break emotional ties to their biological family. Sometimes cults use language that implies that they function as a family (father, children, etc.) (Whitsett & Kent, 2003).

Many members and supporters of cults are not aware of the extent of manipulation or exploitation that may be occurring within a particular group. Michael Langone has developed a checklist to be considered when analyzing the health and safety of any group:

- The group displays excessively zealous and unquestioning commitment to its leader.
- Questioning, doubt, and dissent are discouraged or even punished.
- Mind-altering practices are used in excess and serve to suppress doubts.
- The leadership dictates how members should think, act, and feel.
- The group is elitist, claiming a special exulted status or mission.

- The group has a polarized us-versus-them mentality in conflict with the wider society.
- The leader is not accountable to any authorities.
- The group teaches or implies that its exalted ends justify whatever means it deems necessary.
- The leadership induces feelings of shame or guilt to control members.
- Subservience to the leader requires members to cut ties with family and friends.
- The group is preoccupied with bringing in new members.
- The group is preoccupied with bringing in money.
- Members are expected to devote inordinate amounts of time to the group.
- Members are encouraged or required to live with/socialize only with group members.
- The most loyal members feel there can be no life outside the context of the group.

Source: This checklist is taken from Lalich and Tobias (2006).

In making decisions as a group, people often make different decisions than they would make if they were acting alone. This phenomenon is known as **group shift** and may appear as **risky shift** and **cautious shift** (Stoner, 1968). When risky shift occurs in decision making, group members may assume that the other group members hold more extreme views, causing them to adjust their views in favor of a more radical view than their own. Risky shift causes group members to take more risks as a group than they would if they were making an individual decision.

> *Darrin has been working in maintenance most of his adult life. In high school, he began working at the local grocery store, helping the maintenance director with various jobs after school and on weekends. After high school, he was hired as one of the maintenance personnel for the largest industry in the region. Twenty years later, he is still in the same job. Darrin has contemplated starting his own maintenance company but has never really acted on it. Recently, he expressed his dream to his brother at a family reunion. After talking about it for a few minutes, his brother gathered other relatives, and soon the whole room was buzzing with ideas for Darrin. "You would be a great boss," his brother said. His cousin said, "You know everything there is to know about maintenance; after all, you have done it for 20 years—you could write the book on maintenance!" Leaving the reunion, Darrin was ready to initiate the plans to quit his job and start his own company. His family had given him the confidence to finally take the first step.*

Darrin was making a risky shift in his decision to start a business. Although he would lose his stable income and start a business that had the potential to fail, he took the plunge because the group had given him confidence, and their collective attitude seemed to take away some of the burden of the decision. As with groupthink, Darrin may be making a mistake if he doesn't make his decision based on information that rationally and systematically guides him to the best outcome.

Cautious shift reflects the opposite effect within the group. A group can be overly cautious in their decisions as well, especially following group discussion.

> *Antonio is getting married in 6 weeks. His fiancée is a beautiful girl whom he has known since sixth grade. His coworkers tease him that he is the luckiest man alive, but lately he has been having some doubts about his decision to marry. One night while with his family, he expresses his concern. They all agree that he is mature, financially secure, and emotionally stable. His concerns lie in the uncertainty of marriage. Antonio agonizes, "Will I be a good husband? Will I be able to commit to this relationship long term? What if I find someone else?" Although his family feels that these fears may be a bit of cold feet, they listen and contemplate his dilemma. After much discussion, they agree that Antonio is not ready to marry. The following day, Antonio calls off the wedding.*

Group shift: when making decisions as a group, people make decisions differently than they would if they were acting alone

Risky shift: the group collectively agrees on a course of action that is more extreme than what they would have chosen if asked individually

Cautious shift: the result of group social influence when individual group members become cautious

Antonio's decision was made on the side of caution. Although later he may decide to marry, his family helped him make a decision that was right for him at the time. His family gave him courage to make a decision that he did not feel comfortable making himself.

Myers and Lamm (1976) suggest that a result of group shift may have a polarized effect. They note that the decisions made after discussion tend to be more extreme to one side than the average of the opinions of individual group members before the discussion.

LEADERSHIP

Leadership:
the ability of an individual to influence, motivate, and enable others to contribute toward the effectiveness and success of the groups of which they are members

Every group, including a family, has leaders. Leadership is one of the most important functions of any organization. However, **leadership** is difficult to define. Nall (2005) provides a definition from the 1920s, suggesting that a leader imposes his or her will on those led. That is a different definition from that of Langone (2004), who defines a leader as one who sets the "future direction for an organization. Leadership involves looking at the environment and the organization's mission or purpose and making decisions about which visions, activities, and goals to pursue" (p. 82). It is the leader who makes sure that the goals of the organization are accomplished. It is the leader who affects the behaviors, attitudes, and actions of those who follow him or her. Although families are not typically thought of as organizations, there are some similarities in that an important goal of both groups is that of sustainability over time.

Blank (2001) proposed that the skills of natural-born leaders can be divided into three categories: foundational skills, leadership direction skills, and leadership influence skills. Blank proposes that *foundational skills* are necessary for all other leadership skills and form the foundations for success. These skills are self-awareness, or the ability for people to understand their own behaviors; building a rapport, or the ability to work with others; and an ability to clarify the expectations of the group so that everyone understands. These skills may explain why some leaders successfully rise to the top from among the low-level workers. Those people easily understand the followers and are able to speak their language.

Leadership direction skills are those that provide guidance. Often, in the face of problems or change, it is hard for followers to take action. The effective leader provides that direction. Leadership direction also includes the ability to develop leaders from within the group. These skills are those that allow someone to think on his or her feet—to be an excellent problem solver even in the face of crises.

Leadership influence skills include those that build a base of commitment to the group and create motivation to move forward. Good leaders will influence by commitment rather than force. These skills involve a sense of trust that is built between leaders and their followers. The group is motivated by a common goal for the good of all.

One of the most important components in becoming a good leader is attitude. Attitude can spill over into actions and affect the outcomes of the organization. Maxwell (2003) explains that attitudes such as the inability to admit mistakes, not wanting to forgive, jealousy, arrogance, being critical, and a need to take all the credit keep a group from succeeding. Leaders must also keep the attitudes of their followers in check. When attitudes are positive, the group can use its potential toward success. A bad or negative attitude is contagious and can hamper motivation to move forward. A good leader is fully aware of human behavior and understands why people do what they do.

Within the organization of the family, parental leadership is important. Crittenden (2004) proposes that being a parent prepares people for leadership roles with four transferable skills: multitasking, interpersonal skills, growing human capabilities, and building strengths of character or virtue. Of course, multitasking is evident for parents who must juggle home and work life. She suggests that "the ability to handle irrational and immature individuals of every age; understanding the importance of win-win negotiation; the ability to listen to others' concerns; to practice patience; express empathy; and respect individual differences" (p. 8) are all skills necessary for good leadership. Good leaders in the workplace as well as good parents are able to develop strengths in others by growing their capabilities. Good leaders are able to let people grow from their mistakes but still provide the structure and feedback they need within a safe environment. Finally, a good leader and a good parent model integrity and accurate perspective, which help build character in others.

What is the difference between leadership in an organization and leadership in a family? Hyde and Thomas (2003) suggest that in organizations, roles are more complex. Changes in leadership are much more likely because people are moving in and out of the environment more frequently. In families, the same players are present unless death or divorce occurs. The stability of the organization is not threatened by the loss of one individual, as it would be within a family, unless the leader was a dominant figure in the organization. However, the boundaries will need to be renegotiated, and an adjustment to relationships will probably have to take place.

It is easy to assume that parents, as adults, will be the natural leaders within family decision making. Multigenerational family structures, however, bring multiple sets of adults and parents together at times. Leadership is still necessary.

> *Grandma Ruby is 83 and a widow. She has 5 grown children and 22 grandchildren and great-grandchildren. Just recently, her health has indicated that she should move from her home of 50 years to a facility that would provide some general supervision for her safety. Ruby has designated her youngest daughter, Elle, as her power of attorney for healthcare, but doesn't want to burden her with more legal obligations, so she asks the remaining four children to determine who will help her decide which housing option she should select and to help her with the formalities of selling her home and entering into a housing contract. The only son assumes he should have the job. The three remaining daughters argue and refuse to accept his leadership. Elle, noticing her mother's despair at the behavior of her siblings, steps in and takes charge. Although she is the youngest, and female, Elle's social skills and her education have always set her apart from the others. Ruby, and her older children, will be more likely to accept decisions made by Elle.*

Although research on leadership in the family is limited, it is logical that leadership principles would be similar rather than different. Effective parenting, strong families, efficient management, and other family functions suggest that family life requires intentional leadership.

Theories

Before exploring family leadership, we explore some leadership theories. Most theories of leadership can be divided between the two camps of behavioral theory and situational theory. Behavioral theories of leadership are based on the idea that a leader's personal qualities and techniques drive the kind of leader they become. As early as the 1950s, McGregor (1960) and others began to develop a model of leadership based on the question of whether leaders were born or made. The investigation on leadership resulted in the theory of X and Y as a method of effective leadership. According to this theory, the integration of both X (the organization's needs) and Y (the employee's needs) is necessary, and the effective leader is able to accomplish both. McGregor concludes by saying, "Management is severely hampered today in its attempts to innovate with respect to the human side of enterprise by the inadequacy of conventional organization theory" (p. 245). In addition, the work by Fleishman (1953) in The Ohio State University Leadership Studies was among the first to identify the role of culture and climate in organizations.

Other behavioral research in the 1950s led to a "newer theory of management" (Likert, 1961) that includes the principle of supportive relationships. Likert stated, "The leadership and other processes of the organization must be such that . . . each member will . . . view the experience as supportive and one which builds and maintains his sense of personal worth and importance" (p. 103). Likert (1967) identified four main styles of leadership that focused on decision making. Although these styles—exploitive authoritative, benevolent authoritative, consultative, and participative—incorporate the degree of participation within the group, they generally still view the leader as making the final decision.

Recently, Lefton and Buzzotta (2004) proposed a model of leadership behavior that incorporates four basic patterns. Based on the earlier research conducted in the 1940s and 1950s, the **dimensional model** has two dimensions (see Figure 11.1). One dimension is represented by dominance and submission, whereas the other dimension is represented by hostility and warmth. Dominance represents people who take control and lead. They want to have power over those around them. At the other end of the continuum is submission. These are people who want someone to tell them what to do. They do not want to control others or make decisions. Hostility includes self-absorption and insensitivity to other people's needs. Warmth, in contrast, is a consideration for others coupled with optimism. Hostile people tend not to trust others, whereas warm people are more open-minded about others. These dimensions then form four quadrants or four leadership styles.

Autocratic leaders (Q1) use power and intimidation to control others. This type of leadership style has one leader who makes all the decisions and is more concerned with outcomes than the process used to get there. Although much can

Dimensional model: a model of leadership behavior that incorporates the dimensions of dominance, warmth, submissiveness, and hostility

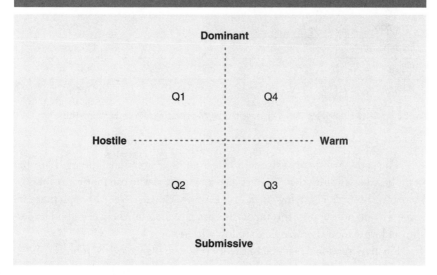

Source: Lefton, R. E., & Buzzotta, V. R. (2004). *Leadership Through People Skills*. London: McGraw-Hill.

be accomplished, the cost is high in terms of how people feel about the organization and how long they stay. Unassertive leaders (Q2) avoid true leadership by procrastinating, passing off decisions, and staying with traditional or old ways of doing things. They do not take risks and are often apathetic to what is going on around them. They tend to neither reward nor punish, which often causes those around them to be apathetic as well. Easygoing leaders (Q3) concentrate their leadership style on morale. They favor relationships rather than rules. Productivity is not as important as keeping people happy in the organization, which leads them to not value productive behavior and ambiguity. No one knows how well they are doing because praise is so easily given that they don't really know when their performance is unsatisfactory. Collaborative leaders (Q4) have the ideal leadership style. These leaders set goals and expect results while creating a positive environment where others feel valued and competent. The collaborative leader takes responsibility for the organization, but knows when to step in and when to back away.

Situational theories of leadership focus on the situational or outside factors that predict effective leadership. The contingency model, developed by Fiedler (1967), examines the relationship between the leadership style and leader effectiveness while being aware of the situational control of the leader. Situational favorability, or how much power and control a leader will have, is influenced by how much the group accepts and supports the leader, how the leader is able to explain and carry out goals (structured tasks), and how much authority the leader is able to have over the group (see Figure 11.2). The leader's influence is a key component in this theory. The more influence someone is able to have over the group, the more favorable the situation for them as a leader. In addition to the leader's influence, the theory also brings in the idea that human relations are important for effective leadership. The leader must be aware of what is going on within the organization.

Figure 11.2 Contingency Model

Unfriendly	1	2	3	4	5	6	7	8	Friendly
Uncooperative	1	2	3	4	5	6	7	8	Cooperative
Hostile	1	2	3	4	5	6	7	8	Supportive
Guarded	1	2	3	4	5	6	7	8	Open

Source: Fiedler, F. E. (1967). *A Theory of Leadership Effectiveness.* New York: McGraw-Hill.

The path–goal theory (House, 1971) is another situational theory. This theory is based on the idea that effective leaders are those who can motivate others by increasing rewards, clarifying goals, or meeting personal needs. Although there are some who do not support this theory, it does provide a link between good leadership and what motivates people to follow a leader.

Finally, situational leadership theory (Hersey, Blanchard, & Johnson, 1992) is rooted in the idea that effective leadership can be measured by the relationship between the leader's actions and the followers' readiness. Using a matrix, task behavior and relationship behavior are used to form four leadership styles: the leader who participates in and facilitates decision making, the leader who explains decisions and clarifies if necessary, the leader who makes the decisions and supervises tasks, and the leader who gives the task to the followers to make decisions on their own. Maturity is another aspect that is considered because the leader must decide whether the follower has the ability (willingness, confidence, responsibility, education, experience, etc.) to carry out the task.

Leadership and Parenting Styles

Today, the development of our understanding about leadership style tends not only to incorporate but also to expand on these theories from the past. Three leadership styles seem to emerge as those relevant to predict leadership effectiveness. They are transactional, transformational, and laissez-faire. **Transactional leadership** is often used to describe a combination of both leader behavior and situational details from both camps of theory. The transactional leader is one who uses interactions with followers to help make decisions, but is ultimately the one in control and usually commands the power in the organization. Leaders provide the incentives and regulation according to the performance of the followers, regardless of the outcomes of the organization. This leadership style is often found in top-down organizations where there is a definite hierarchy of structured leadership.

Although transactional leadership style has been effective in the past, the **transformational leadership** style has become more common and is desired in the workplace. It is not enough just to lead and to make decisions; the transformational leader casts the vision and provides the inspiration for the organization. Often the transformational leader is charismatic and able to empower followers to work beyond their potential. Bass and Avolio (1997) identified five characteristics of the

Transactional leadership: guidance based in contingency, in that reward or punishment is contingent on performance

Transformational leadership: behavior that is founded on the belief that leaders and followers can raise each other to higher levels of motivation and morality

transformational leader. These characteristics are (1) idealized attributes: influences others, is credible, has integrity, is
authentic, is willing to make sacrifices,
and encourages; (2) idealized behaviors:
models behaviors that encourage others to look up to or want to emulate; (3)
inspirational motivation: motivates others by increasing awareness and understanding of the goals, is able to express the
purpose and meaning of goals, and is able
to create vision; (4) intellectual stimulation: teaches followers to think beyond

©iStockphoto.com/gmalandra

▶ **Photo 11.3**
Transformational
leadership
involves teamwork.

the ordinary and encourages them to develop independent thinking; and (5) individualized consideration: mentors others and provides opportunities that foster growth.

Another contemporary leadership style is the **laissez-faire leadership** style.
In this style, the leader's involvement is decreased, especially in decision making,
which allows followers to have more control over the outcomes of the organization. At first glance, this style appears to be a positive method of leadership for the
followers, allowing them to have control over their work environment. However,
certain factors must be present within the organization for the outcomes to be
positive. People must be competent and motivated to make their own decisions
and must be able to work well outside the watchful eye of the leader. This style also
requires that the group does not need coordination of efforts, where each task is
dependent on the other tasks for the job to be successful.

**Laissez-faire
leadership:** a
leadership style
where the leader
allows the followers
to have more control
over the outcomes
of the organization

What style of leadership is best for the family? Let us take a look at the three
contemporary leadership styles (transactional, transformational, and laissez-faire)
and see how these leadership styles affect family functions. Transactional leadership is most often associated with the traditional family, where the father is
the identified leader and the mother carries out the decisions of the father and
enforces those decisions with the children.

> *The Osawa family consists of a father, mother, and two school-age chil-*
> *dren. Mr. Osawa works as an electrical engineer, and Mrs. Osawa is a full-*
> *time homemaker and mother. Mr. Osawa is the identified head of the*
> *house and makes the majority of the decisions. Although Mrs. Osawa is*
> *the one who purchases most of the food, clothing, and household items,*
> *Mr. Osawa controls the budget and pays the bills. If the children behave*
> *badly, Mr. Osawa is the one who decides what course of discipline is*
> *needed. If the children have consequences, it is up to Mrs. Osawa to make*
> *sure that they are carried out. Although Mr. Osawa asks for and listens to*
> *Mrs. Osawa's opinion, he makes the final decisions for the family. The Osawa*
> *family exhibits transactional leadership style.*

Problems associated with the transactional leadership style within a family
are similar to the problems of this style in a nonfamily organization. The divide

between the leader and followers may be wide if the followers sense that the leader is not looking out for their best interest. When this happens, trust is broken between the two, and a lack of motivation to work toward a goal may result. In the case of the Osawa family, when the children became teenagers, the transactional model that worked before will not be as effective.

> *Jerek Osawa just turned 17 and enjoys being with his friends and fellow soccer players. In fact, he would spend all of his free time with them if his father would allow it. Although Jerek understands that there are times when he needs to be with his family and help out by doing chores around the house, it seems to him that he has more responsibility than his sister. He has started to resent the fact that he works harder and tries to find more excuses to be away from the house. Jerek avoids seeing his dad because he doesn't want to risk being given yet another job. He can't wait to turn 18 so that he can move out of the house and be on his own. Mr. Osawa is annoyed that Jerek is never around to help out and that Jerek takes offense to everything he asks him to do. Mr. Osawa recalls that he would have never questioned his own father's authority; even though he didn't always agree, he feared the consequences of disrespecting his father. What makes the transactional style of leadership less effective in both the workplace and the family today?*

The family that exemplifies a transformational leadership style demonstrates a sense of shared purpose. Together, the family will discuss ways to solve problems collaboratively. Although the leader (or leaders, as in egalitarian relationships) will ultimately be the one to make the final decision, the family will work to meet each member's needs in a way to mutually benefit the whole family. In return, members trust and respect the leader because they know there are benefits.

> *The Garcia family consists of parents, Ric and Gloria, and their three children. The Garcias have always made decisions together, including how to raise their children. When a family situation arises, the Garcias sit down together and each person expresses his or her opinion and desires openly. Ric and Gloria then weigh the information and together as coleaders make a decision. Although not all problems are resolved just the way each one would like, they all have a sense that this approach is best for the family. Recently, 15-year-old Julia was invited to a friend's birthday party sleepover. When she asked her parents if she could go, they hesitated because they needed her to watch her younger brother and sister the morning after the sleepover. They knew she would be too tired and it would be difficult for her to be home by the time they needed to be at work the next morning. Julia was upset that she would miss her friend's party, even though she knew that her role as caregiver for her siblings was important to the family. The family was able to collaborate together toward a solution: They decided that Julia would go to the party in the evening, but would not stay overnight. This solution was acceptable for all, and a sense of family unity was maintained.*

Galbraith and Schvaneveldt (2005) suggested that there are many benefits for families that model the transformational leadership style, including

> the involvement of children in a shared vision or cause; positive role modeling; family unity, trust, cooperation, and teamwork; a sense of responsibility among family members; the use of power in healthy ways; and a collective sense of ownership for overcoming problems and working toward positive individual and family outcomes. (p. 236)

Within the discussion of the transformational leadership style, a new and emerging concept of authentic leadership has developed (Luthans & Avolio, 2003; Walumbwa, Avolio, Gardner, Wernsing, & Peterson, 2008). Avolio, Walumbwa, and Weber (2009) suggest that authentic leaders include those who practice good decision making, use moral standards to self-regulate behavior, openly share information and feelings, and are aware of their strengths and weaknesses as well as their own worldview. Families need good leadership just as much, if not more than, any organization. This type of leadership strengthens families and enables family members to successfully adapt to and change in response to the environment around them.

Although the laissez-faire leadership style is not recommended for families, it is identified and practiced in many families. In fact, it may even be referred to as nonleadership, because someone using this style resists taking the role of leader altogether. Within a family, the laissez-faire leader passes off dealing with important issues, postpones making decisions, and avoids getting involved in day-to-day family life (Galbraith & Schvaneveldt, 2005).

Gary and Janice Williams have been married for 28 years. Janice grew up in a traditional family. Her father was the "head of the house" and dictated the direction of the family. In her teen years, Janice resented her father's heavy hand and her mother's submissiveness. She vowed never to marry a man like that, and she didn't. Throughout their marriage, Janice has had to make most of the decisions. It has been difficult to get Gary to take a stand on anything. Janice feels uncomfortable in making decisions; although she didn't like the model of her own parents, she feels that her husband should take an interest at least some of the time. Early in their marriage, Janice would ask Gary's opinion. Gary didn't usually have an opinion and one day finally said, "Janice, I don't care what you do. Don't bother me with the details!" Although Gary doesn't want to make the decisions, he certainly lets Janice know when she makes a mistake. A few years ago, Janice gave their 16-year-old daughter permission to attend a party at a friend's house. It was there that their daughter began a long and painful journey into drugs. Ever since that night, Gary has reminded Janice that it is her fault. "If you would have just paid a little more attention to what you let her do, she wouldn't be in this mess."

Although the laissez-faire leadership style may work in some corporate settings by allowing capable and motivated people to make their own decisions, this style is often detrimental to a growing family. Because a family includes both adults and children, the laissez-faire leadership style affects the entire family. All family members go unsatisfied. In the previous scenario, Gary is unhappy with the decisions of Janice, and Janice is unhappy with Gary's lack of involvement. The children have missed the interaction of their father, have been affected by the conflict of their parents, and will not have a positive model of leadership to carry to their own families.

As presented earlier in this chapter, parental approaches to disciplining can also be applicable to the discussion of family decision making. Professionals often refer to four specific parenting styles: authoritarian, authoritative, permissive, and uninvolved. Each approach to discipline and guidance has specific consequences, and often families develop a unique combination, or strategy, that allows them to consider the individual and the situation before determining the appropriate method.

Authoritarian parenting:
parenting with high expectations and low responsiveness

Authoritarian parenting is reflected in a rigid expectation that children will follow rules to the letter without questioning the adult's motive or situation. In this environment, children will have no involvement in the decision making for resource management. Decisions made by adults will be accepted with little or no challenge. One drawback to this type of parental leadership is that children have very limited opportunity to develop problem-solving skills or the ability to negotiate.

Authoritative parenting:
parenting with reasonable demands and high levels of responsiveness

Authoritative parenting, or family leaders, have rules and expect members to follow these rules, but if children or family members request reasons or challenge limits, their voices are heard. Children from authoritative family structures are better at making decisions and avoiding risky situations. They are more likely to express their opinions and practice responsible social behaviors.

Permissive parenting:
parenting with low demands and high responsiveness

Family members in **permissive parenting** homes are likely to engage in risky behaviors. Parents are lenient and do not exert authority until a serious problem presents. There are few consequences for misbehavior. Often, permissive parents seek the role of friend, rather than parent. Because they are not given adequate limits, children in these situations often feel anxious and insecure. They are forced to make decisions because the adults avoid taking the lead. They may lack the maturity or cognitive ability to make the best decisions and suffer the consequences.

Uninvolved parenting:
neglectful parenting characterized by a lack of responsiveness to the child's needs

Uninvolved parenting can also be characterized as neglectful parenting. This neglect stems from an inability to meet basic needs and to make good decisions based on a lack of information or impaired functioning—substance abuse or mental health issues. Younger family members are forced to assume the adult role and decision making without the necessary maturity to be successful. They may need to step into a faux-parent role to take care of the needs of the parent.

There are other factors that affect leadership within the family. Yu and Miller (2005) found that different generations prefer different leadership styles. Of course, this would be important to know in an organizational or business setting, but it is also important within the family setting where several generations are present. The **Baby Boom generation** (those born between 1946 and 1964) has lived during a period of time that includes more than one phase of leadership style. In the early years, leadership probably focused on control and supervision. As a result, Baby Boomers tend to value loyalty to a leader and expect a chain of command within organizations.

Generation Xers (those born between 1965 and 1980) tend to value personal satisfaction and freedom, rather than loyalty. They are not afraid to change jobs several times because they are used to change and are more flexible. **Millennials** are just now entering into the world of adulthood. They require even different criteria in leadership. Yu and Miller (2005) point out that they are as technologically savvy as those before them, but they have become so at a younger age. They are generally better educated, and they tend to be more articulate in expressing themselves and what they want. They are more interested in a more collaborative type of leadership and will follow someone if they have a need to learn from them. In a family, leadership where there is more than one generation can be a challenge.

No one style of leadership is better than another. Each situation and group's needs will determine the best leadership style. This is true for families as well. Over time, the position-based leadership style, often referred to as *top–down leadership*, will probably be replaced with a more information-based or cooperative leadership style. Some may argue that this would be detrimental for families.

> *Misha and her husband have been married for almost 10 years and have two children, who are now 5 and 8. When her children were born, Misha vowed never to repeat the kind of discipline style that her parents had while she was growing up. Misha's dad was authoritarian and a strict disciplinarian. When a rule was broken, there were consequences. Once, when Misha was 16, she was a few minutes late coming home. When she tried to explain that her car had a flat tire on the way home, her dad just put up his hand and said, "I don't want to hear it!" Even though Misha could see that her mother was sympathetic, her mother never questioned her husband's judgment. Misha's dad was the leader of the home. He made all the decisions and handed down all the discipline. Now that she has children of her own, Misha allows everyone in the family to make their own decisions. She and her husband have decided that a team approach is the best way for the family to live. Both children get to decide when, where, and what they would like to eat; when to sleep; and what they will do each day. Will this style of leadership work for the family? Why or why not?*

In addition to generational leadership styles, there are also gender differences between the leadership styles of men and women. Although there is controversy as to whether men and women inherently have different leadership

Baby Boom generation: people born between (and including) 1946 and 1964

Generation X: the generation following the Baby Boom; people born between 1965 and 1980

Millennials: the generation born in the 1980s and 1990s

styles or they come as a result of what is expected of individuals because of their gender, there are some characteristics that cause men and women to lead differently. Eagly and Johannesen-Schmidt (2001) have suggested that men exhibit more agentic characteristics, such as assertiveness, confidence, and competitiveness. Women exhibit more concern for others and are described as helpful and kind, which are more communal characteristics. Women tend to be more transformational and tend to be less likely to exhibit laissez-faire in their leadership style. More recently, Barbuto, Fritz, and Matkin (2007) found that there were greater differences between the leadership styles of men and women among those with lower education levels, with women using more pressure tactics to motivate.

What is the difference between managing and leading? Ricketts (2009) suggested that a manager needs technical skills, such as knowledge and proficiency; human skills, such as the ability to work with people; and conceptual skills that involve taking a concept and implementing it. A leader is the one who inspires others and is the one who has the vision and long-term focus. How does this work within the family? Is there a difference between a family manager and a family leader?

> *The Clements and the Lees are middle-class families that live in a large metropolitan area. Both families have similar household incomes, with all four parents working full time. Mrs. Clement is a manager. She is a master at scheduling, arranging, purchasing, and organizing. Although she performs much of the work herself, she does enforce the chores and responsibilities that she has implemented over the years. In contrast, Mrs. Lee serves as a leader in her family. On Saturdays, Mrs. Lee gathers the whole family around the breakfast table to divide the weekly tasks and listen to the concerns of the family members, and together they make plans for upcoming events. What is the difference between the leadership style of Mrs. Clement and Mrs. Lee? If Mrs. Clement and Mrs. Lee are suddenly faced with life-threatening illnesses, what consequences will each family face in their effort to maintain family functions?*

IN THE NEWS

Who Really Controls What Families Buy?

The advertising industry has a long history of researching consumer demand and decision making. The influence of children on family purchases is important to product marketing. So, just how important are children in the consumer market? One study in 2012 showed that parents let their children decide what they will eat for breakfast about a third of the time, and when lunchtime rolls around, one out of four children is given choices. Purchase control increases drastically when families are eating fast food. Kids pick their meals 85% of the time at these locations.

And it's not just selection of food that falls to these young consumers. They are collaborating with their adults on clothing, shoes, and vacation purchases. Another national survey found that half of 6- to 12-year olds had a full-sized iPad on their Santa List. In 2012, a large advertising agency reported that children have more than $1 trillion in buying power each year. And this is not just American children—the phenomenon on a global scale has been supported by several studies.

Children, as consumers, pack a one-two punch! Get their attention and loyalty now, and you will have an advantage when they cross over to adult goods and services. Kids are big business. So, what has happened to parental leadership and control? Are families functioning more and more like democracies by giving children the key to the store?

Sources: Nielsen Company (2012); White (2013).

WORLDVIEW

Gender differences in family leadership and decision making are complex across cultures. Families have many tasks to accomplish as they strive to sustain their well-being. Decisions as to who should be responsible for which tasks, especially as time constraints become more intense, can cause family conflict and increase family stress.

How parents negotiate time in paid and unpaid work can reflect gender inequality. The majority of studies report that mothers spend a higher proportion of their time in unpaid work compared to fathers (Chesley & Flood, 2017). Power within families is reflected in the division of labor—home maintenance and childcare. When women have more opportunities and bring money into the family unit, they can bargain more easily for equity.

Qian and Sayer (2016) completed a cross-national comparison of gendered interfamily housework expectations in four East Asian societies (urban China, Japan, South Korea, and Taiwan). They report that traditional marriage in East Asia is built on gender hierarchy, patriarchy, and strictly gendered marital roles. Women in these societies still shoulder the majority of routine housework. Japanese women in their study experienced the greatest discrepancy between their wish for gender equity and the actual division of labor—reporting the lowest level of marital satisfaction. Although at lower levels than Western reports, Chinese and Taiwanese married women and men enjoyed higher marital satisfaction than those in Japan and shared housework more equally.

Gracia and Kalmijn (2016) found that mothers in Spain, across all paid work categories, were more involved in parent-child interaction. Fathers' childcare involvement was much less impacted by the mothers' work schedules than their own. This reflects the "traditional" gendered division of labor in the Spanish work-family system. Another variable in that country is the fact that most working parents rely on grandparents to provide childcare, and if they must use daycare, those facilities are not in sync with work schedules.

Gender and gender expectations impact the ability of adults to assume leadership and to participate equally in the decisions of resource management. Culture and tradition support and promote these practices. As globalization expands our access to and interaction with others, the importance of cultural awareness becomes crucial.

SUMMARY

Leadership is an important function of any group, including families. A leader is one who can set the direction for the group and effectively lead the group in decision making. Leaders need foundational, direction, and leadership influence skills. A good leader is also aware of how attitude affects the outcome of the organization. Effective family leaders possess additional skills, including multitasking, interpersonal skills, growing human capabilities, and building character. Some leadership theories include the theory of X and Y, the three-factor theory, the dimensional theory, the contingency model, the path-goal theory, and the situational leadership theory. Leadership effectiveness can be predicted by the transactional, transformational, and laissez-faire leadership styles.

Most family decisions are made by the group process. This process differs from that of nonfamily groups because of the presence of characteristics such as love, attachment, and a lifelong investment in the group. Within the group process, families may make decisions based on social class, cultural or ethnic norms, communication styles, power structures, and past experience.

Families may be subject to groupthink when they fail to employ vigilant decision-making practices. To prevent faulty thinking, the group needs to establish an environment where alternatives are welcomed. Groups can make different decisions than they would if they were acting along. This process is known as group shift and can involve either risky shift or cautious shift.

QUESTIONS FOR REVIEW AND DISCUSSION

1. How does an effective leader in the family differ from the leader in other organizations?

2. How does the leadership style of a parent influence his or her parenting style?

3. Discuss how the dynamics of a family can affect their decision making.

4. What are the consequences for a family caught in groupthink?

5. What type of family would opt for risky shift in making decisions? Cautious shift?

IMPLEMENTING AND EVALUATING DECISIONS

The Decision-Making Process

- Recognize existing needs
- Identify alternatives to fulfill needs
- Evaluate identified alternatives
- Select and implement alternatives

Chapter 12. Making It Happen

- Reflect on and evaluate the alternatives selected

Chapter 13. Defining Success

Chapter 14. Current and Future Challenges

CHAPTER TWELVE

MAKING IT HAPPEN

Objectives
Implementation
  Strategies
  Delegation
  Accountability
  Motivation
Estate Planning
Family Business Succession
Risk Management
  Insurance
  Health Insurance
Reality Check
  Life Insurance
  Automobile Insurance
  Home Insurance
Worldview
Completion and Reflection
In the News
Summary
Questions for Review and Discussion

Objectives

- Understand the need for flexibility in the implementation process.

- Explore the importance of motivation to plan success.

- Differentiate among different types of implementation strategies.

- Understand the need for accountability of those responsible for plan implementation.

- Become aware of the processes and importance of estate planning and risk management.

- Understand the value of post-implementation evaluation.

- Understand risk management and methods used in family management.

If you can't fly, then run; if you can't run, then walk; if you can't walk, then crawl; but whatever you do, you have to keep moving forward.

—Martin Luther King, Jr.

Decisions rarely stand alone, disconnected from future processing. Usually, one decision leads to others, creating a continuous process that requires monitoring and adjustment. To reach goals, families must purposefully strive to fulfill objectives. In a dynamic environment, these objectives may require revision to reach ultimate success.

> *The Ito family decided to reduce its utility bills and use the savings to strengthen their retirement funds. Their objectives included reducing the electric and gas bills by 25%. Methods used to reach that reduction included (a) weatherizing the doors and windows, (b) installing dimmers and timers on major household lighting, and (c) adjusting temperature thresholds for heating and air conditioning. The first year after implementing these measures, the Itos realized a savings of almost 30%. The next year, however, utilities increased rates by 15%, and it was an especially hard winter, requiring more heat than usual. The family's efforts are still important and are resulting in savings, but their objectives will need to be adjusted in light of the rate changes, which are uncontrollable factors. The plan is still working, but the expectations must be lowered or methods of reduction must be increased.*

Family decisions and the resulting plans are not created or implemented in a vacuum. They are impacted by social, economic, and political changes. If members are unrealistic about the flexibility required to reach goals, they will become frustrated, and their participation may wane. Plans requiring group members' support are vulnerable to the attitudes and behaviors of individual members.

IMPLEMENTATION

Employer wellness programs emerged during the 1970s and gained momentum after the 2010 Affordable Care Act (Obamacare) was implemented. The belief was that health insurance costs would be reduced by creating healthier employees. Recent studies have called into question the effectiveness of these programs. Shephard (1996) found that within 6 months, up to half of employee participants drop out. In 2013, only about 45% of households ages 25 to 64 had any money saved in retirement accounts other than their Social Security funds (Biggs, 2016). Although the need to plan ahead is substantiated, failure to implement plans is evident in many facets of contemporary family management. Why do individuals and families create plans and then fail to implement them? There are several possible explanations.

Most individuals and families have too many goals for their limited resources. When that happens, choices must be made about which goals are most important. In the process of prioritizing, some goals, and the plans to implement them, are abandoned altogether. Some are postponed to be revisited at a later, more conducive time.

> *Max had planned to finish college in eight semesters. Shortly after the second semester, he realized that to pay for tuition, books, and living expenses, he would need more money than he originally budgeted. He decided to take a semester off and work full time to boost his bank account. He is determined to resume studies next semester.*

In this situation, Max is not abandoning his goal of obtaining a college education. He is postponing it—adjusting for reality factors. Should Max secure a full-time job that he likes and that has future potential, he may revisit his college goal and may decide not to go back to school.

Another reason why families don't fully implement plans is crisis management. Because a family operates in a dynamic, ever-changing environment, sudden, unexpected emergencies occur. Long-awaited vacation plans may be abruptly abandoned when a medical emergency or death occurs. Saving for new appliances may give way to repairing a family automobile. Job loss may derail many long-term plans. Resources must be diverted to handling these crises, and less important goals will be delayed or forgotten.

A third reason why family plans may not be fully implemented is attributed to **Gresham's law of planning**. This phenomenon (see Chapter 9) occurs when short-term, more immediate needs shift priorities and extend deadlines away from established plans and into these short-term situations. Remodeling of a kitchen may be delayed when undetected water damage is discovered in the home's foundation.

Gresham's law of planning: a general tendency for programmed activities to overshadow nonprogrammed activities

Another reason for plan failure is loss of motivation. Chapter 11 discussed the complexity of group decision making. The same factors present during the decision and planning phases exist at implementation. It is important for all family members impacted by a plan to feel ownership of that plan. A leader will emerge with the authority and responsibility necessary to monitor, adjust, and complete the plan. His or her leadership style must be appropriate for the plan and for all individuals involved. A common, shared vision must exist for members to maintain their motivation and level of effort toward goal completion. Four important concepts—strategy, delegation, accountability, and motivation—are keys to successful plan management.

Strategies

Recent research in positive psychology (Seligman, 2002) and emotional intelligence (Bar-On & Parker, 2000) provide support for three groups of strategies: affect regulation, interpersonal strategies, and problem solving/task management. **Affect regulation** deals with the emotional reactions experienced by family members during the implementation phase. Goals are often blocked or threatened, and people must learn to manage negative reactions such as anxiety, depression, and anger. Children may be expected to throw tantrums and express frustration vocally, but developmental theory suggests that there are different levels of behavior expected in times of disappointment. Adults usually have a repertoire of coping strategies that allow them to express affective thoughts and feelings. Relaxation, meditation, and stress-reduction skills are often part of successful strategies for managing affect during implementation. Optimism is an inherent desire to expect the best of things (Seligman, 2002). This affective tendency can be useful if it includes a rational evaluation of each situation. Pessimism is the tendency to believe that things will always turn out negatively. This affective reaction is not productive, and those expressing pessimistic attitudes almost always guarantee a drag on successful implementation.

Affect regulation: self-regulation of emotions

Optimists report better adjustment to many types of stressors, including transition to college, pregnancy, chronically ill family members, and personal health threats (Jackson, Weiss, Lundquist, & Soderlind, 2002). Feather (1990) found that when people are confident that goals can be met, they are more likely to act and persist toward goal fulfillment. It is of interest to note that Jackson et al. (2002) also found that optimistic individuals are more likely to be married than are pessimists.

> *When informed that a new test had been implemented to determine proficiency in their foreign language course, Kale and Tristan react differently. Kale tells her friends that she is capable and willing to give the test her best shot. Tristan complains that everyone is out to get him, and he will never have time to adequately prepare for the test.*

Kale's optimism will set her up for success if she is rationally assessing the circumstances—strong language skills and capability. It sets her up for disappointment, however, if she doesn't actually have what it takes. Tristan's pessimism will negatively impact his preparation and attitude toward the testing procedure, but it also provides him with an excuse if he does indeed fail. If family leaders can enhance the perceptions of mastery by communicating that the plan is sound, that members have adequate resources, that personal input and eventual rewards are valued, and that progress is being made, the probability that members will remain engaged toward the completion of the goal is greatly enhanced.

Interpersonal strategies incorporate assertive communication without dominance of others involved. Using this strategy requires expression of one's willingness to cooperate and work with others toward a common goal. Active listening is part of this approach, as is offering support or seeking it from others when needed. **Problem-solving strategies** (or task-management strategies) involve self-monitoring and continual monitoring of the environment. Problems encountered during the implementation phase are viewed as nothing more than discrepancies between what is perceived and what is desired in terms of progress toward goal achievement.

Interpersonal strategies: use of assertive communication without dominance to encourage others to be involved

Problem-solving strategies: a collection of strategies used to complete the problem-solving process

> *Vernon is a problem solver. When his debate team seems to be falling apart after months of success, he looks first at his own performance and effort and then at the differences in the competitions, past and recent. Juliette uses interpersonal strategies in her efforts to understand the problem with the same team. She calls a meeting to discuss team members' concerns and to explore the possibility of a group effort toward improvement. James, also a member of the team, is more likely to use affect regulation, exploring emotions expressed by himself and other team members to find reasons for the recent failures. All three have different approaches, but their strategies will be helpful if the goal is viewed to be the same—a stronger team effort.*

Resilience is the ability to rebound from adversity, overcome obstacles, and achieve success, even when one has experienced great losses in the past. Amatea, Smith-Adcock, and Villares (2006) present the family resilience perspective. This approach to understanding how family members and family units can succeed, even in adverse situations, considers each interaction between the home and outside environment as an opportunity to strengthen that family's ability to overcome adversity and fulfill family goals. Research focusing on obstacles faced by low-income families has supported this resilience perspective, citing a surprising resilience and creativity in these families when building strategies to help children in poverty overcome negative life situations.

Strategies for achieving goals are influenced by available resources, opportunities, and sources of support (Griffith & Graham, 2004). It is not enough just for a strategy to be in place. Day-to-day stress and competition for family resources can sap the energy out of any plan of action. It is important to make the strategy a priority by engaging all involved before and throughout implementation. This process requires clear communication of the plan's intent and structure and connecting each individual involved to the plan by defining his or her role and benefits expected on completion. Another important component of any strategy is continual assessment and feedback to all concerning the progress and necessary adjustments made along the way.

> *Brett, 5 years old, has just been diagnosed with juvenile diabetes. His condition reached a level of hospitalization, and a recovery and maintenance plan has been established for his situation. His mother insists on controlling the plan entirely, feeling that Brett's siblings are too young to handle it and that her husband has enough responsibility outside of the home. Shortly after Brett's return home, the stress level within the family peaks, and his maintenance plan is threatened. There have been no changes in the rest of the family's diet and exercise, and his siblings and friends don't understand the importance of his continual blood monitoring. They start to avoid him, and he becomes isolated and depressed. His father realizes that something must be done but doesn't have the knowledge or skills to step in and work with his wife.*

When any one individual in a family faces lifestyle changes, he or she needs the support of all other family members. They need to understand why and how these changes can impact everyone. They need to celebrate the successes and shoulder some responsibility for failures. Implementing any new type of behavioral change requires flexibility and a willingness of everyone in the family to adapt to change. Change brings about a measure of discomfort within the family, but is ever-present and necessary for family survival. Communication, engagement, and a shared vision help families implement important short- and long-term plans. Strategies that bring about success often become established patterns of actions and behaviors of individuals and family (Griffith & Graham, 2004).

Resilience: the ability to adapt and to move forward

▶ **Photo 12.1**
Resiliency in
adverse situations
is key to success.

Delegation:
the assignment
of authority and
responsibility to
another person to
carry out specific
activities

Delegation

An important part of engagement of individuals during implementation is **delegation** of activities and responsibilities. Delegation is not "dumping" tasks on others, but rather an opportunity for leaders to help develop the skills of others involved in the implementation of a plan (Green, 2008). By delegating parts of the implementation plan to others, the leader will be able to focus time and energy on other matters, and all members will grow and mature by fulfilling assigned responsibilities. They will also feel more connected to the entire plan when they are responsible for at least a part of it. Delegation is a complex activity, however, and there are some basic principles that will enhance the success of that process:

- Determine what requires your own attention and action and those things that may be accomplished by others without your direct supervision. Consider the mental and social maturity of those to whom you wish to delegate responsibilities.

- Realize that delegated actions may not always rise to meet your own personal standards. A younger child may not make perfect rows while mowing the grass. Ask yourself if these "imperfections" will critically harm the implementation process. If not, acknowledge progress, not the procedure.

- Don't underestimate the abilities of others. They may require some instruction and supervision, but each delegated task they accomplish prepares them for future, more complicated tasks.

- Focus on communication during the delegation process. Be clear and concise when expressing your expectations. Explain why you are delegating this task to the other person. Be open to questions the individual may have at the time he or she is given the responsibility and at intervals during the rest of the implementation process.

- Make delegated assignments easy enough to complete, but challenging and enjoyable at the same time.

- Because all decisions require future decisions, include assignments that require the other person to make some decisions and give him or her sufficient authority to do so.

- Always support and monitor family members involved in implementation. Remember to hold them accountable, but only for what is in their control. Avoid micromanaging them, but inform them of when and in what form you expect reports about their progress.

- When the implementation process has been completed, be fair and honest in the assessment of both the effort and end product of your delegated tasks. Compliment when appropriate, and give constructive criticism when necessary. Be sure to include all participating members in the celebration of completion (Webb, 1991).

Throughout this discussion about successful implementation, the importance of good communication continues to surface. Cipriano (2010) found that communication is also essential for successful delegation. The success or failure of delegation depends on a positive two-way relationship and communication of mutual respect and trust between the person responsible and the assistant. Leaders would like others to take more initiative and a more active role in decision making but are not always comfortable giving control of the task to others. Some group members perceive that the leader wants them to follow orders and to be conservative in doing so. These members, however, report that they would like more latitude in how they complete the tasks and more shared decision making. Untapped potential exists, but perceptions prevent implementation—a real possibility in family settings. Underestimating the actual capabilities of younger and older family members reduces total family productivity when delegation to these members is constrained.

Accountability

All members involved in the implementation of a plan should have a balance between responsibility and authority. No one should be held accountable for something over which he or she has no control. Delegated tasks should reflect this balance. The distribution of responsibility across family members for the success of any plan should follow general guidelines of accountability:

- Ensure that each member fully understands his or her tasks within implementation and that each possesses the necessary resources to accomplish those tasks.

- Communicate expected feedback intervals and clarify who should be notified if something goes awry.

- Provide frequent feedback on the progress that results from the members' efforts, and balance positive and constructive criticism carefully.

An essential expectation of parenting and mentoring is that of guidance. Children and young adults learn responsibility by watching older family members and completing supervised tasks requiring developmental and age-appropriate levels of responsibility. A great deal of research and many educational programs address the concept of **empowerment** and the perceived benefits it provides to individuals within family and work settings.

Quinn and Spreitzer (1997) found two competing definitions of empowerment among business executives. One group believed that empowerment was

Empowerment: to give official authority or legal power to

about delegating decision making within a clear set of boundaries. The other group saw it more as risk taking, growth, and change. Empowerment is not something a manager or leader does to subordinates, but rather a mind-set that individuals have about their role in the implementation process. Ghazavi, Minooei, Abdeyazdan, and Gheissari (2014) found that family empowerment interventions are successful in increasing quality of life of chronically ill patients and their families. Empowered family members see themselves as having choices, being personally connected to the family unit, being confident about their abilities, and being capable of having an impact on the family's progress.

Motivation

When an individual is part of a family group, his or her actions impact the outcomes of the other group members and the group as a whole (Dewitte & De Cremer, 2001), which creates a conflict between pursuing one's own self-interest and the group's interest. Dewitte and De Cremer refer to this as a **mixed-motive situation**. Self-control and **delayed gratification** become important in these situations. The ability to sacrifice for the group's long-term benefit will delay the possibility of reaching some short-term personal goals. When a family member can understand and conceptualize the future benefit to both him and her and the family unit, he or she is more likely to support the group's plan of action.

Long-term plans are especially vulnerable to delays and obstacles. Family members will be motivated toward goal achievement by all of the factors discussed earlier in this chapter. Specific strategies, however, are often necessary for certain groups. Adolescents, for example, have been found to be best motivated when they are given explanations for why a goal is valuable to them and how it will **intrinsically** benefit them or their families. **Extrinsic** motivators, such as financial success, power, and image, are less effective in goal accomplishment. Vansteenkiste, Simons, Lens, Soenens, and Matos (2005) believe that extrinsic motivators during adolescence shift the focus to a more rigid, narrowly focused, and superficial involvement. They also found that adolescents are more motivated when they can identify with the personal importance of the activity with appropriate levels of **autonomy** within the tasks expected of them. Adults are more likely to respect the needs of other adults in terms of autonomy but need to strive toward similar approaches when dealing with adolescent family members.

> Marcus is 15 years old and working part time during the school year. His father insists that Marcus save 75% of his earnings. He wants his son to attend an Ivy League college and continually stresses how expensive that will be. Marcus' mother encourages him to save his money so that he will have more options when he is ready to decide where he will go to college.

According to research on intrinsic and extrinsic goal motivation, Marcus will probably be more likely to save his money if he believes it will provide him with choices later. His mother's encouragement is based on intrinsic and autonomous factors. His father is more concerned with image (extrinsic) and uses a more controlling approach.

Mixed-motive situation: a situation where someone's personal actions impact the outcomes of the other group members and the group as a whole

Delayed gratification: the ability to wait in order to obtain something that one wants

Intrinsic: a characteristic or property of some thing or action that is essential and specific to that thing or action and that is wholly independent of any other object, action, or consequence

Extrinsic: a characteristic that is not essential or inherent

Autonomy: self-directing freedom and especially moral independence; a self-governing state

Children develop self-control, independence, and strategies to correct poor behavior through experiences with unpleasant circumstances and by making mistakes (Lynch, Hurford, & Cole, 2002). Parental **enabling**, or overprotectiveness and manipulation to insulate children from these uncomfortable learning experiences, has been found to negatively impact a child's ability to take responsibility for his or her behavior. Another similar concept, **locus of control** (Rotter, 1973), refers to one's belief that one has the ability to control the outcome of a task one has been assigned. Children and adults with an external locus of control believe that the environment and others in that environment have a substantial impact on their ability to achieve. Those with an internal locus of control believe they have control over what happens to them. An internal locus of control has been linked to resiliency in both children and adults.

ESTATE PLANNING

One of the most important and involved planning and implementation processes an individual or family undertakes is that of distribution of accumulated assets to the next generation. **Estate planning** is a process used to manage a family's future financial health and well-being. This concept is a reflection of the belief that future generations should profit from the work and savings plans of current family members. At times through recorded history, a family's holdings were passed to specific members of the next generation, often first-born males. Contemporary beliefs favor a more equitable distribution across genders. There are complex legal methods that will be applied to estate distribution if a family has not created a plan prior to the death of a family member.

An individual's **estate** consists of everything he or she has accumulated to date that has value, including property such as homes, vehicles, and furnishings. An estate also includes all financial holdings—certificates of deposit, stocks, bonds, and cash. To determine what someone's estate is worth, a list of assets is compiled and those current values are adjusted by the liabilities or credit owed against those assets. This final figure is often referred to as an estate's **net worth**. In essence, this is what an individual will pass on to his or her heirs on death. This inheritance can be managed prior to the owner's death to minimize the tax liability for future heirs and ensure that the estate is both protected and invested well.

Inheritance tax has fluctuated greatly at the federal level during the last decade. Laws were passed to eliminate it over time, but money and property passed to another through legal wills or court proceedings may be taxable. It is important for those inheriting things of value to consult with professionals for current requirements. **Gift tax** is another important factor to consider when planning estate giving. Each year an individual is permitted under law to give up to a certain amount of money to as many people as desired without those recipients being taxed on the gifted funds. Currently, around $14,000 (2016) is the maximum allowed for gifting without tax liability.

> *Georgia has gifted each of her five grandchildren and two of her close friends $10,000 during 2012. She plans on doing the same in 2013 and 2014. Her*

Enabling: doing for others what they can and need to do for themselves

Locus of control: a theory in psychology that originally distinguished between two types of people: *internals*, who attribute events to their own control, and *externals*, who attribute events in their life to external circumstances

Estate planning: the process of planning for the efficient transfer of assets at one's death

Estate: the degree, quality, nature, and extent of one's interest in land or other property

Net worth: the total assets minus total liabilities of an individual or a company

Inheritance tax: a tax levied on property received by inheritance or legal succession, calculated according to the value of the property received

Gift tax: a graduated federal tax paid by donors on gifts exceeding $10,000 per year, per donor recipient

grandchildren and friends do not have to pay taxes on these gifts, totaling $30,000 each over the 3-year period. If Georgia had given $30,000 to each in her will, upon her death, that entire amount may have been taxable under current tax law.

Estate taxes are complicated and vary from location to location. It is an important part of an estate plan to research these taxes, and professional guidance is available.

Individuals who die without legally qualified estate plans filed will be considered as intestate. Under these circumstances, there are complex legal steps that will be followed to settle the estate of the deceased. If an individual wishes to have more control over the disbursement of his or her estate, legal steps must be taken before death. A will is a legal document that explains how an individual wants to distribute his or her assets on death. Beneficiaries, similar to insurance terms, will be designated, and terms of distribution among those individuals will be stipulated. To handle the process of distribution, an executor is named in the will. That person is responsible for carrying out all wishes explained within the legal will. A will is an important estate planning technique; however, anything within a will must go through the probate process, the validation and legal processing of the will, and this process is often slow and costly.

There are two other important legal documents that should be considered in the estate planning process. A durable power of attorney is a document that protects your estate if you should become unable to make decisions on your own behalf due to physical or mental problems. This person, chosen by the individual, can act as his or her representative in a legal capacity. This role does not impact an existing will, only the actual time of incapacitation while an individual is still alive. Another more specific legal designation that provides for important decision making when someone is deemed unable to make medical decisions for him- or herself is referred to as a living will. In this document, a healthcare proxy is designated to make life-support decisions for an individual who has lost the capacity to make those types of decisions. Such a document is often requested on hospital admittance, although it is not required for treatment.

Understanding current laws regarding transfer of assets is a major factor for success within estate planning. A few are presented here, but it is important to seek legal counsel when contemplating sound estate plan decisions. Types of ownership and the use of trusts impact estate distribution in unique ways.

Joint ownership with right of survivorship is a method of transferring property without tax implications. When an asset, such as a home or vehicle, is owned jointly, that asset is automatically transferred to the surviving owner without probate. Community property is another form of joint ownership falling under marital laws of states. Community property in these states is anything acquired during a legal marriage. On death of either the husband or wife, the survivor will receive one-half of community property, and the other half will be disbursed through the plan within a will or state inheritance laws.

A trust is a legal entity created by the grantor to hold and manage inheritance property or money on the behalf of another person. If someone is concerned that one of his or her designated beneficiaries might be unable to manage inheritance, such a legal situation may be helpful.

Grantor: somebody from whom something is transferred in a legal transaction

> *Fred has accumulated a great deal of money during his adult life. He married late, and at age 70 he has two children still in elementary school. His wife died recently, and his health is failing. Fred is concerned about how his young children might survive if something happens to him, so he creates a trust fund for both of them. If he dies before they reach the age of 25, the money he has willed to them will be managed by his good friend and legal counsel, Rico. Through this legal arrangement, all living expenses will be provided through their inheritance on the approval of Rico until they reach the age stated in the trust documentation (25), at which each will gain full control of the money in his or her account.*
>
> *Aspen is the single mother of Jacque, an adult with Down's syndrome. To ensure that Jacque will have adequate care if she should die first, Aspen has created a trust that will hold any life insurance paid out on her death in his name, available to help pay for the care and supervision he may need after her death.*

Trusts ensure guidance and supervision of estate inheritance. They are especially useful in the following situations:

- To bypass the probate process

- To avoid legal challenges that wills often experience

- To reduce estate taxes

- To ensure professional management for those who are not deemed knowledgeable or responsible by the grantor

- To ensure confidentiality, as a will becomes public record and trusts do not

- To provide for survivors with special needs

- To keep money responsibly until a child reaches the age of maturity

- To provide uncontestable inheritance to children from a marriage that is currently dissolved

There are several types of trusts that can be legally established during the estate-planning process. Each type specifically answers tax or responsibility issues faced by the planner. Due to the complexity of establishing and implementing a trust, it is strongly advised that legal and financial expertise be used.

Most people recognize the importance of estate planning, but many do not develop or implement strategies that are in the best interest of them and their survivors. Any individual with responsibility toward others—partners, children, parents, siblings—should have a legal will drafted and on file. Beyond that component, the size of the estate and the complexity of relationships will determine the intricacy of one's estate plan.

FAMILY BUSINESS SUCCESSION

Attitudes and behavior toward inheritance are changing, shifting the ways that families manage family-based businesses and how they engage in training of their successors ("Planning for Your Successor," 2005). Without adequate planning, family disputes and mismanaged estate tax issues may force family businesses to be broken into pieces or be sold in entirety to outside bidders when family founders are incapacitated or die. The transfer or distribution of a family business upon the death of older members often strains family relations. There is a difficult balance to negotiate between business strategies to ensure current and future business success and the need to distribute assets fairly and equally to all survivors.

©iStockphoto.com/mediaphotos

▶ **Photo 12.2**
Family businesses have been an important part of the nation's economic history.

Planning for the transfer of a family business is essential for two important reasons. First, when families are mourning the loss of a parent or other family member, emotions are high. Second, dealing with complex business decisions and issues of future business leadership may be too much for family members to bear at this time, and decisions made under such stress may be challenged at a later time, pitting some family members against others. Succession planning should be an integral part of any family business. These plans should be shared and understood by all members who will be impacted.

> *Terri decided to create an investment strategy to protect the money that she and her late husband had accumulated through decades of running a family construction company. Because that money had already been taxed upon earning, she wanted to restructure the business so that her children would assume her shares of ownership equally when she passed. Filing the proper paperwork and legal documents, she is now assured that upon her death, her part of the business will transfer directly to the children with no need for probate or legal action.*

> *Lila was the executor of her mother's estate. Her mother had warned her that a sibling, Leroy, would cause trouble during the estate's distribution. Lila did not believe that her brother would be unreasonable. However, within weeks of her mother's death, Leroy had hired an attorney to challenge his mother's will. Lila has not spoken to her brother for more than 10 years because of this.*

RISK MANAGEMENT

Most decisions contain a degree of uncertainty, and successful implementation of any plan includes assessing possible risks and consequences (Heller, 1998). Williams et al. (2006) define *risk management* as a systematic process of identifying, assessing, managing, and monitoring risks and uncertainty in an effort to plan for and cope with possible negative outcomes. Risk can be managed by intuition or unconscious reasoning based on affect. Past experience provides a more understandable method of analyzing possible future risks; however, intuition is often credited for important decisions.

Williams et al. (2006) suggest three important steps in risk management:

1. Risk recognition

2. Risk prioritization

3. Risk management

Risks within the context of the family include damaged relationships, financial insecurity, and family unit instability. These risks must be analyzed for possible consequences and likelihoods of actuality. Realizing that a family operates under continual risk possibilities, members must determine how much risk is acceptable to members. Unacceptable risks can be handled in one of four different ways. The situation or behaviors can be terminated. They can be treated or managed with control measures or contingency plans. The family may decide to accept the risk and live with whatever outcome occurs, or the family may transfer or move the risk impact to another entity, such as insurance.

> *Missy and Earl own and occupy a home on the California coastline. Neighboring homes have fallen into the ocean over the last few years. Their risks in this situation include danger to life, loss of the family's home, or possible damage to the existing structure. Realizing the risk factors, they can move from the home and try to sell it or parts of it (terminate). They can invest in structural reinforcement to try to prevent future damage (treat). They can try to convince themselves that whatever happens will happen and they will figure out how to deal with it at the time (tolerate). If possible, they may invest in an insurance policy that will pay damages if they do, indeed, occur (transfer). If the risk is too high, it is unlikely that an insurance company will offer coverage on the home.*

There are always choices in situations of risk, and the level of acceptance will differ from family to family.

Worldview (see Chapter 1) presents another way to understand the levels of difference in risk assessment among families and cultural groups. If you do not believe you have control over natural processes, such as erosion and hurricanes, you will not spend time and money trying to manage potential risk from those phenomena. Decisions made by families to not carry insurance are not always based on financial inability or lack of intelligent decision making. Different perspectives lead to different choices in similar situations.

Insurance

Many risks exist for individuals and families over time. Fire, accidents, illness, and legal problems threaten the security of families on a daily basis. As part of the risk management used by contemporary families, insurance plays an important role in resource management. From a worldview perspective, insuring people and things against loss stems from a belief that there is and should be a level of control over the unknown. The insured believe that future loss can be compensated, and that such monetary replacement will make things right again, at least to some degree.

Insurance: an arrangement by which a company gives customers financial protection against loss or harm—for example, theft or illness—in return for payment or premium

Premiums: payments made to an insurance company to buy a policy and to keep it in force

Insurance is based on the concept of risk pooling, or the sharing of financial risks among many group members (Keown, 2003). Those purchasing insurance pay premiums to companies and receive the promise of future payment if they experience a catastrophic situation that is covered by that insurance policy. Chances are that they will never actually face that catastrophe. Insurance companies offer policies based on a calculated risk of their own. Mathematically, the probability that your family home will be destroyed is small. If you and 1 million of your neighbors purchase home insurance, you are pooling your premiums through the insurance agency. That agency has calculated the possibility of home loss among policy owners and has set the premium price to cover the expected claims each year.

> *Insurance Company A has sold home insurance policies to 2,000 families in New Port. Each family pays an average of $1,200 per year for this coverage ($2,400,000 total). Last year, two homes insured by A were ruined by fire, with an insurance payout of $800,000. The $1,600,000 difference between payouts and premiums collected represents a profit for the company, which is then used to employ agents in the community and to finance the overall company's expenses. However, if this community experienced the ravages of a hurricane or tornado, claims could exceed premium income by several million dollars. Insurance companies use mathematical formulas to hedge their own risks.*

Deductible: the billed amount that is the patient's responsibility before insurance coverage will activate

Copayment: the amount the insured pays in addition to the deductible of any judgment or settlement

Of course, in the previous example, the 1,998 families that did not collect money from their insurance policies have paid $1,200 and have received only the security of knowing they are covered just in case such a disaster hits them personally. There are several types of insurance available to families seeking to protect themselves from possible devastating losses. Some commonalities across insurance providers are deductibles, copays, and stop-loss limits. As discussed in Chapter 8, a deductible is the amount the patient is responsible for before insurance coverage will activate. A copayment is the amount of money expected from the patient in addition to the insurance payment. A **stop-loss limit** is the total amount an insured person will be expected to pay in a designated time period.

Stop-loss limit: the maximum amount under traditional insurance for which benefits are calculated on a proportional basis; after the stop-loss is met, coverage is paid at 100%

> *Rogene has an automobile policy that has a $500 deductible. When a rock breaks her windshield, she discovers that the replacement cost of the glass is $450. She must pay the entire amount to repair the windshield, and she probably won't even contact her insurance company, because she is responsible for the first $500 of each repair incident. Her health insurance policy has a $250 annual deductible. Each year she must pay the first $250 of medical expenses before her insurance coverage initiates. After meeting her deductible, she has a copay of 20%. A $100 medical bill, after the deductible has been met, will cost her only $20. The other $80 will be paid by her insurance carrier. Her policy also has a $1,000 stop-loss feature. Once the $250 deductible has been met and she has paid 20% of charges, up to $750 total, her insurance will begin to pay 100% of future bills during that same designated time period (usually an annual cycle).*

Health Insurance

Most **health insurance** policies include a combination of hospital, surgical, and physician expense coverage. Hospital insurance will cover some of the costs resulting from a hospital stay, such as room charges, care and medication costs, and surgical facility usage. Most health insurance plans have limits set on acceptable fees charged their clients and on the length of hospital stay for each visit. Surgical coverage will pay a percentage of expenses for necessary operations that have been approved by the company. This coverage usually does not include experimental treatments. Policies may also cover doctor fees incurred outside of the hospital, such as office visits and lab fees.

Health insurance: insurance against loss caused by sickness or bodily injury

Individuals and families without medical insurance face two possibilities in the event of a health emergency: do without treatment or access public assistance/private foundation funds to pay for treatment. General healthcare is lower among those who are uninsured than those with even minimum insurance support. An important part of most healthcare insurance plans is payment for regular health checkups to identify possible problems early or to avoid the development of disease and sickness later.

Specific insurance for dental and vision health coverage is available for additional premium payments. Those concerned about developing cancer during their lifetimes may purchase insurance plans to cover expenses associated with those kinds of illnesses and treatments. Once basic health insurance has become part of a family's overall life plan, money available for additional coverage (often referred to as *riders*) will impact the decision-making process. It is important that the need for these types of special plans be reevaluated over the life changes of a family.

> *When Barry, the youngest Kohn child, married, Mr. and Mrs. Kohn analyzed their new health insurance needs. Both parents use reading glasses, but do*

not need glasses for other types of functioning. Because the vision insurance plan they had covered one examination annually and one pair of glasses each year, it became obvious that this plan was no longer needed. At $20 per month ($240 per year), Mr. and Mrs. Kohn would be paying more to keep the policy than they would need to pay for two eye exams each year. The plan had been useful when their two youngest children were under their coverage because both required glasses or contacts at all times.

Managed healthcare:
a service that is provided by a hospital or other group of clinics, which may be managed by an external company

Managed healthcare is a concept that stems from the growing need of companies to provide health insurance coverage to employees. To reduce insurance costs and claims, medical providers are recruited who will agree to lower charges per visit or treatment with the advantage of volume numbers of guaranteed patients. Those using a managed healthcare plan are limited to those physicians on a preapproved list. Some are given the right to choose others with additional costs or higher copayments.

There are two distinct types of managed healthcare plans: health maintenance organizations (HMOs) and preferred provider organizations (PPOs). HMOs are prepaid insurance plans that allow members to use the services of participating doctors and medical facilities. Members pay a flat fee to belong, and copayments may be required. HMOs are efficient, saving up to 40% of medical costs (Keown, 2003). The perceived drawbacks to HMO plans include limited choices of providers, impersonal care, and complicated referral requirements.

PPOs fall somewhere between traditional healthcare plans and HMOs. Employers negotiate reduced rates with a group of physicians and facilities, creating a list from which their employees can choose. If the insured insist on using care providers who have not contracted with the insurance group, they will have to pay a higher copay or penalty charge.

Health insurance is available through employers, associations, professional groups, and individual plans. Group plans cost about 25% less than similar individual policies because larger groups have more bargaining power to reduce service costs. Lower costs equate lower premium needs from participants. When insurance is not available through employers, individuals can seek other group affiliations (clubs, financial institutions, and professional organizations) to take advantage of these pooled, lower-rate plans.

REALITY CHECK

Impact of Medical Crises on Family Resource Needs

Earlier this year, Jessica and Brandon faced fear and braced for the battle of their lives. Brandon, fresh from a restaurant management training program, collapsed in the bathroom of their new home. Jessica, newly employed herself, received a memorable phone call later that day.

Brandon had been diagnosed with leukemia. Within the week, Brandon was fully immersed in an aggressive treatment program in a hospital 200 miles from their home and employers. Jessica, torn among her husband's care regime, their 18-month-old daughter's needs, and the responsibilities of her new job, felt her world tilt on its axis.

Understanding our health insurance coverage was one of the first things on our minds. How much is this going to cost us, and how are we going to pay for it? I honestly can't say what we would have done without insurance. I suppose we would have had to sell our house and declare bankruptcy. We didn't have the money in savings to pay for the extremely high medical bills.

At first there was a $500 deductible that we had to meet. This was virtually met with just the doctor visits leading up to the diagnosis. Second, there was a $1,500 stop-loss, which meant that we would have a total of $1,500 out-of-pocket expenses (deductibles and copays) before the insurance company would begin paying 100% of the medical costs. What a relief that was to know that we only had to come up with $1,500. That is much better than the $248,000 spent over the first 6 weeks for Brandon's treatment and care.

Medical costs were just part of the financial problems within this family's crisis. Brandon was 200 miles away from home. Jessica had personal expenses just trying to be with him, care for their daughter, and meet the needs of her job.

Luckily, I am an educated person, and I knew about other resources available. Insurance does not pay for the spouse's food or lodging. The hospital social worker made funds available for these expenses. Reducing those concerns allowed me to focus on my husband's needs and those of our daughter.

In times of family crisis, money is not the only resource necessary for survival. Jessica found that her social networks of family, friends, and colleagues were helpful.

My workplace policies allowed me to put my husband's health as top priority. I left my office immediately after the diagnosis, knowing that my colleagues would cover for me as needed. I was allowed to do much of my normal workload via the computer and Internet. My employer provided me with the laptop computer, also. That allowed me to be near my husband and continue working when things slowed down. Working was routine, and I needed routine to balance the helplessness of the situation and the lack of control I felt.

After a bone-marrow transplant, Brandon was able to return home. Jessica still bears the full responsibility of wage provider and insurance source. An expected full recovery will eventually see this family back on their original track—a dual-career, two-wage family. Until that time, they continue to draw from the resources that emerged during the crisis. Risk management paid off for them in many ways.

Health insurance is available to all in the United States with access to funds, policies, and qualifying states of health. Often young adults ages 18 to 30 view the chances of experiencing devastating illness and injury as improbable. They elect to use their money in more real-life ways, such as consuming goods and services. Although the possibility of illness and disability increase more quickly after age 30, it is unfortunate for those under 30 who have elected to forgo health insurance who do fall ill or suffer catastrophic injury. The lack of health insurance could have derailed Brandon and Jessica's future and forced them to accept less expensive, possibly less effective, treatment options.

Life Insurance

Life insurance: a
contract between the
policy owner and the
insurer, where the
insurer agrees to
pay a sum of money
upon the occurrence
of the insured's
death

Life insurance provides protection against loss of income due to death. When family members are dependent on the income of an adult member, loss of that income would create economic strain. A single person with no dependents would not need more life insurance than would be necessary to cover his or her last expenses. A married person with small children may see life insurance as a way to partially replace income he or she might have contributed to the family if death had not occurred. On the death of the insured, a lump sum payment or installments are paid to the designated **beneficiary.** That person or persons can use that money to replace the lost income of the deceased.

Beneficiary: the
person designated
to receive the
income of a trust
estate; the person
named (as in an
insurance policy) to
receive proceeds or
benefits

If an individual determines that he or she should have life insurance, the next decision involves the amount of coverage desired. Experts suggest that an individual purchase enough life insurance to cover 5 to 15 years of lost income. A more complicated, but focused, approach is to forecast future needs of survivors.

> *Andrew Saw is 65 years old with no surviving spouse or debts. His end-of-life needs are simply burial expenses. If he does not have enough money saved for that, he may want to have a life insurance policy that will cover those costs. Anything above that amount would be distributed among his surviving family members. His son, Tan, is 40 with a wife and three children under the age of 10. Tan's wife does not work outside of the home, and their savings are still quite small. Tan may want to have enough life insurance to replace his income until his youngest child has completed his or her education. Other future costs he may wish to cover would include education, mortgage, and costs associated with replacement of his physical contributions to his family, such as lawn care and home maintenance.*

Term insurance:
low-cost insurance
that is valid only
for a stated period
of time and has
no cash surrender
value or loan value

There are three primary types of life insurance: term, whole, and universal. **Term insurance** is the simplest form of life insurance. You pay a set premium based on your life expectancy, as determined by statistical analysis of your risk factors. In return, your beneficiaries will receive a set amount of money on your death. These types of policies are only in effect for a limited amount of time or a certain term, such as 10 years. Once the term has expired, your insurance carrier may increase the amount of the premium without increasing the policy's value. The original policy may be cancelled at that time if you choose not to agree to pay the increased premium. If you did not die during that term of coverage, none of the money paid in premiums is available to you.

**Whole life
insurance:** an
insurance policy
with cash value
before it becomes
payable upon death
or maturity

Whole life insurance provides both death benefits and an opportunity to accumulate savings through payment of premiums over time. The company invests a small portion of each premium into a savings account that grows with each premium and interest earned over time. This savings account is referred to as the **cash value** of the insurance policy. The policy owner can borrow against this cash value and retain the insurance or he or she may terminate the policy and collect the amount of money in the savings plan.

Cash value: the
amount of money
paid into a life
insurance policy that
is available to the
consumer

Universal life insurance combines term insurance and cash-value, tax-deferred savings. Premium payments are broken down into three parts: term insurance payment, savings, and administrative costs. The insured person can increase or decrease the premiums. A higher payment will result in larger amounts being deposited into the savings plan. A lower payment will result in less savings, and if the payment is too low to cover the administrative costs and term insurance portion, the shortfall can be pulled from accumulated savings, thus ensuring that the life insurance remains in effect. This type of plan requires dedication and continual decision making on the part of the insured party. Temptation to pay less over extended periods of time could result in policy lapse if not monitored closely.

Should adults in the family decide to hedge the risk of death with life insurance, deciding how much to purchase and what type to buy are important decisions. Paying premiums can be done automatically through bank drafts, payroll deductions, or company-supplied coupons. Insurance payments are expenses for families and must be folded into regular family budget plans. Missed payments can result in insurance cancellation, and to reinstate policies, individuals may have to prove insurability at the present time.

> *Bruce and his wife have been struggling to make monthly debt payments. They decide to let his life insurance policy lapse for a time and reapply when their finances stabilize. Three months later, Bruce is diagnosed with cancer. His health records will be reviewed by any life insurance company before he is issued a policy. Chances are low that any company will agree to provide him with coverage, even at high premium rates.*

Automobile Insurance

In the United States, there are 30 million automobile accidents each year (Keown, 2003). That statistic implies that each driver has about a 20% chance per year to be involved in some type of automobile altercation. Automobile insurance is not an optional expense if an individual purchases a vehicle with the intention of driving that automobile on public streets and highways. All states require proof of insurance before vehicles can be licensed for operation. Coverage required differs from state to state, but there are two basic types of auto insurance available to consumers: liability and collision.

Liability coverage provides protection from lawsuits rising from an automobile accident. It will cover bodily injury to people physically hurt and resulting property damage. Medical expense coverage will pay medical bills and funeral expenses of passengers and the driver up to a predetermined limit. Uninsured motorist protection coverage is required in many states, protecting the victims should the responsible driver not have insurance.

Collision coverage provides monetary payment should your vehicle be stolen or damaged. Comprehensive physical damage coverage includes damage from fire, storms, and other major catastrophes. This type of coverage pays for losses regardless of who is determined to be at fault for the damage. It is recommended that

Universal life insurance: a type of flexible permanent life insurance offering the low-cost protection of term life insurance as well as a savings element (like whole life insurance), which is invested to provide cash value buildup

the amount of coverage carried equal the cash value of the automobile, and most policies include a deductible.

The cost of automobile insurance is determined by many things, some under the control of the insured and some determined by statistical calculations of the insurance provider. The most important determinants of price include the following:

- *Type of automobile.* Insurance companies determine the risk of specific models of vehicles and factor that into the insurance premium. Style, power, and even color impact this determinant.

- *Use of automobile.* The probability of an accident increases with the type of driving and the frequency of use.

- *Driver characteristics.* Based on research data, insurance companies have determined the lifestyle or demographic risk factors that predict accidents. Young, unmarried males have a statistically greater chance of being in an accident; thus, they pay higher premiums for coverage. Age, sex, and marital status are factors folded into the premium prices.

- *Driver's past record.* Traffic violations and previous accidents and arrests will result in higher insurance rates.

- *Geographic location.* The more dense the population in an area, the greater the possibility of accident. Those living in urban areas will generally pay more for automobile insurance than those in less dense areas. Types of driving surfaces will also factor into the equation because rough, gravel-covered roads may result in more body damage during general use than will smoother, paved roads.

Discount: a reduction made from the gross amount or value of something; a reduction made from a regular or list price

There are many **discounts** available to automobile drivers to reduce premium prices. Companies offer different types, but common discounts include those for good driving records, multiple automobiles under the same policy, completion of defensive driving courses, and good high school and college student records. Other methods of reducing premium costs include selecting higher deductibles, improving one's driving record, and selecting models that are less costly to insure.

Home Insurance

Home insurance: an insurance policy that combines insurance on the home and its contents, as well as liability insurance for accidents that may happen at the home

Owning a home increases liability for families. Injuries sustained by nonfamily members while visiting are legal issues. Homeowners can be held responsible for injuries of all visitors occurring on their property, regardless of permission or knowledge. Aside from liability, fires, flooding, and other catastrophes can damage or destroy homes, creating enormous physical and emotional stress for families. **Home insurance** is available to consumers to help manage such risks. Often referred to as *homeowner's insurance*, these policies cover more than just the dwelling. Sold in different combinations, insurance is available to cover loss due to natural disasters, manmade perils, and possible liability claims.

Property coverage under homeowner's insurance may include the cost associated with replacement of the dwelling, other structures on the property, personal property within the dwellings, and the loss of use of the dwelling during the time required to replace or repair the home. Not all policies include all of these issues, and it is important that homeowners fully understand the terms of the policy they purchase. There are also additional types of supplemental coverage available for specific situations. **Floaters** provide extended coverage for personal property such as jewelry, silver and gold articles, and valuable collectibles.

Because replacement cost is difficult to determine at the time of insuring and at the time of destruction, companies encourage owners to fully cover their dwellings. Many companies require that owners carry at least 80% of their home's full replacement cost (80% rule).

▶ **Photo 12.3**
Insurance eases the trauma of a crisis.

The St. Claires' home is valued at $200,000. Their insurance company requires that they carry at least a $160,000 policy. A recent storm resulted in $150,000 in damage. The insurance payment will cover the entire loss. If less than 80% of the replacement cost is purchased, the homeowner must pay a coinsurance provision.

Floaters: extended coverage for personal property

The liability insurance within a homeowner's policy protects the policyholder and his or her family from financial loss if someone injured on their property sues for damages and/or medical expenses. Although families rarely anticipate nasty legal battles over such things, this type of insurance hedges risk in a time when liability cases are at an all-time high. It is especially important if the family home has a swimming pool, hot tub, trampoline, or elevated exterior living areas.

The major determinants of policy cost are (a) the location of the home, (b) the home's structure, and (c) the level of coverage and type of policy desired. Geographic location determines the probability of loss due to certain kinds of weather conditions and levels of theft, vandalism, and general crime. Older structures and homes made from less durable materials are more costly to cover. Those constructed with above minimum standard or code-required materials and specifications may qualify for premium discounts. The more comprehensive the policy and the higher the replacement cost of the home, the larger the premium will be. There are a few ways to reduce costs, however. Selecting higher deductibles, installing security features, and using the same insurance provider for multiple policies (auto, homeowners, and health) will lower the premium costs.

WORLDVIEW

Hurricanes, Disaster, and Insurance

The morning of August 29, 2005, Hurricane Katrina struck the Gulf Coast of the United States. The storm, dangerous itself, triggered levee breaches and massive flooding in Louisiana, Mississippi, and Alabama. Beyond the loss of life, structures, and belongings was a long road to recovery. Insurance companies were impacted with subsequent claims by those survivors who had insurance coverage in place.

As this area and its people worked to restore commerce, residential housing, and lives, the reality that natural disasters, and flooding in particular, are not usually covered by general property insurance set in. The Euro-American worldview assumes that humans have a right to control the impact of weather as much as possible with manmade inventions. It also assumes that risk management, or things like insurance, are necessary to make sure that the future is protected. Without that belief in the need and the ability to control the future, people will not invest in products such as insurance. To many of the people directly impacted by Katrina, it came as a surprise that their insurance companies would not be responsible for claims—human and property damage resulting from this natural disaster was, for the most part, not protected by insurance. Some estimates of actual damages were more than $100 billion. Federal relief funds were allocated to help victims, but the financial impact will continue to unfold for years to come.

COMPLETION AND REFLECTION

Why are so many plans—well designed or not—unsuccessful for individuals and families? Plans cease to exist due to three conditions: (1) They are abandoned, (2) they are modified or re-created into a new set of objectives and goals, or (3) they reach completion. Not all plans should be pursued, especially when the monitoring process illuminates flaws in the plan or new circumstances that negate the plan. Abandoning a plan is the right thing to do if it no longer meets the needs of the individual or family or if it places the family in any type of jeopardy. A marathon runner preparing for an upcoming race may have to pull out of that race if he or she experiences physical injury. Abandonment is not always failure. When family members or individuals discard a plan, it may be due to the inappropriateness of the plan or the lack of commitment of those involved. Loss of commitment or motivation may illuminate flaws within the plan.

The planning process exists in a dynamic environment, and both needs and resources continue to change over time. Those changes may result in a misfit between the original plan and current circumstances. Many plans can be adjusted during implementation without completely abandoning them.

> *Shirley is a single female with a long employment history and a healthy retirement savings account. Her original will left her estate to her siblings, in equal amounts. Now, at the age of 60, she has lost two of those siblings to early death. Both in-laws remarried and had children with their second spouses. If*

Shirley left her will as it were, those previous in-laws could petition the courts for the part of her estate that would have gone to their spouses, Shirley's brothers. One of Shirley's living siblings has experienced a severe stroke and will require medical and care services for the rest of her life. Shirley creates a new will, redistributing her estate among her living siblings, but places the majority in a trust to care for her ill sister.

The original will was a good, solid plan. The circumstances, however, have changed, and the changes made in the new version prevent future problems and help address new needs identified.

Completion is a natural end to a plan well implemented. The decision-making process does not stop at that point, however. An important step is that of evaluation. A plan is not a success just because it has been successfully implemented. If the end result is not what was originally desired or if the individual's or family's needs have not been completely and positively met, acknowledging the flaws within the plan or within the implementation process is an important part of future planning. Repetition of past mistakes is detrimental to the health and well-being of a family. Learning from one's mistakes is important at all levels.

IN THE NEWS

Of Debt and Deficit: Could Budgeting Help?

Headlines and news reports herald the looming crisis facing the United States treasury—deficit spending and mounting international debt:

> US Budget Fight Threatens World Food Security: Agriculture Research Could Be Casualty in Debate Over Borrowing Limit

> Lawmakers Burdening Future Generations With Mountain of Debt!

> What Does the US Budget Stalemate Mean for Research?

> US Budget Woes Could Hit European Missile Defense!

Imagine that you spend more money this month than the amount on your paycheck stub. You would have a budget *deficit*. To remain flush, you could borrow (e.g., through a credit card or short-term loan). The amount you borrowed (and now owe) is your *debt*. Interest is charged to you for this debt. If you have a *deficit* every month, you keep borrowing and your debt grows. Now the amount you pay monthly for interest is larger than any other item in your budget. Eventually, all you can afford each month is the interest payment. You are poised now to declare bankruptcy.

This scenario is a simplistic representation of how the United States deficit has come to be what it is—trillions of dollars and growing. It would be irresponsible for you to spend beyond your means. Why can the government? Shouldn't a balanced budget be required?

A budget is a plan for spending based on income, obligations, needs, and wants. For individuals and families, it is difficult enough to plan for contingencies and to adhere to a formal plan of spending. Federal governments have income (taxes) and obligations (interest on the debt and social programs) like families

(Continued)

(Continued)

do. However, the contingencies and unforeseen catastrophic events faced by big governments make budgeting much more difficult.

Imagine implementing a balanced-budget amendment to the U.S. Constitution. When the income is depleted, which looming crises will be ignored? Not requiring the "balancing act" that most citizens work within allows the flexibility within governmental spending that is necessary in times of security crises and natural or manmade disaster response. Should the nation come under attack by another country or military organization, immediate response in terms of military and ammunition spending can be implemented. Citizens would not accept the response of "no can do" because it wasn't originally in the budget.

This doesn't prevent adjustments to and revision of the annual and long-term budget plans of the government. The stalemate often encountered in that process is disagreement about what is essential and what is not. Until agreement can be reached and citizens embrace some very painful sacrifices, the deficit and resulting interest payment debt will remain a major threat to progress.

SUMMARY

Implementation of a decision is the setting of a plan into motion. Successful completion is dependent on many factors—the actual plan, the motivation of family members involved, and the changing context over the time necessary for completion. Risk management is necessary during creation of the plan and throughout implementation. Change is a complicated process for individuals and family units. Efforts to minimize stress and maximize benefits are important. Plans may fail or cease to be useful over time. Flexibility and continual monitoring are necessary at all times. Once completed, lessons learned during the implementation process should be used in future decision-making situations.

QUESTIONS FOR REVIEW AND DISCUSSION

1. Strategy is an important concept in plan implementation. Give examples of two types of strategies presented in the chapter.

2. College can be a stressful time, full of planning and adjustment. What role would a person's resilience play in the event of a health crisis during his or her last semester?

3. At this point in your life, is a legal will important? Why or why not?

4. What types of insurance are essential for contemporary families? Which are discretionary? What differentiates the two?

5. Recall a plan you created that was eventually abandoned. What were the primary problems you experienced? Were they part of the planning process or did they evolve during the implementation process?

CHAPTER THIRTEEN

DEFINING SUCCESS

Objectives
Societal Responsibility
Reality Check
Worldview
Family Responsibility
  Social Wellness
  Occupational Wellness
In the News
  Spiritual Wellness
  Physical Wellness
  Intellectual Wellness
  Emotional Wellness
Individual Responsibility
Summary
Questions for Review and Discussion

Objectives

- Be aware of the responsibility society has for the environment.

- Understand the concept of sustainability and why it is important for the future.

- Recognize the role that ethics plays in social responsibility.

- Identify the responsibility that family has in society.

- Be aware of different aspects of wellness and how it affects the family and society.

- Appreciate the responsibility of the individual to the family and society.

- Realize how happiness and personal satisfaction affect the individual and others.

Success is a journey, not a destination. The doing is often more important than the outcome.

—Arthur Ashe

There are many ways to define success. Building wealth or fame is often what comes to mind when talking about success. Success can also include intangible elements as well, such as self-confidence or standing up for what you believe. Any decision that is made must be evaluated to determine whether it has been success-ful. Families who have made good choices and feel good about the decisions they

Social responsibility: a sense that consumers must act with concern and sensitivity, being aware of the impact of their actions on others, particularly the disadvantaged

have made are more likely to feel a **social responsibility** to contribute to others around them. But social responsibility is highly subjective. How can we measure who does and does not contribute to society?

> *Harold and Jean are active in their community. They volunteer for several causes through their service organizations and collect money in their neighborhood for heart disease, diabetes, and muscular dystrophy. They are active in their church and political party affiliation and actively participate in the voluntary recycling program in their city. Harold and Jean would be considered socially responsible to their community and world.*

Corporate social responsibility: the awareness, acceptance, and management of the implications and effects of all corporate decision making

What makes this couple more socially responsible than the couple who live next door and have taken on the responsibility to care for their elderly parents on a daily basis for the past 10 years? Is a person who volunteers his or her time to work with nonprofit groups, but does not have time to give to his own family members, socially responsible? Questions such as these are the subject of this chapter.

SOCIETAL RESPONSIBILITY

Artificial obsolescence: the phenomenon of industry's creating a new need for consumers that produces demand by creating dissatisfaction with past models

Corporate social responsibility has been identified and studied within corporate America and around the world for some time. In his review of the history of corporate social responsibility, Carroll (2015) finds at least 37 different definitions. Early definitions urged business to consider its impact on society. In our global world today, most definitions include two main facets of protecting society and improving the welfare of society. Maintaining the health and safety of workers, protecting the resources of our planet, ethical reporting, and production of a quality product are components of the expectations placed on a socially responsible business.

REALITY CHECK

Artificial Obsolescence

Corporate America is always looking for ways to get customers to buy more of what they already use. Artificial obsolescence is the yearly introduction of changes in style, color, and small improvements in order to lure status-conscious consumers into replacing perfectly functional products. Did you know that this is not new? This practice actually dates back to the 1920s. Here is just one example.

In the early 1960s, Alka-Seltzer, the fizzy heartburn and acid indigestion pain-relief tablet, needed an update. Most people recognized Speedy, the "cartoon disk with a squeaky voice and pop eyes," who had been introduced in the early days of TV. However, by the 1960s, Alka-Seltzer had fallen out of favor with the younger drug-buying consumer. Alka-Seltzer's customers were mostly older people, and the product was not attracting many new buyers. It had become associated with people who drank too much and ate too much and was not appealing to that younger consumer.

Up to that point, pain-relief products had been advertised in commercials filled with negatives that would have given you pain if you didn't already have it. People ran around groaning, holding their heads and stomachs. In one commercial, a poor man went through a series of tortures, including hammers pounding his head and straitjackets tying him up. People did not watch unless they already had a headache or stomach problem and were looking for relief, so most of the time, from the advertiser's point of view, advertising was ineffective.

Finally, Tinker & Partners advertising think tank solved the problem by coming up with different reasons for people to take Alka-Seltzer and fashioning a series of entertaining commercials around those themes.

> [We] created the kickoff commercial that set the style for all the variety of commercials that followed. It was a truly wonderful, iconic commercial, an ovation to stomachs, a sweet-natured montage of big ones, little ones, slim ones, fat ones, all filmed at stomach level. There was a street digger's jackhammer stomach, a young chick's bare midriff, two men talking, facing each other, one with a flat stomach and one with a big round one, an array of stomachs presented with self-deprecating humor and sweet humanness to a happy, bouncy tune. "No matter what shape your stomach's in" was its opening phrase. Self-deprecating humor was new and popular in the sixties and unheard-of in drug commercials, when it appeared it was news. It was followed by 16 completely different commercials, each entertaining and stylish, each giving you a different reason to take Alka-Seltzer.

One of these commercials was based on an "Alka-Seltzer on the Rocks" theme that showed an appealing visual of nothing but two Alka-Seltzers dropping into a crystal glass of water.

The important thing about this new commercial was that there were two Alka-Seltzers. Before that, both the Speedy commercials and the label on the package only promoted using one tablet at a time:

> We met an attractive doctor at Miles [Laboratories], Dorothy Carter, who demonstrated to us that in order for aspirin to break through the pain barrier it often required two aspirins, not one, to do the job. Because aspirin is one of the ingredients that make Alka-Seltzer effective, we asked her whether two Alka-Seltzers would be better than one. Yes, two would work better than one.

> But the directions on the package said to take only one. And all the old Speedy commercials demonstrated only one fizzing in water. [We] did a little dance with Dorothy Carter in the laboratory. What a stroke of good fortune that was! We changed the directions on the packages and began showing two Alka-Seltzers dropping into a glass of water in every commercial. Miles created portable foil packs that held two Alka-Seltzers each and sold them in new places, magazine stands, bars, fast-food restaurants, powder rooms—they became ubiquitous—and, naturally, Miles began selling twice as much Alka-Seltzer.

Alka-Seltzer's large sales increase was directly related to consumers' using two tablets instead of one. In addition to an increase in the number of tablets used, Alka-Seltzer's new image was later fortified with the catchy and enduring "Plop, plop; fizz, fizz" jingle, which led consumers to believe that no one had ever used anything less than two Alka-Seltzers at a time.

Source: From *A Big Life in Advertising* by Mary Wells Lawrence, copyright © 2002 by Mary L. Book Corp. Used by permission of Alfred A. Knopf, a division of Random House, Inc.

Business and the environment are linked because not only does it make sense to invest in the future through sustainability; it is also good for business when customers are attracted to companies that care about their environmental footprint. As more and more people become concerned about issues such as global warming, clean air and water, and energy consumption, the business community wants to avoid being seen as contributing solutions to the problem. Branding (logos and other promotional material) that reflects products as being "green" or environmentally friendly has become an important business practice. A recent report shows that almost two-thirds of American consumers are more likely to buy products if they believe in the company's cause (Bonnell, 2015). According to Nielsen (2014a), 55% of global online consumers across 60 countries say they are willing to pay more for products that contribute to positive social and environmental outcomes. In his *Newsweek* article, Adler (2006) writes about how business is looking at the "budget-conscience masses" and is "gathering cachet among an affluent new consumer category which marketers call 'LOHAS': Lifestyles of Health and Sustainability. 'The people who used to drive the VW bus to the co-op are now driving the Volvo to Whole Foods,' exults David Brotherton, a Seattle consultant in corporate responsibility" (p. 48). While some may buy green products for the benefit of our environment, there is also some evidence that doing so may be associated with status, as people want others to know that they have the resources to contribute (Griskevicius, Tybur, & Van den Burgh, 2010).

Society as a whole has a responsibility to the planet ultimately for the benefit of those who inhabit the earth. How this is accomplished is a debate that rages on between environmentalists and those who want to use the land for economic gain. Politicians are often forced to take a stand when it comes to the environment and social responsibility involving resources. Presidents are rated on their environmental stance and at the same time are also being closely watched by those who make their living from the land.

One area where the two groups differ significantly is in food production. Product labeling can be confusing with words such as *environmentally safe*, *organic*, and *homegrown*. Many consumers don't know the difference, and there are vast differences in the products. **Ecolabels** are a voluntary labeling system that implies that the food was produced in an environmentally preferable way. There are several benefits associated with food carrying ecolabels. Production that decreases water pollution and soil erosion, as well as being safe for wildlife, is an environmental benefit. It also involves non-environmental benefits, such as animal rights and promoting local agriculture. Ecolabels promote social responsibility by requirements such as decent treatment of farmworkers and fair trade practices that help small farmers remain competitive. These components do not help the food taste better or help protect resources, but they are socially responsible.

In 2013, organic sales represented 5% of U.S. food sales. Although the organic food industry has been operating since the beginning of the 20th century, it wasn't until 1990 that the Organic Foods Production Act (OFPA) was enacted to establish national standards for the organic market, and policies set within the states differ considerably (Mosier & Thilmany, 2016).

Ecolabels:
labels or logos that indicate that a product has met a set of environmental standards

Another controversial food production topic involves the **genetically modi-fied organism (GMO)**. GMOs are present in the majority of processed food in the United States. They are genetically modified to reduce the use of pesticides, and while they increase crop production and lower costs, there is suspicion that they may be harmful to humans and the environment. Consumer demand for non-GMO products has increased, and mandatory labeling is on the horizon. Those who support the use of GMOs point out that Americans have been using GMO products for years and that there is still no credible evidence that they cause harm (Consumer Reports, 2015).

In an effort to combat the obesity problem in the United States, and to comply with mandatory legislation enforceable by the U.S. Food and Drug Administration (2016), many restaurants and fast-food companies are including nutritional infor-mation on their menus. The menu labeling rule applies to restaurants that are part of a chain of 20 or more locations with the same name and having the same menu. Restaurants must list calorie information and a statement about suggested daily caloric intake. Other information, such as total calories, calories from fat, total fat, saturated fat, trans fat, cholesterol, sodium, total carbohydrates, fiber, sugars, and protein, must be available upon request. Food vending machines will also be required to post calorie information.

Soil **conservation** is much less of an issue, especially to those who live in urban areas. However, those who understand the significance of the Dust Bowl have an appreciation for this form of preservation. April 14, 1935, known as "Black Sunday," is a day especially important to remember when it comes to soil conser-vation. It was on that day that a large part of the Great Plains was covered with dust so thick that it blocked out the sun. It was caused by plowed fields and a devastating drought that resulted in blowing and drifting soil, similar to the effect of a blizzard. It was estimated that the fertile farmland of the Plains lost 850 mil-lion tons of soil during that time. As a result, the government established the Soil Conservation Service.

Improvements in soil practices have prevented soil loss; however, today there are new threats to the land. As the population grows, consumers demand more food production at lower prices while encroaching land development demands that this food be grown on small amounts of land. American farmers have successfully been able to produce the most inexpensive food in the world, but not without conse-quences. Although the government has established set-aside programs at a cost of $1.7 billion annually to withhold approximately 32 million acres of cropland from production (U.S. Department of Agriculture, 2011), soil depletion is a problem.

Water conservation is of more concern because everyone needs water. Water is essential to life. Humans need water not only to live, but also for the mainte-nance of many other ecosystems. Fresh water represents only a small amount of the world's water, and its availability is a limited and finite resource. Fresh water is found as surface water (lakes, rivers, reservoirs, etc.) or ground water (under-ground aquifers). Managing water resources is difficult. Competing users, espe-cially in urban areas, stress the availability of water.

Legislation is sometimes necessary to arbitrate water rights and allocation of resources. Legal questions focus on the ownership of moving water. Does the

Genetically modified organism (GMO): any organism whose genetic material has been altered using engineering techniques

Conservation: the preservation of a physical quantity during transformations or reactions

state where the water originated own the water that flows through another state? Also, uncontrolled use of groundwater has caused water tables to fall, and it is estimated that we are removing twice as much water as is being replaced. For example, the High Plains (Ogallala) aquifer, which lies under parts of South Dakota, Nebraska, Colorado, Kansas, Oklahoma, New Mexico, and Texas, has decreased by 35% since 1950 and is being depleted faster than it is being replaced (Konikow, 2013). As the population grows and as irrigation and industrial uses for water increase, conservation of water could become a major crisis. The Organisation for Economic Co-operation and Development believes that water is one of the critical environmental priorities for the next 30 years, predicting that 40% of the world's population will have issues with water by the year 2050 (OECD, 2012). The political fallout in 2016 from unacceptable levels of lead in Flint, Michigan's public water system illustrate the negative impact of budgetary decisions on public health. Most of us take it for granted that when we turn on the faucet, water will be available, clean, safe, and tasteful. According to the U.S. Geological Survey (Maupin et al., 2014), the United States uses about 355 billion gallons of water per day. Most of this is not consumed, but used for other purposes, such as industry and irrigation. Most people think nothing of letting water run while brushing their teeth or peeling vegetables. To find your water footprint, use the water footprint calculator (www.h2oconserve.org/home .php?pd=index).

Liz is in her senior year of college and has moved into a one-bedroom apartment. She previously lived in the dorms since beginning college and wanted to get away from the noise and roommates to concentrate on her studies. During the first night in her new apartment, she noticed a dripping sound while she was lying in bed, but she soon fell asleep. She didn't think about it again until the next night when she got up and discovered that her kitchen faucet had a slow, steady drip. She decided to call her landlord in the morning and shut her bedroom door to cut out the sound of the dripping. It was more than a week before Liz got around to calling her landlord. He said he would take a look at it the following week because he would be out of town. Two weeks later, she called again, but got no answer. As the semester got busy, she didn't think too much about the drip, and she found that if she left the sponge under the faucet, she couldn't hear the dripping. By the end of the year, she had forgotten all about the annoying drip. As long as it didn't keep her awake at night, it wasn't a problem. What Liz didn't think about was the wasted water over that year's time. The average leaky faucet can waste from 1,000 to 2,000 gallons of water per year! Whose responsibility was the leaky faucet?

The debate about energy conservation is decades old. Once again, it is often the consumer who drives the debate when prices cut into their budget. Whether it is home heating oil, natural gas, or gasoline, America is dependent on energy. The debate involves our dependence on oil-producing countries, whether oil drilling should be allowed where the environment will be affected, the depletion of nonrenewable energy sources, the profits of oil refineries, and other concerns.

Although efforts have raised awareness about conserving energy, some efforts do not produce results. For example, the *Annual Energy Outlook 2016* report (U.S. Energy Information Administration, 2016) projects that energy consumption will decline through 2040 due to technological improvements and increased EPA standards. Despite the reduced energy consumption, not all costs will continue to rise. Between 2003 and 2008, average U.S. gasoline retail prices more than doubled, from $1.77 to $4.10 per gallon (Litman, 2011); however, the price has declined each year since 2012, to a low of $1.99 per gallon at the beginning of 2016 (DeHaan & Laskoski, 2016). When gas prices are low, there is less motivation for people to want to conserve energy, and consumers will buy fewer energy-conscious cars.

The Energy Star program is a voluntary governmental program that helps business and individuals protect the environment through energy efficiency. The Energy Policy Act of 2005 provided initial tax credits for home improvement, efficient cars, solar energy systems, and fuel cells. A number of tax credits are renewed each year and are scheduled to continue until 2021. Results show that by using Energy Star products and practices since 1992, Americans have saved nearly $362 billion on their utility bills (EPA, 2016).

What is more important is that some of those costs are associated with wasted energy. Leaving lights on and a lack of insulation both contribute to higher costs. Americans also have a frustration with what seems like a governmental lack of initiative in addressing the problems associated with energy consumption. Everyone agrees that new and emerging energy technologies such as wind, solar, and fuel cells are needed. Yet only 12% of our electricity comes from renewable energy sources, far less than many other developed nations. Elliott (2013) suggests that frequent changes in government control and shifting policies are to blame for the lack of a consistent national renewable energy policy. Making dramatic changes in our energy consumption will take time and money. Americans will have to be committed to making the changes necessary and waiting for the results.

The use of resources leads to the need for disposal. America is known as a throwaway society. We buy too much food and too many clothes, and our products become obsolete too quickly. Even the packaging that the products come in accounts for almost one-third of the trash discarded. According to the EPA (2015), in 1 year, Americans generated 254 million tons of garbage, including

- 37,060,000 tons of food

- 15,130,000 tons of clothing and other textiles

- 11,540,000 tons of glass beer and soda bottles and other glass products

- 32,520,000 tons of plastic wrap, bags, and other plastics

- 68,600,000 tons of paper and paperboard

Over the past three decades, the amount of garbage generated in the United States has increased. When we think of conservation and social responsibility with

▶ Photo 13.1
Recycling reflects
an obligation to
future generations.

Recycling:
reprocessing of
materials into new
products

Greening:
creating a world
with minimum
negative impact on
our environment

regard to trash, we may think of **recycling**. While the average American produces 4.4 pounds of garbage each day, the amount of recycling waste has also increased, from less than 10% in 1980 to more than 34% in 2013 (EPA, 2015).

The number of people who participate in recycling has remained constant over the past few years, and efforts to increase recycling are being explored. Although most believe that recycling is important, not everyone participates. Some may think of the messy job of separating trash into bins or bags, hauling it to a recycling center, remembering the recycling pickup day, and other time-intensive ways that we dispose of household waste. The majority of Americans say they would recycle if it were more convenient, including accessibility to recycling collection sites (LeBlanc, 2016).

Feldman and Perez (2012) found that providing incentives to recycle were more successful than punishing people for not recycling. They also discovered differences between those who are motivated intrinsically (by internal rewards, from doing something good) or extrinsically (by monetary rewards or economic gain). For example, older Americans are more likely to recycle, believing that it is the right thing to do (LeBlanc, 2016). They suggest that local governments would benefit from examining the motivations of their own community before setting recycling policies to increase participation.

Although we think of recycling as a process of sorting trash and recyclables, it can include many other ways of reusing resources. The idea that "one man's trash is another man's treasure" seems to describe a good attitude about recycling. There are many ways to find a home for used and surplus goods. Selling items at garage or tag sales or donating them to nonprofit organizations and charities is better for our environment than sending them to the local landfill. The Internet has also emerged as a distribution system for recycling goods, with several sites devoted to selling used goods, including eBay and Craigslist.

The **greening** of America generally means some form of conservation. It can take many forms. When a company announces that it is "going green," it means that it is actively looking for ways to conserve natural resources, uses products that are environmentally friendly, or is searching for ways to reutilize resources. There are numerous ways that this can be accomplished. Examples are using heat- or motion-activated lights to save energy, installing low-flow faucets and toilets to save water, and using building materials and cleaning supplies that are nontoxic. Leadership in Energy and Environmental Design (LEED)–certified buildings are changing the way buildings are constructed and how communities are designed. According to the U.S. Green Building Council (2016), green building is cost-effective because upfront costs are expected to pay for themselves in just seven years. It also uses natural resources efficiently, depleting fewer non-renewable resources and minimizing waste.

Other attempts at adding "green space" are becoming part of community development. Some cities have required set-aside space, including grass and trees for all new construction, or they have adopted conservation easement programs to preserve existing green space. Some communities around the country are discovering that land deemed unusable is finding new life when it is reclaimed as green space that not only adds aesthetic value but can help with conservation.

Ultimately, society has a responsibility to maintain the earth, but at the same time, we must live on it and use its resources to survive. The balance between the two needs is known as **sustainability**. Sustainability allows the resources of the earth, the people who inhabit the earth, and the economic activity that brings the resources to the people to all benefit without harm. The United Nations (2015) has set forth a comprehensive agenda for sustainable development by 2030. Included in the agenda are 17 goals:

Sustainability: to endure without giving way or yielding

1. No poverty

2. Zero hunger

3. Good health and well-being

4. Quality education

5. Gender quality

6. Clean water and sanitation

7. Affordable and clean energy

8. Decent work and economic growth

9. Industry, innovation, and infrastructure

10. Reduced inequalities

11. Sustainable cities and communities

12. Responsible consumption and production

13. Climate action

14. Life below water

15. Life on land

16. Peace, justice, and strong institutions

17. Partnerships for the goals

What is necessary to bring society to a point where sustainability is valued and economic development follows these ideas as best practices? In the past, legislative laws or governmental regulations have forced these changes. Creating an endangered species list is an example of this. Americans are slowly becoming aware of the environmental costs of economic development. Because of our insatiable consumption of resources, incentives will need to be set out for us to stop and take a look at the consequences to our world.

> *Carl and his family live on the edge of a small town. Carl thinks of himself as a good citizen. He pays his taxes and provides for his family. A few months ago, a new town ordinance was enacted to prohibit burning within the city limits. Carl had opposed the ordinance, saying, "I have burned my trash out behind the garage for years. It isn't hurting anybody, and I have a right to continue to do whatever I want on my own property." Beyond the convenience of disposing of their own trash, Carl and his family would now have to drive the trash to the waste disposal and recycling center a few miles away and pay a small fee. He noticed that his property taxes would also be going up to help pay for the new center.*
>
> *Against his wife's protests, Carl continued to burn his own trash. Although he was careful to burn when the wind was calm, one day the fire got away from him and began to burn in an adjacent field. Because there were plans to develop the field into property lots for new housing, the field that was once planted with crops was now covered with stubble and dry weeds and it burned quickly. The fire headed for the new houses nearby. The local fire department was finally able to contain the fire, but Carl was cited for his actions.*
>
> *Although Carl has the right to own and use his own property, he failed to recognize that the new ordinance was for the benefit of everyone, including himself. As the town expanded, there was a new risk for open fires getting out of control. The fumes from some of the products that were being burned were also a hazard to the people around him, including his family. Finally, the town was beginning to take responsibility for renewable and reusable resources by beginning a recycling program.*

Most of what has been presented so far in this chapter has focused on the economic aspects of social responsibility. There is more of a motivation to make decisions and changes in our world if there is a cost involved or if it will ultimately benefit us economically. A good example of this is the understanding behind NIMBY (not in my backyard). Many people are in favor of something that seems to benefit the world or environment as long as it doesn't affect them personally. If it will cost them something or inconvenience them, they are against it. However, economics is not the only consideration necessary for community development. Hochachka (2005) advanced the idea of **interiority** as important to the sustainability of society. Interiority includes ethical or cultural needs that are less noticeable, but are necessary for social responsibility.

Interiority: consideration of ethical and cultural needs before economic considerations

Making decisions that are ethical and that take into account the cultural history of society is as important as whether things make sense economically. Will the economic benefits of a new business outweigh the ethical concerns about their products? Will providing family services obtained by state and federal funding be worth it when the families they were meant to serve find them culturally offensive?

One ethical issue involves the social responsibility of protecting the weak, which is controversial and is debated at all levels of society. Issues such as protecting children from predators or prosecuting those who take advantage of the elderly seem clear. However, issues such as stem-cell research, euthanasia, or abortion are not, and opinions change and sway over time.

Public opinion often reflects the influence of contemporary politics; however, many believe that society should have an attitude of concern and responsibility for the weakest among humans, regardless of the political climate. Giving voice to those who are less likely to be heard, but are affected by decisions made by others, is a social responsibility. These include not only the vulnerable mentioned earlier, but others such as the mentally challenged, the homeless, and immigrants.

E-waste: electronic waste, including computers, entertainment electronics, mobile phones, and other items that have been discarded by their original users

WORLDVIEW

Recycling E-Waste

Most Americans believe that it is cheaper to buy a new computer rather than upgrade the old one. The United States discards millions of computers and phones each year. What do we call this electronic refuse? It is called **e-waste**. Although the Electronic Waste Recycling Act of 2003 did identify and regulate the disposal of certain products, little is ever recycled. The Environmental Protection Agency estimates that only 15 to 20% of e-waste is recycled; the rest of these electronics go directly into landfills and incinerators (LeBlanc, 2016).

What is even more disturbing is that the majority of the e-waste slated for recycling is exported to areas such as China, India, or Pakistan. E-waste makes its way to remote villages, where people are paid very little to break

discarded computers and other electronic equipment into component materials to be recycled. Workers are exposed to toxic chemicals such as lead beryllium, cadmium, and mercury, and the chemicals find their way to the water and soil of the region. In 2016, PBS published "Where Does America's E-Waste End Up? GPS Tracker Tells All" (Campbell & Christensen, 2016), which tells the story of a 2-year investigation by the Basel Action Network, a Seattle-based e-waste watchdog group. See the article and video chronicling their findings at www.pbs.org/newshour/updates/america-e-waste-gps-tracker-tells-all-earthfix.

What is our responsibility regarding our own waste? What is our responsibility for ensuring a safe world? Does the Information Age have a dark side?

FAMILY RESPONSIBILITY

Social responsibility and family responsibility are similar in that they both require those involved to take a look at how actions affect others. Families are responsible for their members. A family member is irresponsible when he or she makes a decision that negatively impacts others in the family.

> *Mark and Shelly have been married for 14 years and have two children ages 8 and 10. Over the past year, Shelly started to examine her life because she was struggling with feelings of not being wanted or needed. After her examination, she made some changes in her life. First, she decided to spend more time with a man from work who had been encouraging her. Second, she decided to join a health club and a cycling club to get into shape and feel better about herself. Although Shelly began to have more confidence and was feeling better physically, she had made decisions that impacted her family negatively. Mark was jealous of the time she was spending with the man from work, and he had a hard time trusting her because he was sure that the relationship was more than a friendship. Her children noticed that she was never around to help them or attend their activities because she was always at the health club or at a cycling event. Although Shelly's decisions were important to her well-being, they were irresponsible as a family member. Shelly should have considered her own well-being, as well as that of the entire family.*

Wellness: an interactive process of becoming aware of and practicing healthy choices to create a more successful and balanced lifestyle

To consider a family's well-being, we must examine wellness. Good health is more than physical well-being. It also includes life satisfaction. H. Dunn (1961) was the first to coin the term **wellness** and defined it as "an integrated method of functioning which is oriented toward maximizing the potential of which the individual is capable" (p. 4). Others followed with definitions that included the idea that wellness is a chosen lifestyle that can be defined as the active process of becoming aware of and making choices toward a more successful existence. Most definitions also incorporate the idea that wellness includes the total person, involving the body, mind, and spirit.

Wellness, as a concept in the study of individuals and families, has been applied in several different theoretical models in the literature. Most of these models include the concepts of wellness in one's social, occupational, spiritual, physical, intellectual, and emotional realms. Viewed as a systemic, interdependent idea, the belief is that healthy functioning of each and every one of these components is important to the overall health and well-being of individuals, and ultimately their families. Deficits in any of the areas will impact the family in negative ways. Figure 13.1 illustrates the integration of these components. In other words, when a change takes place, it affects the other parts. It is necessary to understand this when we recognize how wellness changes over time and across the life span.

Wellness is a topic being considered in all aspects of society. Whether it is found in the workplace or within the medical community, it seems that wellness is

Figure 13.1   The Wheel of Wellness

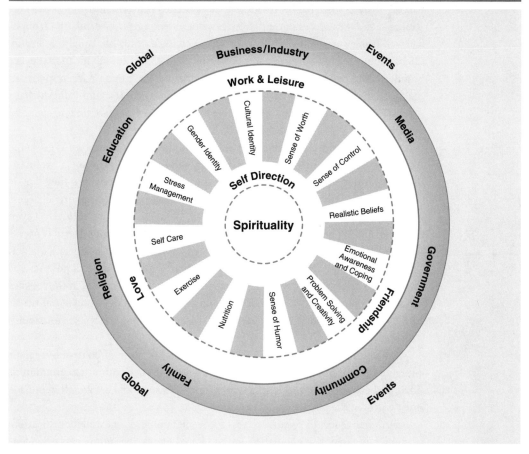

Figure 13.1   The Wheel of Wellness

Source: From *Counseling for Wellness: Theory, Research and Practice* by J. E. Myers and T. J. Sweeney. Alexandria, VA: American Counseling Association, 2005. Reprinted with permission.

being publicized as the answer to the problems of individuals, families, and society. Although wellness is an issue for all of society, we focus most of our discussion on the family's responsibility for wellness and use the tasks identified previously to focus on six areas of wellness: social, physical, occupational, spiritual, intellectual, and emotional.

Social Wellness

Social wellness involves many factors for a family. The conditions in which a family lives and works play a big part in the well-being of the family. Their connections to the community where they live provide a sense of belonging and provide them with security. A social network of friends and acquaintances can be called on for help when a family is experiencing difficulties. We have all witnessed countless fundraisers that are conducted by friends and neighbors who want to help a family that is going through a difficult time with medical bills or after a house fire.

Social wellness: being aware of, participating in, and feeling connected to your community

The quality of the living environment is important for individuals. Research has shown that a green environment has a relationship with health and well-being. Access to green space has been shown to be associated with better mental health outcomes, such as less depression and stress, as well as direct and positive impacts on physical well-being, such as lower blood pressure (Bowler, Burung-Ali, Knight, & Pullin, 2010; Cohen-Cline, Turkheimer, & Duncan, 2015). This doesn't mean that every family should live in rural areas outside the urban environment. Green space can be found in cities in the form of parks and recreation areas. If a family doesn't have its own green space or a park nearby, they may want to designate time to spend in green space.

Social wellness also includes social capital available for families. We assume that a family that is below the poverty level will experience low social wellness; however, it depends on the resources within the community where they live. If there are adequate resources, such as low-income housing, food pantries, access to services, and other capital, the family will be more likely to survive or even move forward. The family that lives in an isolated setting where poverty is prevalent and services are not readily available will be less likely to succeed. King and Ogle (2014) found that certain environments with a concentration of poor households contribute to negative health results. However, social capital in the form of resources is not the only factor. Social support in the form of strong social ties to the community as well as cooperation and trust among neighbors also contributes to social wellness.

Much of social wellness depends on the family's sense of control over their situation. Racial discrimination, disrespect among groups within the community, income inequality, and residential segregation are situations that are often outside the control of the people involved.

Another aspect of social wellness for some families is cultural identification. Although the majority population in the United States does not necessarily identify with a particular cultural heritage, minorities are more likely to identify and find belonging with a certain ethnic group.

Although cultural groups may experience discrimination and segregation, which can hinder wellness, some immigrant groups have formed strong and interdependent cultural networks that benefit families.

Occupational Wellness

Occupational wellness: wellness within the workplace

Wellness within the workplace (**occupational wellness**) is important for family life because it may be difficult to separate the two settings. For many family members, the work role consumes a good deal of their time, and this is only increasing. The concept of spillover is based on the idea that there is overlap between work and home. Promoting employee wellness can best be achieved by increasing employees' control over their own schedule and by reducing negative work and home spillover. The conflict that can be created between work and home has been associated with a variety of negative outcomes, including poor family relationships at home and lower production at work.

> *Just before the end of the day, Celia's boss demanded that she finish a very detailed report by the time she left for the day. It meant that Celia had to drop the other project that she was working on and rush through the report to finish on time. Not only was it frustrating; it put Celia in a bad mood, and she was mad at her boss. When she got home, she barked orders to her children and yelled at her husband, Brent, for not helping around the house. The rest of the evening was a disaster. Everyone was irritable until they all went to bed for the evening. The next day, Brent was still upset about what had happened the night before. He thought that Celia's accusations were unfounded and, as a result, he hadn't gotten much sleep. On his way to work, he made a plan to discuss his concerns with Celia that evening. At work, he found it hard to concentrate and snapped at his secretary for not being able to find a file that he needed. At lunch, he lost patience with his coworkers' comments about his mood and stormed out of the lunchroom. The last 24 hours for Celia and Brent can be characterized as spillover. Celia's problem at work spilled over into her home life, and Brent's problem at home spilled over into his work life.*

Although most of the time the spillover effect is presented as harmful for families, Grosswald (2003) believes that it may not necessarily always be negative. She points out that talents and skills developed in both worlds can benefit each other. For example, skills such as negotiation learned in the workplace and the ability to organize and multitask learned at home can benefit both situations interchangeably.

Most people recognize that their occupation and their family life are connected, and that their satisfaction is essential to their life. A person's satisfaction with his or her work can be directly related to the meaning that he or she attaches to work. Based on the Meaning of Work International Research Team, there are five major dimensions of the meaning of work (Snir & Harpaz, 2002):

- Work centrality: Work is a life role and is the most basic of activities for people within society. It is more important than leisure time.

- Economic orientation: People work for and are motivated by the income that results from work. The reason that we work is to sustain life and meet our needs.

- Interpersonal relations: Humans need interaction and a place to belong. We work for the satisfaction of being with others.

- Intrinsic orientation: Individuals need challenges and strive to show competence in their work. They work because it creates interest and self-determination.

- Entitlement/obligation: People work because they should work. It is expected within society, and they have a right to work.

By understanding their own orientation to work, individuals can create more realistic expectations of work that should lead to greater satisfaction. Marriage partners also need to understand the work orientations of each other to avoid misunderstandings. If both partners have a work centrality orientation, for example, it will not be a problem when one has to miss a family reunion because of work.

Although conflict between work and home can be a problem for both men and women, women seem to be affected more. The majority of the demands of both home and work life, especially if children are in the home, still fall on the woman. There are two models that explain the relationship between multiple roles and well-being that help understand how women negotiate the demands of multiple roles.

The scarcity hypothesis says that human energy is limited and, when overloaded, presents conflict that results in guilt and anxiety. Therefore, according to this hypothesis, the more roles one has, the less one will experience well-being. In contrast, the enhancement hypothesis proposes that being able to handle multiple roles results in status, increased self-esteem, and privilege, which seem to compensate for the strain that multiple roles presents. Rao, Apte, and Subbakrishna (2003) suggested that most working women fall into the enhancement hypothesis because they seem to report higher well-being and lower psychological stress than women who stay home with their children. However, these researchers also pointed out that the kind of job women have, the working conditions of that job, the amount of control they feel that they have, and the support they feel from both coworkers and family members, including their husband, make a difference in their well-being. Women who do not have favorable conditions and support may not have the same positive experience in the workplace.

Employers are beginning to recognize that wellness in the workplace is a great benefit to them. One way to attract and retain employees is to allow them to control the balance between their work and home life. Family-friendly policies that allow employees to choose alternative work arrangements, which include flexible hours, working from home, a compressed workweek, or onsite childcare, are valued by workers with families. Employers realize that when there is a lack of work and family balance, employees are less satisfied with the job, and there may be an increase in negative job behaviors such as absenteeism, poor performance, or turnover. Another problem that is making waves in the business world involves "presenteeism," which represents the problems associated with workers who come to work but are not fully functioning because of an illness or medical condition that hinders their performance. If a worker has a severe medical problem, he or she usually stays home (absenteeism), but presenteeism has to do with chronic conditions that may not require missing work, such as allergies, back pain, headaches, and even depression. It is estimated that depression causes absenteeism and reduces performance at work by $51.5 billion per year (Greenberg, Fournier, Sisitsky, Pike, & Kessler, 2015). Because presenteeism is likely to indirectly cost employers more than the direct medical costs that they pay, it is to an employer's advantage to emphasize wellness in the workplace. Helping employees identify strategies that help them cope and learn to care for themselves in stressful situations is beneficial, not only to the worker but to the workplace as well. In addition, individual wellness and family wellness are interconnected. When adults work for companies that care about wellness, regardless of the motivation, families will be better served.

Scarcity hypothesis: the idea that human energy is limited and, when overloaded, presents conflict that results in guilt and anxiety

Enhancement hypothesis: the idea that being able to handle multiple roles results in status, increased self-esteem, and privilege that compensates for the strain

Absenteeism: prolonged absence of an owner from his or her property; chronic absence (as from work or school); also, the rate of such absence

Presenteeism: the problems faced when employees come to work in spite of illness, which can have negative repercussions on business performance

Is the United States Ready
for a 6-Hour Workday?

According to Peters (2015), businesses in Sweden are trying out the concept of a 6-hour workday, and the preliminary results are positive. More and more people in Sweden want to spend more time with their families and have more free time for themselves. It's a trend that an increasing number of companies are testing not only in Sweden, but around the world, too.

The 6-hour workday is nothing new. According to Savage (2015), trials of shorter workdays have been going on since the 1990s, but no data previously had been available to measure the shorter day's success. However, there are now data to show the benefits. The first and most obvious benefit is that employees are able to spend more time with family and friends, as well as have more time to relax.

Greenfield (2016) reveals that the 6-hour workday in Sweden shows that employees use less sick time and are happier, and that productivity increases as a result. One study shows that productivity actually declines as workers increase their workday, especially around the 50-hour-per-week mark.

In the United States, the idea of the 6-hour workday may not work the same way. Savage (2015) reports that the workplace differs in Sweden, where respect for coworkers outside of the workplace is greater than in the United States. There is little contact made between coworkers after hours, whereas in the United States, phone calls and e-mails are more common in the evenings and during weekends. In addition, many workplaces in Sweden ask workers to stay away from social media and personal calls while at work, increasing their productivity during the hours they are working.

Some suggest that this idea will never work in the United States because it is a nation of workaholics. Greenfield (2016) reports that "Americans work around 38.6 hours per week, according to the Organization for Economic Cooperation and Development. They get, on average fewer than eight paid vacation days a year; only about three-quarters of workers get any paid time off at all, according to the U.S. Bureau of Labor and Statistics." According to data from the U.S. Bureau of Labor Statistics, overall output from Americans working has increased almost every year since 1947 (Block, 2015).

One way to begin to change our thinking about work in the United States is to start with subtle changes, allowing the employee more control over their work life. Flexibility in the workplace can help families prioritize and make choices to spend the time needed with their children. Separating the ideas of productivity and time may also change the way we think about how work is accomplished. Future generations will continue to grapple with this work and family balance issue.

Sources: Adapted from Block (2015); Greenfield (2016); Peters (2015); and Savage (2015).

Spiritual Wellness

Spirituality is acknowledged by many professionals in the area of wellness as an essential part of balance. It is difficult to characterize spirituality because it has different meanings and is highly personal for each individual. The spiritual dimension can include aspects of purpose in life, moral or ethical beliefs, and the view of a person's place in the world. These ideas will permeate everything in life and become the foundation for decisions and behaviors.

Although most people equate spirituality and religion, there are distinctions. Religion is a part of spirituality. For many, religion is the way that they express their spirituality. It also means that practicing religion can expand a person's understanding of spirituality. That does not mean that those who choose not to participate in religion are not spiritual. *Inward spirituality* refers to comfort, peace, or an inner strength. *Outward spirituality* usually describes a connection to others or a feeling of being one with the world.

In the past, religion and medicine have had separate spheres. It was widely believed that religion would focus on the inner self, whereas medicine would focus on the physical self. Recently, spirituality has gained a place in wellness and health. Although the power of faith in healing has been an idea that has existed for a long time, more and more people are beginning to consider its benefits, although they don't understand it.

The Holistic Flow Model of Spiritual Wellness (Purdy & Dupey, 2005) describes the components of the spirit and how they affect life tasks. The model includes a belief in an organizing force in the universe, connectedness, faith, movement toward compassion, the ability to make meaning of life, and the ability to make meaning of death. It is thought that the person who is healthy in spirit will be more likely to integrate activities into his family life that develop and strengthen the components of spirituality.

What is the benefit of spiritual wellness for the family? Families that have tapped into spiritual wellness have created a foundation to form attitudes, behaviors, and purposes used in understanding themselves as individuals and in their interactions with others. A good example of this comes when a family faces adversity.

> *Ricardo and his family were going through a difficult time. Ricardo had recently become a U.S. citizen after moving his family from Mexico. At first it was difficult to find housing and a job, but they were eventually able to find a small house to rent not far from the distribution company where Ricardo worked. Recently, Ricardo heard rumors that his company would be laying off 20% of its employees, and because he was one of the most recent to be hired, he figured that he would be among those laid off. Every day he went to work he expected to get a notice from his boss. In addition to the stress of uncertainty with his job, last week his oldest daughter, who had been experiencing some health problems, was diagnosed with a rare and serious lung disease. Ricardo and his family recognize the role of spirituality in their lives. Although these things are never easy, they understand that life is always uncertain and that things happen for a reason. Ricardo is experiencing what is known as spiritual transcendence, which involves moving beyond the limits of human understanding. To get through this difficult time, Ricardo and his family need to draw their strength from their faith, their family, and their friends.*

Physical Wellness

When someone says "wellness," the first things that come to mind are the physical aspects of nutrition and exercise. Healthcare costs are high and rising, and the consequences of poor health for the family are loss of income and increased risk of poverty. The early work of the World Health Organization (1947) defined *health* as "a state of . . . well-being," rather than a definition of someone who simply was not sick or did not have disease. The idea that health should involve proactive prevention has not been the norm for most Americans, however. Understanding the differences in people's willingness to support the idea of wellness can be illustrated along a continuum, where at one end medicine is used to treat problems and the other end represents active prevention strategies.

Such a continuum is consistent with Haber's (2002) assessment of three types of prevention attitudes. Primary prevention represents the kind of interventions that target specific problems and implement exercise, good nutrition, stress management techniques, and immunizations in an effort to prevent disease or illness. Secondary prevention includes interventions such as screenings, which are designed to catch or detect early symptoms of disease or illness. Tertiary prevention is used to treat health issues after they have become a problem and focuses on treatment and stopping the further progression of the disease or illness. Promoting good health and wellness has many benefits for society as well as the family. However, it is often difficult to get people to choose prevention when they do not see an immediate need to change. Often by the time a change in diet or lifestyle is needed, it is already too late to make a difference.

In addition to the attitudes about health and wellness, there are other factors that families need to consider that affect the physical health of individual family members. Where the family is living and working, their skills and abilities to make good decisions, the genetic predisposition of the family, and the availability and competence of the healthcare system in their geographic location will all have an impact on the health of the family. Risk factors such as poverty, unemployment, inadequate transportation, social isolation, and lack of adequate healthcare have been identified as relevant to health and affect many American families (Abbott & Williams, 2015).

One of the most pressing concerns for health in the United States today is obesity. According to the Centers for Disease Control and Prevention (2015), more than one-third of U.S. adults and 17% of children are obese. Health risks such as hypertension, diabetes, and sleep apnea are common for those who are obese. Even weight cycling (repeatedly gaining and losing weight) and the use of some diet treatments are associated with obesity, eating disorders, type 3 diabetes, and hypertension (Montani, Schutz, & Dulloo, 2015). Besides the physical health risks, obese individuals suffer mental health risks associated with the stigma associated with their size. The wellness approach puts the emphasis not on weight loss, but on prevention and reducing risk factors. Using this focus, a healthy lifestyle is the goal and leads to a more positive attitude.

©iStockphoto.com/vgajic

▶ **Photo 13.2**
Exercise improves family wellness in multiple ways.

Exercise is an important aspect of wellness because of the physical and psychological benefits. Obviously, physical activity aids in weight reduction and helps in overall health, but it also serves to lower risk factors associated with poor health.

Research suggests that exercise offers mental health benefits. However, participation in physical wellness programs also shows mixed results in terms of success. Although more wellness programs are being implemented in the workplace and the return on investment for the company can be as high as 6 to 1, not everyone participates. A recent Gallup poll reports that only 24% of employees participate in their company wellness program (O'Boyle & Harter, 2014).

Intellectual Wellness

In society, intellectual wellness is one aspect of the social capital within a community. Many rural communities are concerned about the "brain drain" of the educated young people who move to urban areas in search of better positions. This leaves a community with fewer resources or social capital. Within a family, intellectual wellness involves the preparation and improvement of life skills. It is natural to think first about the skills and knowledge that can be gained through education. However, other skills that are learned through relationships and life experience are also important to intellectual wellness.

We are living in the information age, and education can provide students with the information they need to succeed. Education is not only important for learning that will be needed throughout life (such as reading); there are additional social skills that are learned as a result of the process of education. The National Academy of Sciences (Pellegrino & Hilton, 2012) indicates that noncognitive social skills learned in school are divided between intrapersonal (how people manage themselves) and interpersonal (how they interact with others).

There are disagreements about how education should prepare students for the future. Some believe that children need only basic knowledge, whereas others believe they need a variety of competencies, including technological skills. There are many parents who are concerned about whether the educational system is doing a good job. Some parents opt to teach their own children to ensure that they are taught the basics, usually within a certain set of values that are important to them. Whether parents opt to send their children to public school or private school, or whether they choose to homeschool, it is important that they are involved with the education of their children.

Parents who expect schools to meet all their children's educational needs will be disappointed in how well prepared they are for the future. It is parents' responsibility to teach or reinforce social skills, expose them to new ideas, and provide them with opportunities to work up to their potential. The key to this is a parent who is willing to spend time with his or her child.

It is especially important for parents to learn and practice good problem-solving and decision-making skills and then model them for their children. Families who go through difficult situations need good problem-solving strategies to succeed.

Jami and Delmar are wrestling with a situation concerning Delmar's mother, Margaret. Margaret is 83 years old and still lives in her home, although Jami and Delmar are worried that it is becoming more and more dangerous for her to live alone, because she has fallen twice in the last month. Delmar wants to make sure that Margaret is safe, but is also concerned that she has a part in the decision making about her own future.

One evening, they all sit down to discuss the options. Over the course of the evening, they calmly look at all the ways that Margaret could be safe, yet maintain her independence. They arrive at a solution that empowers them to make a rational decision that fits the needs of everyone concerned. Although the discussion is among the three of them, Jami and Delmar's two daughters witness the entire discussion. Although they do not have any input, the model that they have seen will help them make good decisions themselves in the future.

Economically, education contributes to wellness by adding resources to the family and, ultimately, to society. According to The Georgetown University Center on Education and the Workforce, over a person's lifetime of work, high school graduates earn an average of $1.3 million, associate's degree holders earn about $1.7 million, and bachelor's degree holders earn about $2.3 million (Carnevale, Rose, & Cheah, 2011). There is a downside to viewing education only from an economic point of view. Hargreaves (2003) suggested that the "knowledge economy" is one where knowledge and education focus on the pursuit of growth and profit, which leads down a path of corruption and greed. He proposed that the rise in corporate scandals and secrecy, as well as the widening gap between the rich and the poor, is a result of placing the emphasis on economics.

Unlike some of the other components of wellness discussed, intellectual wellness is difficult to measure. Social wellness can be measured in services that are offered, and physical wellness can be measured in longer life expectancy, whereas intellectual wellness is dependent on numerous other variables. Some of these are the socioeconomic level of the family, the attitudes about formal education, the problem-solving abilities of the adults in the family, or the relationship between parents and children.

Emotional Wellness

A large part of emotional wellness is the ability to be comfortable with your own emotions, whether they involve anger, fear, or love. This means being able to understand your feelings and appropriately express them to others. The best setting in which to practice emotional health is in the family. Children learn to manage their emotions in the safety of their own home. They usually learn, over the course of time, that throwing a tantrum to get what you want doesn't work or that getting angry in response to disappointment doesn't solve the problem and could lead to worse consequences.

▶ **Photo 13.3**
Community service provides opportunities for family growth.

©iStockphoto.com/Wavebreakmedia

Adults who have trouble identifying and expressing their emotions may choose to find other ways to manage their emotions, such as engaging in risky behaviors, which leads to emotional stress and possibly even health problems.

> *Tony was driving home from work on a crowded tollway. Although it was the fastest route home, he dreaded the stop-and-go traffic and tollbooth delays. This day was particularly frustrating because there were a couple of car accidents that made travel even more difficult.* Why can't people just keep moving along? They don't need to know what happened! *he thought to himself as his lane slowly crept along past the wrecked cars and flashing lights. Finally, a break in the traffic allowed Tony to maneuver in and out of the lanes, picking up speed as he went. Things were looking up, and he could taste the cold brew he knew was waiting for him at home. Just as he reached the maximum speed, a car pulled in front of him and seemed to slow down, causing Tony to have to brake. He felt his temper flare. He had always had trouble with his temper. He had been kicked off the playground in elementary school, he had been kicked off the football team in high school, and his ex-wife had kicked him out of the house, all because of his temper. The car in front of him was not going to get away with cutting him off! He accelerated and rammed the car in front, causing them both to career off the road, rolling both cars, and killing both drivers. Tony's road rage was the result of emotions that were out of control.*

Emotional wellness also means that you have to accept yourself, including your limitations. Feeling that you have failed in your life is a sign of low self-esteem. Feelings of failure are painful and can interfere with enjoyment of life and well-being. It can cause problems with friendships and relationships. It can create anxiety, stress, loneliness, and depression. Good self-esteem requires individuals to live consciously aware of themselves and the world, accept themselves as they are, realize that they are responsible for their choices, stand up for their beliefs and values, identify and work toward goals, and honor their commitments (Branden, 1995). Self-esteem is basic to psychological health, achievement, personal happiness, and positive relationships in and outside the family.

Difficult situations disrupt emotional balance. There are times when anger, grief, jealousy, or other negative emotions come into our lives and can damage our personal and family relationships. Individuals and families who are able to adjust to change, cope with stress in a healthy way, and enjoy life regardless of its disappointments and frustrations are able to master emotional wellness.

The family that is resilient is able to make adjustments and changes that, although difficult, they know will benefit them in the long run. For example, although numerous studies have highlighted the negative effects of divorce on children, there are ways that families can turn this devastating period of life around. Using practical steps may reduce some of the anxiety and stress of the situation and can help family members cope with the circumstances.

Humor is an emotion that can be a part of wellness but is often overlooked. A sense of humor is more than being funny; it is a way of seeing the world. The American Association for Therapeutic Humor reported that happiness is directly related to humor; those who can laugh at life's circumstances are 30% more likely to be happy than those who can't see the humor in life. There are many benefits of humor in our lives. Laughter can reduce stress, stimulate your immune system, reduce blood pressure, and lift your spirit. Sometimes we are so serious about our daily activities and work that we forget to have fun.

A healthy sense of humor can be a stress reliever and a valuable tool in relationships. The ability to laugh can help a person put problems in a more realistic perspective. Humor is important in marriage, both emotionally and physically. Humor in marriage brings couples closer together and keeps the relationship fresh. Family members who can laugh at themselves or at their situation usually feel stronger when problems arise. Everyone can relate a time in his or her life when, during a tense situation, it was humor that brought the levity needed to resolve the conflict and release the tension. To add humor to relationships, look for funny moments as you go through the day and share them with each other, recall humorous or embarrassing moments that have happened in the past, watch funny TV shows and movies together, and repeat funny words or phrases that have meaning only for the family.

INDIVIDUAL RESPONSIBILITY

Responsibility from an individual viewpoint takes many forms. Giving back to the community, nation, or world can be accomplished by contributions of money, time, or other resources. Volunteer workers contribute billions of dollars into the economy each year. Yet there never seem to be enough volunteers to cover the need. As discussed in Chapter 6, even though volunteerism is changing, it is still strong and will continue.

According to Rossi (2001), there are three primary sociodemographic variables that play a part in an individual's social responsibility: education, sex, and age. Those who have more education are more likely to be connected to social circles that are larger than those who are not educated beyond the high school level. They are more likely to contribute to society by volunteering, participating in service organizations, and giving to worthy causes financially. The higher the education of a person, the more he or she feels the need to be responsible to society without feeling the need to gain anything in return.

Gender is also a variable in individual social responsibility. Although both men and women contribute to social responsibility, it appears that there are some differences. Men are more likely to contribute money and financial resources, whereas women are more likely to contribute personal time. This finding would be consistent with the fact that women spend much of their lives as caregivers.

Age also plays a role in an individual's social responsibility. Throughout the life cycle, an individual's inclination to contribute to society increases. At midlife, when a person's work and family obligations may be decreasing, his or her desire and willingness to give back to society increases. This may be a result of maturation or generativity (i.e., mentoring, advising). The typical American volunteer is middle aged, politically active, keeps up on current events, participates in one or more groups (especially within their community), actively engaged with friends and family, connected to the Internet, lives in the Midwest, and is religiously involved (Corporation for National and Community Service, 2010). As individuals, is it our responsibility to maintain our own personal satisfaction and happiness? Is it socially responsible to keep our personal well-being in check? It may be more beneficial to ask whether it is socially irresponsible to be unhappy. According to Erikson's (1963) psychosocial theory of development, humans move through a series of stages that are each marked by a crisis that leads to the need for resolution.

In adult life, the stages begin to focus on purpose and fulfillment in life. Those in early adulthood are either productive or they become bored and self-indulgent. At this stage of their lives, they either contribute to society, which leads to a sense of personal fulfillment, or they become a burden to society.

As adults age, this stage gives way to two groups of people. There are those who face old age with integrity, knowing that they had a positive influence on others. The other group enters old age with regrets. They feel despair that there is not enough time left for another chance to make a difference. The first group comprises members who have taken responsibility for their own happiness and have gained wisdom in the process. The second group of people ends up blaming themselves and others.

Unhappiness contributes negatively to society. Unhappiness in the workplace leads to loss of productivity and high turnover. Unhappiness in family life results in divorce. Unhappiness in one's personal life causes individuals to shift resources toward things that we think will make us happy.

> *Nancy is concerned about her husband, Doug. Over the past 2 years, she has noticed that Doug is less interested in doing what he used to do for fun, and he seems generally unhappy most of the time. The effects of his unhappiness are far-reaching. Personally, he has refused invitations from his friends to play golf, attend ball games, and go fishing. Most of the time, he sleeps or watches TV. As a result, he has gained a significant amount of weight.*
>
> *Nancy wants to be supportive, but Doug gets mad every time she suggests a solution. Emotionally, she is worried and hurt, and recently she began to confide in a couple of friends about the problem. She has stopped trying to reason with Doug and feels that their marriage is in jeopardy.*
>
> *Doug has become increasingly agitated with his teenage children. His reaction toward them has caused them to avoid any contact with him. They often sneak out of the house to prevent confrontation. At work, his boss has noticed his lack of productivity and pride in his work. His coworkers also avoid confrontation with him. Not wanting to fire him, his boss has recommended a transfer. Does Doug have a responsibility to himself, his family, and his employer to be happy? What are the costs for his unhappiness?*

According to the U.S. Constitution, the pursuit of happiness is our right, although happiness may be highly subjective and hard to measure. What makes one person happy may not be the same for the next person. Many people think that money is the key to happiness. No doubt, those who are struggling to make ends meet would feel better if they could pay their bills. However, there are rich people who are miserable and poor people who are happy. For some, winning the lottery has turned out to be a nightmare as they watch the money fly through their fingers as fast as it came.

Money is not the only measure of happiness. Measures of desire, intelligence, genetics, friendship, marriage, faith, charity, age, and positive attitude are also used to determine happiness (Davidhizar & Hart, 2006; Mohanty, 2014). Research shows that whether these measures cause happiness often depends on the individual and his or her circumstances. Physical health, stress, self-esteem, and personality can all affect someone's ability to be happy. One question that needs to be asked is whether these measures make someone happy or whether they are the choices of a happy person.

> *Emma and Jill were sisters. Both of them grew up in the same loving and encouraging family. Both were married to supportive husbands. Both of them received a good education and were successful in their careers. The only difference was that Jill was unhappy most of the time. It seemed that no matter what she did, she was never satisfied. When she got a raise, it was not enough. When she got a promotion, it was not enough. Jill was a perfectionist, and in many ways, it contributed to her unhappiness. Her happiness seems to be directly related to her personality style.*

Money or income gained is usually as a result of work. Does moving up the pay scale make someone happier? The idea of the "hedonic treadmill" supposes that as income rises, expectations also rise, and we end up always wanting more by setting our benchmarks higher (Easterlin, 2001). Research also shows that job satisfaction may be more related to job status than the salary (Henry, 2011).

Should an individual's work life play more of a role in social responsibility? Many people today seem to be struggling with the meaning that work has in their lives and have lost the significance that the contributions of work have within society. Taking pride in paid work can be as important to society as the work that is volunteered. The work that is accomplished builds the economy and provides an important social good. Individuals who view work as a negative and enjoy only the weekends or time away from work are missing the sense of community and common purpose that work can inspire.

Finally, as a family member, it is the individual's responsibility to create and maintain a healthy family life. If the family is the basic unit of society, it becomes the foundation from which society builds. The breakdown of the family is the beginning of a breakdown in society, and the burden created by family problems falls on society. According to the structural-functional family theory discussed in Chapter 2, the family performs basic functions within society. When the family does not carry out these functions, society has to step in and use resources to meet the needs of that family. Although this safety net that is provided by society is necessary in some cases, if all families failed to take responsibility for their members, there would be chaos. Consider what would happen if all noncustodial divorced parents decided not to take responsibility to pay child support. The hardship created on society to meet the needs of these children would be overwhelming, and the government as well as the economy would be in serious trouble.

Taking responsibility for our families, our world, and ourselves is essential for survival. It is also the responsible family that feels successful.

SUMMARY

Society has a responsibility to maintain the planet ultimately for the benefit of those who live on the earth. Individuals as well as business and industry must take responsibility for the sustainability of our future resources. Care must be taken to make sure that our food, soil, water, and energy are used wisely and that they are being conserved or replenished for the next generation. Interiority includes ethical or cultural needs that are less noticeable but are necessary for social responsibility. Families are responsible for their members. This responsibility includes different aspects of wellness: social, physical, occupational, spiritual, intellectual, and emotional. Individuals are also responsible for themselves. They must realize how happiness and personal satisfaction affect not only themselves but those around them and, ultimately, society.

QUESTIONS FOR REVIEW AND DISCUSSION

1. Why is social responsibility important?

2. Why should the corporate world have responsibility to society?

3. What are the arguments between environmentalists and business? How can they reach a compromise?

4. Which environmental issue is most important for our world: food, soil, water, or energy?

5. What steps should America take to end the image of the "throwaway society"?

6. How does green space affect you? Is it necessary for society?

7. Is sustainability being accomplished in the United States? Around the world?

8. Why is interiority as important as economics to sustainability?

9. In what area of wellness does the American family need the most help? Why?

10. Does money make people happy?

CHAPTER FOURTEEN

CURRENT AND FUTURE CHALLENGES

Objectives
Technology
   Lifestyle Changes
Worldview
   Healthcare
   Education
   Impact of Technology
In the News
Family Structure
   Marriage and Committed Relationships
   Children
   Divorce
Reality Check
Natural Resources
Changing Demographics
   Diversity and Immigration
   Economic Divide
   Aging Population
   Geographic Location and Housing
Summary
Questions for Review and Discussion

Objectives

- Be aware of the impact that technology has on family resources and decisions.

- Recognize possible future changes to family structure.

- Identify current trends with possible future ramifications for family resource management.

- Understand the current and future challenges of managing natural resources effectively.

- Be aware of the forecasted changes in population demographics and possible changes associated with those shifts.

**In every conceivable manner, the family is link to our past,
bridge to our future.**

—Alex Haley

Chapters 1 through 13 explored both the context and progression within the decision-making process. This final chapter provides a view into the future of family decision making and family resource management. Change is always a constant for families. Although challenging and uncomfortable, change provides the impetus for better decision making and the motivation to seek answers and enhance problem-solving skills.

What are the major changes forecasted that will impact family life in the near and distant future? Technology, family structure, availability of natural resources, and changing demographics will all force change in social policy, economic policy, and family functioning.

TECHNOLOGY

Before you even finish reading this paragraph, there will be new innovations announced in the field of technology. These newer, faster, more sophisticated tools will improve, complicate, and probably harm individuals and families in some way. There is no going back, however. Technology is embedded in business, politics, and family life.

Lifestyle Changes

You are shutting down your laptop at work and ready to head out the door. Before you do, you hit a button on your computer that will automatically activate the thermostat in your apartment, switch your refrigerator drawer into an oven mode to heat your dinner, turn on entryway lighting, draw the curtains, and start filling your bath. It is all currently possible with the proper wiring and equipment. In the future, you can expect even more changes to your lifestyle. Smartphones and other devices allow you to connect to your smoke alarms, humidity detectors, and vibration sensors. You can track who has been inside your house, turn on lights when you enter a room, and shut windows and doors when you leave. You can create your own products, custom designed to the way you want them to look using a 3D printer.

Not only useful to busy adults, these innovations might possibly enable elderly and disabled individuals to function independently at much higher levels. Technology can be used to lessen the most dangerous obstacles, such as loneliness, isolation, and mobility. Constant supervision and social interaction can be provided through camera systems, e-mail programs, and audiovisual equipment. Groceries and medical supplies can be ordered and delivered easily. Motorized chairs, food preparation equipment, and cleaning appliances can lessen dependency on care providers.

The idea of shopping online has surpassed everyone's expectations in terms of the number of purchases that are made online as well as how it has changed our way of thinking and everyday living. Even businesses that rely on the customer to walk in the store offer ways to streamline that experience. Customers can preorder and pick up curbside or have items delivered to shorten the time it takes to shop. Travel is also at your fingertips. Booking tickets online and checking in by phone allows a more smooth transition at the airport or train station.

WORLDVIEW

10 Obscure Technologies That Could Change the World

In the tech world, there is no shortage of products that make our lives better. Some may never be well known, but they have the power to change the world. Here are some that you may never hear about.

- Lifestraw: This is an ingenious product capable of filtering water of contaminants, making it safe and drinkable. This product could help prevent waterborne diseases such as dysentery and cholera around the world.

- SCiO Pocket Molecular Sensor: This product lets users scan and obtain information about the chemical makeup of objects. This device can scan food, medicines, plants, oils, and other items to make identification immediately available in areas where information is limited.

- Sugru: A little like Play-Doh, this product is capable of being molded and manipulated to build, seal, and bind objects together. After 24 hours, it becomes extremely durable, flexible, and waterproof, solving emergency problems quickly.

- Liftware: This product can be attached to objects to create a stabilizing handle using motion sensors. For individuals around the world with mild to moderate tremors, it can be very helpful when completing daily tasks such as eating.

- Kevo Bluetooth Lock: This lock system syncs with an iOS or Android device. Security and safety can be managed from anywhere.

- XStat Syringe: This device provides a quick way for wounds to be treated. A syringe is filled with tiny sponges that expand, apply pressure, and stop bleeding. Applications are many for war zones, accidents, and natural disasters, just to name a few.

- Circuit Scribe: This silver ink allows users to learn and create by drawing circuits. Applications include modeling, innovation, and education.

- Foldscope: This is a foldable paper microscope with implications for education and global health.

- Foldable Bike Helmet: The safety of travel will be enhanced by this new helmet that is foldable and easy to transport.

- Virtual Keyboard: A laser projection system can turn any flat surface into a virtual keyboard. Information can be transmitted instantly through a smartphone or other device anywhere in the world.

Source: Adapted from Heisler, Y. (2015, February 11). 10 obscure technologies that could change the world. *Network World.* http://www.networkworld.com/article/2881908/software/10-obscure-technologies-that-could-change-the-world.html#slide11.

Healthcare

Individuals and families living in the United States already expect the highest level of healthcare available. Although the United States spends more per capita on healthcare than is spent on healthcare around the world, it ranks 38th when compared with other developed nations for health outcomes (Vitalari, 2014). Although mandatory health insurance was designed and implemented so that all Americans could have affordable healthcare, there are still those who fall through the cracks and others whose benefits have decreased. The debate about national healthcare will probably continue for some time.

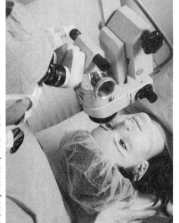

▶ **Photo 14.1**
Medical technology presents opportunities and challenges.

The latest developments in care, management, and medicines continue to feed consumers new hope. Struggles escalate between special interest groups lobbying for increased federal research spending on their particular disease. Resources are obviously not in step with demand or need. What does the future hold in terms of healthcare?

Americans now anticipate that over the next 50 years, the ability to create custom organ transplants will be possible (Smith, 2014). Growing replacement organs such as kidneys, livers, and hearts would allow many people who are on waiting lists to get relief more quickly, and the fear of organ rejection would be eliminated. Even artificially growing new ears, noses, and skin could be possible in the future. These advancements can also help manage certain diseases, such as diabetes.

Another health issue is the banking of umbilical cord blood. Blood found in a child's umbilical cord can be collected at birth and stored for future use. Storage can be in either a private or public bank. Once this blood is collected, it can be accessed when needed for medical treatment of the donor or other patients. If the blood is stored in a private bank, it can be accessed only for that individual unless permission is given for another to use it. These blood cells can treat a growing number of diseases and disorders. If a child has a family history of these medical problems, it may be a safety precaution for the family to bank the blood for possible use in the future. Banking is entirely up to the family. Because it does cost to contract for private storage, the practice

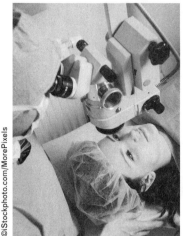

▶ **Photo 14.2**
Advancements in healthcare will improve quality of life for an aging population but will also increase medical spending.

is most common among those with monetary resources. The possibilities raise the ethical question of privilege.

Stem-cell research is both hotly debated and scientifically intriguing. Medical research has the potential to extend the renewing capability of stem cells into treatments for several conditions—brain and spinal cord injuries, heart disease, neurological disease, and countless other types of diseases. Controversy about the source of these cells, especially when taken from human embryos, presents ethical questions that must be considered. As medical technology continues to provide new opportunities at ever-increasing speed, decisions about how, what, and why these new techniques should be utilized must be carefully analyzed.

On the other end of the life span, healthcare of the elderly is expected to be challenging in the next few decades as the population is aging rapidly. Although they will be the healthiest group of elders in history, aging bodies require increased physical and mental health care. While dementia has always been a common health issue facing the elderly, the World Health Organization (2016) predicts that the number of people who suffer from it will nearly triple by 2050.

Advances in medicine, such as joint replacements and neurosurgical procedures, will increase both demand for and use of financial resources for medical expenses. Chronic diseases increase with age, and the demand for pharmaceuticals to relieve symptoms, and even to cure those diseases, will tax the public program dollars.

Education

How will technology influence the future of education? Computerized instruction has already had a tremendous impact on university course and program offerings. Online courses provide opportunities for study to those in remote geographic locations and those with job and other time constraints. Increased demand for and use of higher education courses and programs offered in an online format will ultimately change the college experience. The tension between brick-and-mortar university sites and tightening education budgets creates an environment of increased dependence on off-campus programming.

There is little doubt that technology and education will combine in a powerful way in the future. The *Huffington Post* (2014) proposes some of the changes they believe are on the horizon. Technology will increase in the classroom with integrated touchscreens and interactive curriculum. It is predicted that massive open online courses (MOOCs) are going to continue and expand to connect students to information around the world, changing the look of formal education and the cost of a college education. As new technologies are developed, teaching and learning will need to adapt to those changes.

The increasing dependency on technology for information access and exchange is not without its problems, however. Access to new technology in schools and private homes (or lack of it) creates an economic divide that unfairly polarizes students at all educational levels in their ability to obtain necessary information.

Impact of Technology

Although advances in technology provide many benefits, there are drawbacks. **Technostress** is used to describe information overload in a world where information is continuously a part of our lives. It may come from a feeling of entrapment caused by unrealistic expectations of constant connection to technology with little time to think or analyze (Tarafdar, Tu, Ragu-Nathan, & Ragu-Nathan, 2011). Recent research finds that certain psychological traits may cause some people to be more negatively affected by technostress than others. Lee, Chang, Cheng, and Lin (2016) found that those with poor time management, social dysfunction, or other related side effects, such as lack of sleep or shyness, were experiencing signs for technostress.

Technostress: the negative psychological link between people and the introduction of new technologies

Advances in "time-saving machines" meant to save time may actually result in increased standards. The computer was touted as the way to a paperless society. That was believed to be environmentally beneficial. Many debate whether computers have actually reduced the use of paper or ultimately have increased its consumption as well as disposal problems such as e-waste.

Multiple computers, TVs, and video game systems have created a separatist environment in many homes. Individuals spend increasingly greater amounts of time separated, in different rooms, attending to individual tasks alone. Younger generations are often more comfortable using technology, and the balance of power can be shifted when they have knowledge necessary to use new products while their parents and grandparents feel helpless and unprepared.

Fifty-three percent of Americans are skeptical about the future of technology (Smith, 2014). Technology that allows information to be automatically shared can create vulnerability to fraud and deception. As the demand for devices to get smaller and more accessible grows, it is anticipated that the creation of a body implant or other device to allow continuous connection may create even more chances for vulnerability.

IN THE NEWS

Technology Use Among Seniors

Although seniors consistently have lower rates of technology adoption than the general public, this group is more digitally connected than ever before. In fact, some groups of seniors—such as those who are younger, more affluent, and more highly educated—report owning and using various technologies at rates similar to adults under the age of 65.

Still, there remains a notable digital divide between younger and older Americans. And many seniors who are older, are less affluent, or have lower levels of educational attainment continue to have a distant relationship with digital technology.

With smartphone ownership in the United States more than doubling in the past 5 years, Americans are embracing mobile technology at a rapid pace. And while adoption rates among seniors continue to trail those of the overall population, the share of adults ages 65 and up who own smartphones has risen 24 percentage points (from 18% to 42%) since 2013. Today, roughly half of older adults who own cell phones have some type of smartphone; in 2013, that share was just 23%.

As is true of the population as a whole, Internet adoption among seniors has risen steadily over the last decade and a half. When the Pew Research Center began tracking Internet adoption in early 2000, just 14% of seniors were Internet users. But today, 67% of adults ages 65 and older say they go online.

The share of seniors who subscribe to home broadband services has also risen—albeit at a slower rate than Internet use. Around half of seniors (51%) now say they have high-speed Internet at home. This represents a modest uptick from 2013, when 47% of older adults were broadband adopters.

Social media is increasingly becoming an important platform where people find news and information, share their experiences, and connect with friends and family. And just as Internet adoption and smartphone ownership has grown among seniors, so has social media use.

Today, 34% of Americans ages 65 and up say they use social networking sites like Facebook or Twitter. This represents a seven-point increase from 2013, when 27% of older adults reported using social media. Still, a majority of seniors do not use social media, and the share that do is considerably smaller than that of the general population.

One challenge facing older adults with respect to technology is the fact that many are simply not confident in their own ability to learn about and properly use electronic devices. Hand in hand with this lack of confidence in their own ability to use digital technology, seniors are also more likely than those in other age groups to say they need others to show them how to use new devices. Older adults may also face physical challenges that might make it difficult to use or manipulate devices.

Once online, most seniors make the internet a standard part of their daily routine. Roughly three-quarters of older Internet users go online at least daily, including 17% who say they go online about once a day, 51% who indicate they do so several times a day, and 8% who say they use the Internet almost constantly. Among older adults who own smartphones, this figure is even higher: 76% of these smartphone-owning older adults use the internet several times a day or more.

Source: "Tech Adoption Climbs Among Older Adults," Pew Research Center, Washington, D.C. (May 2017), http://www.pewinternet.org/2017/05/17/technology-use-among-seniors/.

FAMILY STRUCTURE

The increase and eventual leveling off of divorce rates over the last 50 years has already demonstrated a marked impact on family structure in the United States. The emerging trends of cohabitation, single parenting, and same-sex marriage have challenged existing policies and opinions. Future projections indicate that by 2030, single-parent families will increase by 12%, couples without children will increase by 37%, and one-person households will increase by 35% (Organization for Economic Co-operation and Development, 2011). It is reasonable, based on historical analysis, to expect evolving changes in family structure over time. These changes will ultimately impact family resource management.

Marriage and Committed Relationships

The institution of marriage in the 21st century has changed. While about 80% of today's young adults say that marriage is in their future (Hymowitz, Carroll, Wilcox, & Kaye, 2013), it seems that that path is taking longer for a variety of reasons. Cherlin and others (2014) believe that a shift in the transition to adulthood is one reason for this. Thirty-four percent of people report that financial security is a barrier to marriage (Wang & Parker, 2014). Marriage, as well as childbearing, has been postponed, especially among those with education. Economically, this expands the gap between young educated professionals and their counterparts with only a high school degree who marry younger and have children sooner in the future.

Cohabitation as an alternative to marriage has increased, as discussed in Chapter 2. While many see cohabitation as a pathway to marriage, the intentions of the partners and their experiences vary widely. In the future, the rates of cohabitation may not continue to rise as dramatically as in the past, as attitudes and personal beliefs will continue to influence this trend.

Cohabitation: to live together as or as if a married couple

Another emerging relationship gaining visibility in Western societies is living apart together (LAT). These relationships are generally found with older couples who do not want to live together but want to be identified as a couple. Couples choose this committed relationship because it allows them to share intimacy, yet maintain financial independence at the same time. Benson (2015) reports that it is difficult to identify the number of those who choose this type of relationship. More studies need to be conducted on this type of relationship to predict future trends.

It is anticipated that over the next 40 years, class, racial, and regional differences will continue to increase and change family formation and structure because of growing economic inequality (Cahn, Carbone, & Lavine, 2016). The highly educated upper middle class may pull further away from the rest of the population as they adopt new strategies and build on opportunities they have available. This group is predicted to be more marriage-centered and to have lower divorce rates.

Children

Delaying marriage, access to birth control, and the increasing number of women in the workforce have contributed to a drop in fertility rates over the last 30 years. Rates of childlessness have increased since the 1970s and now represent about 20% of women in their early 40s. A desire to develop partner relationships is often a reason to remain childless; however, developing emotional relationships with pets may also be important for some adults. In addition, while voluntary childlessness has been seen as abnormal in the past, that may be changing, especially among those with higher economic status (Blackstone, 2014).

For some, the thought that parenting means more debt, smaller savings, and an inability to live within a certain lifestyle is enough to influence their childbearing decisions. Recent events such as terrorist acts and school shootings may also influence the decision to become a parent. It may be useful to apply this situation to the **principle of revealed preferences**. According to this principle, consumer behavior reveals true preferences. In this case, although many say they value the family and desire children of their own, their true values are revealed by the lower statistics on childbearing. One could argue that economics alone should not be used to predict the trends of childbearing because it is only based on the costs of parenting and not the emotional rewards.

Principle of revealed preferences: the inclusion of mental preferences in economic models to explain choices made

More women are choosing to become a parent before they marry. According to the National Marriage Project, by age 25, 44% of women have had a baby, while only 38% have married, and by the time women turn 30, about two-thirds of first babies are born to unmarried women (Hymowitz et al., 2013). According to Cherlin et al. (2014), there has been a dramatic lengthening of the transition to adulthood, and this new definition of early adulthood will continue into the future with an education gap that will continue to contribute to widening income differences. Researchers predict a continuation of family instability that will result in adverse well-being for children in the future (Lundberg, Pollak, & Stearns, 2016).

Perhaps more significant than fertility rates and timing to the future of the family are the changes in the social climate of parenting. This change in attitude can be found in many aspects of life within the United States. The advantages to being childfree are everywhere. From housing that emphasizes the amenities of single living to TV programs that portray parents as fools and glamorize the single life, there seems to be an apparent preference shift from a child-raising society to a childfree adult society.

Despite the recent trends and seemingly negative research on the benefits of parenting, people have not given up on becoming parents. However, consumer research shows that more and more parents are "outsourcing" family life as they try to find a balance between home and work life. Hochschild's (2012) work documents how parents use the market for almost every aspect of their personal lives. Epp and Velagaleti (2014) suggest that outsourcing family life comes as a result of working parents who have time constraints and less access to extended family, and rising standards for parenting. While outsourcing can include less significant tasks, such as house cleaning, it may also apply to childcare, especially when parents view the care given to their children as equal to their own caregiving.

Divorce

Although divorce rates rose sharply in the 1970s and 1980s, they have leveled and declined slightly over the last two decades. Two factors seem to contribute the most in reducing the number of divorces. The age at marriage and higher educational levels contribute to the stability of marriage (Hymowitz et al., 2013). Steverman (2016) indicates that the average marriage is lasting longer and that younger couples are divorcing less than those in the Baby Boom generation. If current trends remain, divorce will continue to decline in the future.

One issue that seems to be a source of controversy and likely will be a topic of discussion in the future in regard to divorce is the provision of the no-fault divorce law. During the 1970s and early 1980s, the divorce laws underwent what is commonly known as a divorce "revolution," where most states enacted no-fault laws as grounds for divorce. Until this time, spouses could initiate divorce proceedings only if they had proof that their spouse was guilty of marital misconduct. Reasons for the movement toward no-fault divorce included a desire to unburden the court system of divorce proceedings, promote more fairness in division of marital assets, and allow former partners the freedom to remarry. Legal costs of divorce have fallen, as couples no longer need to prove the guilt of the other. Negotiations can take place with a mediator outside of the courtroom rather than with a judge or jury.

Family scientists are more concerned about the consequences of divorce for children and their future relationships. Almost every study about the effects of divorce on children points to some negative effects; however, most have concluded that the effects do not have a universal impact on all children (Amato, 2010; Ribar, 2015). Income, the father's involvement, parents' physical and mental health, parenting quality, and family stability seem to be some of the best predictors of emotional and social well-being for children in all family structures. Ribar (2015) suggests that even if interventions or policies were in place to raise income, increase the amount of time parents spend with their children, or provide other in-kind services for children of divorcing parents, it only partially substitutes for the intact marriage itself.

REALITY CHECK

In the world of marketing we spend a lot of time thinking about what individuals want and what they care about. But no man is an island. How we behave and the decisions we make collectively are equally important to our quality of life and highly relevant to brands seeking to create a more meaningful connection with their customers.

Married couples with 2.4 kids don't really exist: today, only a quarter of families could be termed "nuclear". Exploring the changing dynamics of the family provides a fascinating context for understanding individuals' choices and the changing role of brands in society.

We've spent the last four months identifying the influencing factors that will shape the family of the future. We have established a set of six forces that are dramatically altering what we will come to define as a "family".

Some of the highlights from the six forces give us an indication of the changing nature of the family: growing megacities with space an absolute premium; collective responses to water, escalating demand for energy and food; evolving career expectations; changing definitions of quality of life.

These forces are creating a diversity of family units that are not necessarily defined by marriage or blood-ties and are unlikely to fit into any of today's consumer segmentations.

By applying these forces, we have created a future segmentation of five families of 2030, which challenge brands to consider what they should be doing today to attract customers of tomorrow.

Tandem Tribes: two single parent families sharing one family home

Each with their own private space within the house, the Tandem Tribes come together to share living and kitchen/dining space. The single parents have a partnership of convenience, living a lifestyle that wouldn't be possible alone, which provides a positive, flexible environment for bringing up children.

A Tandem Tribe home is often part of a micro-community featuring communal facilities such as shared DIY tools and a fleet of electric cars, all in the name of encouraging low-cost, enjoyable, collaborative living.

Modular Movers: nomadic professionals living in convenient, high-service, low-ownership homes

Our single person family, Modular Movers are nomadic. Living in flexible spaces around the world, they don't want baggage or clutter as they move from Sao Paulo to New York to Bangalore whenever they need to.

Home is more like a hotel. They crave practicality—location and convenience are more important than a feeling of home sweet home. Modular living means they choose the add-ons to their living space—if they want a kitchen, for example, or a home office. The megacity is their playground—there's always a reason to be out and about.

Silver Linings: the 70 years+ generation

The Silver Linings are determined to grow old positively. They want to have a laid-back lifestyle with a genuine interaction between generations. They are happy to trade-in previous living arrangements for a worry-free lifestyle that means more stability and simplicity. They use their experience and skills to contribute to the local community and economy. The income they receive in return helps support their day-to-day activities.

Ruralites: hyper-connected families living in rural communities.

The Ruralites are entrepreneurial with comfortable, hyper-efficient and tech-orientated homes. They are close to self-sufficiency in food production and make full use of all available resources, including the production of energy, which ensures they make money from energy rather than paying money for it. Their 3D printer keeps the home working, producing replacement parts for all appliances. The environment that surrounds the Ruralites' homes ensures that kids grow up with imaginations that work on overdrive.

Multi-gens: Multiple generations living under one roof

Their homes may be crowded, but these families depend on support from one another, enabling each family member to pursue their own goals and lead independent lives. Each person pitches in and does their bit so life runs smoothly. These families make use of services like cloud-based family hubs, which divide up tasks and responsibilities between all family members. In some ways they run more like an efficient business than a classic family.

The families of the future raise many questions for sustainability professionals and marketers. How can a brand adapt to families as they form and re-form over time? What opportunities arise from personal space being highly limited? How can we make collaborative consumption a desirable benefit, not a sacrifice? And what will it mean for a brand when the key decision-maker in a family is no longer a single person?

Source: Bennie, Fiona. (2014, October 24). Meet the families of 2030: The factors shaping future generations. *The Guardian.* https://www.theguardian.com/sustainable-business/families-of-the-future-brands-marketing. Copyright Guardian News & Media Ltd 2017.

NATURAL RESOURCES

The availability of natural resources is a very important issue to consider, both now and in the future. Natural resources are usually defined as food, water, energy, and minerals. Everywhere around the world, these resources are critical to sustaining life as we know it. The World Economic Forum (2014) reveals four paradigms that emerge in looking at the future availability of natural resources and suggests some challenging scenarios that will unfold over the next 20 years.

First, there should be a focus on the exhaustion of natural resources. There is a finite supply that is being used at an alarming rate, and the demand continues to grow. Currently, the development and adoption of new technologies to address this is not fast enough to meet the coming needs. Second, there is a need to address the rising costs of natural resources. Not only do prices rise because the supply is running out; increased regulation, higher costs of production, and riskier development sites are also driving prices higher. Third, there should be incentive to innovate with new sources or alternative resources. Fourth, social injustice allows allocation of natural resources to be distributed unfairly. "One in seven people on the plant go hungry every day despite the fact that the world is capable of feeding everyone" (p. 14). Populations who control access to resources will benefit and may see it as their right to more of the world's share. These issues lead to challenges in the future. Politics and fears cause widespread changes for the availability of resources. For example, economic sanctions can be imposed that not only trigger panic in one part of the world but cause effects to be felt in other parts of the world, too. Social consequences that come from decisions are also a challenge. For example, "fracking" to expose shale gas deposits will make more of that natural resource available but may affect nearby water supplies. Finally, new technologies that are needed to make the transfer to more and more renewable resources take time to develop and are expensive. For example, while new technologies are being developed, traditional sources must still be kept in place. During this transition, there are still questions about whether the new technology will be cost effective or if it will even be able to provide the needed resources.

Automobiles are utilizing alternative forms of energy already. Ethanol, recycled cooking oil, and electricity are fuels in a limited number of vehicles on the road. Manufacturers are developing new, more efficient automobiles that will be capable of using these alternative fuels. Urban areas are increasing efforts to expand public transportation, hoping to reduce the use of personal automobile congestion on roadways. It is not anticipated that individuals and families will ever purposefully reduce their desire to travel. Air travel will continue to increase as businesses and families expand geographically. Increasing numbers of older adults will pursue travel in their retirement.

A growing dependency on electricity must also be addressed. Harnessing wind and surf energy and converting those into useable forms of electricity are two important areas of research and design in the field of engineering. An emerging interest in portable energy sources parallels consumer demand for wireless technology and flexible products. Rechargeable fuel cells are gaining impetus in many areas of product design.

Food and water shortages are two of the greatest challenges for the planet in the future. Wutich and Brewis (2014) suggest that although the United States does not have chronic hunger or issues with access to safe drinking water like other parts of the world do, there is some resource insecurity. Being able to recognize the early warning signs and making a plan for the future would be helpful in prevention and intervention should conditions such as climate change or population growth change our ability to access resources. With expanding development of housing and industrial complexes, land available for food production is dwindling. New methods of food production that increase quantity without depleting soil sources must continue to emerge. Efficient methods of waste management will also be necessary. Chapter 13 explained social responsibility. The future will be positively or negatively impacted by the acceptance or rejection of this important concept.

CHANGING DEMOGRAPHICS

Using demographic information is an important tool in not only understanding the changes that are taking place, but in helping policymakers and community leaders make informed decisions. Demographic forecasting is possible when emerging trends are identified from changing demographic information. The changing face of America shows a population that is getting older, is becoming more diverse, is less religiously affiliated, and is becoming more liberal. These demographic studies show that the gaps that cause conflict between young and old, poor and rich, and political parties are widening (Taylor, 2014).

Diversity and Immigration

The term *third demographic transition* (Coleman, 2009) refers to the societal transformation in the United States from a mostly low-fertility, native-born population to a high-fertility population that is culturally and ethnically diverse. In 1900, 88% of immigrants were from Europe, and now only 12% come to the United States from those countries (Pew Research Center, 2013). These changes will have a dramatic impact on key discussions such as poverty, equality, and policy.

▶ **Photo 14.3**
Immigration presents economic and social controversy.

Projections indicate that within the next century, white Americans will represent only 43% of the total population of the United States (compared to 85% in 1960). Hispanic and black Americans will make up 45% of the population during this same period of time (Restuccia, 2014). Today, more than 50% of immigrants are from Latin America (Pew Research Center, 2013).

Interracial marriage has also contributed to demographic change. As discussed in Chapter 5, nearly one in six newlyweds marry outside of their racial or ethnic group, in contrast to 50 years ago, when it was still illegal to marry outside of your racial group in many states (Taylor, 2014). As diversity and interracial marriage increases, racial categories may not make much sense in the future. The U.S. Census Bureau now allows individuals to identify their own racial or ethnic background, rather than requiring them to pick from predetermined categories when completing a census survey.

Despite the arguments on immigration following recent terrorist attacks, controversy surrounding legal and illegal immigration continues to be the source of a great deal of debate among politicians and the public. There are no easy solutions, and the debate will likely continue into the future. During the last few decades, immigration played a major role in changing the racial and ethnic composition in the United States. America is one of the most diverse countries in the world, and the open-door policies of immigration have made it possible for people from all over the globe to come and make a life in the United States.

Recognizing and understanding the shift in the demographics of diversity is critical as we prepare for the future. The growth of diversity changes the dynamics of communities. Food migrates with people, but the authenticity of it changes when mixed with the likes and dislikes of others. Think of all the fast-food restaurants that serve an "Americanized" version of an ethnic food. Salsa has taken over ketchup as the number-one condiment, and tortilla chips are sold more than potato chips (Laboy & Hirsch, 2013).

Goods and services will need to change to meet the needs of the diverse groups. Business strategies and practices must change to fit the unique characteristics of the target market. Over time, the political process in America may also change, with immigrants playing a more significant role in creating new laws and policy. The

Hispanic culture, now one of the largest minority groups, has already changed American society. The Spanish language has been introduced in many ways, from advertising and labeling to children's programming on TV. The world of music, entertainment, and sports includes Latino talent, with names such as pop star Jennifer Lopez, actress Sofia Vergara, and Major League Baseball's Alex Rodriguez.

Economic Divide

The American dream has always been associated with the idea that anyone can become successful, no matter where you begin; however, the divide between those who have and those who don't is widening. Saez (2013) reports that income inequality is now the highest it has been since 1928, prior to the Great Depression. What is causing this growing economic divide, and will it continue in the future? Research points to several reasons for the phenomenon.

First, family incomes have declined for the poorest third of children, particularly in single-parent families. Gillespie (2013) reveals that income for the poor and working-class families has decreased, while the top 5% "economic elite" have experienced an increase. Despite the idea of the United States being the land of opportunity, social mobility is now less likely. Those who grew up well off are more likely than those who grew up poor to be well off as adults. Family resources that are not available to less affluent children can delay their ability to move forward economically as adults.

Second, the racial and ethnic income gap has been increasing since the recession of 2007–2009. More than half of all children growing up in low-income families are racial/ethnic minorities (Population Reference Bureau, 2015). While improving slightly over the past few years, black income is still only 63% of white income (Pew Research Center, 2013). Unless policies that address access to education and training for these groups are set in place, the gap will continue into the future.

Third, income inequality has been linked to the growing divide in educational opportunities, and there is a widening gap in the investments that parents make in their children. These opportunities include enrichment expenses, such as private lessons and tutors, and funding children's college education. In addition to money, time commitments are also a way to invest in children. Mothers with a college degree spend 4.5 hours per week more with their children than do those with a high school education or less (Guryan, Hurst, & Kearney, 2008), resulting in larger vocabularies and other benefits for the children.

Finally, there is a significant difference in the debt ratio between the two income groups (Gillespie, 2013). The U.S. financial system allows consumers to be dependent on debt to fulfill their needs. During economic prosperity, Americans have increased their spending using credit that is easy to obtain. During the last recession, many people were already deeply in debt. This debt, in combination with the dramatic decline in housing prices, increased the already large gap between the rich and poor in the United States (Mian & Sufi, 2014).

Aging Population

The population of Americans 65 years old and older is expected to crest 70 million by 2030 (American Geriatrics Society, 2016). It is almost certain that the demographics of our society will continue to change, not only economically but in many other ways. It is evident that the changes in economic security, health, and longevity will give those who are aging considerable social power as they enter the next phase of their lives. Business and industry are already taking note of the likes and dislikes of the Baby Boom generation and are targeting them for a larger share of the consumer market. In the coming years, advertisers may need to switch from products that target only youth to products that target older, more affluent, more technically savvy, and more health-conscious adults than previous generations at that age.

The end of the 20th century brought a reversal in the trend toward early retirement. The age of retirement rose and is predicted to continue due to changes in Social Security that may force many to stay employed longer, technological advances that improve working conditions, and better health of older Americans. The American Association of Retired Persons (AARP) (Peterson, 2015) reports that Social Security will be needed in the future because it provides at least half of the income for one in two older Americans and provides most of the income for one in four. It is likely that this will not change in the future because other financial supports in retirement have not increased. Pensions and individual retirement accounts are not adequate as replacements for Social Security. According to the National Institute on Retirement Security (Rhee & Boivie, 2015), the medium retirement savings balance for those who are near retirement age is only $14,500. In addition, 62% of working households who are near retirement age have retirement savings of less than their annual income for only one year.

While Social Security has allowed the elderly to benefit economically, the economic stress it presents to younger working generations will eventually have the opposite effect. Ten thousand Baby Boomers will begin receiving Social Security and Medicare every day between now and 2030 (Taylor, 2014). This large group of retirees will tax the ability of younger workers to support them as they age.

The United States of Aging Survey (2015) finds that older Americans have some concerns about the future, including maintaining their physical and mental health, increasing costs, remaining independent, and receiving needed support. Older Americans are looking for ways to stay healthy and sharp, and keeping a positive attitude is part of their strategy. Being able to stay at home and independent are goals for aging adults. Many report that while they are able to make home improvements to help them age in place, they also recognize that some of their own community's infrastructure is not acceptable. Older adults are confident that they will be able to find help and support when they need it, even though they believe that young people are less supportive of the elderly than in the past. Also represented in this report are professionals who work with the elderly. These professionals differ in their evaluation of the future for the elderly, and they express concerns about increasing financial scams and access to affordable housing. They also are less confident that older American are prepared for the aging process.

Geographic Location and Housing

Changing demographics of the typical household and other population shifts have led to changes in housing and urban development. In the next 25 years, there will be some changes in where we live and the way we live. The quality of the environment is a top priority for 87% of adults when choosing a place to live (Urban Land Institute, 2015).

Although urbanism previously was said to be an emerging trend for those who wanted to move away from the suburban "sprawl," it appears that most Americans still prefer to live in the suburbs, and there may be less desire for downtown revival and trendy loft spaces. Other factors, such as safety and better education systems, are concerns for families with children (Kotkin, Cox, Schill, & Modarres, 2015). Among Millennials, 75% want to live in single-family homes and 66% want to live in the suburbs. While only 10% of Millennials want to live in the city center, more live in the city center than do other generations, especially singles (Urban Land Institute, 2015). The Nielsen Company (2014b) reports that Millennials who don't live in the city still want that "metropolitan feel." This includes the convenience of having entertainment venues, shops, and restaurants nearby and within walking distance. Just over half of all Americans and 63% of the Millennial generation would like to live in a place where they do not need a car (Urban Land Institute, 2015). Revitalizing small town main streets, bringing business and industry outside the city, and building a sense of community are ways to make suburban living more appealing.

Following the housing "bubble" and burst in 2008 that led to a recession, homebuilding continued to be slow, even though housing price inflation reemerged. Household expenses for housing account for approximately 35% of spending, up from 30% in 1985. Rent has also risen sharply, with renters spending as much as 50% of their income on housing in some urban centers (Kotkin & Cox, 2015). It doesn't look like this will change or improve in the future, with many people still unable to afford to buy housing combined with an affordable housing shortage (White, 2015).

Changes to the housing market and homebuilding will change as Millennials begin to buy their first homes. According to the National Association of Home Builders (2015), homes in the future will be smaller, home technology will increase, and homes will be more energy efficient. Millennials want larger closets and more storage space, along with a separate laundry room, but they are less interested in outdoor kitchens, two-story foyers, or separate family rooms. They also are willing to drive further and have less space if they can't afford a home near their work; however, they are not willing to compromise on quality of materials. They prefer mixed housing types (single-family homes, condominiums, and apartments) and would rather live in a community with a mix of ages and prefer a mix of cultures and backgrounds (Urban Land Institute, 2015).

The housing needs of the elderly will focus on maintaining their own homes with coordinated support services and physical modifications. Although they don't want or need a large, suburban home and choose to downsize to a smaller home that requires less maintenance, they are still more likely to buy a suburban home rather than one in an urban area. As Baby Boomers become empty nesters, they realize that the income from their large homes allows them to downsize in style and are choosing luxury over space in their new environments. However, while most are confident they will be able to afford the homes they want in the next 5 years, nearly a quarter of those over 68 years old say they are not confident that they will be able to do so (Urban Land Institute, 2015).

A new housing trend is emerging for families to cluster together geographically close or even in a multi-generational household. Not only does this allow generations to pool their resources; it reflects their desire to enhance family relationships (Kotkin, Cox, Schill, & Modarres, 2015). As a result, in the future there may be more homes with multiple living spaces, separate in-law suites, or onsite cottages for extended family.

Wherever Americans live, there are also future implications for the way that they choose to engage with their families and their communities. In the future, Millennials are more likely to want to be linked to others than the previous generation, resulting in more family-oriented housing and more connected communities. Decentralizing the workplace to include working from home and flexible hours will increase as parents put more emphasis the balance of work and family life. Working from home at least once a week is already up almost 40% from 20 years ago (Kotkin, Cox, Schill, & Modarres, 2015).

SUMMARY

Families and how they manage the resources necessary to meet their needs and wants are dynamic in nature. Changes within the unit and changes in the external environment impact future needs and decision-making processes. Although it is impossible to predict the future, analysis of current trends allows projection of possible shifts. Technology is sure to continue bringing constant and confounding changes to individuals and families at many levels. Family structures have been and will probably continue to evolve to meet societal expectations and circumstances. Expected future crises in terms of natural resource demands and supply will present challenges. Alternative sources must be developed. Changes within the population will create new opportunities and problems for families to address. Change is both stressful and functional. Needs and resources available to meet those emerging needs will continue to be a primary function of the family unit.

QUESTIONS FOR REVIEW AND DISCUSSION

1. In what ways have recent advances in technology impacted your personal life? Your educational experience?

2. Have new inventions typically increased leisure time and activity?

3. How has technology shaped the educational process you are pursuing?

4. What major shifts in family structure will have the greatest impact on resource management?

5. What are some strategies that might increase participation in recycling efforts?

6. List five long-term effects on family resource management that may result from the aging of the general population.

CASE FAMILY INFORMATION

The information presented here is necessary to complete the 10 case assignments within *Family Resource Management*. This family is completely fictitious, and any and all documents and reports created using this information are for educational purposes only.

FAMILY NAME ALPHA

Adult Family Members: Mother, Father (divorced from Mother and remarried), Husband/Stepfather, Oldest Son

Ages: Mother, 46; Father, 48; Husband/Stepfather, 45; Oldest Son, 22

Employment and Relevant Information

Mother is a registered nurse who has been employed at the same hospital for 15 years. She works four 10-hour days weekly. Her hobbies include reading and a weekly movie night with friends. Father is in mid-level management at a manufacturing plant. He does not pay child support, but does provide money for the necessities of the youngest son as needed. Current Husband/Stepfather is a musician, currently unemployed and currently in a rehabilitation facility for drug and alcohol detoxification. Oldest Son is deployed to Europe with the U.S. Navy. The family has one elderly cat.

Other Family Members and Relevant Information

Level One: Youngest Son, 17 years of age. He attends high school, is not employed, and has chronic asthma. He enjoys attending sporting events, playing video games, and camping with his father on the weekends.

Level Two: Oldest Son's Girlfriend and mother of a 3-year-old grandchild.

Family Assets: The family's home value is three times Mother's annual gross income. There is no mortgage, as per the divorce agreement. Mother's car is valued at half Mother's annual gross income. Youngest Son's car is worth half Mother's annual gross income; it was received as a gift from Father, with no loan. Mother's retirement fund is currently worth two times her annual gross income. There is a liquid savings of $1,400. Mother's paid-up life insurance is worth $50,000 upon her death, and a separate policy worth 1 year's salary would be paid completely by her employer.

Family Debts: The house is insured for replacement value, with monthly premiums due. Mother's car is financed with a 5-year auto loan (at a 5% interest rate) for 90% of its value. Car insurance and annual licensing are required. Youngest Son's car requires insurance and annual licensing. Mother has credit card debt (at a 12% interest rate) equal to two times her monthly gross income and is also responsible for current Husband/Stepfather's credit card debt of $4,000 (at a 15% interest rate). Mother adds 5% of her gross income to her pension monthly.

FAMILY NAME BETA

Adult Family Members: Mother, Father

Ages: Mother is 36 years old. Father is 36 years old.

Employment and Relevant Information

Mother is a medical laboratory technologist and has worked at the same facility for 12 years. She is active in the parent organization at the children's school, belongs to a women's health club, and is taking coursework for an advanced degree. She works Monday through Friday, 8:00 am to 4:00 pm. Father is a city policeman with 8 years in his current position. His work schedule rotates three 12-hour days (6:00 am to 6:00 pm) on duty and three days off-duty. He enjoys coaching his children's sports activities, attending sporting events at the local college, and participating in golf and community projects. The family has a small dog and an aquarium with fish. They belong to the local YMCA.

Other Family Members and Relevant Information

Level One: Daughter is 10 years old. She participates in dance, swimming, and soccer. Oldest Son is 8 years old. He plays ice hockey and baseball and is a member of the local scouting organization. Youngest Son is 5 years old. He plays t-ball and is also a Scout.

Level Two: Mother's parents live 200 miles away. Father's parents live 500 miles away. Aunts and uncles are at least 200 miles away.

Family Assets: The family bought a newly constructed home 3 years ago. Its current value is three times the combined annual gross income of both adults. The family owns two vehicles—a 3-year-old pickup worth two times Father's monthly gross income, with no loan attached, and a new sports utility vehicle worth half the annual combined gross salaries of the parents. Both adults have life insurance policies worth their annual salary, with premiums paid by their employers. Both adults have pension plans, with current balances equal to 2 years' worth of salaries.

Family Debts: The SUV has a 4-year loan against it for 75% of its current value (at a 5% interest rate). There is a 30-year (4% interest rate) home mortgage for 80% of the home's current value. The family has a credit card balance (10% interest rate) of $6,000 and a revolving furniture credit purchase balance (1 year at 0% interest, then 12% thereafter) of $5,000. Home taxes, insurance, and upkeep are required. Homeownership also requires utility payments monthly. Cars must be insured and licensed annually. Memberships must be paid monthly. Both parents add 5% of their monthly gross income to their retirement/pension plans.

FAMILY NAME OMEGA

Adult Family Members: Husband, Wife, and Wife's Mother

Ages: Husband is 68 years old and recently retired from a career as a pharmacist. Wife is 65, and Wife's Mother is 87.

Employment and Relevant Information

Husband is collecting his Social Security monthly payments of $2,200 and has Medicare coverage. He spends his free time golfing and gardening. Wife is an elementary art teacher and has been at the same school for 30 years. She is active in her church and a few other civic organizations. Both belong to the community theater, hold season tickets to the local university's sporting events, and enjoy their membership in the country club. Wife's Mother collects $1,000 in Social Security monthly and is covered by Medicare. She is in the late stages of Alzheimer's disease and is homebound, except for occasional outings with her daughter and son-in-law. The family utilizes Medicaid-sponsored home nursing services 3 days per week. They have an elderly dog.

Other Family Members and Relevant Information

Level One: Two adult, married children, with a total of four grandchildren, all within 250 miles.

Level Two: Wife has three living siblings. Husband has no living siblings or parents.

Family Assets: The couple owns a home worth four times Wife's annual gross salary. They have a $50,000, 5-year (3% interest rate) mortgage against the home. Husband drives a small pickup worth $6,000, and Wife drives a sedan worth her annual salary. Husband has a retirement fund with a current value of five times his last annual income before retirement. He can draw on that money at any time. Wife's pension has a value of four times her annual income. They have liquid savings of $85,000.

Family Debts: Wife's sedan has a 4-year loan (6% interest) for half its value. Their memberships must be paid monthly. Home taxes, upkeep, and insurance must be budgeted, and auto insurance and licensing is necessary. Mrs. Omega continues to add 3% of her gross monthly income to her pension, but can stop at any time. She can retire whenever she chooses.

FAMILY NAME TAU

Adult Family Members: Grandmother and Mother

Ages: Grandmother is 55 years old. Mother is 32 years old.

Employment and Relevant Information

Grandmother is employed by a local hotel chain as a housekeeping manager. She works Monday through Friday, 6:00 am to 2:00 pm, and every third Saturday morning, from 6:00 am to noon. She is widowed and very active in her neighborhood and elementary school organizations. She has a large extended family within a 2-mile radius. Her daughter, Mother of her three grandchildren, is serving a 5-year prison sentence, 80 miles away, and has given guardianship of those children to Grandmother, Mrs. Tau. The family visits Mother every other weekend. The children qualify for Medicaid health coverage and receive a total monthly state-funded living support allowance of $450.

Other Family Members and Relevant Information

Level One: Granddaughter, age 13, attends the local middle school approximately 1 mile from home. Her hobbies and activities include reading, watching television, and spending time with her friends and cousins in the neighborhood. Oldest Grandson, age 9, attends the neighborhood elementary school three blocks from home. He enjoys playing with neighboring children, YMCA sports programs, and riding his bike. Youngest Grandson is 7 years old, and he attends a school for special needs children across town. He has behavioral and developmental disorders and requires medication and therapy treatments. He enjoys walks in the park, playing with Legos, and listening to music.

Level Two: Neighbor woman with two children of her own. She and Mrs. Tau share childcare coverage. Neighbor helps Mrs. Tau's grandchildren get ready for school and supervises their transport to school. Mrs. Tau picks up all five children after school and watches them until Neighbor finishes work at 6:00 pm. Neighbor also supervises children on Mrs. Tau's working Saturdays.

Level Three: Mrs. Tau has two adult nieces and one older sister within 1 mile of her home. They are a very close, supportive family. The children's father has not maintained contact since the birth of the youngest child and does not provide any financial support.

Family Assets: Mrs. Tau inherited full ownership of her home when her husband died. His life insurance paid the remaining mortgage. The current value of the home is equal to 2.5 times Mrs. Tau's annual income. She inherited her older brother's 15-year-old sedan when he passed away. It has a current value of $4,000. Her retirement pension account has a current balance equal to two times her annual salary. She has liquid savings of $2,000. Her car requires annual licensing and insurance coverage and has been experiencing increasing mechanical difficulties.

Family Debts: The home requires upkeep, taxes, and insurance coverage. There are no outstanding credit card balances. Mrs. Tau did take a home equity loan of $40,000 to pay for her daughter's legal fees. It is a 10-year loan with an interest rate of 8%. Mrs. Tau continues to add 4% of her monthly gross income to her retirement fund.

FAMILY NAME ZETA

Adult Family Members: Mr. Zeta and his cohabitating partner, Ms. X

Ages: Mr. Zeta is 38 years old and is divorced from his first wife. Ms. X is 33 years old and divorced from her first husband and the father of her two daughters.

Employment and Relevant Information

Mr. Zeta has worked for a local car dealership as a certified mechanic for 10 years. He works Monday through Friday, 7:30 am to 5:00 pm, and every Saturday morning from 7:00 am to noon. He enjoys spending time with coworkers, bowling, attending auto races, and riding his mountain bike in competitions. Ms. X works 4 hours per day, Monday through Friday, as a receptionist. She has custodial rights for her daughters. She enjoys scrapbooking, cooking, and watching movies. Her ex-husband pays $250 total per month in child support, and his employment benefits provide full health and dental insurance for their daughters.

Other Family Members and Relevant Information

Level One: Ms. X's two daughters live with them. The oldest is in third grade, and the youngest is in first grade. Mr. Zeta's son is 12 years old and lives with his mother 500 miles away.

Level Two: Mr. Zeta's ex-wife and son live 500 miles away. He travels to see his son once a month and brings his son to stay over the summer school break. Mr. Zeta is expected to provide health insurance coverage for his son. Mr. Zeta's parents live in another state.

Level Three: Ms. X has two sisters living within 2 miles. Ms. X's ex-husband is very dependable with child-support payments, but does not have contact with his daughters.

Family Assets: Mr. Zeta has a 10-year-old pickup that is debt free. He also has $750 in liquid savings. He withdrew all of his retirement savings to pay for the divorce. Ms. X has a 5-year-old van with no outstanding loans.

Family Debts: The family lives in an apartment with a monthly rent equal to one-third of Mr. Zeta's gross monthly income. He can match his employer's 3% addition to his retirement pension and plans to do that from now on. Ms. X has no retirement savings or health, dental, or life insurance. The vehicles must be maintained, insured, and licensed. They would like to have renters' insurance, but haven't filed the paperwork yet.

CASE ASSIGNMENTS

Check the schedule of due dates on the syllabus. These completed assignments will be submitted as attachments to an e-mail. They will be returned ASAP so that you can begin the next case.

Make sure you have your name, the date, and your case family's name at the top left corner of all submitted assignments.

Case 1

You will be entering dollar amounts onto the accompanying budget spreadsheet. When completed, you should have figures in every spot labeled "Case 1." Save this budget sheet to your desktop or to an external drive to use with subsequent cases. Your completed assignment will consist of a copy of that budget sheet and your short report e-mailed to the instructor. Make sure your name is on the spreadsheet and the report.

- To determine the gross annual income of employed adults, visit the website provided in class or www.bls.gov/ncs/ncswage2014. Consider information provided in your case family description. Assume that this family lives in the same community you do (i.e., the city of your educational institution). Do not consider employee taxes at this point. They will be handled in a later case.

- Refer to your case family description and use a calculator to determine all other Case 1 spreadsheet amounts. If your family does not have anything to enter in one of those spots, just enter 0 (zero).

- Use a website or local auto dealership to determine the type of vehicles your case family owns. Based on the value formula in the family description, select the make and model of the vehicles you have imagined for your family members. Print that information and keep it for later reference.

- Visit a local realty website and find a house with a similar value to that of your case family's house. Print that information and keep it for later. If your family is the Zeta family, use a local rental website to find an apartment with at least three bedrooms in your city. Print that information and keep for later.

- If you have the Omega family, determine Mr. Omega's income before he retired and keep it to use at a future time.

- Analyzing the income and outflow of monetary assets, identify current and possible future challenges your case family might face. Discuss any possible advantages your family has, based on both financial and human resources available to them. Be careful not to be judgmental in your report. You will complete this entire budget sheet over the next few weeks, so save all entries from this point on.

Case 2

You have explored the identification of family needs, real and perceived. Society's standards and expectations often help determine the kind of large-scale purchases families make. Homes and automobiles are two examples of this concept. Your case family has made decisions about housing and transportation. They may also have credit card debt or other long-term loan commitments.

Using a debt calculator (bankrate.com or similar sites have these available), determine the monthly payments your family must budget based on their current debt load. *If the case family description does not have specific durations and percentages,* automobile payments should assume 5-year payoff periods and 5% interest. Credit card balances will require your personal estimations for how quickly these balances should and can be paid. Assume an 11% interest rate on all credit card and other revolving balances. Enter these monthly payments on the budget spreadsheet. Calculate their "debt load" by adding all monthly debt payments and dividing by the family's total gross income. Many professionals encourage families to keep that load to under 0.50. Do you think your family has a healthy load? Be objective and avoid being critical. Create a one- to two-page summary of your findings and your professional analysis of the family's debt load. Revisit the information in Chapter 2 about the **symbolic interactionism framework**. How does "impression management" impact your case family's housing, automobile, and general spending decisions?

Case 3

The budget category of "soft goods" includes many types of expenditures. Food and clothing purchase behaviors of families have been researched over time, and while families are unique in their consumption patterns, an overall percentage of income can be used to approximate these expenses for your case family. American families typically spend between 13% and 16% of their gross income on food. This includes both in-home dining and out-of-home dining. Please distribute your estimations of both to the appropriate spreadsheet lines. Remember that school-age children may eat breakfast and lunch at school or may bring their lunches. Visit local school websites for meal prices and explain in your report how you determined these figures. Typically 18% of a family's gross income is spent on clothing and furnishings. Another 1% is spent on personal care items such as cleansers, hair care, laundry, and other hygiene supplies.

To fill in the "Soft Goods" section of your case family budget sheet, first calculate the amounts using the percentages in the previous paragraph. Then cross-check the food amount by creating a 1-week menu/eating plan for your family and estimating the actual cost. Use grocery advertisements to make a shopping list with prices. Multiply this plan by four to see how close it is to the monthly amount you calculated with the percentages given. Make adjustments as you determine might be necessary. Enter the figure you determined using the percentage, the adjusted amount you determined from the food list you created, or something in the range between. Explain fully why you selected the monthly expense entered on your spreadsheet. You also need to split the food amount and put part of that into the dining-out category, explaining this in the report.

In this case report (one to two pages), include your calculations, menu plan with grocery list and prices, and any adjustment justifications you might have made. Revisit the information in Chapter 2 about **family development theory**. Discuss the impact of your case family's "family stage" on their food consumption decisions.

Case 4

Maintaining a home is a complex, continual process. Families will manage and exchange many types of resources to accomplish this. Much of home maintenance can be done by family members if necessary. Contemporary families, however, have accepted the exchange of money for public or private services. For example, families could physically haul the garbage they generate in their homes to the public garbage facilities and pay a small fee to dispose of it there. Or they could subscribe to a garbage pickup service, public or private, and have their garbage physically removed from their home on a regular basis. They can pool their physical attributes and clean the premises and do the laundry themselves, or they can contract those chores out for a fee.

To complete the "Home Expenses" portion of the case family budget sheet, you will decide who is responsible for home maintenance and how often certain services are required. The mortgage, if required, was part of a previous case assignment. "Upkeep" is a general term used to describe physical maintenance requirements, such as exterior and interior painting, repair of the living premises, and any exterior renovations necessary. Renters have very little responsibility for upkeep of their rental unit. Any damage caused by members of the family, however, are the responsibility of the renter. It is wise to anticipate some minor repairs (curtain rods, etc.). Newer homes require less upkeep than older homes. Put at least 5% of the monthly mortgage payment or 1% of the rental payment aside for possible maintenance. Depending on the weather patterns of your location, lawn care, snow removal, and leaf removal will vary. Explore such service providers in your community and determine how much to allot for these things. Explain your decision-making process in this case report.

Renters do not have to pay real estate tax, but homeowners do. To determine the appropriate real estate tax for case families who own homes, access the local county assessor's webpage and obtain the tax rate of your community. Take that and multiply it by your home's total value. That will determine annual tax liability. Divide that amount by 12 and enter that figure in the taxes column of your budget spreadsheet. For the Betas and Omegas, figure 2% of their mortgage payment and enter that under monthly homeowner association fees. Many neighborhoods collect these fees to fund common use areas like tennis courts, signage, and necessary risk insurances.

Utilities vary dramatically from home to home. Families make very different decisions about types of energy to use, types of utilities to subscribe to, and what level of service they will require. Explore utility options on your city's webpage and use information on those utility providers' webpages to estimate your family's monthly utility expenses. Some real estate webpages list average utility consumption with information about homes they are selling. If you can find something similar to your case family's home, this could be helpful. You may also find family and friends to be useful resources when completing this section of the budget. Complete all categories under "Home Expenses." Briefly describe and support your decisions in the report.

Revisit the information about **social exchange theory** in Chapter 2. Briefly discuss how your "family members bring to the family unit personal resources that can be used to maintain that unit" in relation to each family member's ability to contribute to the upkeep and functioning of the home.

Case 5

Your case family has vehicles that are used to transport family members to necessary work sites, appointments, and leisure activities. Families in large metropolitan areas can avoid this expense category when a dependable mass transportation system is available. Fees to use that system would need to be budgeted instead. Most Americans would find the lack of vehicle availability limiting, however.

You have already determined the value and the debt associated with your case family's vehicle(s). Other necessary budget items to maintain automobile ownership and use include fuel, taxes/licensing fees, and repairs/general maintenance. You can estimate fuel costs by calculating average miles driven on a weekly basis and multiplying that by four. Online vehicle sites can provide you with estimated mileage per gallon of fuel. Use these figures to determine approximately how much your family would need to budget for automobile fuel monthly and enter that amount on the budget sheet.

New automobiles usually have a warranty for repairs and recalls. They would require only regular maintenance, such as oil and fluid changes and cleaning. Older vehicles will require additional funds for parts and replacement of tires. Using the information provided in the family description, and accessing online automobile maintenance information or seeking assistance from family or professionals in auto mechanics, determine a reasonable amount your family should set aside monthly to cover these anticipated costs. The Taus must make a decision in this case to either invest 20% of the grandmother's monthly gross income in car repairs, or to purchase a newer vehicle.

Annual taxes and licensing fees vary by location. Check your local governmental office webpage to determine the process for figuring these expenses. Enter those amounts on the budget. Remember to enter monthly budget amounts, not annual.

Using **family systems theory**, explain how your case family's needs for transportation will evolve with time and how such changes will impact, or "ripple" through, the experiences of other family members.

Case 6

As a family and its individual members interact within their social realm, that social group impacts the family decision-making process. Case 6 explores the impact of taxes on a family. Employment taxes are generally figured and subtracted from an employee's check, but it is important for individuals to understand how and why that money does not find its way into the family budget. Using the current Social Security tax and Medicare tax rates (6.2% for Social Security and 1.45% for Medicare), calculate how much will be deducted from the family wages earned. Explore state income tax rates in your area and determine the liability for this as well. Take the gross income of each family member and multiply by that state rate. For ease of application across income levels, assume that the federal income tax rate is 18% (this would actually be determined by reducing the gross income through a series of allowable deductions and searching a tax rate table provided by the government each year).

Gross Income – (Social Security Tax + Medicare Tax + State Tax + Federal Tax) = Income After Taxes

- **If you use annual income, be sure to divide by 12 before entering this calculation amount.**

If family members receive state assistance (as with the Taus), you will need to enter that as monthly income, too.

Entertainment expenses are also part of the family's social interaction. To figure the budget amount needed for this, consider movie theater and concert tickets, cable or streaming services, and other types of entertainment family members may select. Consider the description of your family carefully for clues to what they might enjoy doing.

If your family members belong to clubs, sports teams, or athletic support clubs, visit similar websites to determine what the membership and participation fees would be. Ask friends and family for insights as well. Remember to convert annual fees into monthly amounts before adding information to the spreadsheet.

Travel is a difficult category to estimate. Plan at least one annual family excursion fully and divide that cost by 12 to determine the monthly budget amount needed to fund such travel. Consider holidays, birthdays, and other special events that might require travel expenses.

In this case report, explain the choices you have made for this family and discuss constraints and conflicts you encountered in the process. Being realistic and avoiding passing judgment on this family may be challenging. If this family has more or fewer resources than your family of origin, be objective when considering their expectations.

Applying **family ecological theory**, explore how dramatic changes in the tax system could impact your case family.

From this point forward, the budget spreadsheet will be creating an automatic calculation of "spending money." This figure is the amount remaining as expenses are taken from the family income. It may become negative during the next few cases. Do not adjust it until instructed to do so in Case 10. Continue to make the best decisions for your family as you work through the case information, regardless of whether they have the money available on the spreadsheet.

Case 7

The planning process is an important tool for family resource management. All resources can be used in this process, although the most easily identifiable application is financial planning. You have entered asset values and retirement pension plan balances in Case 2. Case family members who are contributing to retirement plans must also enter monthly contribution information as described in the case details. That amount should be placed under "Savings," retirement. Liquid savings amounts are also presented in the case family information and should appear on the budget sheet as assets. If you believe that your family should be setting aside a certain amount of money each month in savings that can be easily accessed in case of emergency, put that amount on the budget sheet under "Savings" in the liquid spot. Some financial specialists suggest that a family should have 6 months' worth of income in savings as a safety net for large-scale emergencies. How might you accomplish this with a savings plan?

Are there possible large-cost purchases in your family's future? Car? Home? If you believe there may be, how would you suggest they save on a monthly basis to meet these goals?

If your family has children, should the adults be saving money on a regular basis to build a fund for educational expenses in the future? If so, indicate an amount for that purpose under "other" savings. If your family has money in savings that could be used to meet monthly expenses or to pay down credit liabilities, how would you allocate such withdrawals? If there are elderly members of your family, should funds be available for future care needs?

The case report for this assignment should be created in a financial analysis format. Begin by discussing the strengths present in the family's financial plan. Then present immediate and forecasted challenges. Provide practical advice to family members on how they might address these needs with a financial savings plan. Do not assume that the reader of this assignment has any prior knowledge of the family's position. Be thorough and professional in reporting.

Case 8

To complete the "Miscellaneous Expenses" portion of the budget sheet, be realistic and thorough. You have previously looked at the credit card debt and calculated a monthly payment. If you feel this needs adjustment, do so at this time. Explain this in your report. Child support is part of the Zeta family's information, and governmental support is part of the Tau family's situation. There are no outstanding education loans, but if you believe family members should be pursuing educational opportunities, add tuition expenses and explain this in the report. Family pets (when included in the family description) require different levels of care for health and grooming. Fully explain your monthly expense decisions.

Beauty expenses include haircuts, styles, and coloring as well as makeup, skincare products, and manicures and pedicures. Some view these expenses as necessary; others view them a luxuries. Try to decide this based on each family member's social expectations and age. Remember to use monthly figures only. Gifts are also discretionary expenses. Consider both the reasons for giving and the family's resources. Be realistic. Families are invited to weddings, showers, friends' celebrations, and even work-related events that require gift-giving. Estimate yearly ranges and convert these to monthly amounts.

Contributions include any money paid to organizations for support of programming, such as church philanthropies, and public service programs (Humane Society, etc.). Some families set aside a flat percentage annually; others preselect charities and amounts. Some just give when the opportunity presents itself. When financial support is not possible, many individuals donate time and energy. Giving back to others is an important value, and you should assume that these families practice this behavior.

Considering **conflict theory**, discuss how decisions about these discretionary expenses can cause conflict between and among family members.

Case 9

This case assignment will complete the insurance section of the family's budget sheet. Health/medical insurance is available as described in your case family's description. If the adults in your case family have health insurance available, assume that their options are exactly the same as those in UNK's employee benefit package for full-time employees. You can access that on UNK's webpage in the Human Resources area. If more than one adult has insurance available, it is not necessary to carry more than one complete coverage package per family. If the adults in your family are over the age of 63, they are eligible for Medicare. They may choose to continue regular insurance coverage to fill in the "gaps" and deductibles. Read through the options available carefully and select the policy that you think fits your family's needs. Determine the monthly premium required for that coverage and add that to your budget sheet. Divide the family's annual deductible by 12 to make sure it is budgeted and available when needed.

For life insurance, use the same university options. Determine the monthly premiums required for the coverage you wish and add that to the budget sheet. Some case family members may already have life insurance, as described in the family information. If you think they need additional coverage, add that and explain this in the report.

Disability insurance, dental and vision insurance, and accidental death insurance are also available. Explain your choices in the report.

If your case family owns a home, it is advisable that they have insurance coverage. If they have a mortgage, it is mandatory. Find a webpage that does not require you to share your personal information to figure the amount of coverage you need and the monthly premium. Use the home's value (from Case 1) to determine how much coverage you need. If your family rents, they will want insurance to cover their possessions, as the landlord is not required to have that coverage.

Automobile insurance is required in most locations before licensing is allowed. View online links to determine what is required in your community. If there is an outstanding loan, replacement insurance is usually required. Determine the monthly payments necessary to cover all automobiles and enter that figure on your budget sheet.

Explain your decisions thoroughly in this case report and submit an updated budget sheet. You will make all necessary adjustments in the next case to bring the budget into balance.

Case 10

Through the last nine cases, you have been discovering the needs and the resources within your assigned case family. This final case is reserved for you to adjust your budget sheet as necessary to balance it (i.e., to have a positive number on your "spending" line) and to summarize what you have learned about the process of family resource management.

Apply the family strengths framework to your case family as you "reassign" this family to someone new. In a two- to three-page report, provide all the important information about your family and explain the final budget sheet to your successor. Provide insight and suggestions for how that person can continue to strengthen this family's resource management skills.

GLOSSARY

Absenteeism (13): prolonged absence of an owner from his or her property; chronic absence (as from work or school); also, the rate of such absence

Accessibility (1, 6): the ability to obtain something when needed

Accommodate (7): to make fit, suitable, or congruous; to bring into agreement or concord

Adaptive (9): showing or having a capacity for or tendency toward adaptation

Affect regulation (12): self-regulation of emotions

Affective resources (10): resources that relate to feelings, preferences, and values

Affluenza (5): an extreme form of materialism resulting from the excessive desire for material goods

Agentic traits (4): characteristics that focus on independence, control, and completion of tasks, which are more associated with men than with women

Agreement (10): the act or fact of agreeing; harmony of opinion, action, or character

Artificial obsolescence (4, 13): the phenomenon of industry's creating a new need for consumers that produces demand by creating dissatisfaction with past models

Assimilate (5): to take into the mind and thoroughly comprehend; to make similar; to absorb into the culture or mores of a population or group

Attitude (5): a mental position with regard to a fact or state; a feeling or emotion toward a fact or state

Authoritarian parenting (11): parenting with high expectations and low responsiveness

Authoritative parenting (11): parenting with reasonable demands and high levels of responsiveness

Authority (4): (a) a conclusive statement or set of statements (as an official decision of a court); (b) a decision taken as a precedent; (c) testimony; (d) an individual cited or appealed to as an expert

Autonomy (12): self-directing freedom and especially moral independence; a self-governing state

Availability (1): the ability to be used as needed

Baby Boom generation (11): people born between (and including) 1946 and 1964

Bargaining (10): to negotiate over the terms of a purchase, agreement, or contract; to haggle; to come to terms

Barter (7): to trade by exchanging one commodity for another; to trade or exchange

Base period (8): a period of time that is used as a measurement yardstick for economic data; a base period may be a month, a year, or an average of years

Behavior (5): the manner of conducting oneself; anything that an organism does involving action and response to stimulation; the response of an individual, group, or species to its environment

Beneficiary (12): the person designated to receive the income of a trust estate; the person named (as in an insurance policy) to receive proceeds or benefits

Benefit packages (6): services an insurer, a government agency, a health plan, or an employer offers under the terms of a contract

Brainstorming (9): a group problem-solving technique that involves the spontaneous contribution of ideas from all members of the group; the mulling over of ideas by one or more individuals in an attempt to devise or find a solution to a problem

Budget (9): a plan for the coordination of resources and expenditures; the amount of money that is available for, required for, or assigned to a particular purpose

Budgeting (9): allocating funds; planning or providing for the use of funds in detail

Bureaucratic (3): of, relating to, or having the characteristics of a bureaucracy or bureaucrat

Business (1): a commercial or mercantile activity engaged in as a means of livelihood

Cafeteria plans (6): employee benefit plans that allow employees to select among various group programs to best meet their specific needs

Capitalism (5): an economic system characterized by private or corporate ownership of capital goods, by investments that are determined by private decision, and by prices, production, and the distribution of goods that are determined mainly by competition in a free market

Cash value (12): the amount of money paid into a life insurance policy that is available to the consumer

Cautious shift (11): the result of group social influence when individual group members become cautious

Certainty (6): the quality or state of being certain, especially on the basis of evidence

Circumstances (4): conditions, facts, or events accompanying, conditioning, or determining one another

Code of ethics (5): a set of moral principles to guide group behavior

Coexistence (10): to exist together or at the same time; to live in peace with each other, especially as a matter of policy

Cognitive resources (10): mental-skill abilities, such as concentration, memory, problem solving, and reasoning

Cohabitation (1, 2, 14): to live together as or as if a married couple

Collective socialization (6): a process by which children within a community social network are influenced by common behavioral expectations

Commodity (3): an economic good

Communal traits (4): characteristics that are related to forming and maintaining social relationships with others, which are more common for women than for men

Communication (10): a process by which information is exchanged between individuals through a common system of symbols, signs, or behavior

Community property (12): property held jointly by husband and wife

Companionate family (2): a family where husbands and wives were partners who married because they loved each other, rather than out of a sense of moral duty

Competitive symmetry (10): an interaction between two people where both want to define the interaction or dominate

Complementary interaction (10): when each person in an interaction adopts a different tactic of conversation, with one being dominant and the other submissive

Compulsory education (8): schooling required by law

Conceptual framework (2): a framework used in research to outline possible courses of action or to present a preferred approach to a system analysis project; built from a set of concepts linked to a planned or existing system of methods, behaviors, functions, relationships, and objects

Concreteness (6): characterized by or belonging to the immediate experience of actual things or events

Conflict (10): the opposition of persons or forces that gives rise to the dramatic action in a drama or fiction; a state of disagreement or disharmony

Conflict resolution (10): the process of consensus arrived at after discussion of a disagreement between people

Conformity orientation (10): parental assertion of power and control of communication in the family

Consensual families (10): families that stress both the socio- and concept-orientation dimensions of communication, with the result that children are encouraged to explore the world about them, but to do so without disrupting the family's established social harmony

Conservation (13): the preservation of a physical quantity during transformations or reactions

Conspicuous consumption (2): spending large quantities of money, often extravagantly, to impress others

Consumerism (7): the promotion of the consumer's interests

Consumer protection (8): government regulation to protect the interests of consumers, for example, by requiring businesses to disclose detailed information about products

Contingency plan (9): a plan designed to deal with a particular problem, emergency, or state of affairs if it should occur

Conversation orientation (10): a situation where family members of all ages have the freedom to express their opinions openly and freely

Copayment (12): the amount the insured pays in addition to the deductible of any judgment or settlement

Corporate social responsibility (13): the awareness, acceptance, and management of the implications and effects of all corporate decision making

Cultural rituals (4): practices that serve to unite a particular group by preserving cultural identity and heritage

Cultural transmission (4): how culture is passed on through learning from one generation to another

Culture (1): a set of learned beliefs, values, and behaviors of the way of life shared by the members of a society

Currency (7): something (e.g., coins, treasury notes, banknotes) that is in circulation as a medium of exchange

Cyclical unemployment (7): the increase in unemployment that occurs as the economy goes into a slowdown or recession

Deductible (12): the billed amount that is the patient's responsibility before insurance coverage will activate

Deficit (9): an excess of expenditure over revenue; a loss in business operations

Delayed gratification (12): the ability to wait in order to obtain something that one wants

Delegation (12): the assignment of authority and responsibility to another person to carry out specific activities

Demand (7): the quantity of a commodity or service wanted at a specified price and time

Democratic family (2): a family that emerged at the end of the 18th century as a separate and private group in society where mates were selected through preferences and children were nurtured

Dependent (2): a person who relies on another for support

Digital divide (4, 10): the gap between those people and communities who can access and make effective use of information technology and those who cannot

Dimensional model (11): a model of leadership behavior that incorporates the dimensions of dominance, warmth, submissiveness, and hostility

Directional plan (9): a strategic plan that guides the future of decision making

Direct mail marketing schemes (8): misleading marketing programs using advertising that is distributed via the mail system

Disability benefit (8): a benefit paid to active members when they are totally disabled and unable to work at any job for which they are qualified based on education, training, or experience

Discipline (1): an academic area of research and education

Discount (12): a reduction made from the gross amount or value of something; a reduction made from a regular or list price

Distorter (10): an element of communication that convinces the sender and/or the receiver that a message has a hidden meaning

Distributive justice (6): justice dispensed in the community to confer maximum value to those in need through the notions of fairness and consistency

Diversity (1): the inclusion of diverse people (as people of different races or cultures) in a group or organization

Domestic partners (2): the personal relationship between individuals who are living together and sharing a common domestic life together, but are not joined in any type of legal partnership, marriage, or civil union

Durable goods (7): goods that have a life span of 3 or more years

Durable power of attorney (12): a written legal document by which an individual designates another person to act on his or her behalf

Ecolabels (13): labels or logos that indicate that a product has met a set of environmental standards

Economic resources (6, 10): the basic inputs or component parts of an economy, such as land, labor, and capital

Economics (7): a social science concerned chiefly with description and analysis of the production, distribution, and consumption of goods and services

Effectiveness (1): producing a decided, decisive, or desired effect

Efficiency (1): being or involving the immediate agent in producing an effect

Empowerment (12): to give official authority or legal power to

Enabling (12): doing for others what they can and need to do for themselves

Enhancement hypothesis (13): the idea that being able to handle multiple roles results in status, increased self-esteem, and privilege that compensates for the strain

Environmental resources (6): anything an organism needs that can be taken from the environment

Estate (12): the degree, quality, nature, and extent of one's interest in land or other property

Estate planning (12): the process of planning for the efficient transfer of assets at one's death

Esteem needs (4): needs for being respected, having self-respect, and respecting others

Ethics (5): the discipline dealing with what is good and bad and with moral duty and obligation

E-waste (13): electronic waste, including computers, entertainment electronics, mobile phones, and other items that have been discarded by their original users

Executor (12): the person appointed by a testator to execute a will

Expenses (9): payments disbursed to secure a benefit or bring about a result

Extrinsic (12): a characteristic that is not essential or inherent

Family (1, 2): the basic unit in society, traditionally consisting of two parents rearing their children

Family goals (9): broad statements of ideal future conditions that are desired by a family

Family stage (2): an interval of time in which the roles and relationships within the family change in observable ways

Family values (5): values, especially of a traditional or conservative kind, that are held to promote the sound functioning of the family and strengthen the fabric of society

Fashion (7): a distinctive or peculiar and often habitual manner or way; mode of action or operation

Filter (10): a way to convince the sender and receiver that the message wasn't intended in its true form

Financial plan (9): a budgetary planning document reflecting the way an organization plans to use its financial and human resources in a given year

Five-step decision-making process (1): a flexible decision-making framework that incorporates recognizing existing needs, identifying alternatives to fulfill needs, evaluating identified alternatives, selecting and implementing alternatives, and reflecting on and evaluating the alternatives selected

Fixed expenses (9): those expenses that remain the same regardless of circumstances

Flexibility (9): a ready capability to adapt to new, different, or changing requirements

Floaters (12): extended coverage for personal property

Frictional unemployment (7): workers who have decided to leave one job and look for another; typically, frictionally unemployed workers are out of the labor market for short periods of time

Functional value (7): having a practical application or serving a useful purpose

Generations (5): groups born in different time periods

Generation X (11): the generation following the Baby Boom; people born between 1965 and 1980

Genetically modified organism (GMO) (13): any organism whose genetic material has been altered using engineering techniques

Gift tax (12): a graduated federal tax paid by donors on gifts exceeding $10,000 per year, per donor recipient

Goal (9): something that somebody wants to achieve

Grantor (12): somebody from whom something is transferred in a legal transaction

Greening (13): creating a world with minimum negative impact on our environment

Gresham's law of planning (12): a general tendency for programmed activities to overshadow non-programmed activities

Gross family income (9): family income before taxes are removed

Group shift (11): when making decisions as a group, people make decisions differently than they would if they were acting alone

Groupthink (11): conformity in thought and behavior among the members of a group, especially an unthinking acceptance of majority opinions

Head of household (2): the person whose name appears first in the census enumeration of a family or group of people living together

Health insurance (12): insurance against loss caused by sickness or bodily injury

Hierarchy of needs (4): Maslow's theory of motivation, which states that we must achieve lower-level needs, such as food, shelter, and safety, before we can achieve higher-level needs, such as belonging, esteem, and self-actualization

Home insurance (12): an insurance policy that combines insurance on the home and its contents, as well as liability insurance for accidents that may happen at the home

Homogamy (5): purposeful selection of a mate who has similar characteristics to your own

Household (7): a group of individuals occupying a house, apartment, group of rooms, or a single room that is considered a housing unit

Human resources (6): human wisdom, experience, skill, labor, and enterprise

Human rights (5): the rights one has because one is a human being; the right to life, freedom, and human dignity

Hypercoordination (10): when smartphones are used for coordination of activities and the development of group norms through emotional and social communication

Implementation power (6): responsibility for day-to-day decisions

Impression management (2): the process by which people try to control the impressions that other people form of them

Income (9): the amount of money received over a period of time as payment for work, goods, or services, or as profit on capital

Independent activities (9): activities that are unrelated to each other

Industrialization (7): the adoption of industrial methods of production and manufacturing by a country or group, with all the associated changes in lifestyle, transport, and other aspects of society

Inflation (7): an increase in the supply of currency or credit relative to the availability of goods and services, resulting in higher prices

Inheritance (2): the succession of money, property, or a title that has been passed on from generation to generation

Inheritance tax (12): a tax levied on property received by inheritance or legal succession, calculated according to the value of the property received

Insurance (12): an arrangement by which a company gives customers financial protection against loss or harm—for example, theft or illness—in return for payment or premium

Intangible (7): without material qualities, and so not able to be touched or seen

Interactivity (10): the way in which a family communicates

Interchangeable (6): resources that can be exchanged or substituted as a means to gain assets

Interdependent activities (9): activities that are dependent on each other and are sequence-specific

Interfaith (2): involving or occurring between people of different religious faiths

Interiority (13): consideration of ethical and cultural needs before economic considerations

Intermediate goals (9): goals that will be accomplished in less than 1 year

Interpersonal strategies (12): use of assertive communication without dominance to encourage others to be involved

Intersubjectivity (10): communicating shared meanings

Intestate (12): a person who dies owning property without having made a valid will or other binding declaration

Intrinsic (12): a characteristic or property of some thing or action that is essential and specific to that thing or action and that is wholly independent of any other object, action, or consequence

Intuition (9): understanding without apparent effort; quick and ready insight seemingly independent of previous experiences or empirical knowledge

Investment scams (8): illegal programs designed to entice individuals to invest large sums of money in fraudulent funds

Joint ownership with right of survivorship (12): a provision stating that property that is owned by two or more people will pass to the survivor upon the death of one

Labor force (7): people ages 16 years or older who are employed or looking for work

Laissez-faire family (10): a family where members do not communicate with or connect to each other

Laissez-faire leadership (11): a leadership style where the leader allows the followers to have more control over the outcomes of the organization

Leadership (11): the ability of an individual to influence, motivate, and enable others to contribute toward the effectiveness and success of the groups of which they are members

Life insurance (12): a contract between the policy owner and the insurer, where the insurer agrees to pay a sum of money upon the occurrence of the insured's death

Life span (4): the period or length of time in which a person lives

Liquid (7): *see* Liquidity

Liquidity (9): an asset's ability to *quickly* be liquidated or converted through an action of buying or selling without causing a significant movement in the price and with minimum loss of value

Living wage (6): the minimum hourly wage necessary for a person to achieve some specific standard of living

Living will (12): a legal document that covers specific directives as to the course of treatment to be taken by caregivers

Locus of control (12): a theory in psychology that originally distinguished between two types of people: *internals*, who attribute events to their own control, and *externals*, who attribute events in their life to external circumstances

Long-range goals (9): goals that usually require more than 1 year to complete

Manageability (6): something that is capable of being managed or controlled

Managed healthcare (12): a service that is provided by a hospital or other group of clinics, which may be managed by an external company

Management (1): the act of directing and controlling a large group of people for the purpose of coordinating and harmonizing the group toward accomplishing a goal beyond the scope of individual effort

Membership group (11): a group where people belong as a result of birth or life circumstance

Microcoordination (10): when smartphones are used only to coordinate activities

Millennials (6, 11): the generation born in the 1980s and 1990s

Mixed-motive situation (12): a situation where someone's personal actions impact the outcomes of the other group members and the group as a whole

Modern family (2): a family that consists of a bread-winning husband, a housewife, and their children

Money (7): a good or token that functions as a medium of exchange that is socially and legally accepted in payment for goods and services and settlement of debts

Morals (5): ethics, codes, values, principles, and customs of a person or society

Motives (5): a thought pattern with feelings and values that leads to energized behavior

Multitasking (9): a human being's simultaneous handling of multiple tasks

Mutual definition (2): a definition shared by or common to two or more people or groups

Need (4): the psychological feature that arouses an organism to action toward a goal and the reason for the action, giving purpose and direction to behavior

Net income (9): the money available after tax liability is removed from gross income

Net worth (12): the total assets minus total liabilities of an individual or a company

Neutralized symmetry (10): a situation in which neither person in a conversation seeks to be dominant

Nondurable goods (7): items that generally last for only a short time (3 years or less)

Nonrenewable resources (6): resources such as coal, oil, and other fossil fuels that are finite in supply and replaced so slowly that they are soon depleted

Nontraditional family (1): a family that doesn't fit the social norm of the traditional family

Normative resources (10): family power that is given to those within the family who are identified by culture or society as having a particular type of authority

Nuclear family (2): the family group consisting of parents (usually a father and mother) and their children in one household

Objectives (9): specific and measurable means for accomplishing goals

Occupational wellness (13): wellness within the workplace

Old money (5): families that have been wealthy for several generations

Opportunity cost (7): an opportunity forgone; what is lost because a decision is made

Optimization (3): the process of finding the solution that is the best fit to the available resources

Orchestration power (6): responsibility for major decisions that often determine the lifestyle of the family

Orientation (1): an awareness of self in relation to time, place, and person; an integrated set of attitudes and beliefs

Overscheduling (9): family activities where members are too busy; a contemporary problem for many families

Particularistic (6): the exclusive devotion to the interests of one's own group

Permissive parenting (11): parenting with low demands and high responsiveness

Personal goals (9): goals that are specific to the individual

Personality (4): the consistent emotional, thought, and behavior patterns in a person

Personal resources (10): resources that are inherent in the personality or appearance of a family member

Philanthropy (5): the act of donating money, goods, time, or effort to support a charitable cause, usually over an extended period of time and in regard to a defined objective

Physiological needs (4): a person's most basic needs: food, shelter, and clothing

Plan (9): a proposed or intended method of getting from one set of circumstances to another

Planned obsolescence (4): the conscious decision on the part of a manufacturer to produce a consumer product that will become obsolete and/or nonfunctional in a defined timeframe

Planning process (9): a process that begins with a decision and includes identification of a situation that requires action, a formulation of a plan, and the implementation of that plan

Pluralistic family (10): a family that communicates but does not expect everyone to agree

Polygyny (2): the practice of a man having more than one wife at the same time

Postmodern family (2): the contemporary family that is more diverse than in the past in terms of family structure and relationships

Power bases (10): positions where individual family members have power when making decisions that impact other family members

Predispositions (5): inclinations beforehand to interpret statements in a particular way; dispositions in advance to react in a particular way

Preference (7): a real or imagined "choice" between alternatives and the possibility of rank ordering these alternatives, based on the happiness, satisfaction, gratification, enjoyment, and utility they provide

Premiums (12): payments made to an insurance company to buy a policy and to keep it in force

Presenteeism (13): the problems faced when employees come to work in spite of illness, which can have negative repercussions on business performance

Pricing (7): the manual or automatic process of applying prices to purchase and sales orders

Principle of least interest (10): a phenomenon where the partner with the least interest in continuing the relationship has the most power in that relationship

Principle of revealed preferences (14): the inclusion of mental preferences in economic models to explain choices made

Private programs (8): privately funded assistance programs

Proactive plans (9): plans that are designed with forethought and consideration of anticipated events

Probate (12): the legal process of settling the estate of a deceased person

Problem-solving strategies (12): a collection of strategies used to complete the problem-solving process

Production (4): the making or creation of something; the process of manufacturing a product for sale

Protection (9): the act of preventing somebody or something from being harmed or damaged

Protective family (10): a family that does not communicate but expects everyone to follow the rules

Public programs (8): publicly funded assistance programs

Pyramid schemes (8): schemes where participants make money only by recruiting more members

Qualitative research (2): a research method that measures information based on opinions and values as opposed to statistical data; data can be collected through open-ended interviews, review of documents and artifacts, participant observations, or practice

Quality circle (3): a group composed of workers who meet together to discuss workplace improvement and make presentations to management with their ideas

Quantitative research (2): research that examines phenomena through the numerical representation of observations and statistical analysis; data can be collected through structured interviews, experiments, or surveys and are reported numerically

Rapport talk (10): conversation meant to strengthen intimacy; typically used by women

Rationing (4): the controlled distribution of resources and scarce goods or services

Reactive plans (9): plans that are spontaneous and without forethought

Recycling (13): reprocessing of materials into new products

Reference group (11): a self-selected membership from which one receives feedback on his or her actions

Relative deprivation (4): a lack of resources to sustain socially expected levels of status or consumption

Renewable resources (6): resources that can be used and will not be depleted, or those that can be used over and over again

Report talk (10): conversations meant to convey information; typically used by men

Reproduction (4): a copy of something in an earlier style; the act of reproducing something

Resilience (12): the ability to adapt and to move forward

Resource-allocation behavior (6): the outward observable behavior exhibited when people make decisions about how they use resources

Resourcefulness (6): having inner resources; being skillful or imaginative

Resources (1, 6): commodities and human resources used in the production of goods and services; anything identified to meet an existing or future need

Risk (6): the probability of a known loss

Risky shift (11): the group collectively agrees on a course of action that is more extreme than what they would have chosen if asked individually

Safety needs (4): safety and security rank above all other desires and include physical security (safety from violence, delinquency, and aggressions), moral and physiological security, family security, security of health, and security of personal property against crime

Scarcity hypothesis (13): the idea that human energy is limited and, when overloaded, presents conflict that results in guilt and anxiety

Schedule (9): a plan for carrying out a process or procedure, giving lists of intended events and times

School voucher (8): a certificate by which parents are given the ability to pay for the education of their children at a school of their choice, rather than the public school to which they were assigned

Selective interpretation (5): purposeful dissemination of certain information in ways advantageous to the individual

Selective memory (5): purposeful retrieval of certain information while ignoring other information stored in memory

Self-actualization (4): a driving life force that will ultimately lead to maximizing one's abilities and determine the path of one's life

Sequencing (9): doing things in a logical, predictable order

Services (7): the nonmaterial equivalent of a good

Shortage (7): when there is excess demand and limited supply

Short-term goals (9): goals that will be achieved in the near future

Situation (5): the general conditions that prevail in a place or society; the circumstances that somebody is in at a particular moment

Social needs (4): needs related to interaction with other people, including the need for friends, the need for belonging, and the need to give and receive love

Social resources (6): resources that are felt and collectively owned

Social responsibility (13): a sense that consumers must act with concern and sensitivity, being aware of the impact of their actions on others, particularly the disadvantaged

Social wellness (13): being aware of, participating in, and feeling connected to your community

Societal goals (9): goals that are reflected in rules and expectations within larger social groups

Socioeconomic status (4): the hierarchical distinctions between individuals or groups in societies or cultures based on social rank and monetary advantage

Standards (9): a degree or level of requirement, excellence, or attainment

Stop-loss limit (12): the maximum amount under traditional insurance for which benefits are calculated on a proportional basis; after the stop-loss is met, coverage is paid at 100%

Strategic plan (9): a tool used to outline a group's priorities and future goals

Structural unemployment (7): unemployment caused by basic changes in the overall economy, as in demographics, technology, or industrial organization

Submissive symmetry (10): an interaction where each person accepts the other's definition of interaction or submits

Substitute (1, 7): to replace something with another similar product or good

Sufficiency (1): judged as being adequate

Supply (7): a quantity of something on hand or available, as for use

Surplus (7, 9): something that remains above what is used or needed

Survivor benefits (8): Social Security taxes that are used to provide insurance for a worker's family should he or she die

Sustainability (13): to endure without giving way or yielding

Sustainable development (4): any construction that can be maintained over time without damaging the environment; development that balances near-term interests with the protection of the interests of future generations

Symbiotic (7): any interdependent or mutually beneficial relationship between two persons, groups

Symbol (2): something that represents something else by association, resemblance, or convention

Symmetrical conversations (10): conversations that are balanced in regard to dominance

Taste (7): a personal preference or liking

Tax efficiency (9): financial planning that involves consideration of tax liability

Technostress (14): the negative psychological link between people and the introduction of new technologies

Telemarketing (8): solicitation of business using the phone or Internet conferencing

Term insurance (12): low-cost insurance that is valid only for a stated period of time and has no cash surrender value or loan value

Theoretical perspective (2): one's preference for a particular theory

Theory (2): a broad generalization that explains a body of facts or phenomena

Traditional family (2): a married couple and their biological child or children in one household

Transactional leadership (11): guidance based in contingency, in that reward or punishment is contingent on performance

Transferability (6): the quality of being exchangeable

Transformational leadership (11): behavior that is founded on the belief that leaders and followers can raise each other to higher levels of motivation and morality

Trust (12): something committed or entrusted to one to be used or cared for in the interest of another

Uncertainty (6): a perception that ranges from falling short of certainty to an almost complete lack of conviction or knowledge especially about an outcome or a result

Unemployment rate (7): the percentage of people seeking employment but without work at the current time

Uninvolved parenting (11): neglectful parenting characterized by a lack of responsiveness to the child's needs

Universal life insurance (12): a type of flexible permanent life insurance offering the low-cost protection of term life insurance as well as a savings element (like whole life insurance), which is invested to provide cash value buildup

Universal values (5): beliefs existent or operative everywhere or under all conditions

Utility (6): the quality or condition of being useful; usefulness

Value (5): worth in usefulness or importance to the possessor; a principle, standard, or quality considered worthwhile or desirable

Value congruence (5): the degree to which all members of the group agree on values about group processes and group work

Variable expenses (9): costs that are not always consistent and that change due to circumstances within and external to the family

Vegetarian (5): one who subsists on a diet composed primarily or wholly of vegetables, grains, fruits, nuts, and seeds, with or without eggs and dairy products

Vocational (3): relating to, providing, or undergoing training in a special skill to be pursued in a trade or occupation

Volunteerism (6): contributing one's time or talents for charitable, educational, social, political, or other worthwhile purposes, usually in one's community, freely and without regard to compensation

Want (4): something desired, but not necessary

Wellness (13): an interactive process of becoming aware of and practicing healthy choices to create a more successful and balanced lifestyle

Whole life insurance (12): an insurance policy with cash value before it becomes payable upon death or maturity

Will (12): a legally enforceable declaration directing the disposal of a decedent's property

Worldview (1): the common concept of reality shared by a particular group of people, usually referred to as a culture or an ethnic group; an individual as well as a group phenomenon

WEB RESOURCES

CHAPTER 1

www.ncfr.org

CHAPTER 2

www.census.gov

www.childtrends.org/publications/world-family-map-2015-mapping-family-change-and-child-well-being-outcomes

www.irs.gov

CHAPTER 3

www.aafcs.org/

CHAPTER 4

http://menzelphoto.photoshelter.com/gallery/Hungry-Planet-Family-Food-Portraits/G0000zmgWvU6SiKM/C0000k7JgEHhEq0w

http://news.yahoo.com/why-daily-deal-sites-stay-opinion-183659994.html

CHAPTER 5

https://www.census.gov/newsroom/releases/archives/2010_census/cb12-68.html

CHAPTER 6

www.nelp.org

https://www.bls.gov/careeroutlook/2016/data-on-display/education-matters.htm

https://www.ssa.gov

CHAPTER 7

https://www.census.gov/topics/income-poverty/income-inequality/data/data-tables.html

https://www.dol.gov/general/topic/unemployment-insurance

https://www.bls.gov/opub/ted/2015/time-spent-working-by-full-and-part-time-status-gender-and-location-in-2014.htm

https://www.census.gov/housing

CHAPTER 8

www.irs.gov/pub/irs-pdf/fw4.pdf

http://taxfoundation.org

https://www.ssa.gov

www.hhs.gov

https://www.usda.gov

www.fda.gov

https://www.ftc.gov/about-ftc/bureaus-offices/bureau-consumer-protection

https://www.ftc.gov/policy/federal-register-notices/division-consumer-business-education-agency-information-collection

www.ed.gov

CHAPTER 9

https://www.bls.gov/news.release/cesan.nr0.htm

http://www.redcross.org/get-help/prepare-for-emergencies/be-red-cross-ready

CHAPTER 10

https://www.gottman.com/blog/the-four-horsemen-recognizing-criticism-contempt-defensiveness-and-stonewalling

https://www.ftc.gov/enforcement/rules/rulemaking-regulatory-reform-proceedings/childrens-online-privacy-protection-rule

www.wwcd.org/action/ampu/crosscult.html

CHAPTER 12*

https://www.irs.gov/businesses/small-businesses-self-employed/estate-and-gift-taxes

CHAPTER 13

https://www.nal.usda.gov/afsic/organic-productionorganic-food-information-access-tools

https://www.nrcs.usda.gov/wps/portal/nrcs/main/national/about/history

http://www.h2oconserve.org/home.php?pd=index

https://www.epa.gov/

http://www.calrecycle.ca.gov/electronics/act2003

www.pbs.org/newshour/updates/america-e-waste-gps-tracker-tells-all-earthfix

www.today.com/money/millennials-eye-better-work-life-balance-us-ready-6-hour-t54886

CHAPTER 14

http://www.networkworld.com/article/2881908/software/10-obscure-technologies-that-could-change-the-world.html#slide11

www.newsweek.com/internet-making-us-crazy-what-new-research-says-65593

https://www.theguardian.com/sustainable-business/families-of-the-future-brands-marketing

---

* Chapter 11 does not have any web resources.

REFERENCES

Abbott, L. S., & Williams, C. L. (2015). Influences of social determinants of health on African Americans living with HIV in the rural southeast: A qualitative meta-synthesis. *Journal of the Association of Nurses in Aids Care, 26*(4), 340–356.

Adler, J. (2006). Going green. *Newsweek*, 43–52.

Aldrich, N. W. (1996). *Old money: The mythology of wealth in America*. New York, NY: Allworth.

Allport, G. W. (1935). Attitudes. In C. Murchison (Ed.), *A handbook of social psychology* (pp. 798–844). Worchester, MA: Clark University Press.

Amatea, E. S., Smith-Adcock, S., & Villares, E. (2006). From family deficit to family strength: Viewing families' contributions to children's learning from a family resilience perspective. *Professional School Counseling, 9*, 277–313.

Amato, J. (2011, July 5). Why daily deal sites are here to stay. *Mashable*. Retrieved from **http://news .yahoo.com/why-daily-deal-sites- stay-opinion-183659994.html**

Amato, P. R. (2010). Research on divorce: Continuing trends and new developments. *Journal of Marriage and Family, 72*, 650–666.

American Association of Family and Consumer Sciences (AAFCS). (2001). *The essence of family & consumer sciences: State of the profession at the dawn of the 21st century*. Alexandria, VA: Author.

American Federation of State, County and Municipal Employees (AFSCME). (2017). *AFSCME's Comprehensive Guide to Understanding the Family and Medical Leave Act*. Retrieved June 1, 2017, from **www .afscme.org/news/publications/ health-care/afscmes-comprehen sive-guide-to-understanding- the-family-and-medical-leave- act/general-provisions**

American Geriatrics Society. (2016). Fueling future progress for 46 million older adults at 2016: AGS annual scientific meeting. *Science Newsline: Medicine*. Retrieved from **http://www.sciencenewsline.com/ news/2016041312580004.html**

Anderson, G. L. (1997). *The family in global transition*. New York, NY: Paragon House.

Anderson, J. R., & Doherty, W. J. (2005). Democratic community initiatives: The case of overscheduled children. *Family Relations, 54*, 654–665.

Andreasen, M. (2001). Evolution in the family's use of television: An overview. In J. Bryant & J. A. Bryant (Eds.), *Television and the American family* (pp. 3–30). Mahwah, NJ: Lawrence Erlbaum.

Archibold, R. C. (2011, January 13). Haiti: Quake's toll rises to 316,000. *New York Times*. Retrieved June 27, 2017, from **http://www .nytimes.com/2011/01/14/world/ americas/14briefs-Haiti.html**

Arvey, R. D., Segal, N. L., Bouchard, T. J., & Abraham, L. M. (1989). Job satisfaction: Environmental and genetic components. *Journal of Applied Psychology, 74*, 187–192.

Asay, S. M., Younes, M. N., & Moore, T. J. (2006). The cultural transformation model: Promoting cultural competence through international study experiences. *International Family Studies: Developing Curricula and Teaching Tools*, 84–99.

Aulette, J. R. (2002). *Changing American families*. Boston: Allyn & Bacon.

Avery, R. J., & Stafford, K. (1991). Toward a scheduling congruity theory of family resource management. *Lifestyles: Family and Economic Issues, 12*, 325–344.

Avolio, B., Walumbwa, F., & Weber, T. J. (2009). Leadership: Current theories, research, and future directions. *Annual Review of Psychology, 60*, 421–449.

Bade, R., & Parkin, M. (2015). *Essential foundations of economics* (7th ed.). Upper Saddle River, NJ: Pearson.

Bakan, D. (1966). Behaviorism and American urbanization. *Journal of the History of the Behavioral Sciences, 2*, 5–28.

Barbuto, J. E., Fritz, S. M., & Matkin, G. S. (2007). Effects of gender, education, and age upon leaders' use of influence tactics and full range leadership behaviors. *Sex Roles, 56*, 71–83.

Barge, J. K., & Loges, W. E. (2003). Parent, student, and teacher perceptions of parental involvement. *Journal of Applied Communication Research, 31*, 140–163.

Bar-On, R., & Parker, J. (2000). *The handbook of emotional intelligence: Theory, development, assessment, and application at home, school, and in* the workplace. San Francisco, CA: Jossey-Bass.

Barsade, S. G. (2002). The ripple effect: Emotional contagion and its influence on group behavior. *Administrative Science Quarterly*, *47*, 644–677.

Bass, B. M., & Avolio, B. J. (1997). *Full range leadership development: Manual for the multifactor leadership questionnaire*. Redwood City, CA: Mind Garden.

Baumle, A. K. (2009). The cost of parenthood: Unraveling the effects of sexual orientation and gender on income. *Social Science Quarterly*, *90*(4), 983–1002.

Baxter, L. A., & Braithwaite, D. O. (2002). Performing marriage: Marriage renewal rituals as cultural performance. *Southern Communication Journal*, *67*, 94–109.

Beblo, M. (2001). *Bargaining over time allocation economic modeling and econometric investigation of time use within families*. New York, NY: Physica-Verlag.

Becker, G. S. (1991). *A treatise on the family*. Cambridge, MA: Harvard University Press.

Beder, S. (1998). Is planned obsolescence socially responsible? *Engineers Australia*, *52*.

Beecher, C. E. (1869). *The American woman's home*. New York, NY: J. B. Ford.

Bem, D. J. (1972). Self-perception theory. *Advanced Experimental Social Psychology*, *6*, 1–62.

Bennett, F. (2013). Researching within-household distribution: Overview, developments, debates, and methodological challenges. *Journal of Marriage and Family*, *75*, 582–597. doi:10.1111/jomf.12020

Benson, J. J. (2015). Living-apart-together (LAT) relationships. *The Encyclopedia of Adulthood and Aging*. doi:10.1002/9781118521373 .wbeaa261

Bertalanffy, L. V. (1969). *General system theory*. New York, NY: G. Braziller.

Bertocchi, G., Brunetti, M., & Torricelli, C. (2012). *Is it money or brains? The determinants of intra-family decision power*. Bonn, Germany: Institute for the Study of Labor (IZA).

Bickham, D. S., & Rich, M. (2006). Is television viewing associated with social isolation? Roles of exposure time, viewing context, and violent content. *Archives of Pediatrics & Adolescent Medicine*, *160*(4), 387–394.

Biggs, A. (2016). How many Americans are saving for retirement? How many should be? *Forbes*. Retrieved from https:// www.forbes.com/sites/ andrewbiggs/2016/09/20/ how-many-americans-are-sav ing-for-retirement-how-many-should-be/#4aff7f406705

Bindley, K. (2012, June 1). Domestic partner health insurance benefits grow for heterosexual couples, too. *The Huffington Post*. Retrieved from http://www.huff ingtonpost.com/2012/06/01/ domestic-partner-health-insur ance-unmarried-heterosexual-couples_n_1532584.html

Bjornholt, M. (2010). Like father, like son? The transmission of values, family practices, and work-family adaptations to sons of work-sharing men. *Fathering*, *8*, 276–284.

Blackstone, A. (2014). Doing family without having kids. *Sociology Compass*, *8*(1), 52–62.

Blackwell, D. L., & Lichter, D. T. (2004). Homogamy among dating, cohabiting, and married couples. *Sociological Quarterly*, *45*, 719–737.

Blank, W. (2001). *The 108 skills of natural born leaders*. New York, NY: AMACOM.

Blau, F. D., & Kahn, L. M. (2016). *The gender wage gap: Extent, trends, and explanations* (discussion paper No. 9656). Bonn, Germany: Forschungsinstitut zur Zukunft der Arbeit Institute for the Study of labor. Retrieved from http://ftp .iza.org/dp9656.pdf

Block, J. (2015, November 9). As millennials eye better work-life balance, is the US ready for a 6-hour workday? *Today Money*. Retrieved June 28, 2017, from www.today .com/money/millennials-eye-better-work-life-balance-us-ready-6-hour-t54886

Blood, R. O., & Wolfe, D. M. (1960). *Husbands and wives: The dynamics of married living*. Glencoe, IL: The Free Press.

Blum, R. W. (2002). *Mother's influence on teen sex: Connections that promote postponing sexual intercourse*. Minneapolis, MN: Center for Adolescent Health.

Bond, A. E., Mandleco, C. L., & Donnelly, M. (2003). Needs of family members of patients with severe traumatic brain injury: Implications for evidence-based practice. *Critical Care Nurse*, *23*, 63–74.

Bonilla-Silva, E., & Forman, T. A. (2000). I am not a racist but . . . : Mapping white college students' racial ideology in the U.S.A. *Discourse and Society*, *11*, 51–86.

Bonnell, A. (Ed.). (2015). *The state of sustainability in America 2015: Trends and opportunities*. Rockville, MD: Market Research.com.

Bornstein, M. H., Cote, L. R., Haynes, M., Hahn, C.-S., & Park, Y. (2010). Parenting knowledge: Experiential and sociodemographic factors in European American mothers of young children. *Developmental Psychology*, *46*, 1677–1693.

Boscia, T. (2013). Elevating home economics. *Human Ecology*, *41*, 18–21.

Bossard, J. H., & Boll, E. S. (1943). *Ritual in family living*. Philadelphia, PA: University of Pennsylvania Press.

Bowler, D. E., Buyunk-Ali, L. M., Knight, T. M., & Pullin, A. S. (2010). A systematic review of evidence for the added benefits to health of exposure to natural environments. *BMC Public Health, 10,* 456–466. doi:10.1186/1471-2458-10-456

Branden, N. (1995). *The six pillars of self-esteem*. New York, NY: Bantam.

Brazelton, B. T., & Greenspan, S. (2000). Your child—learning: Our window to the future [Special issue]. *Newsweek,* 34–36.

Bristow, D. N., & Mowen, J. C. (1998). The consumer resource exchange model: Theoretical development and empirical evaluation. *Marketing Intelligence & Planning, 16,* 90–99.

Bronfenbrenner, U. (1994). Ecological models of human development. In *International encyclopedia of education* (Vol. 3, 2nd ed.). Oxford , UK: Elsevier.

Brooks, J. (2013). The process of parenting (9th ed.). New York, NY: McGraw-Hill.

Brown, A. (2011). Relationships, community and identity in the new virtual society. *The Futurist, 45*(2), 29–34.

Brown, P. L. (2000). Silicon Valley wealth brings new stresses on children. *New York Times,* p. 1A.

Bryant, C., DeWalt, K., Courtney, A., & Schwartz, J. (2003). *The cultural feast* (2nd ed.). Boston, MA: Thomson Learning.

Bryant, W. K. (1990). *The economic organization of the household*. New York, NY: Cambridge University Press.

Bubolz, M. M., & Sontag, M. S. (1993). Human ecology theory. In P. G. Boss, W. J. Doherty, W. R. LaRossa, W. R. Schumm, & S. K.

Steinmetz (Eds.), *Sourcebook of family theories and methods a contextual approach* (pp. 591–625). New York, NY: Plenum.

Buckley, W. (1967). *Sociology and modern systems theory*. Englewood Cliffs, NJ: Prentice Hall.

Burgess, E., & Locke, H. (1945). *The family: From institution to companionship*. New York, NY: American Book.

Cahn, N., Carbone, J., & Lavine, H. (2016). *Two perspectives on demographic change and the future of the family*. Washington, DC: The Center for American Progress, the American Enterprise Institute, and the Brookings Institution.

Campbell, K., & Christensen, K. (2016). Where does America's e-waste end up? GPS tracker tells all. *PBS Newshour*.

Carnevale, A. P., Rose, S. J., & Cheah, B. (2011). *The college payoff*. Washington, DC: The Center on Education and the Workforce.

Carroll, A. B. (2015). Corporate social responsibility: The centerpiece of competing and complementary frameworks. *Organizational Dynamics, 44,* 87–96.

Catsanos, R., Rogers, W., & Lotz, M. (2013). The ethics of uterus transplantation. *Bioethics, 27,* 65–73.

Caughlin, J. (2003). Family communication standards: What counts as excellent family communication and how are such standards associated with family satisfaction? *Human Communication Research, 29,* 5–40.

Centers for Disease Control and Prevention (CDC). (2015). *Overweight and obesity data and statistics*. Atlanta, GA: Author.

Chelsey, N., Siibak, A., & Wajcman, J. (2013). Information and communication technology use and work-life integration. In D. A. Major & R. Burke (Eds.), *Handbook*

of work-life integration among professionals: Challenges and opportunities (pp. 245–266). Cheltenham, UK: Edward Elgar.

Cherlin, A. J., Talbert, E., & Yasutake, S. (2014). *Changing fertility regimes and the transition to adulthood: Evidence from a recent cohort*. Paper presented at the Annual Meeting of the Population Association of America, Boston, MA.

Chesley, N., & Flood, S. (2017). Signs of change? At-home and breadwinner parents' housework and child-care time. *Journal of Marriage and Family, 79,* 511–534.

Cipriano, P. (2010). Overview and summary: Delegation dilemmas: Standards and skills for practice. *OJIN: The Online Journal of Issues in Nursing, 15*(2). Retrieved from **http://nursingworld.org/Main MenuCategories/ANAMarket place/ANAPeriodicals/OJIN/ TableofContents/Vol152010/No2 May2010/Overview-and-Summary-Delegation-.html**

Clarke, R. (1973). *Ellen Swallows: The woman who founded ecology*. Chicago, IL: Follett.

Cohen, R., & Roosevelt, E. (2002). *Dear Mrs. Roosevelt: Letters from children of the Great Depression*. Chapel Hill: University of North Carolina Press.

Cohen-Cline, H., Turkheimer, E., & Duncan, G. E. (2015). Access to green space, physical activity and mental health: A twin study. *Journal of Epidemiology and Community Health, 69,* 523–529. doi:10.1136/jech-2014-204667

Coleman, D. (2009). Divergent patterns in the ethnic transformation of societies. *Population and Development Review, 35,* 449–478.

Collinge, R. A., & Ayers, R. M. (2000). *Economics by design principles and issues.* Upper Saddle River, NJ: Prentice Hall.

Consumer Reports. (2015). *GMO foods: What you need to know.* Retrieved from http://www.consumerreports.org/cro/magazine/2015/02/gmo-foods-what-you-need-to-know/index.htm

Coontz, S. (2000). Historical perspectives on family studies. *Journal of Marriage and the Family, 62,* 283–297.

Cordry, S., & Wilson, J. D. (2004). Parents as first teacher. *Education, 125,* 56–57.

Corporation for National and Community Service. (2010). *Civic life in America: Key findings on the civic health of the nation.* Washington, DC: Corporation for National and Community Service.

Coverdill, J. E., Lopez, C. A., & Petrie, M. A. (2011). Race, ethnicity, and the quality of life in America, 1972–2008. *Social Forces, 89*(3), 783–805.

Crainer, S. (2000). *The management century: A critical review of 20th century thought and practice.* San Francisco, CA: Jossey-Bass.

Crittenden, A. (2004). *If you've raised kids, you can manage anything: Leadership begins at home.* New York, NY: Gotham Books.

Crosswhite, J. M., Rice, D., & Asay, S. M. (2014). Text messaging among US young adults: An exploratory study on texting and its use within families. *The Social Science Journal, 51*(1), 70–78.

Curtis, K. T., & Ellison, C. (2002). Religious heterogamy and marital conflict. *Journal of Family Issues, 23,* 551–576.

Cushman, E. M. (1945). *Management in homes.* New York, NY: Macmillan.

Davenport, T. H., & Prusak, L. (1998). *Working knowledge: How organizations manage what they know.* Boston, MA: Harvard Business School Press.

Davidhizar, R., & Hart, A. (2006). Are you born a happy person or do you have to make it happen? *The Health Care Manager, 25,* 64–70.

Deacon, F. M., & Firebaugh, R. E. (1975). *Family resource management: Principles and applications.* Boston, MA: Allyn & Bacon.

DeFrain, J., & Asay, S. M. (Eds.). (2007). *Strong families around the world: Strengths-based research and perspectives.* London, UK, and New York, NY: Routledge, Taylor & Francis.

DeFrain, J., & Stinnett, N. (2002). The family strengths perspective. In J. J. Ponzetti (Ed.), *International encyclopedia of marriage and family relationships* (pp. 637–672). New York, NY: Macmillan.

DeHaan, P., & Laskoski, G. (2016). *Gas Buddy fuel price outlook 2016.* Boston, MA: Gas Buddy.

DeLorey, C. (2003). The health consequences of being female or male. *Healthcare Review, 16,* 12.

Desimone, L. (1999). Linking parent involvement with student achievement: Do race and income matter? *Journal of Educational Research, 93*(1), 11.

Deutch, P. J. (2005). Energy independence: High oil prices have everyone talking about energy independence again. *Foreign Policy, 151,* 20–25.

Dewitte, S., & De Cremer, D. (2001). Self-control and cooperation: Different concepts, similar decisions? A question of the right perspective. *Journal of Psychology, 135*(2), 133–154.

Dickson, A. (2004). 2004 catalyst survey: Most top women execs want CEO job. *InnoVisions Canada.* Retrieved from http://www.ivc.ca/studies/us/index.htm

Doherty, W. J. (1997). *The intentional family: How to build family ties in our modern world.* Reading, MA: Addison-Wesley.

Doyal, L., & Gough, I. (1991). *A theory of human need.* New York, NY: Guilford.

Dubner, S. J., & Levitt, S. D. (2009). *Freakonomics.* New York, NY: Harper Perennial.

Dunn, H. L. (1961). *High-level wellness.* Arlington, VA: R.W. Beatty.

Dunn, J. S., Kinney, D. A., & Hofferth, S. L. (2001). *Parental ideologies and children's after-school activities.* Unpublished manuscript, University of Michigan, Alfred P. Sloan Center for the Study of Working Families.

Dupont, H. (1994). *Emotional development, theory and applications: A neo-Piagetian perspective.* Westport, CT: Praeger.

DuPraw, M. E., & Axner, M. (1997). *Working on common cross-cultural communication challenges (toward a more perfect union in an age of diversity).* Retrieved from http://www.pbs.org/ampu/crosscult.html

Eagly, A. H., & Johannesen-Schmidt, M. C. (2001). The leadership styles of men and women. *Journal of Social Issues, 57,* 781–798.

Easterlin, R. (2001). Income and happiness: Towards a unified theory. *Economic Journal, 111,* 465.

Eaves, L. J., Eysenck, H. J., & Martin, N. G. (1989). *Genes, culture, and personality: An empirical approach.* San Diego, CA: Academic Press.

Edgar-Smith, S. E., & Wozniak, R. H. (2010). Family relational values in the parent–adolescent relationship. *Counseling and Values, 54,* 187–200.

Edleson, J. L., & Tan, N. T. (1993). Conflict and family violence: The tale of two families. In P. Boss (Ed.),

Sourcebook of family theories and methods: A contextual approach (pp. 382–384). New York, NY: Plenum.

Edwards, B., Baxter, J., Smart, D., Sanson, A., & Hayes, A. (2009). Financial disadvantage and children's school readiness. *Family Matters, 83*, 23–31.

Edwards, R., & Hamilton, M. A. (2004). You need to understand my gender role: An empirical test of Tannen's model of gender and communication. *Sex Roles: A Journal of Research, 50*(7–8), 491–505.

Eisenkraft, N., & Elfenbein, H. A. (2010). The way you make me feel: Evidence for individual differences in affective presence. *Psychological Science, 21*(4), 505–510.

Elliott, E. D. (2013). *Why the United States does not have a renewable energy policy.* Washington, DC: Environmental Law Institute. Retrieved from https://www.cov .com/~/media/files/corporate/ publications/2013/02/why_the_ united_states_does_not_have_a_ renewable_energy_policy.pdf

Engelking, C. (2016, June 10). Goodbye to night: 80 percent of humanity lives under light polluted skies. *Discover: Science for the Curious.*

Environmental Protection Agency (EPA). (2015). *Advancing sustainable materials management: 2013 fact sheet.* Washington, DC: Author. Retrieved from https://www.epa .gov/sites/production/ files/2015-09/documents/2013_ advncng_smm_fs.pdf

Environmental Protection Agency (EPA). (2016). *EPA honors 2016 Energy Star partners of the year for outstanding achievements in energy efficiency.* Washington, DC: Author. Retrieved from https://www.epa .gov/newsreleases/epa-honors- 2016-energy-star-partners- year-outstanding-achievements- energy-efficiencyin

Epp, A. M., & Velagaleti, S. R. (2014). Outsourcing parenthood: How families manage care assemblages using paid commercial services. *Journal of Consumer Research, 41*(4), 911–935. doi:10.1086/677892

Erikson, E. H. (1963). *Childhood and society.* New York, NY: Norton.

Fayol, H. (1949). *General and industrial management.* London, UK: Pitman.

Feather, N. T. (1990). Bridging the gap between values and actions: Recent applications of expectancy-value model. In R. M. Sorrentino & E. T. Higgins (Eds.), *Handbook of motivation and cognition foundations of social behavior* (pp. 151–192). New York, NY: Guilford.

Featherman, D. (1980). Schooling and occupational careers: Constancy and change in worldly success. In O. G. Brim & J. Kagan (Eds.), *Constancy and change in human development* (pp. 675–738). Cambridge, MA: Harvard University Press.

Federal Communications Commission (FCC). (2014). *Report of Technological Advisory Council Subcommittee on mobile device theft protection* (version 1.0). Washington, DC: Author.

Feldman, D., Wall, M., Hosea, J., Banker, L., & Ponce, J. (2015). *The millennial impact report: Cause, influence & the next generation work force.* West Palm Beach, FL: Achieve. Retrieved June 22, 2017, from www.themillennialimpact.com/ sites/default/files/reports/2015- MillennialImpactReport_01_0 .pdf

Feldman, Y., & Perez, O. (2012). Motivating environmental action in a pluralistic regulatory environment: An experimental study of framing, crowding out, and institutional effects in the context of recycling policies. *Law and Society Review, 42*(2), 405–442. doi:10.1111/j.1540- 5893.2012.00493.x

Feldstein, S. W., & Miller, W. R. (2006). Substance use and risk-taking among adolescents. *Journal of Mental Health, 15*(6), 633–643.

Fiedler, F. E. (1967). *A theory of leadership effectiveness.* New York, NY: McGraw-Hill.

Fishbein, M., & Ajzen, I. (1975). *Belief, attitude, intention, and behavior: An introduction to theory and research.* Reading, MA: Addison-Wesley.

Fishbein, M., & Ajzen, I. (1980). *Understanding attitudes and predicting social behavior.* Englewood Cliffs, NJ: Prentice Hall.

Fishbein, M., & Ajzen, I. (2010). *Predicting and changing behavior: The reasoned action approach.* New York, NY: Psychology Press.

Fitzpatrick, M. A. (1988). *Between husbands and wives: Communication in marriage.* Newbury Park, CA: Sage.

Fitzpatrick, M. A., & Ritchie, L. D. (1994). Communication schemata within the family: Multiple perspectives on family interaction. *Human Communication Research, 20*, 275–301.

Fleishman, F. E. (1953). Leadership climate, human relations training, and supervisory behavior. *Personnel Psychology, 6*, 205–222.

Foa, U. G. (1971). Interpersonal and economic resources. *Science, 171*, 345–351.

Foa, U. G. (1993). *Resource theory: Explorations and applications.* San Diego, CA: Academic Press.

Folbre, N. (2001). *The invisible heart: Economics and family values.* New York, NY: New Press.

Forgays, D. K. (1996). The relationship between type A parenting and adolescent perceptions of family environment. *Adolescence, 31*, 841–862.

Fox, J. J., & Bartholomae, S. (2000). Economic stress and families. In

P. C. McKenry & S. J. Price (Eds.), *Families and change: Coping with stressful events and transitions* (pp. 250–278). Thousand Oaks, CA: Sage.

Galbraith, K. A., & Schvaneveldt, J. D. (2005). Family leadership styles and family well-being. *Family and Consumer Sciences Research Journal, 33,* 220–239.

Galvin, K. M., Bylund, C. L., & Brommel, B. J. (2004). *Family communication: Cohesion and change* (6th ed.). Boston, MA: Allyn and Bacon.

Galvin, K. M., Bylund, C. L., & Brommel, B. J. (2012). *Family communication: Cohesion and change* (8th ed.). Boston, MA: Allyn and Bacon.

Gasana, P. U. (2009). Relative status and interdependent effects in consumer behavior. *The Journal of Socio-Economics, 38,* 52–59.

Gentzler, Y. S. (2012). Home economics: Ever timely and forever complex. *Phi Kappa Phi FORUM,* 5–7.

Gerbner, G., Gross, M., Signorielli, N., & Shanahan, J. (2002). Growing up with television: Cultivation processes. In J. Bryant & D. Zillmann (Eds.), *Media effects: Advances in theory and research* (2nd ed., pp. 43–67). Mahwah, NJ: Lawrence Erlbaum.

Gerlagh, R., & Sterner, T. (2013). Rio+20: Looking back at 20 years of environmental and resource economics. *Environmental and Resource Economics, 54,* 155–159. doi:10.1007/s10640-012-9627-6

Ghazavi, Z., Minooei, M. S., Abdeyazdan, Z., & Gheissari, A. (2014). Effect of family empowerment model on quality of life in children with chronic kidney diseases. *Iranian Journal of Nursing and Midwifery Research, 19,* 371–375.

Giacquinta, J. B., Bauer, J. A., & Levin, J. E. (1993). *Beyond technology's promise: An examination of children's educational computing at home.* New York, NY: Cambridge University Press.

Gibbs, T., & Campbell, J. (1999). Practicing polygyny in black America: Challenging definition. *The Western Journal of Black Studies, 23,* 144–153.

Gillespie, M. D. (2013). The economic deterioration of the family: Historical contingencies preceding the great recession. *American Journal of Economics and Sociology, 72*(2), 329–360. doi:10.1111/ajes.12007

Goethals, G. R. (2003). A century of social psychology. In M. A. Hogg & J. Cooper (Eds.), *The Sage handbook of social psychology* (pp. 3–23). Thousand Oaks, CA: Sage.

Goode, J. (2010). Mind the gap: The digital dimension of college access. *The Journal of Higher Education, 81*(5), 583–618.

Gordon, L. (1979). The struggle for reproductive freedom: Three stages of feminism. In Z. R. Eisenstein (Ed.), *Capitalist patriarchy and the case for socialist feminism* (pp. 107–136). New York, NY: Monthly Review Press.

Gottman, J. (1995). *Why marriages succeed or fail and how you can make yours last.* New York, NY: Simon & Schuster.

Gottman, J., & Notarius, C. (2000). Decade review: Observing marital interaction. *Journal of Marriage and Family, 62,* 927–947.

Gough, E. K. (1971). The origin of the family. *Journal of Marriage and Family, 33,* 760–771.

Gracia, P., & Kalmijn, M. (2016). Parents' family time and work schedules: The split-shift schedule in Spain. *Journal of Marriage and Family, 78,* 401–415.

Graham, M. (2011). Time machines and virtual portals: The spatialities of the digital divide. *Progress in Development Studies, 11*(3), 211–227.

Green, C. (2008). The importance of delegation. *EzineArticles.* Retrieved from http://ezinearticles.com/?The-Importance-of-Delegation&id=192169

Greenberg, P. E., Fournier, A., Sisitsky, T., Pike, C. T., & Kessler, R. C. (2015). The economic burden of adults with major depressive disorder in the United States (2005 and 2010). *Journal of Clinical Psychiatry, 76*(2), 155–162. doi:10.4088/JCP.14m09298

Greenfield, R. (2016, May 10). The six-hour workday works in Europe. What about America? *Bloomberg.* Retrieved June 28, 2017, from www.bloomberg.com/news/articles/2016-05-10/the-six-hour-workday-works-in-europe-what-about-america

Greenhouse, S. (2001, January 29). Problems seen for teenagers who hold jobs. *New York Times,* pp. A1, A22.

Griep, Y., Hyde, M., Vantilborgh, T., Bidee, J., DeWitte, H., & Pepermans, R. (2014). Voluntary work and the relationship with unemployment, health and well-being. A two-year follow-up study contrasting a materialistic and psychosocial pathway perspective. *Journal of Occupational Health Psychology, 20,* 190–204. doi:10.1037/a0038342

Griffith, B. A., & Graham, C. C. (2004). Meeting needs and making meaning: The pursuit of goals. *Journal of Individual Psychology, 60,* 25–41.

Griskevicius, V., Tybur, J. M., & Van den Burgh, B. (2010). Going green to be seen: Status, reputation, and conspicuous conservation. *Journal of Personality and Social Psychology, 98*(3), 392–404. doi:10.1037/a0017346

Grosswald, B. (2003). Shift work and negative work-to-family spillover. *Journal of Sociology and Social Welfare, 30,* 31–56.

Gupta, S. (1999). The effects of transitions in marital status on men's performance of housework. *Journal of Marriage and the Family, 61,* 700–711.

Guryan, J., Hurst, E., & Kearney, M. (2008). Parental education and parental time with children. *Journal of Economic Perspectives, 22*(3), 23–46.

Gutis, P. S. (1989). Family redefines itself, and now the law follows. *New York Times*, p. 6.

Haber, D. (2002). Wellness general of the United States: A creative approach to promote family and community health. *Family and Community Health, 25*, 71–83.

Habibi, M. R., Laroche, M., & Richard, M. (2016). Testing an extended model of consumer behavior in the context of social media-based brand communities. *Computers in Human Behavior, 62*, 292–302.

Hagelskamp, C., Hughes, D., Yoshikawa, H., & Chaudry, A. (2011). Negotiating motherhood and work: A typology of role identify associations among low-income, urban women. *Community, Work & Family, 14*(3), 335–366.

Hamilton, I. (Ed.). (1992). *Resources and industry*. New York, NY: Oxford University Press.

Hands, B. P., Chivers, P. T., Parker, H. E., Beilin, L., Kendall, G., & Larkin, D. (2011). The associations between physical activity, screen time and weight from 6 to 14 yrs: The Raine study. *Journal of Science and Medicine in Sport, 14*(5), 397–403.

Hanes, S. (2009, June 14). How the recession is reshaping the American family. *The Christian Science Monitor*.

Hargreaves, A. (2003). *Teaching in the knowledge society: Education in the age of insecurity*. New York, NY: Teachers College Press.

Harris, J. L., Schwartz, M. B., & Speers, S. E. (2011). Child and adolescent exposure to food and beverage brand appearances during prime-time television programming. *American Journal of Preventative Medicine, 41*(3), 291–296.

Hawley, A. H. (1986). *Human ecology: A theoretical essay*. Chicago, IL: University of Chicago Press.

Heckert, T. M., Droste, H. E., Adams, P. J., Griffin, C. M., Roberts, L. L., Mueller, M. A., & Wallis, H. A. (2002). Gender differences in anticipated salary: Role of salary estimates for others, job characteristics, career path, and job inputs. *Sex Roles, 47*(3–4), 139–152.

Heller, R. (1998). *Making decisions*. New York, NY: DK Publishing.

Henley, W., Lamond, E., Cunningham, W., & Grosseteste, R. (1890). *Walter of Henley's husbandry*. London, UK: Longmans, Green.

Henry, P. J. (2011). The role of group-based status in job satisfaction: Workplace respect matters more for the stigmatized. *Social Justice Research, 24*(3), 231–238.

Hersch, P. (1998). *A tribe apart: A journey into the heart of American adolescence*. New York, NY: Fawcett Columbine.

Hersey, P., Blanchard, K. H., & Johnson, D. E. (1992). *Management of organizational behavior: Leading human resources* (6th ed.). Upper Saddle River, NJ: Prentice Hall.

Hertlein, K. M. (2012). Digital dwelling: Technology in couple and family relationships. *Family Relations, 61*, 374–387.

Hesiod. (1999). *Theogony: Works and days* (M. L. West, Trans.). Oxford, UK: Oxford University Press.

Hess, B. B. (1995). *Sociology*. New York, NY: Allyn & Bacon.

Hill, R. (1971). Modern systems theory and the family: A confrontation. *Social Science Information, 10*, 7–26.

Hochachka, G. (2005). Integrating interiority in community development. *World Futures, 61*, 110–126.

Hochschild, A. R. (2012). *The outsourced self: Intimate life in market times*. New York, NY: Metropolitan.

Hofferth, S. L. (2003). Parental ideologies and children's after-school activities. *American Behavioral Scientist, 26*, 1359–1387.

Hornby, G., & Lafaele, R. (2011). Barriers to parental involvement in education: An explanatory model. *Educational Review, 63*(1), 37–52.

House, R. J. (1971). A path–goal theory of leader effectiveness. *Administrative Science Quarterly, 16*, 321–338.

Howitt, R. (2001). *Rethinking resource management: Justice, sustainability and indigenous peoples*. New York, NY: Routledge.

Hsiung, R. O., & Bagozzi, R. P. (2003). Validating the relationship qualities of influence and persuasion with the family. *Human Communication Research, 29*, 81–111.

Huffington Post. (2014). *What education of the future will look like*. Retrieved from **http://www.huffingtonpost .com/2014/07/25/education-of-the-future_n_5549193.html**

Hughes, D., & Campbell, P. (1998). *Kids alone: Protecting your children in cyberspace*. Grand Rapids, MI: Revell.

Hughes, K. (2006). *The short life and long times of Mrs. Beeton*. Oxford, UK: Oxford University Press.

Hyde, P., & Thomas, A. B. (2003). When a leader dies. *Human Relations, 56*, 1005–1024.

Hymowitz, K., Carroll, J. S., Wilcox, W. B., & Kaye, K. (2013). *Knot yet: The benefits and costs of delayed marriage in America*. Charlottesville, VA: The National Marriage Project.

Illich, I. (1978). *Toward a history of needs*. New York, NY: Pantheon.

Irvin, B. L., & Acton, G. J. (1996). Stress mediation in caregivers of cognitively impaired adults: Theoretical model testing. *Nursing Research, 45*(3), 160–166.

Isaac, M., & Ember, S. (2016, November 8). For election day influence, Twitter ruled social media. *New York Times*.

Jackson, L. A., von Eye, A., Biocca, F. A., Barbatsis, G., Zhao, Y., & Fitzgerald, H. E. (2006). Does home Internet use influence the academic performance of low-income children? *Developmental Psychology, 42*(3), 429–435.

Jackson, T., Weiss, K. E., Lundquist, J. J., & Soderlind, A. (2002). Perceptions of goal-directed activities of optimists and pessimists: A personal projects analysis. *Journal of Psychology, 136*(5), 521–533.

Jafarov, J. (2015). Factors affecting parental involvement in education: The analysis of literature. *Khazar Journal of Humanities and Social Sciences, 18*(4), 35–44.

Janis, I. L. (1972). *Victims of group-think*. Boston, MA: Houghton Mifflin.

Janis, I. L. (1982). *Groupthink: Psychological studies of policy decisions and fiascoes*. Boston, MA: Houghton Mifflin.

Janis, I. L. (1989). *Crucial decisions: Leadership and policy making in crisis management*. New York, NY: The Free Press.

Janis, I. L., & Mann, L. (1977). *Decision making: A psychological analysis of conflict, choice, and commitment*. New York, NY: The Free Press.

Jenkins, N. H. (2002). *You paid how much for that?! How to win at money without losing at love*. San Francisco, CA: Jossey-Bass.

Johnson, B. R., & Jacobsen, C. K. (2005). Contact on context: An examination of social settings on whites' attitudes toward inter-racial marriage. *Social Psychology Quarterly, 68*(4), 387–400.

Johnson, D. S., Rogers, J. M., & Tan, L. (2001). A century of family budgets in the United States. *Monthly Labor Review, 124*(5), 28.

Johnson, L. (1998). *Strengthening family and self*. Tinley Park, IL: Goodheart-Willcox.

Kanter, R. M. (1985). *The change masters*. New York, NY: Simon & Schuster.

Kantrowitz, M. (2016, January 10). Why student loan crisis is even worse than people think. *Time*. Retrieved from http://time.com/money/4168510/why-student-loan-crisis-is-worse-than-people-think

Kennedy, L. (1991). Farm succession in modern Ireland: Elements of a theory of inheritance. *Economic History Review, 44*, 477–499.

Kenrick, D. T., Griskevicius, V., Neuberg, S. L., & Schaller, M. (2010). Renovating the pyramid of needs: Contemporary extensions built upon ancient foundations. *Perspectives on Psychological Science, 5*(3), 292–314.

Keown, A. J. (2003). *Personal finance: Turning money into wealth*. Upper Saddle River, NJ: Prentice Hall.

Kerr, D. C. R., Capaldi, D. M., & Pears, K. C. (2009). A prospective three-generational study of fathers' constructive parenting: Influences from family of origin, adolescent adjustment, and offspring temperament. *Developmental Psychology, 45*(5), 1257–1275.

Key, R. J., & Firebaugh, F. M. (1989). Family resource management: Preparing for the 21st century. *Journal of Home Economics, 81*, 13–17.

King, K., & Ogle, C. (2014). Negative life events vary by neighborhood and mediate the relation between neighborhood context and psychological well-being. *PLOS ONE, 9*(4). doi:10.1371/journal.pone.0093539

Kluckhohn, F. R., & Strodtbeck, F. L. (1961). *Variations in value orientations*. Evanston, IL: Row, Peterson.

Knoll, M. M. (1963). Toward a conceptual framework in home management. *Journal of Home Economics, 55*, 335–339.

Koerner, A. K., & Fitzpatrick, M. A. (1997). Family type and conflict: The impact on conversation orientation and conformity orientation on conflict in the family. *Communication Studies, 48*, 59–74.

Koerner, A. K., & Fitzpatrick, M. A. (2002). Toward a theory of family communication. *Communication Theory, 12*, 70–91.

Kohlberg, L. (1984). *The psychology of moral development the nature and validity of moral stages*. New York, NY: Harper & Row.

Konikow, L. F. (2013). *Groundwater depletion in the United States (1900–2008)*. Reston, VA: U.S. Department of the Interior, U.S. Geological Survey.

Kotkin, J., & Cox, W. (2015, December 17). The cities doing the most to address the U.S. housing shortage. *Forbes*. Retrieved from http://www.forbes.com/sites/joelkotkin/2015/12/17/the-cities-doing-the-most-to-address-the-u-s-housing-shortage/#1b66d45f7430

Kotkin, J., Cox, W., Schill, M., & Modarres, A. (2015). *Building cities for people*. Orange, CA: Chapman University Press, Center for Demographics and Policy.

Kranichfeld, M. L. (1987). Rethinking family power. *Journal of Family Issues, 8*, 42–56.

Kroesche, M. (2002). *Home economics through the years: 1898–2002*. Lincoln: University of Nebraska Press.

Kurtines, W. M., & Gewirtz, J. L. (Eds.). (1991). *Handbook of moral behavior and development*. Hillsdale, NJ: Lawrence Erlbaum.

Kurtz Landy, C., Sword, W., & Ciliska, D. (2008). Urban women's socioeconomic status, health service needs and utilization in the four weeks after postpartum hospital discharge: Findings of a Canadian cross-sectional survey. *BMC Health Services Research*, *8*(203), 1–9.

Laboy, S., & Hirsch, J. M. (2013, October 17). As US demographics change, so does the menu. *AP News*.

Lacy, E. (2006). University study dispels myths about state's Mexican immigrants. *USC News*. Retrieved from http://uscnews.sc.edu/2006/FORL330.html

Lalich, J., & Tobias, M. (2006). *Take back your life: Recovering from cults and abusive relationships*. Berkeley, CA: Bay Tree.

Lam, N. M., & Graham, J. L. (2007). *China now: Doing business in the world's most dynamic market*. New York, NY: McGraw-Hill.

Lamanna, M. A., Riedmann, A. C., & Stewart, S. D. (2015). *Marriages, families, and relationships: Making choices in a diverse society* (12th ed.). Belmont, CA: Wadsworth.

Langholtz, H., Marty, A., Ball, C., & Nolan, E. (2003). *Resource allocation behavior*. New York, NY: Kluwer Academic Press.

Langone, C. A. (2004). The use of a citizen leader model for teaching strategic leadership. *Journal of Leadership Education*, *3*(1), 82–88.

Lareau, A. (2007). *Unequal childhood: Class, race, and family life*. Berkeley: University of California Press.

LaRossa, R., & Reitzes, D. C. (1993). Symbolic interactionism and family studies. In P. Boss, W. J. Doherty, L. LaRossa, W. R. Schumm, & S. K. Steinmetz (Eds.), *Sourcebook of family theories and methods: A contextual approach* (pp. 135–162). New York, NY: Plenum.

Larson, V. (2011, November 26). Politics, divorce and infidelity: An unhappy marriage? *The Huffington Post*. Retrieved from http://www.huffingtonpost.com/vicki-larson/post_2661_b_1099186.html#s277211&title=19621980

Lauer, S., & Yodanis, C. (2011). Individualized marriage and the integration of resources. *Journal of Marriage and Family*, *73*, 669–683.

Laverie, D. A., Kleine, R. E., & Schultz, S. (2002). Re-examination and extension of Kleine, Kleine, and Kernan's social identity model of mundane consumption: The mediating role of the appraisal process. *Journal of Consumer Research*, *28*, 1–25.

LeBlanc, R. (2016, April 30). Who recycles more, young or old? *The Balance*. Retrieved from https://www.thebalance.com/who-recycles-more-young-or-old-2877918

Lee, Y.-K., Chang, C.-T., Cheng, Z.-H., & Lin, Y. (2016). Helpful-stressful cycle? Psychological links between type of mobile phone user and stress. *Behaviour & Information Technology*, *35*(1), 75–86. doi:10.1080/0144929X.2015.1055800

Lefton, R. E., & Buzzotta, V. R. (2004). *Leadership through people skills*. London, UK: McGraw-Hill.

Lemonick, M. D., Bjerklie, D., Park, A., & Thompson, D. (1999). Designer babies. *Time*, 64–67.

Lenhart, A. (2015). *Teens, social media & technology overview 2015*. Washington, DC: Pew Research Center.

Lenski, G. E., Nolan, P., & Lenski, J. (1995). *Human societies: An introduction to macrosociology*. New York, NY: McGraw-Hill.

Levinson, D. J. (1978). *The seasons of a man's life*. New York, NY: Knopf.

Levinson, D. J. (1990). A theory of life structure development in adulthood. In C. N. Alexander &

E. J. Langer (Eds.), *Higher states of human development* (pp. 35–54). New York, NY: Oxford University Press.

Lewton, A., & Nievar, M. A. (2012). Strengthening families through volunteerism: Integrating family volunteerism and family life education. *Marriage & Family Review*, *48*, 691–712.

Likert, R. (1961). *New patterns of management*. New York, NY: McGraw-Hill.

Likert, R. (1967). *The human organization*. New York, NY: McGraw-Hill.

Lindahl, K. M., & Malik, N. M. (1999). Observations of marital conflict and power. *Journal of Marriage and Family*, *61*, 320–330.

Ling, R., & Yttri, B. (1999). "Nobody sits at home and waits for the telephone to ring": Micro and hyper-coordination through the use of the mobile telephone. *Perpetual Contact*, *30*, 1–27. Retrieved from http://www.mendeley.com/research/nobody-sits-home-and-waits-for-the-telephone-to-ring-micro-and-hypercoordination-through-the-use-of-the-mobile-telephone

Litman, T. (2011). *Appropriate response to rising fuel prices: Citizens should demand, "Raise my prices now!"* Victoria, BC: Victoria Transport Policy Institute. Retrieved from http://www.vtpi.org/fuelprice.pdf

Lundberg, S., Pollak, R. A., & Stearns, J. (2016). Family inequality: Diverging patterns in marriage, cohabitation, and childbearing. *The Journal of Economic Perspectives*, *30*(2), 79–101.

Luthans, F., & Avolio, B. J. (2003). Authentic leadership: A positive developmental approach. In K. S. Cameron, J. E. Dutton, & R. E. Quinn (Eds.), *Positive organizational scholarship: Foundations of a new discipline* (pp. 241–258). San Francisco, CA: Berrett-Koehler.

Lynch, J., Smith, G. D., Harper, S., Hillemeier, M., Ross, N., Kaplan, G. A., & Wolfson, M. (2004). Is income inequality a determinant of population health? Part 1. A systematic review. *Milbank Quarterly*, *82*, 5–96.

Lynch, L. (2015). *Attorney General Lynch announces federal marriage benefits available to same-sex couples nationwide*. Washington, DC: U.S. Department of Justice.

Lynch, S., Hurford, D. P., & Cole, A. (2002). Parental enabling attitudes and locus of control of at-risk and honors students. *Adolescence*, *37*, 527–560.

Macdonald, M. (1995). Feminist economics: From theory to research. *The Canadian Journal of Economics*, *28*, 159–176.

Mannes, G. (2006). Getting back to business: After time off to raise kids, returning to work can solve a host of problems. First step: Rebuild your network. *Money*, *35*(2), 39.

Manning, G. L., & Reece, B. L. (2001). *Selling today creating customer value* (9th ed.). Upper Saddle River, NJ: Prentice Hall.

Marling, K. A. (1994). *As seen on TV: The visual culture of everyday life in the 1950s*. Cambridge, MA: Harvard University Press.

Marshall, C., & Rossman, G. (1995). *Designing qualitative research*. Thousand Oaks, CA: Sage.

Martinez-Torteya, C., Bogat, G. A., Von Eye, A., & Levendosky, A. A. (2009). Resilience among children exposed to domestic violence: The role of risk and protective factors. *Child Development*, *80*(2), 562–577.

Marvin, K. C. (2017). Health information technology: Integration, patient empowerment, and Security. *American Journal of Health-System Pharmacy*, *74*, 36–38.

Marx, K., & Engels, F. (1967). *Capital*. New York, NY: International

Publishers. (Original work published 1867)

Maslow, A. H. (1954). *Motivation and personality*. New York, NY: Harper & Row.

Maslow, A. H., & Frager, R. (1987). *Motivation and personality* (Rev. ed.). New York, NY: Harper & Row.

Maslow, A. H., Stephens, D. C., & Heil, G. (1998). *Maslow on management*. New York, NY: Wiley.

Matheny, K. B., & Curlette, W. L. (2010). A brief measure of coping resources. *Journal of Individual Psychology*, *66*(4), 384–407.

Maupin, M. A., Kenny, J. F., Hutson, S. S., Lovelace, J. K., Barber, N. L., & Linsey, K. S. (2014). *Estimated use of water in the United States in 2010*. Reston, Virginia: U.S. Department of the Interior, U.S. Geological Survey.

Maxwell, J. C. (2003). *Attitude 101: What every leader needs to know*. Nashville, TN: Thomas Nelson Publishers.

Mazurkewich, K. (2010). Mothers who take parental leave see lower wages. *National Post*. Retrieved from http://www.nationalpost.com/Mothers+take+parental+leave+lower+wages+report/3658218/story.html

McCain, J. (2010). National history and universal values: Prioritizing human rights in U.S. foreign policy. *Brown Journal of World Affairs*, *16*, 9–14.

McCracken, G. D. (1988). *Culture and consumption new approaches to the symbolic character of consumer goods and activities*. Bloomington, IN: Indiana University Press.

McDermott, C. J. (2004). *Economics in real time: A theoretical reconstruction*. Ann Arbor, MI: University of Michigan Press.

McDonald, G. W. (1980). Family power: The assessment of a decade

of theory and research, 1970–1979. *Journal of Marriage and Family*, *42*, 841–854.

McGregor, D. (1960). *The human side of enterprise*. New York, NY: McGraw-Hill.

Mead, G. H. (1964). *On social psychology*. Chicago, IL: University of Chicago Press.

Menzel, P., & D'Aluisio, F. (2005). *Hungry planet: What the world eats*. Napa, CA: Material World Press.

Merriam, S. B., Cafferella, R. S., & Baumgartner, L. M. (2007). *Learning in adulthood: A comprehensive guide*. San Francisco, CA: Wiley.

Merton, R. K., & Kitt, A. S. (1950). Contributions to the theory of reference group behavior. In R. K. Merton & P. F. Lazarsfeld (Eds.), *Studies in the scope and method of "The American soldier"* (pp. 40–105). Glencoe, IL: The Free Press.

Meyers, S. A., Varkey, S., & Aguirre, A. M. (2002). Ecological correlates of family functioning. *The American Journal of Family Therapy*, *30*, 257–273.

Mian, A., & Sufi, A. (2014). *House of debt: How they (and you) caused the Great Recession, and how we can prevent it from happening again*. Chicago, IL: University of Chicago Press.

Miles, D. R., Silberg, J. L., & Pickens, R. W. (2005). Familial influences on alcohol use in adolescent female twins: Testing for genetic and environmental interactions. *Journal of Studies on Alcohol*, *66*, 445–451.

Miller, B. C. (2002). Family influences on adolescent sexual and contraceptive behavior. *The Journal of Sex Research*, *39*, 22–27.

Milyavskaya, M., & Koestner, R. (2011). Psychological needs, motivation, and well-being: A test of self-determination theory across multiple domains. *Personality and Individual Differences, 50*(3), 387–391.

Mintz, S., & Kellogg, S. (1988). *Domestic revolutions: A social history of American family life.* London, UK: Collier Macmillan.

Mitchell, J. (1984). *Women: The longest revolution.* New York, NY: Pantheon Books.

Mohanty, M. S. (2014). What determines happiness? Income or attitude: Evidence from the U.S. longitudinal data. *Journal of Neuroscience, Psychology, and Economics, 7*(2), 80–102. doi:10.1037/npe0000019

Molina, B. S. G., Donovan, J. E., & Belendiuk, K. A. (2010). Familial loading for alcoholism and offspring behavior: Mediating and moderating influences. *Alcoholism: Clinical & Experimental Research, 34*(11), 1972–1984.

Molix, L. A., & Nichols, C. P. (2013). Satisfaction of basic psychological needs as a mediator of the relationships between community esteem and wellbeing. *International Journal of Wellbeing, 3*(1), 20–34. doi:10.5502/ijw.v3i1.2

Montani, J. P., Schutz, Y., & Dulloo, A. G. (2015). Dieting and weight cycling as risk factors for cardiometabolic diseases: Who is really at risk? *Obesity Reviews, 16*(S1), 7–18. doi:10.1111/obr.12251

Morin, R. (2011). *The public renders a split verdict on changes in family structure.* Washington, DC: Pew Research Center. Retrieved June 1, 2017, from www.pew socialtrends.org/2011/02/16/the-public-renders-a-split-verdict-on-changes-in-family-structure/?src=family-interactive

Mosier, S. L., & Thilmany, D. (2016). Diffusion of food policy in the U.S.: The case of organic certification. *Food Policy, 61*, 80–91.

Moyn, S. (2010). Human rights in history. *The Nation*, 31–38.

Murray, J. (1987). *The perceptions of sexuality, marriage, and family in early English pastoral manuals.* Unpublished doctoral dissertation, University of Toronto.

Myers, D. G., & Lamm, H. (1976). The group polarization phenomenon. *Psychological Bulletin, 83*, 602–627.

Nall, M. A. (2005). Strengthening families and securing communities. *Journal of Family and Consumer Sciences, 97*, 18–21.

National Association of Home Builders. (2015). *Millennials seek smaller houses, but won't sacrifice details, panelists say.* Retrieved from https://www.nahb.org/en/news-and-publications/press-releases/2015/january/millennials-seek-smaller-houses-but-wont-sacrifice-details-panelists-say.aspx

National Employment Law Project. (2015). *14 cities and states approved $15 minimum wage in 2015.* New York, NY: Author. Retrieved from http:222.n3lpp.org/content/uploads/PR-Minimum-Wage-Year-End-15.pdf.

National Telecommunications and Information Administration. (2013, May). *U.S. broadband availability: June 2010–June 2012.* Retrieved from http://www.ntia.doc.gov/report/2013/us-broadbandavailabilityjune-2010-june-2012

Neumark, D. (2015). The effects of minimum wages on employment. *FRBSF Economic Letter.* San Francisco, CA: Federal Reserve Bank of San Francisco. Retrieved from http://www.frbsf.org/economic-research/files/el2015-37.pdf

Nguyen, L. N. (2010, August 9). Want to win the lottery? Tips from experts who share their stories. *Daily Finance.* Retrieved from http://www.dailyfinance.com/2010/08/09/want-to-win-the-lottery-tips-from-experts

Nielsen Company. (2010). *Television audience 2009.* New York, NY: Author. Retrieved June 7, 2017, from http://www.nielsen.com/content/dam/corporate/us/en/newswire/uploads/2010/04/TVA_2009-for-Wire.pdf

Nielsen Company. (2012, November 20). U.S. kids continue to look forward to "iHoliday." *Newswire.* Retrieved June 27, 2017, from http://www.nielsen.com/us/en/insights/news/2012/u-s-kids-continue-to-look-forward-to-iholiday.html

Nielsen Company. (2014a, June 17). Global consumers are willing to put their money where their heart is when it comes to goods and services from companies committed to social responsibility. *Press Room.* Retrieved from http://www.nielsen.com/us/en/press-room/2014/global-consumers-are-willing-to-put-their-money-where-their-heart-is.html

Nielsen Company. (2014b, March 4). Millennials prefer cities to suburbs, subways to driveways. *Newswire.* Retrieved from http://www.nielsen.com/us/en/insights/news/2014/ millennials-prefer-cities-to-suburbs-subways-to-driveways.html

Nihira, M. A. (2009). Infertility and in vitro fertilization. *WebMD Medical Reference.* Retrieved from http://www.webmd.com/infertility-and-reproduction/guide/in-vitro-fertilization

O'Boyle, E., & Harter, J. (2014, May 13). Why your workplace wellness program isn't working. *Gallup Business Journal.* Retrieved from http://www.gallup.com/businessjournal/168995/why-workplace-wellness-program-isn-working.aspx

Olsen, S. O., Tudoran, A. A., Honkanen, P., & Verplanken, B. (2015). Differences and similarities between impulse buying and variety seeking: A personality-based perspective. *Psychology & Marketing, 33*(1), 36–47.

Olson, D. H., & DeFrain, J. (2003). *Marriages and families: Intimacy, diversity, and strengths* (4th ed.). Boston, MA: McGraw-Hill.

Olson, D. H., DeFrain, J., & Skogrand, L. (2014). *Marriages and families: Intimacy, diversity and strengths* (8th ed.). New York, NY: McGraw-Hill.

Olson, J. M., & Zanna, M. P. (1993). Attitudes and attitude change. *Annual Review of Psychology, 44*, 117–155.

Opt, S. K., & Loffrendo, D. A. (2000). Rethinking communication apprehension: A Myers–Briggs perspective. *The Journal of Psychology, 134*, 556–570.

Organisation for Economic Co-operation and Development (OECD). (2011). *The future of families to 2030: Projections, policy challenges and policy options—A synthesis report.* Paris, France: Author.

Organisation for Economic Co-operation and Development (OECD). (2012). *Meeting the water reform challenge.* Paris, France: Author.

Orth, U. R., & Kahle, L. R. (2008). Intrapersonal variation in consumer susceptibility to normative influence: Toward a better understanding of brand choice decisions. *The Journal of Social Psychology, 148*, 423–447.

Osmond, M. W., & Thorne, B. (1993). Feminist theories: The social construction of gender in families and society. In P. Boss (Ed.), *Sourcebook of family theories and methods: A contextual approach* (pp. 591–625). New York, NY: Plenum.

Otto, H. A. (1962). What is a strong family? *Marriage and Family Living, 24*, 77–81.

Pagan, C. N. (2006). Do you have an emergency plan? *Prevention, 5*, 103–105.

Palomba, C. A., & Banta, T. W. (1999). *Assessment essentials planning, implementing, and improving assessment in higher education.* San Francisco, CA: Jossey-Bass.

Pandya, S. M., & Coleman, B. (2000). *Caregiving and long-term care* (Rep. No. AARP FS82). Washington, DC: Public Policy Institute.

Paolucci, B., Hall, O. A., & Axinn, N. W. (1977). *Family decision making: An ecosystem approach.* New York, NY: Wiley.

Parsons, T. (1968). *The structure of social action.* New York, NY: The Free Press.

Patrick, H., Knee, C. R., Canevello, A., & Lonsbary, C. (2007). The role of need fulfillment in relationship functioning and well-being: A self-determination theory perspective. *Journal of Personality and Social Psychology, 92*(3), 434–457.

Patton, M. (2015, November 19). The cost of college: Yesterday, today, and tomorrow. *Forbes.* Retrieved June 22, 2017, from www.forbes.com/sites/mikepatton/2015/11/19/the-cost-of-college-yesterday-today-and-tomorrow/#532afe966060

Payne, R. K. (1998). *A framework for understanding poverty.* Baytown, TX: RFT Publications.

Pearl, D., Bouthilet, L., & Lazar, J. B. (Eds.). (1982). *Television and behavior: Ten years of scientific progress and implications for the eighties* (DHHS Publication no. [ADM] 82-1195-1196). Rockville, MD: U.S. Department of Health and Human Services.

Pellegrino, J. W., & Hilton, M. L. (Eds.). (2012). *Education for life and work: Developing transferable knowledge and skills for the 21st century.* Washington, DC: National Research Council, The National Academies of Sciences, Engineering, and Medicine. doi:10.17226/13398

Perry-Jenkins, M., Newkirk, K., & Ghunney, A. K. (2013). Family work through time and space: An ecological perspective. *Journal of Family Theory and Review, 5*, 105–123.

Peters, A. (2015, September 29). Why Sweden is shifting to a 6-hour workday. *Fast Company.* Retrieved June 28, 2017, from www.fastcompany.com/3051448/why-sweden-is-shifting-to-a-6-hour-work-day

Peterson, J. (2015). Securing social security's future: 3 reasons why the program will be there for you. *AARP Bulletin.* Retrieved from http://www.aarp.org/work/social-security/info-2015/future-of-social-security.html

Pew Research Center. (2011). *Republican candidates stir little enthusiasm: Candidate traits: D.C. experience viewed less positively.* Washington, DC: Author. Retrieved from http://www.people-press.org/2011/06/02/republican-candidates-stir-little-enthusiasm

Pew Research Center. (2013). *King's dream remains an elusive goal: Many Americans see racial disparities.* Washington, DC: Author. Retrieved from http://www.pewsocialtrends.org/2013/08/22/kings-dream-remains-an-elusive-goal-many-americans-see-racial-disparities

Pew Research Center. (2014a). *Device ownership over time.* Washington, DC: Author. Retrieved from http://www.pewinternet.org/data-trend/mobile/device-ownership

Pew Research Center. (2014b). *The rising cost of not going to college.* Washington, DC: Author.

Pew Research Center. (2014c). *U.S. religious landscape survey.* Washington, DC: Author. Retrieved June 1, 2017, from www.pewforum.org/religious-landscape-study

Pew Research Center. (2015). Parenting in America. *Pew Research*

Center's Social and Demographic Trends. Washington, DC: Author.

Pew Research Center. (2016). *The 2016 presidential campaign—A news event that's hard to miss.* Washington, DC: Author.

Pfeffer, J. (1987). Understanding the role of power in decision making. In J. M. Shafritz & J. S. Ott (Eds.), *Classics of organizational theory* (pp. 309–335). Chicago, IL: Dorsey.

Phillips, K. (2009, June 17). Same-sex partner benefits. *New York Times.* Retrieved from http://thecaucus .blogs.nytimes.com/2009/06/17/ same-sex-partner-benefits

Planning for your successor. (2005). *Farmers Weekly.* Retrieved from http://www.fwi.co.uk/Articles/ 20/12/2005/91534/Planning-for-your-successor.htm

Population Reference Bureau. (2015). *Race/ethnic income gap growing among U.S. working poor families.* Washington, DC: Author. Retrieved from http://www.prb .org/Publications/Articles/2015/ working-poor-families.aspx

Pundt, H. (1980). *AHEA: A history of excellence.* Washington, DC: American Home Economics Association.

Purdy, M., & Dupey, P. (2005). Holistic flow model of spiritual wellness. *Counseling and Values, 49,* 95–107.

Putnam, R. D. (2000). *Bowling alone.* New York, NY: Simon & Schuster.

Qian, Y., & Sayer, L. C. (2016). Division of labor, gender ideology, and marital satisfaction in East Asia. *Journal of Marriage and Family, 78,* 383–400.

Quart, A. (2003). *Branded the buying and selling of teenagers.* Cambridge, MA: Perseus.

Quinn, R. E., & Spreitzer, G. M. (1997). The road to empowerment: Seven questions every leader should consider. *Organizational Dynamics, 26,* 37–49.

Rao, K., Apte, M., & Subbakrishna, D. K. (2003). Coping and subjective well-being in women with multiple roles. *International Journal of Social Psychiatry, 49,* 175–184.

Rauber, P. (2003). When Uncle Sam wanted us. *Sierra, 88,* 32.

Read, C. R. (1991). Achievement and career choices: Comparisons of males and females. *Roeper Review, 13,* 188–193.

Restuccia, D. (2014, April 13). A study on the changing racial makeup of 'the next America.' *Huffington Post.* Retrieved from http://www.huffingtonpost .com/2014/04/13/changing-racial-makeup-_n_5142462.html

Rhee, N., & Boivie, I. (2015). *The continuing retirement savings crisis.* Washington, DC: National Institute on Retirement Security. Retrieved from http://labor center.berkeley.edu/pdf/2015/ RetirementSavingsCrisis.pdf

Ribar, D. (2015). Why marriage matters for child wellbeing. *The Future of Children, 25*(2), 11–27. Retrieved from http://0-www.jstor.org.rosi .unk.edu/stable/43581970

Ricketts, K. G. (2009). *Leadership vs. management* (ELK1-103). Lexington: Cooperative Extension Service, University of Kentucky College of Agriculture.

Rodman, H. (1967). Marital power in France, Greece, Yugoslavia, and the United States: A cross-national discussion. *Journal of Marriage and the Family, 29,* 320–324.

Rosa, H. (2003). Social accelerations: Ethical and political consequences of a desynchronized high-speed society. *Constellations, 10*(1), 3–33.

Rosenbaum, D. (1993). America's economic outlaw: The U.S. health care system. *New York Times,* pp. A1(N)–A1(L).

Rossi, A. S. (2001). *Caring and doing for others: Social responsibility in the domains of family, work, and community.* Chicago, IL: University of Chicago Press.

Rotter, J. (1973). A locus of control scale for children. *Journal of Consulting and Clinical Psychology, 40,* 148–154.

Rubinstein, J. S., Meyer, D. E., & Evans, J. E. (2001). Executive control of cognitive processes in task switching. *Journal of Experimental Psychology, 27,* 763–767.

Saez, E. (2013). *Striking it richer: The evolution of top incomes in the United States.* Berkeley: University of California, Berkeley. Retrieved from http://eml.berkeley.edu//~saez/ saez-UStopincomes-2012.pdf

Safilios-Rothschild, C. (1976). A macro and micro-examination of family power and love. *Journal of Marriage and the Family, 37,* 355–362.

Savage, M. (2015, November 2). The truth about Sweden's short working hours. *BBC News.* Retrieved June 28, 2017, from www.bbc.com/news/busi ness-34677949

Scanzoni, J., & Marsiglio, W. (1993). New action theory and contemporary families. *Journal of Family Issues, 14,* 105–132.

Schaefer, R. T. (2008). *Race and ethnicity in the United States* (7th ed.). Upper Saddle River, NJ: Pearson.

Schein, E. H. (2004). *Organizational culture and leadership* (3rd ed.). San Francisco, CA: Jossey-Bass.

Schermerhorn, J. R., Naumes, W., Naumes, M. J., & Schermerhorn, J. R. (1996). *Management.* New York, NY: Wiley.

Seabald, H. (1986). Adolescents' shifting orientation toward parents and peers: A curvilinear trend over recent decades. *Journal of Marriage and the Family, 48,* 5–13.

Seligman, M. (2002). *Authentic happiness: Using the new positive psychology to realize your potential for lasting fulfillment*. New York, NY: The Free Press.

Seufert-Barr, N. (1994). The smallest democracy: At the heart of society. *UN Chronicle*, 43–45.

Shafer, K., & Qian, Z. (2010). Marriage timing and educational assortative matings. *Journal of Comparative Family Studies, 41*(5), 661–691.

Shephard, R. J. (1996). Financial aspects of employee fitness programmes. In J. Kerr, A. Griffiths, & T. Cox (Eds.), *Workplace health, employee fitness and exercise* (pp. 29–54). London, UK: Taylor & Francis.

Sherif, C. W., & Sherif, M. (1967). *Attitude, ego-involvement, and change*. New York, NY: Wiley.

Shneiderman, B. (2010). The quest for universal usability. In C. Hanks (Ed.), *Technology and values: Essential readings* (pp. 522–530). West Sussex, UK: Wiley-Blackwell.

Siegel, C. (2006). *The end of economic growth*. Berkeley, CA: Preservation Institute.

Signorielli, N., & Morgan, M. (2001). Television and the family: The cultural perspective. In J. Bryant & J. A. Bryant (Eds.), *Television and the American family* (pp. 333–351). Mahwah, NJ: Lawrence Erlbaum.

Simon, S. A. (2010). Addressing broad challenges to universal theories of justice. *The Good Society, 19*(2), 75–78.

Sisson, S. B., Broyles, S. T., Newton, R. L., Jr., Baker, B. L., & Chermausek, S. D. (2011). TVs in the bedrooms of children: Does it impact health and behavior? *Preventive Medicine, 52*(2), 104–108.

Skipp, C., Ephron, D., & Hastings, M. (2006). Trouble at home. *Newsweek*, 17.

Skolnick, A. (1993). Changes of heart: Family dynamics in historical perspective. In P. A. Cowan (Ed.), *Family, self, and society toward a new agenda for family research* (pp. 43–68). Hillsdale, NJ: Lawrence Erlbaum.

Skolnick, A., & Skolnick, J. (2014). *Family in transition* (17th ed.). Glenville, IL: Scott, Foresman.

Smith, A. (2011). Americans and their cell phones. *Pew Internet & American Life Project*. Washington, DC: Pew Research Center.

Smith, A. (2014). *U.S. views of technology and the future*. Washington, DC: Pew Research Center.

Snir, R., & Harpaz, I. (2002). Work-leisure relations: Leisure orientation and the meaning of work. *Journal of Leisure Research, 34*, 178–203.

Social Security Administration. (2016). *A summary of the 2016 annual reports: Status of the Social Security and Medicare programs*. Washington, DC: Author.

Sokalski, H. J. (1994). The international year of the family. In K. Altergott (Ed.), *One world, many families* (pp. 3–7). Minneapolis, MN: National Council on Family Relations.

Soriano, F. I. (2013). *Conducting needs assessments: A multidisciplinary approach*. Thousand Oaks, CA: Sage.

Sorrels, J. P., & Myers, B. (1983). Comparison of group and family dynamics. *Human Relations, 36*, 477–492.

Stalder, D. R. (2007). Need for closure, the big five, and public self-consciousness. *The Journal of Social Psychology, 147*(1), 91–95.

Stanley, S. M., Rhodes, G. K., & Markman, H. J. (2006). Sliding versus deciding: Inertia and the premarital cohabitation effect. *Family Relations, 55*, 499–509.

Stanley, T. J. (2004). *Millionaire women next door: The many journeys of successful American businesswomen*. Kansas City, MO: Andrews McMeel.

Stavrinos, D., Byington, K. W., & Schwebel, D. C. (2009). Effect of cell phone distraction on pediatric pedestrian injury risk. *Pediatrics, 123*(2), e179–e185.

Stein, H. W., & Brier, M. C. (2002). Raising responsible children of wealth. *Trusts & Estates, 140*(6), 42.

Sterner, T. (2003). *Policy instruments for environmental and natural resource management*. Stockholm: Swedish International Development Cooperation Agency.

Steuer, F. B., & Hustedt, J. T. (2002). *TV or not TV: A primer on the psychology of television*. Lanham, MD: University Press of America.

Steverman, B. (2016). *Boomers are making sure the divorces keep coming: The much-reported decline in failed marriages may be misleading. Blame your parents*. New York, NY: Bloomberg. Retrieved from http://www.bloomberg.com/news/articles/2016-06-17/boomers-are-making-sure-the-divorces-keep-coming

Stinnett, N. (1981). Strong families: A national study. In N. Stinnett, J. DeFrain, K. King, P. Knaub, & G. Rowe (Eds.), *Family strengths 3: Roots of well-being* (pp. 33–42). Lincoln: University of Nebraska Press.

Stinnett, N., DeFrain, N., & DeFrain, J. (1999). *Creating a strong family*. West Monroe, LA: Howard.

Stolle, D. (2003). The sources of social capital. In M. Hooghe & D. Stolle (Eds.), *Generating social capital: Civil society and institutions in comparative perspective* (pp. 19–42). New York, NY: Palgrave Macmillan.

Stone, R. (1998). *Human resource management*. New York, NY: Wiley.

Stoner, J. A. (1968). Risky and cautious shifts in group decisions: The influence of widely held values. *Journal of Experimental Social Psychology, 4,* 442–459.

Strong, B., Devault, C., & Sayad, B. W. (2008). *The marriage and family experience: Intimate relationships in a changing society.* Belmont, CA: Wadsworth.

Sugimoto, Y. (1997). *An introduction to Japanese society.* New York, NY: Cambridge University Press.

Szinovacz, M. (1987). Family power. In M. B. Sussman & S. K. Steinmetz (Eds.), *Handbook of marriage and the family* (pp. 651–693). New York, NY: Praeger.

Tadmor, N. (1996). The concept of household-family in eighteenth-century England. *Past and Present, 151*(1), 111–130.

Tannen, D. (1990). *You just don't understand: Women and men in conversation.* New York, NY: Morrow.

Tarafdar, M., Tu, Q., Ragu-Nathan, T. S., & Ragu-Nathan, B. S. (2011). Crossing the dark side: Examining creators, outcomes, and inhibitors to technostress. *Communications of the ACM, 54*(9), 113–120.

Taylor, P. (2014). *The next America.* Washington, DC: Pew Research Center.

Taylor, R. L. (2002). *Minority families in the United States: A multicultural perspective.* Upper Saddle River, NJ: Prentice Hall.

Taylor, W. C. (2011). Prolonged sitting and the risk of cardiovascular disease and mortality. *Current Cardiovascular Risk Reports, 5*(4), 350–357.

Tesser, A. (1992). On the importance of heritability in psychological research. *Psychological Review, 100*(10), 129–143.

Thomson, I. T. (2005). The theory that won't die: From mass society

to the decline of social capital. *Sociological Forum, 20*(3), 421–448.

Timmerman, G. M., & Acton, G. J. (2001). The relationship between basic need satisfaction and emotional eating. *Issues in Mental Health Nursing, 22*(7), 691–701. http://dx.doi .org/10.1080/01612840119628

Tomer, J. F. (2001). Economic man vs. heterodox men: The concepts of human nature in schools of economic thought. *The Journal of Socio-Economics, 30,* 281–293.

Torpey, E., & Terrell, D. (2015). *Should I get a master's degree?* Washington, DC: U.S. Department of Labor, Bureau of Labor Statistics.

Torquati, J. C. (2002). Personal and social resources as predictors of parenting in homeless families. *Journal of Family Issues, 23,* 463–485.

Traut-Mattausch, E., Jonas, E., Frey, D., & Zanna, M. P. (2011). Are there "his" and "her" types of decisions? Exploring gender differences in the confirmation bias. *Sex Roles, 65,* 223–233.

Triplett, N. (1898). The dynamogenic factors in pacemaking and competition. *American Journal of Psychology, 9,* 507–533.

Turner, R. H. (1970). *Family interaction.* New York, NY: Wiley.

Tuttle, C., & Kuhns, A. (2017, May). Percent of income spent on food falls as income rises. *Food price outlook.* Washington, DC: USDA Economic Research Service. Retrieved June 22, 2017, from www.ers.usda.gov/ amber-waves/2016/september/ percent-of-income-spent-on-food-falls-as-income-rises

United Nations. (2015). *Transforming our world: The 2030 agenda for sustainable development.* Resolution adopted by the General Assembly, September 25. Retrieved from http:// www.un.org/ga/search/view_doc .asp?symbol=A/RES/70/1& Lang=E

United States of Aging. (2015, July 8). *Health or finances? Older Americans and professionals who support them disagree on needs of growing aging population.* Minnetonka, MN: United Healthcare and National Council on Aging. Retrieved from https:// www.ncoa.org/resources/usa15-national-news-release-pdf/

University of Nebraska. (2017). *Benefits.* Retrieved June 22, 2017, from www.nebraska.edu/docs/benefits/ benefits_deplife.pdf

Urban Land Institute. (2015). *America in 2015: A ULI survey of views on housing, transportation, and community.* Washington, DC: Author.

U.S. Bureau of Labor Statistics. (2015). Highlights of women's earnings in 2014. *BLS Reports, 1064.* Washington, DC: U.S. Department of Labor.

U.S. Bureau of Labor Statistics. (2016). *Employer costs for employee compensations.* Washington, DC: U.S. Department of Labor.

U.S. Census Bureau. (2015). *Current population survey.* Washington, DC: Author. Retrieved June 22, 2017, from www.census.gov/programs-surveys/cps.html

U.S. Department of Agriculture (USDA). (2011). *Conservation reserve program: 2008 Farm Bill CRP summary.* Washington, DC: Author.

U.S. Energy Information Administration. (2016). *Annual energy outlook 2016 with projections to 2040.* Washington, DC: U.S. Department of Energy.

U.S. Food and Drug Administration (FDA). (2016). *Menu and vending machines labeling requirements.* Washington, DC: Author.

U.S. Green Building Council. (2016). *Benefits of green building.* Washington, DC: Author. Retrieved from http://www.usgbc .org/articles/green-building-facts

Vansteenkiste, M., Simons, J., Lens, W., Soenens, B., & Matos, L. (2005). Examining the motivational impact of intrinsic versus extrinsic goal framing and autonomy: Supportive versus internally controlling communication style on early adolescents' academic achievement. *Child Development, 76*, 483–501.

Vickers, C. (1984). *Themes in home management.* Washington, DC: American Home Economics Association.

Vinski, E. J., & Tryon, G. S. (2009). Study of a cognitive dissonance intervention to address high school students' cheating attitudes and behaviors. *Ethics and Behavior, 19*, 218–226.

Vitalari, N. P. (2014). *A prospective analysis of the future of the U.S. healthcare industry.* Center for Digital Transformation white paper. Irvine: University of California Irvine, Center for Digital Transformation.

Waller, W. W., & Hill, R. (1951). *The family: A dynamic interpretation.* New York, NY: Warner Books.

Walter, S. R., Raban, M. A., Dunsmuir, W. T., Douglas, H. E., & Westbrook, J. I. (2016). Emergency doctors' strategies to manage competing workload demands in an interruptive environment: An observational workflow time study. *Applied Ergonomics, 58*, 454–460. doi:10.1016/j.apergo.2016.07.020

Walumbwa, F. O., Avolio, B. J., Gardner, W. L., Wernsing, T. S., & Peterson, S. J. (2008). Authentic leadership: Development and validation of a theory-based measure. *Journal of Management, 34*(1), 89–126.

Wang, W. (2015). *Interracial marriage: Who is 'marrying out'?* Washington, DC: Pew Research Center. Retrieved from www.pewresearch.org/fact-tank/2015/06/12/interracial-marriage-who-is-mayying-out

Wang, W., & Parker, K. (2014). *Record share of Americans have never married: As values, economics and gender patterns change.* Washington, DC: Pew Research Center.

Ward, K. (2001). Perceived needs of parents of critically ill infants in a neonatal intensive care unit (NICU). *Pediatric Nursing, 27*, 281.

Warschauer, M., Matuchniak, T., Pinkard, N., & Gadsden, V. (2010). New technology and digital worlds: Analyzing evidence of equity in access, use and outcomes. *Review of Research in Education, 34*, 179–225.

Wartella, E., & Jennings, N. (2001). New members of the family: The digital revolution in the home. *Journal of Family Communication, 1*(1), 59–69.

Webb, D. M. (1991). Delegation. *Academic Search Premier, 69*(4), 40–42.

Weir, A. (2001). *Henry VIII: The king and his court.* New York, NY: Ballantine.

Welch, P. J., & Welch, G. F. (2004). *Economics, theory and practice.* New York, NY: Wiley.

Wensley, R. (1996). Isabella Beeton: Management as "everything in its place." *Business Strategy Review, 7*, 37–47.

Westermarck, E. (1971). *The history of human marriage.* New York, NY: Johnson Reprint Corporation. (Original work published 1922)

White, G. B. (2015, September 21). A bleak future for renters. *The Atlantic.* Retrieved from http://www.theatlantic.com/business/archive/2015/09/a-bleak-future-for-renters/406453

White, J. M., Klein, D. M., & Martin, T. F. (2015). *Family theories: An introduction* (4th ed.). Thousand Oaks, CA: Sage.

White, M. C. (2013, April 11). American families increasingly let kids make buying decisions. *Time.* Retrieved June 27, 2017, from http://business.time.com/2013/04/11/american-families-increasingly-let-kids-make-buying-decisions

The White House, Office of the Press Secretary. (2011, May 12). *Fact sheet: The administration's cybersecurity accomplishments.* Retrieved from https://www.whitehouse.gov/the-press-office/2011/05/12/fact-sheet-administrations-cybersecurity-accomplishments

Whitsett, D., & Kent, S. A. (2003). Cults and families. *Families in Society: The Journal of Contemporary Human Services, 84*(4), 491–502.

Whorton, J. C. (2000). Vegetarianism. In K. F. Kiple & K. C. Ornelas (Eds.), *The Cambridge world history of food* (pp. 1553–1564). New York, NY: Cambridge University Press.

Wickrama, K. A., & Bryant, C. M. (2003). Community context of social resources and adolescent mental health. *Journal of Marriage and Family, 65*, 850–866.

Wilkinson, D. (1987). Ethnicity. In M. B. Sussman & S. K. Steinmetz (Eds.), *Handbook of marriage and the family* (pp. 183–210). New York, NY: Plenum.

Williams, C., Rosen, J., Hudman, J., & O'Malley, M. (2004). *Challenges and trade-offs in low-income family budgets: Implications for health coverage.* Washington, DC: The Kaiser Commission on Medicaid and the Uninsured.

Williams, R., Bertsch, B., Dale, B., van der Wiele, T., van Iwaarden, J., Smith, M., & Visser, R. (2006, November 1). Quality and risk management: What are the key issues? *The TQM Magazine, 18*, 67–86.

Woolley, F. (2003). Control over money in marriage. In S. A. Grossbard-Shechtman (Ed.), *Marriage and the economy: Theory and evidence from advanced industrial societies* (pp. 105–128). New York, NY: Cambridge University Press.

World Commission on Environment and Development (WCED). (1987). *Our common future*. Oxford, UK: Oxford University Press.

World Economic Forum. (2014, November). *The future availability of natural resources: A new paradigm for global resource availability*. Geneva, Switzerland: Author. Retrieved July 6, 2017, from http://www3.weforum.org/docs/WEF_FutureAvailabilityNaturalResources_Report_2014.pdf

World Health Organization. (1947). *Chronicle of the World Health Organization: Vol. 1*. Geneva, Switzerland: Author.

World Health Organization. (2016). *Mental health and older adults*. Geneva, Switzerland: Author. Retrieved from http://www.who.int/mediacentre/factsheets/fs381/en

Wutich, A., & Brewis, A. (2014). Food, water, and scarcity: Towards a broader anthropology of resource insecurity. *Current Anthropology, 55*(4), 444–468. doi:10.1086/677311

Yorburg, B. (2002). *Family realities: A global view*. Upper Saddle River, NJ: Prentice Hall.

Young, J. (2013, January 7). Health care spending growth is slow for third straight year. *Huffington Post*.

Yu, H., & Miller, P. (2005). Leadership style: The X generation and baby boomers compared in different cultural contexts. *Leadership and Organizational Development Journal, 26*, 35–50.

Yu, L., Chan, C., & Ireland, C. (2006). *China's new culture of cool: Understanding the world's fastest-growing market*. Berkeley, CA: New Rider's Press.

Zimmerman, E. (1964). *Introduction to world resources*. New York, NY: Harper & Row.

Zuckerman, M. (2000). Are you a risk taker? *Psychology Today, 33*, 52–57.

INDEX

AARP (American Association of Retired Persons), 317
Abandonment of plans, 274
Abdeyazdan, Z., 259–260
Ability as human capital, 116–117
Abraham, L. M., 100
Absenteeism, 292
ACA (Affordable Care Act), 254
Accessibility of resources, 6, 115
Accountability, 259–260
Activity orientation, 14, 15 (table), 16 (table)
Acton, G. J., 77
Adams, John Quincy, 229
Adaption, 195
Addictive behaviors, 233
Adjustment of plans, 274–275
Adler, J., 280
Administration on Aging, 168
Adolescents, 82–83, 149–150, 260
Adulthood transitions, 83
Advertising industry
    Alka-Seltzer, 278–279
    brand preferences, 105
    choosing food based on, 248–249
    claims of, 173
    fraudulent marketing practices, 175
    See also Consumers and consumption
Affective resources, 216
Affect regulation, 255–257
Affluenza, 109
Affordable Care Act (ACA), 254
Affordable housing, 177
Agentic traits, 84
Aging population. See Older adults
Agreement in conflicts, 219
Aguirre, A. M., 43
Ajzen, I., 100, 100 (figure), 101–103
Aldrich, N. W., 108–109
Alka-Seltzer advertisements, 278–279
Allocation of resources, 128–131
Allport, G. W., 17, 100
Alpha Family, 321–322

Amatea, E. S., 257
Amato, J., 86
American Association for Therapeutic Humor, 299
American Association of Retired Persons (AARP), 317
American Recovery and Reinvestment Act, 136
The American Woman's Home (Beecher), 9–10
Ancient cultures, 9
Anderson, J. R., 197
Anger and stress, 298
Annual Energy Outlook report, 283
Anthropology, 18
Apte, M., 292
Archival family function, 123–124
Artificial obsolescence, 86–87, 278
Artificial reproductive methods, 62
Arvey, R. D., 100
Ashe, Arthur, 277
Asians and gender inequality, 249
Assessment of plans, 257
    See also Success of plans
Assimilation, 96
Attitudes
    about, 99–101, 100 (figure)
    behavior and, 101
    culture influencing, 107–108
    leadership and, 238–239
    socioeconomic factors influencing, 108–109
    See also Behavior; Values
Audio streaming, 221
Authoritarian parenting, 246
Authoritative parenting, 246
Authority, 81
Autocratic leadership, 240–241, 241 (figure)
Automobile insurance, 271–272
Automobile purchases, 92, 106–107
Autonomy and motivation, 260
Availability of resources, 6
Avery, R. J., 60
Avolio, B. J., 242–243, 245
Axinn, N. W., 60

Baby Boomers, 98, 247, 317, 318
Bagozzi, R. P., 232
Bakan, D., 84
Ball, C., 129–130
Banking system, 152
Barbuto, J. E., 248
Bargaining conversations, 219–220
Barnard, Chester, 53
Barsade, S. G., 230
Barter system, 151
Basel Action Network, 287
Base period, 166
Base unit of money, 152
Bass, B. M., 242–243
Bauer, J. A., 225–227
Baumgartner, L. M., 83
Baumle, A. K., 120
BCP (Bureau of Consumer Protection),
    172–176
Beblo, M., 117
Beecher, C. E., 9–10
Beeton, Isabella, 9, 51
Behavior
    about, 101–103
    decision making influenced by, 232–233
    family values expressed by, 97
    purchasing decisions and, 104–107, 143–144
    role in accomplishing tasks, 117
    socioeconomic factors influencing, 108–109
    See also Attitudes; Consumers and
        consumption; Values
Beliefs. See Religion; Values
Bem, D. J., 102
Beneficiaries, 262, 270
Benefit packages, 119
Bertalanffy, L. V., 36
Bertocchi, G., 129
Beta Family, 322–323
Bindley, K., 7
Bjornholt, M., 98
"Black Sunday," 281
Blackwell, D. L., 94
Blank, W., 238
Blau, F. D., 120
Blood, R. O., 216
Blood banking, 306
Bogat, G. A., 233
Bonilla-Silva, E., 94
Book of Household Management (Beeton), 9, 51

Bouchard, T. J., 100
Bouthilet, L., 222
Bowling Alone (Putnam), 125
Brainstorming technique, 192–193
Brand Keys Customer Loyalty Index, 105
Brand preferences, 105
Brandweek, 105
Brazelton, B. T., 82
Brewis, A., 314
Brier, M. C., 109
Bristow, D. N., 75
Brommel, B. J., 209–210
Bronfenbrenner, U., 42–43
Brotherton, David, 280
Brown, A., 223
Brunetti, M., 129
Bryant, C. M., 125
Bryant, W., 60
Bubolz, M. M., 42
Budgets and planning, 197–201, 275–276,
    326–333
Building codes, 177
Bureaucratic model of decision making,
    8, 53–54
Bureau of Consumer Protection (BCP),
    172–176
Bureau of Labor Statistics, 120
Burns family example, 56–57
Business management parallels, 7, 52–58
Buzzotta, V. R., 240–241, 241 (figure)
Bylund, C. L., 209–210

Cafeteria plans, 119
Cafferella, R. S., 83
Cain, Herman, 103–104
Calculator prices, 106
Campbell, P., 226
Capitalism, 109
Carl D. Perkins Vocational Education Act, 55
Cash value of insurance policies, 270
Catsanos, R., 62
Caughlin, J., 214, 215 (table)
Cautious shift, 237–238
Cell phones
    etiquette of, 224
    necessity or luxury question, 84–85
    smartphones, 143–144, 222–223, 224, 308–309
Centers for Disease Control and Prevention, 295
Certainty, 129–130

Chang, C.-T., 307
Change
    constancy of, 303–304
    in demographics, 314–319
    in family structures, 309–313
    in lifestyle, 257
    in natural resources, 313–314
    in technology, 304–309
Charter schools, 182
Cheng, Z.-H., 307
Cherlin, A. J., 309, 310
Children
    cell phones as necessity or luxury for, 84–85
    consumer behavior of, 249
    decision to have, 310–311
    developmental programs for, 179–180
    See also Education; Parents and parenting
Children's Online Privacy Protection Act
    (COPPA), 226
Chinese *guanxi*, 107–108
Choices
    educational, 183
    goal implementation and, 254–255
    limited by *tanshin funin*, 155
    marketing industry influencing, 248–249
    needs influenced by, 70–71
    product preferences, 140
    values influencing, 96
    women at work options, 148–149
    See also Plan of action
Church of England, 9
Cipriano, P., 259
Circuit Scribe, 305
Circumstances and perception of needs, 78–79
Class warfare, 138
    See also Socioeconomic status (SES)
Code of ethics, 103
Coexistence after conflict, 220
Coffee prices, 114
Cognitive dissonance theory, 102
Cognitive resources, 216
Cohabitation, 6–7, 97, 309
Coleman, B., 83
Collaborative leadership, 241, 241(figure),
    244–245
Collective identity, 231–232
Collective socialization, 124–125
Collision coverage for automobiles, 271–272
Colonial education, 181

Commodities, 61
Commodity standard, 151
Communal traits, 84
Communication
    conflict and, 218–220
    culture influencing, 220
    decision-making process and, 227
    defined, 209–210
    family dynamics influenced by, 232
    importance of, 123
    interpersonal assertive strategies, 256–257
    patterns in, 212–213, 212 (table)
    process of, 210–212, 210 (figure)
    smartphones and, 143–144
    standards in, 214–218, 215 (table)
    technology and, 221–227
Community, 124–125
    See also Local government
Community property, 262
Competitive symmetry, 217
Complementary interaction, 217, 218
Compulsory education, 183
Computers, 225–227
    See also Internet; Technology
Conceptual frameworks. See Theoretical
    perspectives
Concreteness of resources, 116
Conflict, 218–220, 233, 290–293
Conflict theory, 39–41
Conformity orientation, 212
Consensual families, 212–213
Conservation of resources, 281–284, 314
    See also Sustainability
Conspicuous consumption, 39, 135, 136
Consumer Leasing Act, 173
Consumer Resource Exchange Model
    (CREM), 75–76
Consumers and consumption
    artificial obsolescence, 86–87, 278
    automobile purchases, 92
    beginnings of consumerism, 134–135
    daily deals, 86
    factors in buying behavior, 143–144
    family decision-making process for, 87
    food choices, 96, 141–142, 248–249
    governmental protection of consumers,
        172–176
    household spending habits, 155–156
    income affecting, 80, 141–142

outsourcing of family life and, 311
principle of revealed preferences, 310
purchasing values and behaviors, 104–107
sustainability of resources, 286–287
symbolic interactionism and, 38–39
See also Advertising industry; Preferences;
Supply and demand
Contingency model of leadership, 241–242,
242 (figure)
Contingency plans, 195, 196, 204
Conversation orientation, 212
Coontz, S., 4
Copayments, 165–166, 266–267
Coping resources, 127
COPPA (Children's Online Privacy Protection
Act), 226
Cordry, S., 181
Corporate culture, 55
Corporate social responsibility, 278, 280–287
Crainer, S., 50
Credit Practices Act, 173–174
Credit statutes, 173–174
CREM (Consumer Resource Exchange
Model), 75–76
Crisis management, 255, 268–269
Crittenden, A., 239
Cuban healthcare, 167
Cult involvement, 236
Cultural anthropology, 18
Culture
communication and, 211–212, 220
family dynamics influenced by, 231–232
family management influenced by, 13–16,
15 (table), 16 (table)
family needs influenced by, 81–82
human rights and, 91
identification with, 290
rituals of, 82
transmission of, 81
values, attitudes and behaviors influenced
by, 107–108
Currency, 150–151
See also Inflation
Curtis, K. T., 94
Cushman, E. M., 58
Cyclical unemployment, 145

Daily deals for consumers, 86
D'Aluisio, Faith, 72

Dating websites, 226
Davenport, T. H., 116–117
Deacon, F. M., 58, 60
Death, 102
Debt and deficits, 275–276
Debt ratio, 316
Decision making
communication and, 227
cults and, 236
culture influencing, 220
group dynamics influencing, 229–233
groupthink influencing, 233–238
Knoll's framework, 58
process of, 7–8
resource management and, 58,
127–128, 129
societal needs influencing, 87
taste and, 143–144
worldview influencing, 13–16, 15 (table),
16 (table)
See also Change; Choices; Implementation
of plans; Plan of action
De Cremer, D., 260
Deductibles, 165–166, 266
Deficits, 199, 275–276
DeFrain, J., 43, 219
Delayed gratification, 260
Delegation of activities/responsibilities,
258–259
Demand for goods, 138–140
Demographic changes, 314–319
Department of Agriculture, 168–169
Dependent care, 63–64
Descriptive budgets, 200
Designer families, 62
Design preferences, 106–107
Deutch, P. J., 131
DeVault, C., 210, 211
Dewitte, S., 260
Diamonds, value of, 115
Dickson, A., 149
Digital divide, 81, 226, 308
See also Technology
Dimensional model of leadership, 240,
241 (figure)
Directional plans, 193–195
Direct mail marketing schemes, 175
Disability benefits, 164
Disabled individuals, 304

Disasters, 206–207, 274
   See also Plan of action
Discounts on insurance, 271–272
Distorters in communication, 211
Distributive justice, 131
Diversity, 13, 315–316
   See also Worldview perspectives
Divorce, 311–312
Doherty, W. J., 4, 197
Douglas, H. E., 191
Doyal, L., 77–78, 81
Dunn, H., 288
Dunn, J. S., 197
Dunsmuir, W. T., 191
Dupont, H., 102
Durable goods, 155–156
Durable power of attorney, 262
Dust Bowl Sunday, 281

Eagly, A. H., 248
Early Head Start, 179
Earnings. *See* Income
Easygoing leaders, 241, 241(figure)
Ecolabels, 280
Economic Organization of the Household (Bryant), 60
Economic resources
   about, 76, 118–121, 216
   adolescents on the job, 149–150
   education and, 81, 297
   employment, 144–145
   feminist perspectives, 41
   household data, 154–156
   inflation, 150–153
   monetary planning, 197–201
   preference changes, 143–144
   price of natural resources, 313
   pricing process, 139–140
   protecting, 205
   resources as choices, 137
   stability provided by, 127–128
   supply and demand, 138–140
   sustainability and, 286–287
   tanshin funin in Japan, 155
   unemployment, 144–146
   See also Consumers and consumption;
      Corporate social responsibility; Income;
      Risk management; Socioeconomic
      status (SES)
Edgar-Smith, S. E., 98–99

Education
   alternatives to public education, 181–183
   economic resources and, 81, 297
   federal funding for, 179–180
   history of compulsory education, 178–179
   human resources and, 116–117
   intellectual wellness, 296–297
   mate selection influenced by, 94
   parental influence on attainment of, 99
   skippies, 149
   social responsibility and, 299
   supply and demand in, 183–184
   technological advances and, 307
   value of, 81, 119, 121–122
Edwards, B., 80
Edwards, R., 211
Effort and ability, 117
Electricity, 314
Electronic Fund Transfer Act, 174
Electronic Waste Recycling Act, 287
Elizabeth I, Queen, 135
Elliott, E. D., 283
Ellison, C., 94
Ember, S., 101
Emergency action plans, 207
Emergency budgets, 200
Emotional contagion, 230
Emotional intelligence, 255–257
Emotional resources, 11–12
Emotional wellness, 297–299
Employment, 144–150, 290–293
   See also Income
Employment Act (1946), 136
Empowerment, 55, 259–260
Enabling actions, 261
Energy as human resource, 118
Energy conservation, 282–283
Energy efficiency, 283, 284, 314
Engelking, C., 126
Enhancement hypothesis, 292
Environmental Protection Agency, 287
Environmental resources
   about, 122–123
   conservation, 281–283
   corporate social responsibility and, 280–287
   family management influenced by, 10
   green space, 284–285, 290
   humans and nature orientation, 14,
      15 (table), 16 (table)

EpiPen controversy, 170–172
Epp, A. M., 311
Equal Credit Opportunity Act, 174
Equality, principle of, 131
Equity, principle of, 131
Eras of household management, 53–56
Erickson, E. H., 300
Estate planning, 261–264
Esteem needs, 71, 72 (figure), 74
Ethics, 103
European Medicines Agency, 171
Evans, J. E., 191
Evolutionary theory, 75
E-waste, 287, 308
Exchange of resources, 115–116, 126–128
Exchange theory, social, 37–38, 46 (table), 129
Executors, 262
Exercise, 295–296
Expenses, 198–199
External locus of control, 261
Extrinsic motivators, 260
Eyring, Pamela, 224

Failure, feelings of, 298
Fair Credit Billing Act, 174
Fair Credit Reporting Act, 174
Fair Debt Collection Practices Act, 174
Fair Labor Standards Act (FLSA), 118
Fair trade networks, 114
Faith-based assistance programs, 178
Family
    changes in, 29–30
    cultural context of, 32–33
    defining, 5, 23–28
    functions of, 31–32, 301–302
    goals of, 189
    history of, 22–23
    influence of, 13, 180–181
    researching, 35–45
    time allocation within, 117
    values of, 93–97
Family business succession, 264
Family cases
    Alpha, 321–322
    assignments, 326–333
    Beta, 322–323
    Omega, 323–324
    Tau, 324–325
    Zeta, 325–326

Family development theory, 44–45, 46 (table)
Family ecological theory, 42–43, 46 (table)
Family-friendly employers, 63
Family planning, 62–63
Family research design, 45–46, 46 (table),
    47 (table)
Family resource management
    business management parallels, 52–56
    concept of, 4
    contextual influences on, 8–10
    decision-making process, 7–8
    foundation of, 58–60
    See also Resources
Family responsibility for decisions
    emotional wellness, 297–299
    intellectual wellness, 296–297
    occupational wellness, 290–293
    physical wellness, 294–296
    social wellness, 289–290
    spiritual wellness, 293–294
    wellness as lifestyle, 288–289, 289 (figure)
Family rules, 210
Family stages, 44–45
Family strengths framework, 43–44, 46 (table)
Family structure, 309–313, 319
Family systems theory, 36, 46 (table)
Farm families, 134–135
Fashion, 143
Faucet/drain analogy, 153
Fayol, H., 51
FDA (Food and Drug Administration), 169–172
Feather, N. T., 99, 256
Featherman, D., 99
Federal government
    benefit assistance programs, 125
    budgets for, 159 (figure), 275–276
    Bureau of Labor Statistics, 120
    Department of Agriculture, 168–169
    Food and Drug Administration, 169–172
    food provided by, 168
    Health and Human Services, 167–168,
        168 (figure)
    Medicaid, 167–168, 168 (figure)
    Medicare, 165–168, 168 (figure), 317
    public education, 179–180
    public vs. private assistance programs, 166
    tax system, 92, 158–160, 159 (figure)
    See also Social Security
Federal Trade Commission, 175–176, 223

Feedback on plans, 257
Felchi, Fabio, 126
Feldman, Y., 284
Feminist theory, 40, 41, 46 (table)
Fiedler, F. E., 241–242, 242 (figure)
Filters in communication, 211
Financial management, 64
Financial planning, 201–203, 201 (table)
Financial resources, 11, 219, 309
    See also Economic resources
Firebaugh, F. M., 60
Firebaugh, R. E., 58, 60
Fishbein, M., 100, 100 (figure), 101–103
Fitzpatrick, M. A., 210, 217
Five resource categorizations, 11–13
Five-step decision-making process, 8
Fixed expenses, 198
Fleishman, F. E., 240
Flexibility, 204, 293
Flow resources, 122
FLSA (Fair Labor Standards Act), 118
Foa, U. G., 113, 115–116
Folbre, N., 97
Foldable Bike Helmut, 305
Foldscope, 305
Follet, Mary Parker, 53–54
Food
    choosing, 96, 141–142, 248–249
    governmental assistance for providing, 168
    grocery shopping, 61
    labeling system for, 280–381
    safety of, 170
    shortages in, 314
Food and Drug Administration (FDA), 169–172
Forecasts of demographic change, 314–319
Forman, T. A., 94
Foundational skills, 238
"Four Horsemen of the Apocalypse"
    behaviors, 219
Frager, R., 71
Franklin, Benjamin, 187
Frey, D., 93
Frictional unemployment, 145
Friends, network of, 289–290
Fritz, S. M., 248
Frost, Robert, 209
Functional value of products, 140
Future, management of. *See* Change; Decision
    making; Plan of action

Galeano, Eduardo, 114
Galvin, K. M., 209–210
Gambling, spending for, 142
Garbage, 283–284
Gasana, P. U., 80
Gas prices, 139
Gender differences
    decision making and, 93
    housework expectations, 249
    leadership preferences, 247–248
    needs and, 83–84
    political expectations and, 104
    social responsibility and, 299
    spending behavior, 142
    wages affected, 63–64
    wages affected by, 119–120
    women in the labor force, 146–149, 150
Generational issues
    about, 97–98
    adolescents, 82–83, 149–150, 260
    estate planning, 261–264
    family business succession, 264
    inheritances, 37–38, 120–121, 261, 263
    leadership preferences, 246–247
    multi-gen families, 313
    See also Older adults; Parents and parenting
Generation Xers, 247
Generic drugs, 106, 170–172
Genetically modified organism (GMO), 281
Gentzler, Y. S., 56
Georgetown University Center on Education
    and the Workforce, 297
German healthcare, 167
Gerwitz, J. L., 102
Ghazavi, Z., 259–260
Gheissari, A., 259–260
Giacquinta, J. B., 225–227
Gift tax, 261
Gilbreth, Frank, 53
Gilbreth, Lilian, 53
Gillespie, M. D., 316
Glossary, 335–343
GMO (genetically modified organism), 281
Goals
    choices and, 254–255
    financial, 204–206
    in planning, 188–190
    shifting of, 191–192
Godfrey, Arthur, 158

Gordon, L., 41
Gough, I., 77–78, 81
Gracia, P., 249
Graham, J. L., 108
Gramm–Leach–Bliley Act, 174
Grantors, 262–263
Great Depression, 79–80, 79–80 (box), 136
Great Recession, 136, 150
Greek culture, 9
Greenfield, R., 293
Greening of America, 284–285
Greenspan, S., 82
Gresham's law of planning, 255
Grocery shopping, 61
Grosseteste, Robert (Bishop of Lincoln), 9
Gross family income, 198–199
Grosswald, B., 291
Group dynamics, 229–233
Groupon deals, 86
Group shift, 237–238
Groupthink, 233–238
Guanxi, 107–108
Gupta, S., 45

Haber, D., 295
Habibi, M. R., 105
Hackett, Buddy, 113
Haeckel, E., 42
Haitian disasters, 206–207
Hall, O. A., 60
Hamilton, I., 113
Hamilton, M. A., 211
Happiness, 300
    See also Success of plans
Hargreaves, A., 297
Hawley, A. H., 42
Head Start, 179–180
Healthcare
    Affordable Care Act, 254
    crisis management example, 268–269
    debates about, 306
    EpiPen controversy, 170–172
    generic drug prices, 106
    illness, 78–79
    insurance for, 267–269
    managed healthcare, 268
    Medicare, 317
    safety of medications, 169–170
    supply and demand in, 140

technological advances in, 306–307
worldview perspectives on, 167
    See also Wellness
Health maintenance organizations (HMOs), 268
Heil, G., 71
Henry Kaiser Family Foundation, 99
Henry VIII, King, 51
Hersch, P., 82
Hertlein, K. M., 226
Hierarchy of needs, 71–75, 76
Hill, R., 58, 216
Historical archives of the family, 123–124
Historical perspectives on education, 181
Historical perspectives on resource
    management
    about, 8–10
    contemporary movements, 56
    Era Four, 55–56
    Era One, 53–54
    Era Three, 54–55
    Era Two, 54
    post–Civil War, 51
    turn of 20th century, 51–52
Historical role of women in workplace, 147–148
HMOs (health maintenance organizations), 268
Hochachka, G., 286
Hochschild, A. R., 311
Hofferth, S. L., 197
Holder-in-Due-Course Rule, 174
Holistic Flow Model of Spiritual Wellness, 294
Home and work conflicts, 290–293
Home economics programs, 53–56
Home insurance, 272–273
Home Management House, 53
Homeschooling, 182
Homogamy, 94–96
Hospital stays, 267
Household census data, 154–155
Household management, evolution of, 52–56
Housing, 142, 177, 317–319
Howitt, R., 113
Hsiung, R., 232
Hudman, J., 200
Huffington Post, 307
Hughes, D., 226
Human activity orientation, 14, 15 (table),
    16 (table)
Humanistic approach to management, 55
Human resources, 116–118

Humans and nature orientation, 14, 15 Tab, 15 (table), 16 tab, 16 (table)
Humor, 299
Hungry Planet (Menzel and D'Aluisio), 72
Hurricane Katrina, 274
Hyde, P., 239
Hypercoordination of social groups, 223

IAASTD (International Assessment of Agricultural Knowledge, Science and Technology for Development), 114
Illich, I., 87
Illness, 78–79
Illusion of invulnerability, 234
Immigration, 96, 194, 195, 315–316
Implementation of plans
  accountability, 259–260
  adjustments during, 253–254
  completion and reflection, 274–275
  delegation of activities/responsibilities, 258–259
  estate planning, 261–264
  failures, 254–255
  family business succession, 264
  motivation affecting, 260–261
  strategies, 255–257
  See also Risk management; Success of plans
Implementation power, 129
Impression management, 38–39
Income
  budgets, 197–201
  dependent care affecting wages, 63–64
  educational levels influencing, 121–122
  fluctuations in, 141–142
  inequality in, 316
  inequities between rich and poor, 137–138
  overtime compensation, 198
  wage and salary comparison, 118–119
Independent activities, 191
Individualist society, 231–232
Individual responsibility, 299–302
Industrialization, 136
Industrial Revolution, 9, 179
Inequities, 127, 137–138, 313
Infants, needs of, 82
Infertility, 62
Infidelity scandals, 103–104
Inflation, 150–153
Inheritances, 37–38, 120–121, 263

Inheritance tax, 261
Insurance. *See* Risk management
Intangible resources, 137
Intellectual wellness, 296–297
Interactivity of communication, 211
Interchangeable nature of resources, 115
Interdependence of family and business, 58
Interdependent activities, 191
Interiority, 286–287
Intermediate goals, 188–189
Internal locus of control, 261
Internal Revenue Service (IRS), 159
International Assessment of Agricultural Knowledge, Science and Technology for Development (IAASTD), 114
International Division of Consumer Protection, 176
International study opportunities, 98
Internet, 225–227, 308–309, 345–346
  social media, 101, 108, 225, 308–309
  See also Social media
Interpersonal assertive strategies, 256–257
Interracial marriage, 94
Intersubjectivity, 210–211
Intestate, 262
Intrinsic motivators, 260
Intuition, 192
Investments, 129, 175
In vitro fertilization (IVF), 62
Invulnerability, 234
Inward spirituality, 294
IRS (Internal Revenue Service), 159
Irvin, B. L., 77
Isaac, M., 101
IVF (in vitro fertilization), 62

Jackson, T., 256
Jacobsen, C. K., 94
Janis, Irving, 7, 233–235
Jennings, N., 221
Job satisfaction, 100–101
Johannesen-Schmidt, M. C., 248
Johnson, B. R., 94
Johnson, D. S., 199
Joint ownership with right of survivorship, 262
Jonas, E., 93

Kahle, L. R., 105
Kahn, L. M., 120

Kalmijn, M., 249
Kanter, R. M., 55
Kendrick, D. T., 75
Kevo Bluetooth, 305
Key, R. J., 60
King, K., 290
King, Martin Luther, Jr., 253
Kinney, D. A., 197
Kitt, A. S., 231
Klein, D. M., 44
Kleine, R. E., 39
Kluckhohn, F. R., 13–15
Knoll, M. M., 58
Knowledge economy, 296–297
Koerner, A. K., 210
Kohlberg, 91–92, 91 (table)
Kranichfeld, M. L., 219–220
Kurtines, W. M., 102

Labeling system for food, 280–381
Labor force, 144
    See also Employment; Income
Lacy, E., 194
Laissez-faire families, 213, 243, 245–246, 248
Lake Placid conferences, 10
Lam, N. M., 108
Lamanna, M. A., 63
Lamm, H., 238
Langholtz, H., 129–130
Langone, Michael, 236, 238
Lareau, A., 197
Laroche, M., 105
Larson, 104
Latino immigration, 194
LAT (living apart together), 310
Lauer, S., 129
Laverie, D. A., 39
Law, 92
Law enforcement, 173
Lazar, J. B., 222
Leadership
    moral character and, 103–104
    parents and, 239–240, 242–248
    skills of, 238–239
    styles of, 255
    theories of, 240–242, 241 (figure),
        242 (figure)
Leadership direction skills, 238
Leadership influence skills, 238

Lee, Y.-K., 307
Lefton, R. E., 240–241, 241 (figure)
Lens, W., 260
Lenski, G. E., 70
Lenski, J., 70
Levendosky, A. A., 233
Levin, J. E., 225–227
Levinson, D. J., 83
Lewton, A., 126
Liability coverage, 271, 273
Lichter, D. T., 94
Life course development, 201–203
Life cycles of family financials, 201–203,
    201 (table)
Life insurance, 270–271
Life span changes, 82–83
Life span of consumer goods, 86–87
Lifestraw, 305
Lifestyle changes, 257, 304–305
Lifestyles of Health and Sustainability
    (LOHAS) category, 280
Liftware, 305
Light-polluted skies, 126
Likert, R., 240
Lin, Y., 307
Lindahl, K. M., 40–41
Ling, R., 223
Liquidity of assets, 151, 205
Living apart together (LAT), 310
Living wage, 118
Living wills, 262
Local government, 125, 160–161, 180
Locus of control, 261
LOHAS (Lifestyles of Health and
    Sustainability) category, 280
Long-term goals, 188–189
Long-term plans, 260
Long-term relationships, 230–231
Lottery winners, 137
Lotz, M., 62
Low-income families. See Poverty;
    Socioeconomic status (SES)
Lupkin, Sydney, 170–172
Luxuries, 86–87

Macdonald, M., 41
Maintenance budgets, 200
Malik, N. M., 40–41
Manageability of resources, 115

Managed healthcare, 268
Management as field of study, 50–51, 60–64
   See also Family resource management
Management in Homes (Cushman), 58
Management versus leadership, 248
Manning, G. L., 104–105
Marital power, 127
Marketing practices. *See* Advertising industry
Marriage, 94, 309–310
Martinez-Torteya, C., 233
Marty, A., 129–130
Marx, Karl, 39
Maslow, A. H., 71
Maslow, Abraham, 55, 71–75, 72 (figure), 76
Massive open online courses (MOOCs), 307
Mass production, 136
Mate selection, 94
Matkin, G. S., 248
Matos, L., 260
Maxwell, J. C., 238–239
McCain, John, 90
McCracken, G. D., 135
McDermott, C. J., 123
McDonald, G. W., 216
McGregor, D., 240
Meaning of work, 291–292
Measurement of needs, 77–78
Media, 221
Medicaid, 167–168, 168 (figure)
Medicare, 158, 165–166, 167–168,
   168 (figure), 317
Medications, 106, 169–172
Membership group, 231
Mental resources, 12
Menzel, Peter, 72
Merriam, S. B., 83
Merton, R. K., 231
Meyer, D. E., 191
Meyers, S. A., 43
Microcoordination, 223
Microeconomics of the family, 37–38
Middle class, 138
Military deployment, 10–13
Millennial Impact Report (2015), 125
Millennials, 247, 318, 319
Miller, B. C., 99
Miller, P., 246–247
Mindguards, 234
Minimum wage, 118

Minooei, M. S., 259–260
Minorities. *See* Culture
Miscommunication, 227
Mixed-motive situation, 260
Mobile devices, 222–223
   See also Cell phones; Smartphones
Modular Movers, 312
Monetary planning, 197–201
MOOCs (massive open online courses), 307
Morality, 234
Morals, 103–104
   See also Personal values
Morgan, M., 222
Mothers' workplace penalties, 120
Motivation, 255, 260–261
   See also Pyramid of needs
Mowen, J. C., 75
Moyn, S., 90–91
Multidisciplinary perspectives, 16–19
Multitasking, 191
Myers, B., 230
Myers, D. G., 238

Nall, M. A., 238
Name-brand products, 105
National Academy of Sciences, 296
National Association of Home Builders, 318
National Council on Family Relations, 4
National Institute on Retirement Security, 317
National Marriage Project, 310
National School Lunch Program, 169
Natural resources, 122–123, 313–314
   See also Conservation of resources
Need, principle of, 131
Needs
   assessing, 85–86
   behavior explained by, 102
   changing perceptions of, 78–84
   Consumer Resource Exchange Model, 75–76
   diversity in, 76
   economic needs, 76
   hierarchy of, 71–75, 72 (figure), 76
   measuring satisfaction of, 77–78
   physiological needs, 76
   planned obsolescence, 86–87
   social needs, 77
   wants compared to, 70–71
Neglectful parenting, 246
Net income, 198

Net worth, 261
Neutralized symmetry, 217
New money, 109
NGOs (nongovernmental organizations), 178
Nguyen, L. N., 137
Nielsen Company, 221, 280, 318
Nievar, M. A., 126
NIMBY (not in my backyard), 286
No-fault divorce, 311
Nolan, E., 129–130
Nolan, P., 70
Nondurable goods, 155–156
Nongovernmental organizations (NGOs), 178
Nonleadership families.
    See Laissez-faire families
Nonmonetary resources, 153–154
Nonrenewable resources, 122
Nontraditional families, 5
Normative resources, 216

Obamacare, 254
Obesity, 295
Objectives in planning, 188–189
Obsolescence, 86–87, 278
OCBE (Office of Consumer and Business
    Education), 176
Occupational wellness, 290–293
Oekology, 42
Office of Consumer and Business Education
    (OCBE), 176
Ogle, C., 290
Older adults
    caregiving services, 83
    happiness of, 300–301
    healthcare for, 307
    housing needs of, 318, 319
    increases in, 316–317
    living apart together, 310
    multi-gen families, 313
    Silver Linings, 312
    social responsibility and, 299–300
    technology and, 304, 308–309
    See also Retirement
Older Americans Act, 168
Old money, 108–109
Olson, D. H., 43, 219
O'Malley, M., 200
Omega Family, 323–324
Online media, 221–222

Open Veins of Latin America (Galeano), 114
Opportunity cost of not working, 148
Optimism, 255–256
Optimization of families, 54
Optional benefits, 119
Orchestration power, 129
Organic food, 280
Organizational leadership, 239
Organ transplants, 306
Orth, U. R., 105
Osmond, M. W., 41
Otto, Herbert, 43
Outsourcing of family life, 311
Outward spirituality, 294
Overscheduling problems, 197
Overtime compensation, 198
Ownership of moving water, 281–282

Pagan, C. N., 207
Pandya, S. M., 83
Paolucci, B., 60
Parents and parenting
    decision to have children, 310–311
    educational involvement, 296
    leadership styles, 239–240, 242–248
    mothers' workplace penalties, 120
    technology and, 218
Particularistic nature of resources, 116
Path-goal theory of leadership, 242
Patton, M., 122
Payne, R. K., 11–13, 15, 64
Pearl, D., 222
"Penny candy," 115
Perez, O., 284
Permissive parenting, 246
Personal goals, 189
Personality differences in needs, 80, 84
Personal needs, 232
Personal resources, 216
Personal values, 91–92, 91 (table)
Pessimism, 255–256
Peters, A., 293
Pew Research Center, 101, 103, 308
Philanthropy, 109
Physical resources, 12
Physical wellness, 294–296
Physiological needs, 71, 72 (figure), 73, 76
Pioneer families, 134–135
Planned obsolescence, 86–87

Plan of action
    budgeting, 197–201
    creating, 204–206
    emergency action plans, 207
    financial aspects, 201–203, 201 (table)
    goals and objectives, 188–190
    Haitian disaster example, 206–207
    planning process, 190–193
    scheduling, 188, 190–191, 197
    standards and, 190
    types, 193–196
    See also Decision making; Implementation of
        plans; Success of plans
Pluralistic families, 213
"Plus one" benefits, 6–7
Political model of decision making, 8
Political scandals, 103–104
Politics, 287, 313, 315–316
Positive psychology, 255–257
Poverty, 118, 137–138, 200–201, 201 (table)
    See also Socioeconomic status (SES)
Power
    conflict theory and, 40–41
    family communication and, 214–218
    implementation power, 129
    leadership and, 241–242
    marital power, 127
    orchestration power, 129
    structure of, 232
Power bases, 37, 215
PPOs (preferred provider organizations), 268
Predispositions, 100
Preferences, 105–107, 140, 143–144
Preferred provider organizations (PPOs), 268
Premiums, 266
Presenteeism at work, 292
Prevention attitudes for physical wellness, 295
Price inequality, 114
Price preferences, 105–106
Pricing process, 139–140
Primogeniture, 120
Principle of least interest, 216
Principle of revealed preferences, 310
The Principles of Scientific Management
    (Taylor), 52
Prioritization of plans, 257
Private assistance programs, 166
Private schools, 182–183
Proactive plans, 195, 196

Probate, 262
Problem-solving strategies, 256–257, 296–297
Production, 81
Products, obscure, 305
Profits, 139
Property coverage, 273
Property taxes, 180
Protection of financial assets, 205
    See also Risk management
Protection of resources, 129
Protective families, 213
Prusak, L., 116–117
Psychological needs, 77
Psychology, 17
Psychosocial theory of development, 300
Public assistance programs, 166
Pull factors in immigration, 194
Punctuality as value, 91
Push factors in immigration, 194
Putnam, R. D., 123, 125
Pyramid of needs, 55
Pyramid schemes, 175

Qian, Y., 249
Qualitative methodology, 46, 47 (table)
Quality circles, 55
Quality of education, 183–184
Quality of life, 78
Quality preferences, 105–106
Quantitative research, 45–46, 47 (table)
Quinn, R. E., 259–260

Raban, M. A., 191
Radio, 221
Rao, K., 292
Rapport talk, 211
Rational model of decision making, 7
Rationing of resources/products, 80
Reactive plans, 195–196
Read, C. R., 99
Real estate and financial plans, 206
Real estate taxes, 177
Reality factors, 254–255
Reasoned action theory, 100, 100 (figure)
Recession, 136, 150
Recycling efforts, 284
Reece, B. L., 104–105
Reference group, 231
Regulations for affordable housing, 177

Relationships and resources, 126–127
    See also Power
Relations orientation, 14, 15 (table), 16 (table)
Relative deprivation, 78
Relative resources theory, 126–127
Religion
    faith-based assistance programs, 178
    food selection/consumption influenced by, 96
    government values reflecting, 107–108
    race and, 94
    spiritual wellness, 293–294
Relocation of families, 155
Renewable resources, 122
Report talk, 211
Reproduction and culture, 81
Resilience, 257, 298
Resources
    allocation and use, 128–131
    availability of, 114–115, 313
    categorizations, 11–13
    cognitive resources, 216
    conservation of, 281–283
    defined, 5, 113
    effectiveness/efficiency of, 6
    environmental resources, 122–123
    human resources, 116–118
    management assignments, 326–333
    measurement of, 126–128
    resource theory, 115–116
    social resources, 123–126
    use of, 5–6
    See also Economic resources;
        Education; Needs
Resource theory, 115–116, 216
Responsibility
    individual, 299–302
    social, 278
    See also Corporate social responsibility;
        Family responsibility for decisions
Restructuring of jobs, 145
Retirement
    age of, 317
    income during, 161–163
    in life cycle, 202
    planning for, 203
    See also Social Security
Revenue Act, 121
Ribar, D., 311
Richard, M., 105

Richards, Ellen Swallow, 42, 52
Ricketts, K. G., 248
Riedmann, A. C., 63
Risk factors in physical health, 295
Risk management
    about, 265–268
    automobile insurance, 271–272
    budgeting for insurance, 205–206
    disasters and, 274
    health insurance, 267–269, 268–269
    home insurance, 272–273
    life insurance, 270–271
    resource use and, 129–130
Risky shift, 237
Rodman, H., 127
Rogers, J. M., 199
Rogers, W., 62
Roman cultures, 9
Roosevelt, Eleanor, 79–80 (box)
Rosa, H., 117
Rosen, J., 200
Rossi, A. S., 299
Rubinstein, J. S., 191
Rule activation, 191–192
Ruralites, 312–313

Saez, E., 316
Safety needs, 71, 72 (figure), 73
Safety of products, 169–170
Safilios-Rothschild, C., 129
Salaries, 118–119
Sales tax, 160–161
Savage, M., 293
Sayad, B. W., 210, 211
Sayer, L. C., 249
Scarcity hypothesis, 292
Schaefer, R. T., 194
Schein, E. H., 55
School kids with purchasing power
    (skippies), 149
School vouchers, 183
Schultz, S., 39
SCiO Pocket Molecular Sensor, 305
Seabald, H., 99
Segal, N. L., 100
Selective interpretation, 101
Selective memory, 101
Self-actualization, 71, 72 (figure), 74
Self-censorship, 234

Self-employment, 159
Self-esteem, 298
Self-perception theory, 102
Self-sufficiency, 134–135
Semi-closed system of households, 58
Separatist environment, 308
Sequencing order, 191
SES. *See* Socioeconomic status (SES)
Sexual orientation, 93
Shared meanings, 38–39
Shephard, R. J., 254–255
Sherif, C. W., 99–100
Sherif, M., 99–100
Shortage of products, 138
Short-term goals, 188
Siegel, C., 87
Signorielli, N., 222
Silliman, Ben, 50
Silver Linings, 312
Simon, S. A., 91
Simons, J., 260
Situation, 91
Situational theories of leadership, 241–242,
   242 (figure)
Six-hour workday, 293
Skippies (school kids with purchasing
   power), 149
Skogrand, L., 219
Skolnick, A., 4
Skolnick, J., 4
Smartphones, 143–144, 222–223, 224,
   308–309
Smith, A., 223
Smith-Adcock, S., 257
SNAP (Supplemental Nutrition Assistance
   Program), 168
Social class affiliation, 94
Social exchange theory, 37–38, 46 (table), 129
Social media, 101, 108, 225, 308–309
Social needs, 71, 72 (figure), 73–74, 77
Social psychology, 17
Social Psychology (Allport), 17
Social resources, 123–126
Social responsibility, 278
Social Security, 125, 146, 158, 161–165
Social wellness, 289–290
Societal goals, 189
Socioeconomic status (SES)
   class warfare, 137–138

consumers and consumption, 80, 141–142
   equity debates, 166
   factors impacting values, attitudes, and
      behaviors, 108–109
   family management style differences
      and, 64
   groups affecting family dynamics, 231
   homogamy and, 95
   income inequality, 316
   influencing needs, 80–81
   marriage and childbearing, 309–310
   spending behavior and, 142
   See also Poverty
Sociology, 17
Soenens, B., 260
Sontag, M. S., 42
Soriano, F. I., 85–86
Sorrels, J. P., 230
Spanish work-family system, 249
Spillover, 290–291
Spiritual resources, 12
Spiritual wellness, 293–294
Spouse, as defined by Social Security, 163
Spreitzer, G. M., 259–260
Stafford, K., 60
Standards
   communication, 214–218, 215 (table)
   cultural differences in, 82
   goals and, 190
Stanley, Thomas J., 142
State government, 125, 160–161, 167–168,
      168 (figure), 180
Stein, H. W., 109
Stem-cell research, 306
Stephens, D. C., 71
Stereotypes, 234
Steverman, B., 311
Stewart, S. D., 63
Stinnett, N., 43
Stone, R., 50
Stop-loss limit, 267
Strategic plans, 196, 204
Stress, 297–299, 307
Strodtbeck, F. L., 13–15
Strong, B., 210, 211
Structural unemployment, 145
Subbakrishna, D. K., 292
Subjugation orientation, 14
Submissive symmetry, 217

Substitution of prices, 139
Substitution of resources, 6
Suburbs, 318
Success of plans
    defining, 277–278
    emotional wellness, 297–299
    intellectual wellness, 296–297
    occupational wellness, 290–293
    physical wellness, 294–296
    social wellness, 289–290
    spiritual wellness, 293–294
    wellness as lifestyle, 288–289, 289 (figure)
Sufficiency of resources, 6
Sugru, 305
Supplemental Nutrition Assistance Program
    (SNAP), 168
Supplies acquisition, 207
Supply and demand, 138–140, 183–184
Surplus in budgets, 199
Surplus of products, 138
Survival needs, 109
Survivor benefits, 164
Sustainability, 285–287
Sustainable development, 87
Swedish workday, 293
Symbiotic relationships, 136
Symbolic interactionism, 38–39, 46 (table)
Symbolic resources, 116
Symbols, 38–39
Symmetrical conversations, 217
System boundaries, 59 (figure)
Szinovacz, M., 214–215

Taiwanese healthcare, 167
Tan, L., 199
Tandem Tribes, 312
Tannen, D., 211
Tanshin funin, 155
Task-management strategies, 256–257
Tau family, 324–325
Tax efficiency, 205
Taxes
    federal tax, 92, 158–160, 159 (figure)
    financial plans for, 206
    gift tax, 261
    laws covering, 121
    property tax, 180
    state tax, 160–161
Taylor, Frederick, 51–52, 52

Technology
    changes resulting from, 304–309
    communication and, 221–227
    computers and Internet, 225–227
    digital divide, 81, 226, 308
    drawbacks, 307–308
    educational advancements and, 307
    effects of, 58
    healthcare advances, 306–307
    Internet and, 225–227, 308–309, 345–346
    job restructuring as result of, 145
    natural resources and, 313–314
    older adults and, 308–309
    parenting in the digital age, 218
    scheduling plans with, 197
    social media, 101, 108, 225, 308–309
    time not saved with, 117
    See also Smartphones
Technostress, 307
Telemarketing, 175
Telephones, 222–223
Television, 221–222
"Television Audience 2009" report, 70
Term insurance, 270
Theoretical perspectives
    about, 35
    conflict theory, 39–41
    family development theory, 44–45
    family ecological theory, 42–43
    family strengths framework, 43–44
    family systems theory, 36
    feminist theory, 40, 41
    importance of, 35–36
    social exchange theory, 37–38
    strengths and weaknesses of, 46 (table)
    symbolic interactionism, 38–39
Theory of X and Y, 240
Thomas, A. B., 239
Thorne, B., 41
Throwaway society, 283–284
Time
    allocation of, 117
    cultural views on, 14, 15 (table), 16 (table)
    management of, 61, 183
    as resource, 154
Timmerman, G. M., 77
Tinker & Partners, 279
Tobacco costs, 142
Tomer, J. F., 76

Top-down leadership, 247
Torquati, J. C., 125
Torricelli, C., 129
Tourism tax, 161
Traditional family leadership, 243–244
Transactional leadership, 242, 243–244
Transferability of resources, 115
Transformational leadership, 242–243, 244–245, 248
Transformational leadership style, 236
Transition, families in, 4
Traut-Mattausch, E., 93
Travel, 98, 304, 314
Triplett, N., 17
Truancy, 179
Trust, 82
Trusts, 262–263
Truth in Lending Act, 174
Turner, R. H., 38
Twin study, 100–101

Unacceptable risk, 265
Unassertive leaders, 241, 241 (figure)
Uncertainty, 129–130
Unemployment, 144–146, 166
Uninvolved parenting, 246
United States of Aging Survey, 317
Universal life insurance, 271
Unmarried partners, 6–7, 97, 309
Urbanism, 318
Uterine transplants, 62
Utilitarian thinking, 37–38
Utility of resources, 115

Value of products, 138–140
Values
    across life spans, 97–98
    congruence between generations, 98–99
    culture influencing, 107–108
    human rights, 90–91
    as measurement of exchange, 90
    personal values, 91–92, 91 (table)
    poverty and, 103
    purchasing decisions and, 104–107
    sexual orientation, 93
    socioeconomic factors influencing, 108–109
    universal, 90
    See also Attitudes; Behavior

Vansteenkiste, M., 260
Variable expenses, 198
Varkey, S., 43
Vegetarianism, 96
Velagaleti, S. R., 311
Vickers, C., 53
Victims of Groupthink (Janis), 234–235
Villares, E., 257
Violence, 233
Virtual Keyboard, 305
Vocational framework, 55
Voluntary simplicity, 131
Volunteerism, 125–126, 299
Von Eye, A., 233
Vonnegut, Kurt, 90

Wages. See Income
Waller, W. W., 216
Walter, S. R., 191
Walumbwa, F., 245
Wang, W., 94
Wants versus needs, 70–71
Wartella, E., 221
Water conservation, 281–282, 284, 314
Wealth versus poverty gap, 137–138
Weber, Max, 53
Weber, T. J., 245
Web resources, 345–346
Weir, A., 51
Wellness
    about, 288–289, 289 (figure)
    emotional, 297–299
    intellectual, 296–297
    occupational, 290–293
    physical, 294–296
    social, 289–290
    spiritual, 293–294
Westbrook, J. I., 191
White, J. M., 44
Whole life insurance, 270
Wickrama, K. A., 125
Williams, C., 200
Williams, R., 265
Wills, 262
Wilson, J. D., 181
Wolfe, D. M., 216
Women in the labor force, 146–149, 150
Women's Property Acts, 120

Woolley, F., 129
Work, meaning of, 291–292, 301
Work and home conflicts, 290–293
Workplace issues, 290–293
    See also Income
World Economic Forum, 313
World Health Organization, 295, 307
Worldview perspectives
    changes in families, 28–29
    culture influencing, 13–16, 15 (table),
        16 (table), 211–212
    diet, 72
    disasters, 274
    e-waste, 287
    family decisions, 16
    grocery shopping, 61
    healthcare discrepancies, 167

immigration myths, 194
insurance, 266–267
World War II era, 54, 80
Wozniak, R. H., 98–99
Wundt, Wilhelm, 17
Wutich, A., 314

XStat Syringe, 305

Yodanis, C., 129
Yttri, B., 223
Yu, H., 246–247
Yu, L., 108

Zanna, M. P., 93
Zeta family, 325–326
Zimmerman, E., 113

ABOUT THE AUTHORS

Tami James Moore, Ph.D., CFLE, is Professor of Family Studies at the University of Nebraska at Kearney. She received a Ph.D. in Curriculum and Instruction from the University of Nebraska, Lincoln, in 1995. She is a Certified Family Life Educator (CFLE) through the National Council of Family Relations and served as an FRM content expert during the process of creating the most recent version of the CFLE exam. She has more than 30 years of postsecondary teaching experience and has taught the Family Resource Management course for the past 15 years.

Sylvia M. Asay, Ph.D., CFLE, is Professor of Family Studies and Chair of the Family Studies and Interior Design Department at the University of Nebraska, Kearney. She received her Ph.D. in Community and Human Resources at the University of Nebraska, Lincoln, in 1998. She received her Certified Family Life Educator credentials through the National Council on Family Relations. Her years of postsecondary teaching experience include such courses as Infant Development, Lifespan Development, Human Sexual Behavior, and Marriage and Family Relationships, as well as Family Resource Management.